THE ECONOMICS OF ATTENTION

THE TRIUMPH OF SUBSTANCE OVER STYLE

RICHARD A. LANHAM

THE ECONOMICS OF
{ATTENTION}

STYLE AND

SUBSTANCE

IN THE AGE OF

INFORMATION

The University of Chicago Press

Chicago and London

The University of Chicago Press, Chicago 60637

The University of Chicago Press, Ltd., London

© 2006 by The University of Chicago

All rights reserved. Published 2006

Paperback ediiton 2007

Printed in the United States of America

16 15 14 13 12 11 10 09 08 07   2 3 4 5 6

ISBN-13: 978-0-226-46867-9 (paper)

ISBN-10: 0-226-46867-4 (paper)

Library of Congress Cataloging-in-Publication Data

Lanham, Richard A.

  The economics of attention : style and substance in
the age of information / Richard A. Lanham.

    p. cm.

  Includes bibliographical references and index.

  ISBN 0-226-46882-8 (cloth : alk. paper)

    1. Information society—Economic aspects. 2. Eco-
nomics—Sociological aspects. 3. Information technology—Social aspects. I. Title.

HM851 .L357 2006

303.48'33—dc22   2005022857

⊗ The paper used in this publication meets the minimum requirements of the American National Standard
for Information Sciences—Permanence of Paper for
Printed Library Materials, ANSI Z39.48-1992.

This book is dedicated to VERIP 3.

CONTENTS

ILLUSTRATIONS

This book had its origins in a narrow question: What's new about the digital expressive space and what's not? Yet more narrowly, what happens when words move from printed page to electronic screen? What's next for text? This narrow question expanded, in spite of my best efforts to resist it, into a second and larger one: What's new about the "new economy" and what's not? Seeing clearly what is happening to the word as it moves from page to screen seems, to me at least, to depend on seeing clearly what is happening in the world that expressive field has to express. Both are battles for attention as the scarce resource.

Economics, as we all remember from Introduction to Economics, studies the allocation of scarce resources. Normally we would think that the phrase "information economy," which we hear everywhere nowadays, makes some sense. It is no longer physical stuff that is in short supply, we are told, but information about it. So, we live in an "information economy." But information is not in short supply in the new information economy. We're drowning in it. What we lack is the human attention needed to make sense of it all. It will be easier to find our place in the new regime if we think of it as an economics of attention. Attention is the commodity in short supply.

Since I am not a real economist, I cannot make out quite how far we have moved from stuff to what we think about stuff, how disembodied we have actually become. But to the degree that we have made this shift, to the extent that the attention needed to make sense of information has become our scarce resource, some fundamental changes occur.

The devices that regulate attention are stylistic devices. Attracting attention is what style is all about. If attention is now at the center of the economy rather than stuff, then so is style. It moves from the periphery to the center. Style and substance trade places. And so do real property and intellectual property. In an economy of stuff, the laws of property govern who owns stuff. In an attention economy, it is the laws of intellectual property that govern who gets attention.

The center of gravity for formal inquiry changes places too. In an economy of stuff, the disciplines that govern extracting material from the earth's crust and making stuff out of it naturally stand at the center: the physical sciences, engineering, and economics as usually written. The arts and letters, however vital we all agree them to be, are peripheral. But in an attention economy, the two change places. The arts and letters now stand at the center. They are the disciplines that study how attention is allocated, how cultural capital is created and traded. When our children come home and tell us that they have decided to major in English or art history, no longer need we tremble for their economic future.

In such an economy, who are the economists? No longer will they be found in economics departments but instead in the disciplines that study how attention is allocated. It is a fair guess that neither the old-style economists nor the new ones will welcome this exchange of roles.

In the digital writing space, words no longer have it all their own way. They have to compete with moving images and sounds. This competition leads us, by stages I'll trace later on, to a new theory of communication, a new way to think about being "clear."

So—an attention economy brings big changes with it, changes that these essays seek to describe.

My old Chaucer teacher, Talbot Donaldson, began one of his papers by confessing that, at the outset of his investigation, he had no idea how many books about it he would not have time to read. So it has proved with me. Many paths lead to human attention: through neuroscience, through experimental psychology, through the physiology of vision, through philosophy, through what is now called "behavioral economics." Amid all this wisdom, ignorance as well as caution has kept me, as much as I could manage it, in my own neck of the woods, which is the history of rhetoric.

"Rhetoric" has not always been a synonym for humbug. For most of Western history, it has meant the body of doctrine that teaches people how to speak and write and, thus, act effectively in public life. Usually defined as "the art of persuasion," it might as well have been called "the economics of attention." It tells us how to allocate our central scarce resource, to invite people to attend to what we would like them to attend to. Rhetoric has been the central repository of wisdom on how we make sense of and use information since the Greeks first invented it sometime in the middle of the last millennium before Christ. This body of traditional wisdom does not tell us all we need to know about the economics of attention but it does at least provide a place to start.

How and why "rhetoric" has become the antonym of "true" and "real" will form a main thread of our story. If that antonymy can't be explained and resolved, we'll find ourselves in the marmalade, for our new economics of attention will become synonymous with deception, something that all of us, old economists and new, might wish to avoid.

Before we start, here is an easy way to think about this book: it is a series of variations on a theme and that theme is a rhetorical figure. Rhetorical figures are patterns of speech or writing that provide patterns for thought. Hundreds of them have come down to us, usually under their Greek or Latin names. The one I deploy here, though, is both nameless and an outcast.

The figure itself is dead simple: It is a fundamental template, a basic habit of mind in how we pay attention to the world. Viktor Weisskopf put his finger on it: "We cannot at the same time experience the artistic content of a Beethoven sonata and also worry about the neurophysiological processes in our brains. . . . But we can shift from one to another." We alternately participate in the world and step back and reflect on how we attend to it. We first write, absorbed in what we have to say, and then revise, look at how we have written it.

But why does this fundamental oscillation lurk, an outcast, without a name? Because we don't want to think about it. If we think about how we compose our selves and our world, we're afraid we'll lose our concentration, our jobs, maybe at some primitive level our lives. Yet reflection as well as concentration preserves life. Survival depends on being able to move back and forth from the one to the other. No reason why this fundamental rhythm of attention should not have a Latin name like all the rest: let's call it *oscillatio*, from the Latin word for moving back and forth.

I don't claim for *oscillatio* scientific precision, but it does prove useful, especially when you have to hold two kinds of economy in the mind at once, stuff and fluff.

A note on the "Background Conversations." When you take on a subject like the economics of attention, you charge into that uneasy no-man's-land where ideas from different fields meet. I thought you might want to know some of the company that these ideas have kept, in my mind at least. This company usually emerges as you move back and forth from argument to note or from parenthetical reference (Boondoggle, 1993a) to the works cited to see which of Boondoggle's 1993 offerings is meant. This procedure is essential in the specialized world of modern academic inquiry. It wouldn't work for me here, however, since I was pretty much shut out of the professional economics discussion by my lack of mathematics and because I am by no means expert in many of the other topics I touch on. So, as an experiment, I have chosen to chronicle my pursuit in a more informal, hypertextual way, as a supplement to the main argument of each chapter. In these background conversations, I'll describe some of the places I'm coming from and where you might go if you want to continue the conversation. Certainly this procedure will not be respectable in the eyes of professional economists, or of the many other scholars whose fields I touch on, but it may be useful to the ordinary reader, in whose existence I continue to believe.

Crestwood Hills, Los Angeles, 2005

CHAPTER ONE

{STUFF AND FLUFF}

The age of information has brought with it a strange paradox. Just when we are drowning in stuff, we seem to be abolishing it. Stuff and what we think about stuff seem to be changing places. Never before have so many people bought so many physical objects, so many varied consumer goods, or expressed their personalities so fully through them. Houses get bigger, and one is seldom enough. Cars metamorphose into trucks and, with the Hummer, into tanks. Mail-order catalogs rain down on us. Our garages must have boats and our homes, home theaters. Moralizers preach about the villainies of such rampant consumerism but also complain, oddly enough, that not everyone can afford them. People love stuff and get enormous fun out of it, especially if it is a fashionable brand. But all this stuff, in spite of much whining to the contrary, has not stifled the finer things of life. There have never been so many art galleries, so many symphony orchestras, so sophisticated a life for the senses and the sensitive. And never have the actual physical locations of the world been so venerated or visited. Tourism, by some accounts at least, is the biggest business in the world, and sophisticated travelers search in vain for an island in the South Seas so obscure that the cruise ships don't yet call there. Nor have the resources of the natural world, live and inanimate, ever received such anxious care and loving contemplation as now they receive. You're nowhere if you don't have your merit badge in whale watching.

> For the wit and mind of man, if it work upon matter, which is the contemplation of the creatures of God, worketh according to the stuff, and is limited thereby, but if it work upon itself, as the spider worketh his web, then it is endless, and brings forth indeed cobwebs of learning, admirable for the fineness of thread and work but of no substance or profit.
>
> Francis Bacon, *The Advancement of Learning*

At the same time, the world of real places and the stuff in them seems to be evaporating before our stuff-clouded eyes. Tourism seems an oddly self-destructive business. When that South Seas island is discovered by "the tourists" we say it has been "ruined." It has lost its reality, its genuine substance. It has become an attention structure, a cruise ship stop, the nonstuff of which Disneylands are made. The more cruise ships we launch, the fewer real ports will be left for them to visit. Mountain climbers have to make a reservation for Everest. The Galapagos Islands, the archetypal paradise of unspoiled nature, has had to ration access, too, lest the ecological balance be upset. Every city worth its salt has parked up its "old town" or, if unlucky enough to be new, has invented one. In such a world, all the world does indeed become a stage, staging itself for the visitor's eyes. Dramatic self-consciousness increases like global warming. Tourism, invented to restore our naive wonder at strange places, destroys them instead.

Actual physical location threatens to evaporate everywhere we look. Information, we are everywhere taught, has annihilated distance. Surgeons can cut you open from a thousand miles away. Facsimile Las Vegas casinos deliver Rome and New York on the same daily walk. You don't have to go to the office to go to the office. You can shop in your kitchen and go to school in your living room. And, sadly enough, when you actually do go out shopping, one mall seems much like another. For what actually matters, physicality doesn't matter anymore. Even with money; now, we are told, information about money is more important than the actual green.

So, too, with all the stuff that is so much fun to play with. Products used to be designed to last a lifetime. Now they have a shorter life than young love. For computers, it is three steps from cutting-edge to doorstop. It is the relationship to the consumer that matters now, not the object that engenders it, or the database that such relationships generate that generates value, or the associations that can be built on such relationships, or the brand, the box it comes in. So enamored of brands have we become that we walk around plastered with sponsor decals like a race car. The clothes, the stuff, have become an excuse to display our brand loyalties, what we think about stuff.

Consumerism has become etherealized. The foes of "conspicuous consumption" always juxtapose the life of the mind to such shallow display, but what could be more cerebral than the information that prints out the stuff of the world? Conspicuousness triumphs over consumption. And look at how the automobile has suffered. Never have there been so many neat cars out there, so much new and useful engineering, so many marvelous roads to drive them on (once you get off the freeway, at least). Yet the felt center of the car business has gravitated to design and the brand recognition that design can create. The "art and color" world Harley Earl began many years ago at GM has now moved center stage. Real men engineer brands not engines. And you don't buy a car anymore—you lease it like a piece of software that wears out its welcome in three years.

This paradoxical relation of stuff to nonstuff shows up in the oddest places. When Westminster Abbey decided to replace the chairs for its congregation, a company bought the old ones and sold them for £3,000 each. The interface between this expensive seat and the priceless aura it represents lies in the gold-plated plaque that comes with each one, identifying it (how P. T. Barnum would have loved this) as a "bespoke congregation chair."

Or consider the Swiss cow. Such are the sentimental ties that Swiss citizens have to picturesque dairy farming that the Swiss government now spends, it is estimated, $1,000 per cow in annual subsidies to keep that cow in the pasture for your drive-by. Or we might consider, on a larger scale, the picturesque countryside of rural France. The French have decided, with the financial help of their European brethren, to subsidize their agriculture in order to preserve the appearance of the countryside. The beautiful countryside and its picturesque agriculture—the stuff—is protected, but at the expense of converting it into an unreal tableau, nonstuff, a subsidized attention structure not unlike the Europe Disneyland that French intellectuals take such pleasure in despising.

Or we might consider the *Antiques Roadshow*. This popular TV show is not about antiques so much as about "collectibles." And the range of stuff that people collect is extraordinary, from old stoves to old campaign buttons, from porcelain to piggy banks. We are all, it seems, enamored of all this old stuff. Here is the world of antique virtue, where objects were made to last, when stuff was stuff. Yet what all those apprentice antiquarians who tote their stuff to the *Roadshow* seek, finally, is not stuff but information about stuff. Sure, they want to know what their object is worth, but quite as much they want information about it. How old is it? Where does it come from? Who made it? And, more rarefied yet, What about its style? It is by style that most of the expert identifications are made anyway. The hunger for stuff is paralleled by a hunger for style. Modern "materialism" turns out to be an intellectualized, spiritualized, affair.

This new oxymoronic coupling of stuff and nonstuff is supposed to be the work of the new information economy. Marshall McLuhan said long ago (in

1959) that information processing and packaging was now the chief business of the age. And Peter Drucker, the godfather of business gurus, has written more recently (1993): "The basic economic resource—'the means of production,' to use the economist's term—is no longer capital, nor natural resources (the economist's 'land'), nor 'labor.' It is and will be knowledge. The central wealth-creating activities will be neither the allocation of capital to productive uses, nor 'labor'—the two poles of nineteenth- and twentieth-century economic theory, whether classical, Marxist, Keynesian, or neo-classical. Value is now created by 'productivity' and 'innovation,' both applications of knowledge to work." So much for stuff. It has become a derivative effect like Swiss cows and French farms, forever preserved in picturesque pickle. To the degree that this change has occurred, obviously adjustments will be required. Even the bankers are feeling the heat. Here is the late Walter Wriston, the former chairman of Citibank: "The world desperately needs a model of economics of information that will schematize its forms and functions. But even without such a model one thing will be clear: When the world's most precious resource is immaterial, the economic doctrines, social structures, and political systems that evolved in a world devoted to the service of matter become rapidly ill suited to cope with the new situation. The rules and customs, skills and talents, necessary to uncover, capture, produce, preserve, and exploit information are now mankind's most important rules, customs, skills, and talents." Jeremy Campbell, the British journalist and science writer, paints this change from stuff to information on a broader canvas:

> The view arose of information as an active agent, something that does not just sit there passively, but "informs" the material world, much as the messages of the genes instruct the machinery of the cell to build an organism . . . Thus information emerged as a universal principle at work in the world, giving shape to the shapeless, specifying the peculiar character of living forms and even helping to determine, by means of special codes, the patterns of human thought. . . . Evidently nature can no longer be seen as matter and energy alone. Nor can all her secrets be unlocked with the keys of chemistry and physics . . . A third component is needed for any explanation of the world that claims to be complete. To the powerful theories of chemistry and physics must be added a late arrival: a theory of information. Nature must be interpreted as matter, energy, and information.

OK. If you interpret nature as matter and energy, you create the industrial society within which we have grown accustomed to living. Real persons dig minerals out of the earth's crust and make stuff out of them. Stuff, things that you can drop on your foot, predominates. Our archetype of the brawny blue-collar worker puddling concrete or staring into an open-hearth furnace has been built on this firm substrate of stuff. So a young businessman recently profiled in the *Wall Street Journal:* "My dad always said to me, 'You've got to dig it, grow it, or build it; everything else is just fluff.'" So there you have the three ages of economy, redefined: agriculture, industrialism, fluff.

But when you interpret nature as information, stuff and fluff change places. The "real" world becomes a printout, a printout created increasingly by computer graphics, by digital design. We see this synthetic reality every-where nowadays, from TV commercials to scientific visualization, computer games to military training. In this world, every element has been created from specific information keyboarded by master illusionists. Made objects, from buildings to airplanes, find their beginning and central reality in computer-assisted design and manufacture. The life-giving act inheres in designing the object on a digital screen. The manufacture or "printout" of the object be-comes a derivative function performed slave-like by a computer-controlled machine.

We have always had information as a perspective on stuff, to be sure, and toggled back and forth between the stuff and the information that informs it. You can look at a table and, like an early Greek philosopher, try to see it as a particular collection of atoms, but you seldom do. You can peer inside an amplifier chassis and try to see the circuit schematic that it instantiates. Such reverse engineering used to be uphill work. But now it is much easier. The information economy leaves the toggle switch in the information position. An information economy naturally assumes that pattern, design, comes first. (Perhaps that is why designers of electronic apparatus have started using see-through enclosures to spotlight the circuit boards.) The important people sit at computer screens and make designs. Even that true possessor of the right stuff, the fighter pilot, finds himself seated at a screen and flying a pilotless aircraft with a computer joystick. The great dream of manufacturers, now, is to metamorphose the factory simply by changing the software. The world we stub our foot on is only a printout that happens to have been made from the information available at that time. New information, and maybe we wouldn't have stubbed our foot.

This printout perspective is not new. The Middle Ages conceived the world as existing in the mind of God and having its only true reality there. Everything down here below was a temporary printout indeed, compared to the eternity of Heaven. Or, if we want to search further back into the past, we find the eternity of Plato's world of ideal forms. The ultimate reality of that world was a mathematics similar to the computer code that creates the world of computer graphics. So too, in a different way, the Greek philosopher Heraclitus thought that the ultimate reality of things lay in structure not stuff.

The God-like perspective has been recreated in our own time, in a new form, called, fittingly enough, "artificial life." Artificial life, as a scientific discipline, seeks to evolve biological systems within a computer, create living systems based on silicon (information) rather than carbon (the stuff that makes up us). Christopher Langton, one of the field's founders, explains it: "Certainly life, as a dynamic physical process, could 'haunt' other physical material: the material just needs to be organized in the right way. Just as certainly, the dynamic processes that constitute life—in whatever material bases they might occur—must share certain universal features—features that will allow us to recognize life by its dynamic *form* alone, without reference to its *matter*." Or, as these sentiments were synthesized by computer journalist Steven Levy, "The stuff of life is not stuff." In the great age of materialism, the material seems to be evaporating.

An information economy thus implies a fundamental figure/ground reversal in how we think about the world we live in. We always knew it had form, but the real reality was the stone you kicked with your foot. Now we are back in the Middle Ages, trying to fathom the mind of God. That's proving harder than kicking the stone. Such a reversal leads us to wonder whether "information economy" is the right name for where we find ourselves. Economics, in the classic definition, is the "study of how human beings allocate scarce resources to produce various commodities and how those commodities are distributed for consumption among the people in society." In an information economy, what's the scarce resource? Information, obviously.

But information doesn't seem in short supply. Precisely the opposite. We're drowning in it. There is too much information around to make sense of it all. Everywhere we look, we find information overload. The journalist David Shaw warns that "information inundation imperils our children." And the grownups, too. The designers of police cars complain that there is not enough room in a car for all the communications equipment that needs to fit into it. Ditto for airplane cockpits. The National Security Agency overhears far more information than it can make sense of, as the occupants of the World Trade Center found out. Race car engineers are overwhelmed by the amount of information relayed back to them from sensors on the cars. Oil wells are now so heavily instrumented that they produce geysers of data points that are harder to process than the oil. Data from across the spectrum, X-rays, gamma rays, and the like, shower down on the head of the astronomer. The poor foot soldier, formerly isolated in his foxhole by the fog of war, now has so much information pouring into him that a special project, Force XXI, has been developed to help cope with foxhole overload. A recent effort to measure the amount of new information generated in the world each year came up with these numbers: "The world's total yearly production of print, film, optical, and magnetic content would require roughly 1.5 billion gigabytes of storage. This is the equivalent of 250 megabytes per person for each man, woman, and child on earth—every year!" (A megabyte = a million characters; a gigabyte = 1,000 megabytes.) The World Wide Web is now a document billions of pages long. And, as if digital overload weren't enough, printed books still pour from the presses: over 160,000 new U.S. titles and editions in 2002. No wonder the multitasking soccer mom, driving her SUV while talking on the phone, checking her personal digital assistant, drinking coffee, and coaching the young phenom sitting next to her, still feels frantic for time.

What then is the new scarcity that economics seeks to describe?

It can only be the human attention needed to make sense of information. This need has, in fact, been acknowledged in the current discussion but only in a tacit terminological fashion. Everyone discussing the information society hastens to distinguish between a dyslogistic "raw data" and a more eulogistic term, "true information" or "knowledge"—or sometimes even "wisdom"— which describes the valuable item. But the kitchen that cooks the raw data into useful "information" is human attention. It is the attention economy that has created the paradox of stuff.

So what do we make of this new kind of economy where stuff and fluff change places? Economics is the "study of how human beings allocate scarce resources to produce various commodities." But what if the scarce commodity is not a commodity? Fluff instead of stuff? Not surprisingly, conventional economists have ignored this reversal and treated information as a commodity. That, after all, is what economics is all about. "What companies need," says one business guru, "is a way to navigate in the knowledge economy. To do that, firms must have better devices for measuring knowledge—and their ability to create it and convert it into profits." Such a voice is thinking about knowledge as stuff that gets shipped out on pallets from the shipping dock. It hasn't made the vital jump from information to the attention needed to make sense of it or from the static world of stuff to the volatile world of information and attention that, in our heart of hearts, we still think of as fluff.

The famous economist Herbert Simon considered the attention-economy problem in 1971 and saw it as simply a question of filtering. Computer "knowbots," as we now call them, digital librarians, would organize our attention for us; our news would arrive pre-Googled and personalized. Or we would hire live special librarians to step in where Google fails. And so, at least to some degree, it has worked out. Special librarians are a growing job category. But either way, bots or bodies, the thinking remains "commodity" thinking. We have too many boxes of information arriving at our loading dock. We must find mechanized ways to organize their arrival. A UPS problem.

Human attention is a little more complicated than that. It is more like a poetry reading than a profit-and-loss statement. When stuff and fluff swap places, as they do in an attention economy, some basic changes occur. "Capital" and "productivity" take on more complex meanings. Economists are to be found in strange new places. A different theory of expression, and of digital notation, supervenes. A different balance in educational curriculum is implied. And a different kind of property, intellectual property, comes to the fore. We'll consider these changes in the chapters to follow, but let's begin with an "establishing shot" to get us thinking.

In a stuff economy, what is needed to capture, produce, and preserve goods we usually, if sometimes loosely, call capital. What, in an attention economy, constitutes capital? If we define "capital" simply as any sequestration of current resources for future use, how can such a concept exist in an attention economy? You can't deposit attention in the bank until you need it. Nor can you reallocate it according to your own conception of social justice, as central planners yearn to do with the stuff of the world. And you can't measure it accurately, either, as accountants and stock analysts have been finding out. One scholar has suggested that audits of a company ought to include a category for proclivity to change, proleptic agility. A fighter pilot–theorist has argued that top speed in fighter design is less important than the ability to change states more quickly than your opponent. These are starts. But they take us right into the world of human attention where such proclivities are born. There seems to be—the observation comes from many quarters—some attitude, or talent, lurking out there that can function as a compass for navigation in the new economy, some attention-economy equivalent for an accountant's "feeling for numbers." What else sells all those business-advice books about "navigating your company in the dangerous waters of the future"? But what could this talent be? And how do you apply it when you find it? Obviously, these questions have something to do with the oscillation between stuff and nonstuff that an attention economy creates. But what? Back to capital in this new economy. What is it?

Let me sketch two answers that at least introduce the problem's complexity. The behavioral biologists have sought to describe something called "the human biogrammar." We used to call it "human nature" before the term was disallowed by a social science determined to see us as blank sheets of paper on which it could write utopian designs. But now we are allowed to use the term again, especially since we are beginning to find genetic bases for it. We might think of this inherited set of adaptive patterns, of behavioral inclinations, as the attention capital of humankind. It represents the stored-up impulse to pay attention to certain kinds of things in certain kinds of ways. We might, as an outstanding example, point to the "language instinct" that we possess, apparently from birth. Or our response to some sexual signals more than others. Or any of the myriad other suitcases in our evolutionary baggage. Only a fraction of these inherited capacities can any one of us express in our lives, but they are there for the asking. They constitute behavioral capital, resources stored up in an evolutionary bank and waiting to be allocated to human purposes, proclivities to attend to the world in some ways and not in others. The discussions of human capital in the business world, in as much as it has been given me to understand them, seem to be buzzing around this central assertion. And education has long done so, which might explain why we spend so much money to improve it. We want people to have a fuller sense of what it means, or might mean, to be alive.

Alternatively, we might locate "capital" in this new economy in the literary and artistic imagination, the powers that take the biogrammar we inherit and spin from it new patterns for how to live and to think about how we live. Capital, in this view, lies in the cultural conversation. Hasn't this storehouse always been the fundamental capital, the major stored resource, with which we meet the perpetual novelty of human life? Now that our future is becoming less and less constrained by material circumstance, now that we are less and less compelled to live out one manner of life only, or one job for life, may not this category of capital come to seem primary?

What, we might also ask, constitutes "productivity" in an attention economy? We are trying out one obvious answer to this question by doing more than one thing at once. *Carping* our *diem* with both hands. Or, productivity might mean simply better information filters. Or—a different sort of an-

swer—what about the famous "Hawthorne Experiment"? This classic experiment sought to determine if production on a factory floor increased if the
lighting was brighter. It did. But it also increased if the lighting was dimmer.
The difference lay not in the light but in the workers' being observed. This
is not quite the same thing as being recognized or rewarded, though these
obviously are part of it. When we are observed in our work, we socialize it.
We share it with the observer and by doing so it becomes more real. Because
more real, it becomes more worth attending to, more interesting. And so you
do better work. From this dynamic, all the employee-of-the-month programs
and performance bonuses. In all these programs, more attention makes more
stuff. The productivity enzyme here is theatrical self-awareness.

Like the tourist business that plays such a prominent role in it, an attention economy is irremediably and self-consciously dramatic. It brings with it
heightened dramatic self-consciousness as a central element. But more attention also makes for a more enjoyable life, not only more stuff but more
fluff. A life shared with someone else is not the same life as one lived singly
but one more real, deeper, richer, dynamic, more alive. If attention is the commodity in short supply, then all the debates about "quality of life" come to the
fore. Ecclesiastes' advice, "Better is a handful with quietness than both the
hands full with travail and vexation of spirit," is no longer fluffy proverbial
wisdom. The argument between the arts and commerce begins just here. And
the much older conflict between *otium* and *negotium,* between leisure and a
life of "getting and spending." And the equally venerable "Achilles' choice"
between a short, famous life and a long, prosperous obscurity. Or the conflict,
fundamental to the argument, between substance and style. The conflict between these two kinds of economy, that is, returns us to a cluster of related,
and perennial, topics in the history of Western thought. Each of these fundamental debates, I would argue, is about our two different kinds of economies,
stuff and what we think about stuff or, for the sake of our handy rhyme, stuff
and fluff. Learning how to oscillate between the two categories, loose and
baggy as they are, has been a problem for a long time. It is thus a problem rich
with precedent argument. Pondering these arguments may help us understand the present problem.

Consider, for example, Achilles' choice. A capitalist economy brings with
it a perennial argument, lively again at the present time, about when profit
turns into greed. The same argument has been pursued since Homeric times
about fame. Achilles' choice. Practically every literary hero we know about
has been "greedy for praise," *lofgeornost* as the Anglo-Saxon hero Beowulf is

described. Yet, much more often than not in Western history, we have applauded this "greed," unlike the money kind, as a noble longing, an aristocratic hunger. Why is this?

Modern mass communications have created centripetal attention structures that bottle celebrity, and celebrities, for sale. Centripetal attention structures like these emerge so spontaneously from our behavior that they must be an inherited primate behavior pattern, part of our attention capital. So onward to our adoration of princesses, movie stars, and basketball players. These structures focus attention efficiently but on a very few people. They create machine-made fame.

They also create a winner-take-all society, as a recent book styles it. A few basketball players, opera singers, thriller writers, you-name-its, get all the attention and make all the money. All the world watches the young girl ice-skating at the Olympics do a double-triple backward toe flip. She wins and reaps the rewards. But a painful inefficiency comes with it. What about the rest of us?

Concentrating all the attention in a few hands, a world of celebrities, brings the same misfortunes of maldistributed wealth we know so well from goods economies. What about all the good pianists, violinists, novelists, poets, who are not great, or who have not managed their careers so as to be viewed as great? How do they find a condign place in the sun? Professors, too, are feeling this heat. When education migrates online, one famous professor can replace dozens of us lesser lights. Odd, isn't it? We don't object to these gross inequities in attention (at least if they happen to someone else) nearly so much as we do to similar inequities in stuff. If attention makes life real, if self-consciousness about experience enriches us as we pass through it, then the centripetal structures of modern fame should make us equally vexed. Why don't they?

Well, in a few pathological instances, they do. As I write this, we are in the midst of a worldwide terrorist campaign that seeks, at least as its proximate reward, more attention from "the media." Behind it lie plans, we are told, for eventual worldwide conquest, but the immediate goal is media attention. A more narrowly focused terror campaign was recently pursued by a sniper on the East Coast of the United States who toyed with the media to gain attention. And these two campaigns, large and small, have lots of company in the disgruntled teenager who brings a shotgun to school to kill the teacher and a few classmates and thus gain the attention so churlishly denied him by his peers. Or in the employees, vexed by the daily abrasions of work, who arrive at the same solution. They are all crimes of attention, trying to get more of that commodity, as surely as Jesse James was trying to get more money from banks and trains. They want to prove that they are truly alive, not by getting rich but by being on television.

How on earth (heaven is another matter) do you resolve inequities of attention? Andy Warhol, in suggesting fifteen minutes of fame for each of us, pointed out the paradox in his characteristically indirect way. If you redistribute this subspecies of wealth, fame ceases to be fame. The egalitarian argument makes no sense in an economy of attention. You can't map the one sort of economic thinking directly onto the other.

Nor can you do so in regard to the most fundamental economic category, property itself. Property in a stuff economy means real stuff you can sit on, live in, drive. In a world of stuff, property can have only one owner. I cannot give you my Miata and continue to drive it myself. As the world has discovered from its experiments with the abolition of such private property, a productive economy depends on it. But this fundamental law of property does not work in an attention economy. Because it is built on electronic information as its central wealth, a public good that is effortlessly duplicated and distributed, we can eat our cake, still have it, and give it away too.

This paradox of property has come up before in the Western cultural conversation. An early Greek rhetorician (in a textual fragment usually called *Dissoi logoi* [Opposed arguments]) set for debate the question: "That it is not possible, if you were to hand a thing over to someone else, for you still to have this thing. . . ." Not possible with a car; quite possible with an idea, an argument, a style, a design, an e-mail joke. It may be that this fundamental difference explains the frequent antipathy between the business world and the university. In the world of scholarship, so long as due credit is given, ideas are freely available for others to build on. (That, at least, is how it is supposed to work.)

The law of intellectual property has, as we might expect, been much roiled by this paradox. When copyright law first developed, it aimed to protect written utterance as enshrined in books, physical objects. You could not both keep a book and give it away, and every effort to evade this law of nature, as in nineteenth-century lending libraries, for example, has been opposed by the providers of such fixed-substrate information. But the digital screen finally gives information its condign expressive platform, a "binding" that, unlike the binding of a codex book, exactly fits its inner nature. You can both keep and share such information; both you and the world have an equal chance to turn it into wisdom. The increasingly frantic and avaricious efforts by intellectual property holders to map old conceptions of property onto a new world it does not fit now constitute daily headlines. These headlines tell us that the locus of "property" has moved from stuff to fluff.

The collision of these two kinds of property manifests itself most strongly in the paradigmatic case of an attention economy, the Internet. The biologist Garrett Hardin, in his celebrated essay "The Tragedy of the Commons," made clear how the common ground in an English village, on which all could graze their sheep, speedily became overgrazed because each person had the use of it but none the responsibility for it. The more people grazed their sheep on the common, the more barren it became. (In fact, the villagers introduced laws to meet the problem, a problem that the economist Scott Gordon had more accurately described for the fisheries industry. It is Hardin's attention-grabbing phrase, however, that has gained immortality.) The World Wide Web has created what we might call "the comedy of the commons." It has developed into an ever-richer community resource. The more people graze on it for their own purposes, the bigger it becomes and the greener its grass grows. It thus combines the power of a free market, where individual gain leads to collective benefit, with the cooperative ownership of the cultural conversation.

We don't know how to handle this comedy of plenty in which the more we give away, the more we have. The efforts to absorb it into the alien, stuff, conception of property, to impose on it stuffy sales patterns and profit expectations, have cluttered it up with advertising and finally, perhaps, along with routine human folly, led to the dot-com collapse. These efforts may also, judging by the metastasizing intellectual property claims, strangle it. The Internet models the larger cultural conversation, and when something is put up there, people naturally consider it not as a product but as part of a conversation, whether it be the exchange of embroidery patterns or pop songs. The outraged exclamations that this conversation is "simple thievery" refuse to acknowledge the movement from an economics of stuff to an economics of attention.

In this discussion of changes that come with an economy of attention, I've been following Walter Wriston's admonition to seek out "the rules and customs, skills and talents, necessary to uncover, capture, produce, preserve, and exploit information." But I've left until last the most obvious place where such activity has always occurred: the university. Universities exist to "uncover, capture, produce, and preserve" information. Thus their increasing importance in advanced economies since World War II. But universities have never been simply data-mining and storage operations. They have always taken as their central activity the conversion of data into useful knowledge and into wisdom. They do this by creating attention structures that we call curricula, courses of study. These try to make sense of the world's welter of information for students beginning to make their way in it. They decide how we pay attention to the world of information and hence what use we can make of it, how we can, to pick up Wriston's last word, "exploit" it. Since World War II these debates about the "relevance" and "use" of education have grown increasingly acrimonious. Let me suggest a new way to think about them. They have been, at heart, about the relative importance of an economics of stuff and an economics of attention and, above all, about how to relate them, how to move from one to the other. Not an easy thing to do, this oscillation from stuff to fluff, from the sciences to the arts and letters. This oscillation is not about knowledge per se but about how knowledge is held and used, about wisdom. Back again to our central paradox.

Since the end of the nineteenth century, the world of stuff has gradually come to dominate the university curriculum, at least in America. The sciences needed to analyze the physical world and the business acumen needed to make useful objects from it have constituted the serious subjects of study, the fields you "could make a living with." The traditional attention economists, the practitioners of the arts and letters, have supplied the ornamental frills. These aristocratic remnants have been sustained, when they have survived, by the unanswerable argument of "knowledge for its own sake." This argument, strong to those who already possess the knowledge and find it satisfying, has proved less powerful to those who must be persuaded why they should acquire it. But to the extent that we now live in an information economy, and hence one built on attention engineering, to coin an ecumenical phrase, this relationship must invert. The arts and letters, which create attention structures to teach us how to attend to the world, must be central to acting in the world as well as to contemplating it. The design of an object, in such a world, becomes as important as the engineering of the object. The "positioning in the market" of an object, a version of applied drama, will be as important as either one. The launch of a movie will be as important as the movie itself. No "for its own sake" arguments are required. Such knowledge is immediately useful in the world. A liberal education matters in a world of fluff.

Neither side seems prepared for this figure/ground inversion. The arts and letters have not yet outgrown the antipathy to industrial enterprise, the world of stuff, left over from their nineteenth-century delusions of a static, rural, earthly paradise. The world of affairs is still pretty much the enemy. But the arts and letters, in an attention economy, constitute the world of affairs. For those of us who teach in the humanities, that enemy is now us. But the world of stuff has not gotten the message either. If you start talking about dramatic illusion, about the centrality of design, about the deep paradoxes of "intellectual property" to policy wonks or business execs or copyright lawyers you will not, at least in my experience, ring any bells.

But what about the economists? Where are they, and who are they, in an attention economy? In the twentieth century, the most obvious economists of attention have been the visual artists. The locus of art, for them, became not the physical object that occasioned the aesthetic response but the response itself. The center of art migrated from the object to the attention it required. Asking for instances is like writing the history of twentieth-century visual art. Cubism asked us to look at our seeing as well as the landscape seen and to toggle between the two in a single painting. The Italian futurists created alphabetic collages that asked us to consider letters as physical objects, stuff, rather than as agents of information, to reverse our customary stuff/nonstuff assumptions. Marcel Duchamp made a large career out of manipulating our attention about the modest number of objects he managed to create. Josef Albers in his color-square paintings asked us to look at color rather than through it to the information it conveyed. Robert Irwin created a series of paintings and scrim curtains that aimed to make us see how we see. The pop artists continually manipulated scale to make us recognize the role scale plays in how we apprehend the world. Claes Oldenburg scaled up ordinary objects until they became not ordinary stuff but the way we saw that stuff. Roy Lichtenstein drove the lesson home with a painting of a magnifying glass that magnified the Benday dots out of which he constructed his comic-book paintings. And we could write the same story for music, beginning with John Cage's effort to make us pay attention to daily background sounds by foregrounding them and presenting them as music. He wanted us to hear ourselves hearing.

When this art of attention became tedious, as it often did in percolating down, we could see it more clearly. It was didactic, not revolutionary, and its aim was to teach us how to toggle back and forth between seeing the art object, and hence the world, as stuff and seeing it as attention. It taught an economics lesson. It aimed to train us in the oscillation between stuff and fluff, objects and what-we-think-about-objects, which we are continually required to make in an economy of attention. It told us an economics of attention was coming and it tried to teach us how to behave in it.

Without this background/foreground switch in the premise of art, we would not have had the design revolution that increasingly informs the attention economy. Design is now data driven. If you look at the history of non-representational painting through the eyes of computer graphics, it comes to seem not pure abstraction but the opposite, data-driven pictures of how we see. And looking now the opposite way, the scientific visualizations created by using numerical data often make wonderful nonrepresentational paintings. We can, for example, "see" mathematical equations given visual equivalence on a computer screen, and they turn out to be as beautiful as the mathematicians have always said they were. And self-consciously data-driven art, for example the paintings of Steven Rooke, which are created using genetic algorithms, links the world and our attention to it in fundamentally new ways. All of computer graphics—and that is increasingly how we create images—is data driven. It is made up of algorithms. You see the "information" in the image, the mathematics that inheres in the image. When a computer animator creates an algorithm to draw an image, she has looked at the object as information not as stuff. This oscillation embodies the background/foreground reversal we began with: the object from a stuff economy and the algorithm from the world of nonstuff. The economics of attention finds its center in just this oscillation between the two worlds, in the paradox of stuff.

When I went to a computer graphics meeting a dozen years ago, one of the participants introduced herself as an "information designer." The job description took me by surprise but it should not have. It encapsulates the stuff/fluff paradox. Designers make patterns in the physical world, templates for stuff. But when they design information, they are designing nonstuff, templates for how to think about the world, how to act in it.

Consider, for example, the design of fighter plane cockpits. The speed of encounter and decision that fighter pilots face has created a paradigmatic attention economy. Time is not only money here, it is life itself. The pilot has to allocate power in the world of stuff but to do so must convert masses of data into useful information and act on it immediately. The techniques invented to make this possible have involved superimposing information on the cockpit Plexiglas (the "heads-up display" that has now found its way into automobile windshields) so that the pilot sees the physical world and the information needed to make sense of it in the same visual field and can toggle back and forth between them almost instantaneously. Surely the designer of such a space qualifies as an economist in an economy of attention, figuring out how the scarce commodity is, and should be, allocated.

The fighter cockpit exemplifies the theatrical space of the digital world, and if the literary critics have not seen this, the video game designers certainly have. Not only the flight-simulator games but the entire video game universe aims to make players into acute and swift economists of attention. The designers of motion-based theme park rides have developed the genre in a less involving way. Real-life military training is migrating into electronic theater, too, because training in the physical world is too expensive. War has always been an intensely theatrical experience, but in the Gulf War, the strategists truly began to see themselves as the set designers of the Mideast theater. "Theater of operations" is no longer a metaphor.

In twentieth-century experimental theater, the role of the actor has often conflated with that of the audience. In a "happening," the audience is the cast and writes the script as well. Literary theory has made much of how an audience rewrites the play in its own mind, bringing about the same conflation of roles, author and participant. We can, in video games, see the same conflation. The video gamer acts in his world. It is participatory theater par excellence. But he must also, to improve his performance, become a student of his own attention and the attention structure designed into the game. He must become, that is, an economist of attention, studying his performance even while he is immersed in it or in a high-frequency oscillation between the two states. So, too, with all the soldiers trained with this technology. They become acutely self-conscious of their own behavior, in rapid alternation acting and considering their own actions. The designer of these digital dramas is clearly an economist of attention, then, but so are the players. Parents may not need to worry so much about their children when they play video games. They may be training themselves for a new economy.

The most obvious new group of attention economists may be the computer-human interface designers. This branch of information design subsumes all the efforts at Web site design, amateur and professional, which we encounter on our daily voyages through cyberspace. The Internet constitutes the pure case of an attention economy. "Eyeballs" constitute the coin of the realm. If, as one sometimes reads, Internet companies spend 75 percent of their money on marketing, this only makes sense in a world where stuff has given way to fluff. It should not surprise us that the dominant discipline, the economics that matters in this new theater, is design.

We might look at the present ubiquity of product design as illustrating the paradox of stuff. When design is so big that it makes the cover of *Time* as it did a couple of years ago, the figure/ground relationship between stuff and fluff threatens to reverse itself, design becoming the figure, stuff the background. Yet designed products energize the world of products, of stuff, elevate them to artistic stature, make them more than ever occupy the foreground rather than the background. Foreground and background, stuff and nonstuff, begin to oscillate before our eyes, indeed have to oscillate, if we are to make sense of what is going on.

This should not surprise us. "Design" is our name for the interface where stuff meets fluff. The design of a product invites us to attend to it in a particular way, to pay a certain type of attention to it. Design tells us not about stuff per se but what we think about stuff. It is the interface where the stuff we dig out of the earth's crust meets a fully human reality of feelings, attitudes, and ambitions. The role of design in product development is beginning to reflect an awareness of this interface.

To take one egregious instance, consider automobile design. For the original Henry Ford, it hardly existed. "Any color so long as it is black," he is said to have said. When Alfred Sloan introduced the annual model change, and when changing paint formulations began to make other colors possible, design poked its nose under the tent flap. When Harley Earl came to General Motors to create the Style and Color section and began to make cars lower and sleeker, design got head and neck inside the tent. When Lee Iaccoca sold Henry Ford II on the Mustang, design was all the way inside. Now, it threatens to take over the tent and command the campaign. Cars are built on a small series of platforms and differentiated by design into market niches. The next step, it is prophesied, will be the VBO or Vehicle Brand Owner. This company "will do only the core tasks of designing, engineering and marketing vehicles. Everything else, including even final assembly, may be done by the parts suppliers." The dominant economics in the car business has become an economics of attention rather than an economics of engineering.

The automobile business is not the only business to experience this change of focus from stuff to fluff. The triumph of brand recognition across the world of consumer products testifies to the same reversal. Firms are beginning to outsource the actual manufacture of their products as tangential to their real essence, which is brand development and recognition. Attention engineering is replacing product engineering as the center stage. The CEO of a handheld computer company recently confessed that she has never even seen the factory in Mexico where her product is made. Stuff doesn't matter. The manipulation of attention provides the crucial center. Design school, perhaps combined with library school, may be a better preparation for the felt realities of current business life than the MBA mills dedicated to the economics of stuff. Or, perhaps even better, a degree in the history of drama.

If we are surrounded by information, we are equally surrounded by the notational systems that express it. Here, too, we surprise a fundamental change. The kinds of information vary, as do the kinds of expression, but the one will continue to demand the other. Even if we use raw numbers, information cannot come to us without some expression. No idea comes to us without traces of the company it has kept. We have always wished in the West, and especially in America, that this were not so. We want information to come in neutral packets. Michael Herr, in describing his life as a Vietnam war correspondent, found his way to this hunger: "After a year I felt so plugged in to all the stories and the images and the fear that even the dead started telling me stories, you'd hear them out of a remote but accessible space where there were no ideas, no emotions, no facts, no proper language, only clean information."

But clean information is not the destiny of humankind. Clean information is unnatural and unuseful. Information always comes charged with emotion of some kind, full of purpose. That is why we have acquired it. The only way to make it useful is to filter it. Filtering thus becomes central. And here is where style comes in. We keep striving for "pure information," but the more information we have, the more we need filters, and one of the most powerful filters we have is the filtration of style. So another paradox: the utopia of perfect information brings with it the return of stylistic filtration, of, as it has traditionally been called in Western culture, rhetoric.

"Rhetoric" has not always been a dirty word, the opposite of sincerity, truth, and good intentions. For most of its life it meant the training in expression, spoken and written, that you need to play a useful role in human society. It became a dirty word in the seventeenth century, when science, trying to describe the world of stuff, wanted to abolish the distortions of human attention structures. Human communication ought to be like the United Parcel Service, an efficient mover of information boxes from one destination to the other. This model for human communication gains its power from its narrowness, but we need a wider model for an attention economy. Information does not come in simple neutral boxes and its distribution is a more complex matter altogether. We need a more capacious conception of human communication, one that can accommodate the full range of human purpose.

All the more do we need it because the digital computer has created a new expressive space. The screen works differently from the page. Words don't stay put. They dance around. Images play a major role and they move too. Color is everywhere. And sound, too, spoken and synthesized. Above all, a different expressive economy prevails. The printed page depends on an economics of deprival. No color, no movement, images in careful moderation. All these sacrificed to create an expressive field that encourages concentration on conceptual thought. It is a monopolistic attention economy, directed from the top. The digital screen depends on an economics of plenty. It allows competition between word, image, and sound for our attention. It is a market attention economy, driven from the bottom. You can map onto these two contrasting expressive spaces all the arguments about top-down versus bottom-up, planned versus market, economies. Market economies, like the political democracy that accompanies them, demand a full-range conception of human communication, the kind a rhetorical curriculum has always provided. And this new rhetoric will have to be built on the digital expressive space as well as the printed one, and teach how to move easily from one to the other.

Time now for some "of courses."

Of course, there have always been more things to do than time to do them in. Of course, time has always passed too swiftly. Of course, we have always been surrounded by magnets that pull our attention in a dozen different directions at once. Of course, people have always sought fame, even, as Hamlet says, in the cannon's mouth. Of course, it has always been the case, as Epictetus said long ago, that "it is not things but what we think about things which troubles humankind." Stuff has never been only stuff. It has always, like gold, carried an emotional charge.

Of course, too, we are not going to etherealize into digital spirits who leave the flesh-and-blood world of stuff behind. Driven by our central paradox, the more efficient our instruments of electronic attention become, the more stuff we can, and do, turn out, and the more important it becomes. Being a gregarious lot, we are not going to be content with a world brought to our doorstep by the Internet and UPS. We are carbon-based creatures, not silicon bits, and will continue to take our joys out there in the human barnyard with our carboniferous fellows. The more we seem to float away into informational space, the more we want to hug the ground.

But these of courses don't change the fundamental reversal of focus. Data rain down on us as never before, teraflops from space probes and gigaflops from point-of-sale registers at the Wal-Marts of the world. Scholarly research continues to heap mountain on mountain. And we have never had so many entertaining distractions, or—if you dislike them—distracting entertainments. The biggest one is the world itself, the raw material of the tourist business. Travel as much as environmentalism and global trade has made us self-conscious about living on the planet Earth. Everything going on there now demands our attention. Suddenly we need to know about it not only to be hip but to be saved. Never have we paid so much attention to time, either. Since the dot-com bubble burst, we have heard less about "Internet Time" but surely its speedups continue to work on us. Information, and sometimes—who knows?—wisdom is dispersed into society faster than ever before. It is as if a computer compression algorithm had been applied to life itself.

And—biggest "of course" of all—the topic of human attention is impossibly broad. Cognitive science, neuroscience, and psychology study how human beings see, hear, use language, solve problems. Primatologists study how primates keep their bands together through attention structures. Archaeologists study how "primitive" *Homo sapiens* built unprimitive attention structures like Stonehenge and the Easter Island figures. The arts and letters are wholly occupied with creating attention structures. Each of these disciplines, and many more, have their own ways of narrowing the subject down into manageable size.

My own way here will follow my own discipline, the history of human expression, oral and literate—"rhetoric." It has traditionally been defined as the art of persuasion. It might as well, though, have been called the economics of attention. I argue here that, in a society where information and stuff have changed places, it proves useful to think of rhetoric precisely as such, as a new economics. How could it be otherwise? If information is now our basic "stuff," must not our thinking about human communication become economic thinking?

The following chapters explore some basic questions about an attention economy: Who are the economists? What happens to our expressive space when it moves from the stuff of the book to the volatile fluff of the computer screen? What kind of attention economy prevails there? What happens to our theory of human communication? What happens to universities when they go online, into a pure economy of attention? What happens to our idea of ownership when it moves from physical property to, as the lawyers style it, intellectual property? What, finally, considered in this new light, does the traditional theory of formal rhetoric look like? Can we think of this old body of thought as a new economics? And finally, what happens to how we think about the human self and human society, to morality in a world where stuff and nonstuff have switched places?

To answer these questions we need to learn how to move more adroitly and self-consciously between stuff and fluff. We must understand better than we do now the paradoxical relationship between things and what we think about things. A comprehensive economics of attention will include both these ways of looking at the world and how we are to relate them. It must be built on the perceptual oscillation that allows us to focus both in our minds at once.

We'll begin our inquiry by considering two unlikely economists of attention.

Background Conversations

Rhetoric as an Educational System

Since the word "rhetoric" runs through this book, perhaps our first background conversation might sketch its history. Thinking about human personality, in Western culture at least, begins with the poems of Homer (ca. eighth century B.C.). Homer created two heroes, Achilles in the *Iliad* and Odysseus in the *Odyssey*. Achilles is the ideal blunt, brave warrior, a type as incapable of guile as of cowardice. At one point in the *Iliad,* Odysseus, who appears in that poem as well as his own adventure, tries to persuade Achilles to return to the battle, instead of sulking in his tent nursing his grievances. Only with his help can the Greeks conquer Troy. Achilles replies: "I must without scruple speak out what I think and what will happen. So don't keep sitting by me and pouring first one thing then the other into my ears. Hateful to me as the gates of hell is that man who hides one thing in his breast and speaks another." Hateful to all of us. Odysseus is forever doing just what Achilles hates, hiding one thing in his breast and speaking another. He is famous for it. At the beginning of his own poem, the *Odyssey,* he is called *polytropon,* a man of many turnings. Many times in the poem he has to lie to save his skin, but sometimes he lies just for the fun of it, dwindling from epic hero into improvisational poet. He finally arrives home and, by using a masterful disguise, frees his wife and house from the parasitical suitors infesting it. He would not have gotten home, or reclaimed it, without his fondness for dramatic imposture and ability to tell a good story.

Achilles' sincerity must appeal to all of us. So too his manner of persuasion. He simply says exactly what he feels and lets the chips fall where they may. His follow-up method, though common enough in history, is less appealing. If his enemies persist in disagreement, he kills them. That's one social model. Odysseus's contrasting method—trying to change Achilles' mind by calling attention first to this circumstance then to that result, suggesting that the world might seem different if viewed from a different perspective, that he may have misunderstood Agamemnon, who has offended him, or that Agamemnon is sorry he has hurt Achilles' feelings—whatever argument might work—appeals to us much less. It aims less at finality than at temporary conflict resolution, compromises, sweeping things under the carpet, playing "let's pretend" here and casting a blind eye there, letting bygones be bygones and water flow under the bridge, everything that we mean by "spin," "politics," or—to use our dirtiest word—"rhetoric."

But Achilles' uncompromising sincerity, appealing as it is, seldom works. Achilles has become the model of unforgiving sincerity and, as Robert Frost once said, "to be social is to be forgiving." Brutal sincerity, unvarnished truth, seldom works, even for absolute monarchs. To govern, even kings must employ expedients. But Achilles' philosophy of communication is always the operating system of choice for political dictators and religious zealots and their wars of conquest and religion. As Athenian culture moved toward democracy, Achilles remained its hero but Odysseus increasingly provided its operating system. In a democracy, the voters need to be persuaded not coerced, and they often are as petulant and resentful as Achilles. And, like Achilles, if you don't get them on your side, you are going to lose the war.

Thus there grew up in Athens a body of knowledge about how to get people on your side voluntarily. This body of knowledge speedily became, and remained for more than 2,000 years, the core of Western education. It was called "rhetoric." (*Rhetor* was the usual term in Greek for "politician.") It taught you how to get people's attention and how to argue your case once you had it. Getting people's attention in a predominantly oral culture that worked through direct assembly meant training two vital powers: memory and voice. You had to speak your case, not read it. ("Reading a paper," then as now, was an invitation to slumber land.) That meant a training in memory so thorough that, in our time, it seems incomprehensible. And you had to learn how to speak in public. That meant, in an age before artificial amplification, voice training, and training for volume as well as quality. And you had to learn how to gesture as well, since more people could see you than hear you. From this necessity, grew a whole vocabulary of gestures. Each aimed to create a specific emotion or underline a specific kind of argument. You had to learn, not to put too fine an edge on it, to be an actor. That part of rhetoric, speaking and body language (as we now call it), was called delivery.

Delivery did not deliver its messages as simply as United Parcel or FedEx, which bring the stuff to your door, ring the bell, and leave. It involved communicating the message in such a way that it would be accepted and attended to rather than refused, ignored, or thrown in the wastepaper basket unread. The United Parcel theory of communication fits Achilles very well; it is the physical counterpart to his blunt sincerity. Look, here's what I think, a box of stuff that I drop on your doorstep. Take it or leave it. But that wasn't how Odysseus operated at all. He was trying to convey a different conception of the world and to invite you to live in this changed world. That meant embodying your argument. Rhetorical delivery was a fully social act. The meaning came wrapped in a package of behavioral clues and cues.

What did you deliver? An argument, and so a rhetorical education taught you how to find arguments and how to arrange them. Finding them was, as the rhetorical *paideia,* or method of education, developed, made easier for you by the compilation of lists of possible arguments from which you could select what you needed. These came to be called the "places of argument," locations where you could go to get good arguments, preformed and ready to use. (In much the same way, computer graphics programs have ready-to-use libraries of visual effects, and digital music programs stores of sounds.) This part of rhetoric was called invention, and it brought with it its own assumptions. If delivery assumed that human communication was essentially and inevitably a dramatic act, invention implied that argument was a teachable activity. You did not have to make up your arguments from scratch each time you sought to persuade someone. The kinds of arguments that people would find convincing were limited in number and could be categorized and learned. In this way, you would learn what people were like by learning what kinds of arguments persuaded them of what. People were not all originals and you did not have to be all original either. Thus the implied system of authorship was communal not individual.

You can already see here the birth of the stuff/nonstuff paradox. You would, with messages delivered this way, always be oscillating between message and delivery, stuff and what we think about stuff.

Once you had your arguments in hand, you had to arrange them in a convincing order. You first stated the question to be resolved, and then presented your arguments, the story you asked your audience to believe. Then you tried to refute the other side's story and then you presented a summary that you hoped would stick in your audience's mind. This two-sided argument is so familiar a manner of proceeding that we take it for granted. It is just the way things are. But two-sided argument is not inevitable in human affairs, which come with many sides. Two-sided argument (*Dissoi logoi,* as the Greeks called it) had to be invented as a particular way to structure human attention.

Because it is the basis of our legal system, we assume that it is how argument inevitably must be pursued—every argument has two sides. But we inherited this inevitability from Greek rhetoric, which devised a procedure for solving disputes in a democracy based on attention structures. Two-sided argument allows for resolution. The jury is offered two conflicting stories of what happened, and it has to accept one or the other. Like delivery, two-sided argument is an essentially dramatic method of conflict resolution and hence of governance. That is its enfranchising assumption: resolution comes with a price and the price is dramatic persuasion. Achilles remained the Greek culture hero, but Odysseus founded the legal system.

Two-sided argument emerged as part of rhetoric, a theory of communication that was and remained profoundly social. It was always concerned with returning abstract thought to the three-dimensional world of behavior where it had to work. Some kind of decision had to be reached. Digital expression, as we shall see, tries to do the same thing, to bridge the gap between the abstract world of alphabetic notation and the three-dimensional noisy world of human behavior. Formal rhetoric assumed that the scarce commodity was human attention and that it had to be skillfully allocated. We can think of a legal trial as just such an allocation. Each side presents an attention structure that purports to be what really happened in the "real" world of stuff. Again, that paradox.

But it also emphasized audience awareness. You would always listen to how your audience was responding and adjust your arguments accordingly. You might end up very far from where you had originally planned to be. As Helmuth von Moltke said, and many generals after him, "No battle plan lasts beyond the first day." Your audience often makes links you hadn't thought of, and these links stimulate your creative imagination. We strive for the same results when we reticulate a series of hypertextual "links" into systematic efforts to stimulate creativity with unexpected juxtapositions. Hypertextual linking can move us from one world of discourse to another, and this kind of voyaging has always stimulated creativity. Rhetorical invention was this kind of organized creativity. It coaxed chance, planned for improvisation.

The classical doctrine of arrangement, the organizational plan for an oration, implied the other kind of management, top-down, "table of organization and equipment" thinking. Arrangement supplied the basic pattern for extended conceptual thinking from the classical Greeks onward. It told us how to begin, how to develop, how to end, how to refute objections—and thus how to both hear and evaluate an argument. Listen to a corporate executive try to explain an organizational chart, and she'll explain it to you using the form of a classical oration, whether she knows it or not. It is the archetypal voice of planning. Thus an oscillation was built into the educational system that both encouraged top-down thinking and bottom-up thinking, each when it seemed to work best.

Style, memory, and delivery constituted the package for persuasion in classical rhetoric. Memory allowed you to pretend that you speak spontaneously. Delivery allowed you to distribute the message in person. In preamplification days, this meant a loud voice and commanding gestures. Radio and television provide us with subtler delivery techniques (although they are not always used), but the basic requirement remains the same. You must seem like someone people can trust. Style really includes both of these, now that memory is digitized, voice and image amplified. Style, once again, is ingratiation.

From this educational system emerged the "revisionist thinking" I discuss in the last chapter. It taught its pupils how to revise not only speeches and texts but also attitudes and human relationships. It linked style and behavior; they were part of the same system. The rhetorical educational system taught a way to hold knowledge: tentatively, aware of your motives in holding it, aware of your audience and of the arguments that oppose your own. Aware, above all, that under different circumstances, you might be arguing the opposite case. Such training in rhetoric as has survived into our time usually justifies itself by arguing that you need to learn the methods of argument to defend yourself against your opponents. But, more important, it allows you to defend yourself against yourself, to cultivate an interior countercheck. The more odious you might find that opposing opinion, the more you should seek to know what would make someone hold such an opinion. And the more you should examine the grounds on which you hold your own. This self-examination is, and ought to be, a humbling experience.

Such an education makes you comfortable with a bi-stable grasp of the world. Looking through experience and at it, first one and then the other, comes to seem a natural way of seeing, a habit of perception. Such an oscillation will constitute your characteristic way of looking at the world. Helpful, don't you think, if you have to live in a world where stuff and what we think about stuff are often at odds?

What kind of economy did rhetorical education imply? A market economy, obviously enough. An economy that depends on persuasion. It is the rhetorical habit of mind that creates both the free market and the free market of ideas. The freedom comes from persuasion not coercion, whether you buy a product or an idea. Planned economies constrain attention; rhetorical markets attract it. They do not compel agreement; they invite it.

Think of all the diatribes against "hidden persuaders" that have accompanied the plenitude of goods advanced economies can now provide. If you know what people really ought to buy instead of what they do buy, as cultural critics usually do, you'll always demonize persuasion of any sort, hidden or not. Rhetorical education put its faith in this demon. Persuasion creates markets that embody free choice. A training in persuasion ran both ways; you tried to persuade and you knew persuasion when it was aimed at you. Such a training both defines and refines markets. The more self-conscious the training, the more sophisticated the markets.

We like to think, especially if we are of a scientific turn of mind, that information comes without packages, just the "raw data." Intellectuals like to think that ideas come without packages, that they bear no traces of the company they have kept. That there is a history of ideas, all by themselves. Like the recipients of the Christo joke discussed in chapter 2, they pay no attention to the package and unwrap it to find an idea. But the idea has evaporated when the package was cast aside. Like Christo, the arguments of what we have come to call postmodern thought have all, in one way or another, insisted that ideas do have packages and that the packages are important. So rhetoric has always argued. By the intensity of its training in the means of expression, it lent to the people whom it educated a self-consciousness about how expression affected content, about how knowledge always should be held with an awareness of its container. I think that is what the philosopher and mathematician Alfred North Whitehead had in mind when he defined wisdom as just this—how knowledge is held.

If you want to read up on the history of rhetoric, George Kennedy's two foundational volumes, *The Art of Persuasion in Greece* and *The Art of Rhetoric in the Roman World,* are the place to start. He has also written an abridgement of these two works, *A New History of Classical Rhetoric.* My *Handlist of Rhetorical Terms* introduces a reader to the basic nomenclature and categories and offers short essays on key terms and concepts. The foundational quarrel of intellectual perspectives in Western culture is the one between the rhetoricians and the philosophers. Bruce A. Kimball has written a "history of the idea of liberal education" as the quarrel between the two in *Orators and Philosophers.* The philosophers have gotten most of the praise—think of how Plato's Socrates has become a secular god in liberal education—but the rhetoricians founded the educational system. The best introduction to this system I know is H. I. Marrou's *A History of Education in Antiquity.* G. B. Kerferd has written an incisive short book on the rhetoricians whom Plato denounced, *The Sophistic Movement.* The great explanatory defense of the rhetoricians, however, is Eric A. Havelock's *The Liberal Temper in Greek Politics.* He has also written a corollary book, *A Preface to Plato,* which seeks to explain, among many other things, why Plato hated art. It reads like a mystery story and provides a good introduction to the whole debate.

The argument for a "bottom-up" free-market economy has been made by Friedrich A. Hayek's *The Constitution of Liberty*. He argues for the role of chance in ways strikingly similar to those employed in the "aleatory art" of the twentieth century. I cite him rather than Milton Friedman, or other defenders of the market, because his arguments parallel in many ways the basic assumptions of the rhetorical system of education. He might, in fact, be thought of as a defender of the rhetorical view of society. Or, perhaps we might say, he conceived economics as essentially an economics of attention. Hayek argued that "there is no simple understanding of what makes it necessary for people under certain conditions to believe certain things. The evolution of ideas has its own laws and depends very largely on developments that we cannot predict." Formal rhetorical instruction created market rules for this evolution to occur. It did not argue for one conclusion or another—that was philosophy's job—but rather sought to establish an environment in which argument could persuade by peaceable competition. Hayek stressed the creativity of competition. Techniques of persuasion referee the competition of ideas and from this competition, Hayek argued, evolves the spontaneous development of thought.

Daniel Yergin and Joseph Stanislaw have surveyed the shift, in the last fifty years, from top-down planning to open markets, in *The Commanding Heights: The Battle between Government and the Marketplace That Is Remaking the Modern World*. Robert J. Samuelson's *The Good Life and Its Discontents* talks about this same contention between government planning and the marketplace. It is a carefully argued and balanced book from which much is to be learned, not least about the puzzling mixture of stuff and attention that makes up the modern American economy. Both books, though neither makes the point explicitly, continue the classical dispute between the top-down philosophers and the bottom-up rhetoricians.

The arts and letters world has, at least since Alexander Pope's denunciation of popular taste in *The Dunciad,* despised the bottom-up freedoms of the marketplace in favor of the pastoral stasis of a traditional English country village. Martin J. Wiener's *English Culture and the Decline of the Industrial Spirit* traces this literary resistance to an industrial economy. If you want to know where all the literary clichés about heartless capitalism and sordid profit come from, Wiener is the place to go. He chronicles the Edenic illusion on which so much adverse commentary about an attention economy is based.

The Platonic critique of rhetoric and those who taught it argued that it was a training in lying. Jeremy Campbell surveys the history of lying in *The Liar's Tale: A History of Falsehood,* a book that touches my own argument at many points. It ought to be read in conjunction with Jonas Barish's *The Anti-Theatrical Prejudice.* Between them, they survey all the objections to rhetoric that have made it a dirty word. Campbell discusses a number of issues that I've not had space for here, including the postmodern tolerance for, and sometimes advocacy of, lying. Much of what we think of as postmodern thought amounted to a revival of rhetoric, but the world of literary theory and cultural studies adopted only half of the rhetorical *paideia,* the search for the special interests that lie behind any argument. As often as not, these debunking inquiries have not extended to the writers themselves. "At" vision has been restricted to opponents. They use rhetoric; we only speak the unvarnished truth. Campbell explores these self-contradictions. It is a book whose careful and complex arguments are couched in wonderfully clear prose. An excellent introduction to the "deconstructive" postmodern world by someone with a first-class crap detector that he does not hesitate to use.

I must acknowledge here the "conversation" (through books and, on two notable occasions, in person) of the great American rhetorician and literary critic, Kenneth Burke. He has provided the intellectual framework within which my thinking has developed since I was introduced to his work as a graduate student. Throughout his unorthodox intellectual life he refused to observe the disciplinary boundaries by which, and in which, most academics live, and without his inspiration I never would have had the wit, much less the courage, to try to bring together the various kinds of endeavor and thinking I've drawn on in this book. Burke started out in the thirties as a raging Marxist and remained, throughout his career, a fierce opponent of business and business people and the world of capitalism and profit that they represented. But, at the same time, his final loyalty was to the rhetorical habit of mind, and that habit led inexorably to free markets and the profit-oriented and hierarchical struggles in what he called "the human barnyard." If you are interested in the arguments for rhetoric I've advanced in this book, Burke is the place you should go next. Start with *A Rhetoric of Motives* and persevere. (I've listed his main books in "Works Cited.") He started the rhetorical conversation for our time.

Rhetoric and Economics

The book that first made me think about economics and rhetoric in the same frame was Deirdre McCloskey's *The Rhetoric of Economics,* and I owe it a great debt, a debt that has continued as I read McCloskey's other work: *If You're So*

Smart, Knowledge and Persuasion in Economics, and her later *The Vices of Economists—the Virtues of the Bourgeoisie.* This last book, and its pocket book redaction, *The Secret Sins of Economics,* constitute the best introduction for humanists to the current state of economic thought. *Knowledge and Persuasion in Economics* tells an ordinary reader like me how this current state has come about. McCloskey's prose sparkles with wit and good sense, and no mathematics is needed. She offers that rarest of scholarly combinations, immense intellectual breadth and an ability to go deep to the root of the disagreements that breadth introduces. That she argues for one-quarter of economic activity as rhetorical emboldened me to pursue my argument. That she dismisses much of economic thought in the last fifty years as fundamentally flawed cautioned me to walk carefully in how I did so.

I've knocked on more conventional doors. I started with a textbook by two friends, Jack and David Hirshleifer, *Price Theory and Applications,* which, although clearly written and argued, does require mathematical skills I don't possess. Even nonmathematical readers can learn a lot from it, however, as I have done. William R. Allen's mini-essays on basic economic principles, collected in the three volumes of *Midnight Economist,* constitute an excellent introduction to how economists think (*Midnight Economist: Choices, Prices, and Public Policy, The Midnight Economist: Meditations on Truth and Public Policy,* and *The Midnight Economist: Little Essays on Big Truths*). Allen, the reader should be warned, does not take a cheerful, or a fashionable, view of the present scene. Adam Smith's arguments are presented in the spirit of Jonathan Swift.

Roger E. Backhouse's *The Ordinary Business of Life: A History of Economics from the Ancient World to the Twenty-first Century* provides the neutral survey every beginner needs. Then, since I had taught medieval literature throughout my career, I thought I might read a little bit about medieval economics. Edwin S. Hunt and James M. Murray, *A History of Business in Medieval Europe, 1200–1550,* is a good beginning textbook. So, too, Jean Favier's *Gold and Spices: The Rise of Commerce in the Middle Ages.* Iris Origo's description of the fourteenth-century Italian merchant Francesco di Marco Datini, *The Merchant of Prato,* working in much finer individual detail, provides a good corrective to anyone thinking economic decisions were any simpler, any more rational, or less dominated by time and chance, in the dawn of European commerce than they are now.

It seemed sensible to look at some business case histories written for the common reader, to see what rhetorical ingredients they might possess. I started with a couple of surveys. John Micklethwait and Adrian Wooldridge's *The Company: A Short History of a Revolutionary Idea* is an accessible, plain-language introduction to the subject. Likewise with Joan Magretta's marvel of concise explication, *What Management Is*. These books made me reflect on management as one of rhetoric's descendants, along with advertising, public relations, and the liberal arts curriculum.

Then on to some concrete instances. Since I've always been in love with cars, I started with them: James P. Womack, Daniel T. Jones, and Daniel Roos's *The Machine That Changed the World*. If you want an introduction to the car business, you can't do better than this. Their discussion of lean production, pioneered by Toyota, seemed to me so applicable (if not as yet remotely applied) to academic organizations, that I followed up with Womack and Jones's discussion of *Lean Thinking* and then Edwin M. Reingold's *Toyota: People, Ideas and the Challenge of the New.*

Peter L. Bernstein's *Against the Gods: The Remarkable Story of Risk* would have made perfect sense to Francesco Datini, the merchant of Prato, and teaches a salutary lesson for our security-obsessed age as well. When you risk you sometimes lose, and I read two salutary tales of losers. In the story of computers, *the* story of the second half of the twentieth century, the biggest failure was Xerox's failure to market the Alto computer invented at its research establishment, XeroxParc. This exemplary failure of nerve and imagination is recounted by Douglas K. Smith and Robert C. Alexander in *Fumbling the Future: How Xerox Invented, Then Ignored, the First Personal Computer*. The information economy was a dangerous place even in its inception. Even sadder reading is John P. Hoerr's long history, *And the Wolf Finally Came: The Decline of the American Steel Industry*. The Monongahela Valley was the center of the American stuff economy, "hell with the lid off" when it was thriving, mourned when dead, its shriveled up plants left to rust. If you want to see and feel the complexities of mature industrial enterprise—surely a fundamental part of our economy—you can't do better than a book like this. The steel industry, the backbone of the stuff economy, was not dead, certainly, and *The Renaissance of American Steel,* by Roger S. Ahlbrandt, Richard J. Fruehan, and Frank Giarratani, tells that tale. They quote John Correnti, the CEO of Nucor: "Technology accounts for about 30 percent of Nucor's success. The other 70 percent is our culture and employee relations/employee management practices." Again and again in my reading in industrial enterprise, I found the same observation, or made it myself when the author could not see it. Persuasion and motivation—the center of rhetorical teaching—also stood at the center of business enterprise. The technology that dominates the public conversation—the stuff—is no more important than the fluff—motive, persuasion, communication, style—that makes up a company's management. Style and substance: you can, in studies like these, see them oscillate before your eyes. Some people, like John Correnti, understand what is going on; many in Hoerr's tale don't or can't switch between the two economies.

Books on management have fallen thick as snowflakes in Siberia ever since the change from an economy of stuff to an economy of attention made managers wonder how to be saved in this new world. Management gurus are, in more than one sense, put in their place in John Micklethwait and Adrian Wooldridge's *The Witch Doctors*. Again, it is revealing to read their description of the various diagnoses of "the new economy" in light of an economics of attention. The star of their pantheon is Peter Drucker, who coined the term "knowledge worker" (in 1959). Drucker has spent a long and immensely productive life defining "management" as a broad and humanistic, rather than a narrowly economic, activity. As they say, "Perhaps Drucker's most insightful observation is that management plays a vital role in all spheres of life, not just in business." Just like rhetoric.

Perhaps Drucker's broad culture has made him less than welcome among professional economists, but it makes him the more welcome to a general reader trying to make sense of economic change. Drucker has always been, atop all his other accomplishments, a professional writer addressing a general cultured reader. This broad address has conferred the freedom from academic disciplinary confines needed to understand an attention economy.

Drucker's most important book for me (I have read only half a dozen of them) is his personal memoir, *Adventures of a Bystander*. It is a charming book from start, in his Austrian beginnings, to finish as preeminent American business guru. The chapter titled "The Man Who Invented Kissinger" is a rare and delicate satire on the rhetorical invention of the wise man–foreign minister type. The chapter on the Polanyi family, and their belief in "salvation by society" (in "the quest for the one absolute 'civic religion'; for the perfect—or at least the good—society"), epitomizes the conflict between the planned society's search for perfection and the market economy's willingness to settle for a less perfect, unsettled and unsettling freedom. Once again, the philosopher's design for society contends with the rhetorician's desire to set the rules of the game.

But the chapter I learned the most from was the chapter on Alfred Sloan, the legendary president of General Motors. Drucker's first popular book was his study of GM, *The Concept of the Corporation,* and he tells about writing it in the chapter on Sloan. Drucker argued that a company was a human society and its management involved, and required, all kinds of noneconomic issues. Thus his discussion of the "information economy" came naturally to someone who had been looking beyond the stuff economy from the beginning. At the time he did the study, Drucker was teaching at Bennington College, and Bennington's president then, Lewis Jones, was an economist. He encouraged Drucker to do the study but warned against publishing it. "'You're launched,' he said, 'on a highly promising academic career, either as an economist or as a political scientist. A book on a business corporation that treats it as a political and social institution will harm you in both fields.' Jones was right in this too. When the book came out, neither economist nor political scientist knew what to make of it and both have ever since viewed me with dark suspicion." Study of the attention economy will require the perspective Drucker brought to the subject, a subject that falls into the oubliette lurking between academic specializations. I don't mean, in this discussion, to ignore Drucker's books that bear on an information economy. Two that a nonprofessional reader will find accessible are *Post-Capitalist Society* and *The New Realities*.

When I began thinking about rhetoric as an economics of attention, my thinking about American capitalism, like that of many humanists, stopped with Ida Tarbell's tarring and feathering of John D. Rockefeller and Matthew Josephson's long-lasting calumny, *The Robber Barons*. "The sequence 'Capitalism bad, socialism good' is the most persistent but most damaging *non sequitur* in political science," Arthur Seldon remarks in his defense of free markets, *Capitalism*, but that's about where I began. Of course, central planning made more sense than leaving the fate of the republic to market manipulators like Rockefeller and Morgan.

What jolted me from top-down to bottom-up thinking, though, had nothing to do with economics. It was the arguments for emergent order, "order for free," advanced by the proponents of artificial life and complexity theory. These made me rethink the proposition of control. I started with Steven Levy's *Artificial Life: The Quest for a New Creation* and Mitchell Waldrop's *Complexity: The Emerging Science at the Edge of Order and Chaos*. I kept reading around, moving on to Stuart Kauffman's and John Holland's work, then backward a little to the basic evolutionary thinking in Richard Dawkins's *The Selfish Gene* and *The Blind Watchmaker*. Matt Ridley's *The Origins of Virtue* develops an evolutionary argument for markets as the product of "an exchange organ in the brain." We are wired to make market-exchange calculations. From this wiring develops our talents for social cooperation. Ridley is developing the *Theory of Moral Sentiments* side of Adam Smith. (He titles one chapter "Theories of Moral Sentiments.") Here again I found an economics/rhetoric overlap. Rhetoric developed a framework for competition and from it sought to bring cooperation. If this was not Kauffman's "order for free," it was at least Hayek's "order from the bottom up."

Then I felt ready to take on two volumes from the Santa Fe Institute Proceedings, *Artificial Life* and *Artificial Life II*. From there I moved to a book about mathematics that, for a wonder, I could understand: James Bailey's *After Thought: The Computer Challenge to Human Intelligence*. It's a book that opened my eyes on almost every page, a retrospective history of science that argued for problems solved by cultivating solutions on computers rather than by working them out by propositional reasoning. Mathematics, I suppose you might call it, for a complexity world. Some applications of these new maths for business are suggested in a slender volume, *Embracing Complexity: Exploring the Application of Complex Adaptive Systems to Business*, which summarizes a colloquium on this topic convened by the Ernst & Young Center for Business Innovation in 1996.

I took three reflections from this line of inquiry. One was economic: Here was a powerful argument for free markets, where order, too, was created from below, without central direction. But this argument came from outside economics altogether. The second reflection led back to rhetoric: in human debate, in the endless bickering in the barnyard, order emerged from below, too. The order was messy in origin and forever shifting and growing in content, and this volatile messiness put off Plato and has put off Platonists ever since. But it was, clearly, how governance in a democracy had to take place. Rhetoric had been, for two millennia and more, our means for bottom-up thinking, just as philosophy had been our means for top-down control, all philosophy being, as Whitehead said, but footnotes to Plato, the master of central planning. And here, charging back, came a book I mentioned earlier, Eric Havelock's *The Liberal Temper in Greek Politics*. Havelock argues, in a clarifying first chapter, "The Eden Myth and the Science of Man," that early Greek rhetoric came out of an anthropological, an evolutionary, view of humankind. It was an orderly procedure, that is, for allowing human thought to evolve, for human order to work its way up from individual decisions. So here was an argument, again from outside the field, for rhetoric not as an art of ornamentation but as a way to impose order on the world. The third reflection led me to the world of twentieth-century art. A central thread in that world was the reintroduction of chance into artistic creation. Assemble some ingredients and let the performer put them together in the almost unlimited number of ways they could be combined. Let performances evolve. Here was artistic creation trying to use the "new maths" that Bailey discusses in *After Thought*. An argument for free-market artistic creation. Books on finance tend, not surprisingly, to emphasize its efforts to rationalize human behavior. The aleatory, chance-driven strand in twentieth-century art, on the contrary, went right to the heart of the matter: our love of gambling and of the dramatic intensity it creates.

These reflections led me to ponder government efforts to control this love of risk. I started with a history of the Securities and Exchange Commission, the top-down control mechanism created by the New Deal to regulate the financial markets: Joel Seligman's *The Transformation of Wall Street: A History of the Securities and Exchange Commission and Modern Corporate Finance*. The Pecora Committee's investigation of the House of Morgan, replayed now in the Enron inquiries, led me to Ron Chernow's *The House of Morgan: An American Banking Dynasty and the Rise of Modern Finance*. I found Pierpont Morgan an altogether more interesting figure than the Pecora Committee's demonization, and not only because he was an art collector, museum patron, premier collector of rare books, yachtsman, womanizer, founding patron of the New York hospital that pioneered obstetrics as a medical specialization, amateur Egyptologist, and pillar of the Episcopal Church. Far from being a free-market buccaneer, he was a privatized commissar. As Chernow said of Morgan's steel trust: "It was a form of national industrial policy, albeit conducted by businessmen for private gain." Morgan allocated foreign capital to the industries needing it in the United States in a manner not too different, so far as I could see, from the way the Ministry of International Trade and Industry tried to guide the reconstruction of the Japanese economy after World War II. Only he grew rich doing it. Did Morgan's way of funding American railroads cost the country more than if the federal government had done it? I'm not qualified to say, but it certainly makes the top-down/bottom-up argument more complex if one of the main robber barons was in actuality a social planner. After Chernow's book, I couldn't resist reading Jean Strouse's *Morgan: American Financier*. She makes the same discovery of Pierpont Morgan as central economic planner but can never quite forgive him for not feeling guilty about all the money he was making and all the fun he had spending it.

It wasn't nearly as much money, however, as John D. Rockefeller made by organizing the oil business. Here I depend on another book by Chernow, *Titan: The Life of John D. Rockefeller, Sr.* You learn here why Ida Tarbell hated Rockefeller: he put her father, one of the small Pennsylvania oil producers whose chaotic competition Rockefeller methodized into Standard Oil, out of business. But you also learn that Rockefeller, too, would have made a wonderful central planner. He led the way for American industrial enterprise: "In many ways, Standard Oil's metamorphosis previewed the trajectory of other major American business organizations in the late nineteenth century as they moved from freewheeling competition to loosely knit cartels to airtight trusts. The 1882 agreement introduced the concept of the trust as something synonymous with industrial monopoly." But, as with Morgan, he always felt that he acted in the public interest.

(An assurance not unknown in bureaucrats today.) As Chernow quotes him in a passage immediately before the one just quoted: "I would have every man a capitalist, every man, woman and child . . . I would have everyone save his earnings, not squander it: own the industries, own the railroads, own the telegraph lines." As indeed now, through pension plans, they pretty much do.

Rockefeller's life's work, though, as Chernow describes it, was less making his money than figuring out how to spend it. The list of Rockefeller philanthropies is truly astonishing. The nickel-nursing hard-shell Baptist turned out to be an even greater patron of culture than the cultivated, Europeanized Morgan. And this has been the characteristic pattern of American great wealth: make it and then found a foundation to give it away. This pattern has not been remarked so much as it ought to be. It redefines "property," for a start. Like ideas in the rhetorical marketplace, it is something that you own to make use of, to generate new wealth, not something forever. Rhetorical education has always had two purposes: to train for competition and for cooperation. You see them both in "philanthropic" wealth. Rockefeller was a ruthless competitor, but he was forever stressing the advantages of cooperation. He saw, as rhetorical education has always seen, that the one could create the other. It was not for nothing that Adam Smith taught rhetoric.

The money made in a stuff economy was transferred, via philanthropy, to the stuff that makes up an attention economy: libraries, museums, universities, opera houses, symphony orchestras—the infrastructure of the arts and letters. Jean Strouse remarks, in her Morgan biography: "Capital markets are essentially the organized processes through which money for long-term investment is raised, distributed, traded, and above all *valued*." Think of the cultural conversation as the capital of an attention economy, and notice the fit. It is possible, then, to read these robber baron biographies in quite another light. Economics preoccupies itself with the motives required to make money. It might pay more attention to the motives required to give it away. They testify to an awareness, vague perhaps to these money men but keenly felt, that another conception of economics lay behind the world they worked in.

A revealing glimpse of this other, more complex cluster of motives is offered in Bernice Kert's *Abby Aldrich Rockefeller: The Woman in the Family*. Abby Aldrich married John D. Jr., the conscience-stricken heir to the fortune, and schooled him in social and philanthropic awareness. She also tried, unsuccessfully for the most part, to share her sense of style with his burden of substance. Not until Franklin married Eleanor did style and substance unite in such a public match. Abby Aldrich was, in my view, an altogether remarkable woman who played an equally remarkable role in American philanthropy: think Colonial Williamsburg and the Museum of Modern Art, for a start. But she also spent a lot of money on clothes and houses, expenditures at which the egalitarian temperament will revolt. She was a very stylish lady, good at transferring substantial money to stylish purposes.

Ethos

I grew up with a pathological fear of debt. I still have it. I agree with George Washington: "There is no practice more dangerous than borrowing money." Not a promising attitude to bring to economic reflections of any kind. So, to correct my aberrant vision, I read James Grant's *Money of the Mind: Borrowing and Lending in America from the Civil War to Michael Milken,* a book about "the long-range implications of the socialization of financial risk or the disenfranchisement of character as a competitive element in banking." Rhetoric's term for "character" was "ethos," and ethos was, the rhetoricians argued, a central element in human persuasion and hence human affairs. I was tempted to pursue this theme of debt and character, since it was shared by rhetoric and economics. I stumbled on a striking instance of "the disenfranchisement of character" when I started wondering what "derivatives" were all about. When I learned that their use had led to the fall of an investment company fronted by two Nobel Prize winners, I read all about it in Roger Lowenstein's *When Genius Failed: The Rise and Fall of Long-Term Capital Management.* Long-Term Capital was a hedge fund created by a bond trader named John Meriwether after he had been asked to leave Salomon Brothers as a result of scandalous behavior by a subordinate. It was composed, like the arbitrage group Meriwether had created at Salomon, of "professors" whom Meriwether had plucked from academia. In fact, he had raided the arbitrage group to staff his new firm, adding Nobel high-flyers. Together they had made a great deal of money at Salomon and even more at Long-Term. Without trying to explain how they did it—Lowenstein does this very well—they started by borrowing a great deal of money, much more than such a fund would usually start with. They would then place commensurately big investment bets. Banks lent them the money because they trusted the man who had already made so much money doing the same thing elsewhere. Long-Term recruited a group of a hundred investors, told them that they could not withdraw their money when they wanted to and would not be told what was being done with it. This was, as Lowenstein says, "asking investors to show enormous trust." Meriwether's boys felt that they had conquered risk through mathematical certitude. Their arrogance patronized the investment world. That world bowed down. After all, one of the partners was Nobel-winner and Harvard professor Robert Merton, *the* man in finance. They had the plenary wisdom of mathematical computation on their side. How could they lose?

Lowenstein tells the story of how they did lose, and lose big. It is a medieval tale of the fall of princes who start at the top of fortune's wheel and are inevitably rolled down to the bottom by pride. The wheel was turned, as it always has been, by chance. It measured ethos, character. The ethos of the firm, its collective reputation, attracted all the money. It was not the result of calculation by the banks or the investors because neither was told what was to be done with their money. Its foundation was a rhetorical, not a financial, triumph. Reputation, not calculation, animated these economic decisions. It was run by celebrities, and that was enough for all those banks and rich folks. A salutary lesson: at the top of the rationally calculating economic world stood the celebrity ethos of an attention economy. Rhetoric played as big a role in the story as economics. And an acquaintance with medieval wheel-of-fortune tragedies told you as much about it as a knowledge of derivatives.

Not entirely by chance, perhaps, Lowenstein's previous book had also been a character analysis: *Warren Buffett: The Making of an American Capitalist.* He might have called it, "Where Genius Succeeded." Here's how he begins it: "In the annals of investing, Warren Buffett stands alone. Starting from scratch, simply by picking stocks and companies for investment, Buffett amassed one of the epochal fortunes of the twentieth century. Over a period of four decades—more than enough to iron out the effects of fortuitous rolls of the dice—Buffett outperformed the stock market, by a stunning margin and without taking undue risks or suffering a single losing year." But the ethos here was something entirely different. Buffett started and stayed in Omaha, Nebraska. He lived in an ordinary house and, at least until he got genuinely rich, lived an ordinary life. His favorite drink is Pepsi-Cola. His yearly investor letters are much more Will Rogers than Nobel Prize winner. He was the star pupil of Benjamin Graham, the originator of value-based investing. (Benjamin Graham had argued, in his *The Intelligent Investor,* that the vital factor for a beginning investor was not how much money he had but how much attention he was willing to invest.) But here too it was trust that attracted his first investors and kept them. He has become a mythical figure, a financial celebrity, but the myth has a rhetorical basis: ethos, what kind of person are you? The opposite kind from the Long-Term Capital types, but people needed to know that. Even here, the attention economy is not far away.

When I finished these two books, I realized what I was trying to find out from them. Here were two examples of quintessential buying situations: very sophisticated sellers and very sophisticated buyers. How rational were these decisions? How governed by market information, perfect or otherwise? How much driven by more ordinary, noneconomic decisions about human character and trust, on the one hand, and lust for chance, on the other? About human motive as it operates in the world rather than the world of formal economics.

No one in American finance has been more vilified than Michael Milken, the great proponent of the junk bond. He found his Ida Tarbell in James B. Stewart, whose *Den of Thieves* convinced me, as well as many others, of Milken's depravity. If ever ethos played a role in economic decisions, surely it was here. But something didn't quite fit because junk-bond financing, to my ignorant eye, seemed to promise a salutary democratization of capital access. So I read Daniel Fischel's *Payback,* a defense of Milken and the financial revolution he precipitated. Stewart's argument was not, perhaps, the full story. And the story continues with the Milken Family Foundations and the many good works they perform (a couple of which I've witnessed at first hand). Character stood at the center of the Rockefeller progress from rapacity to philanthropy, and surely Milken's trip on the wheel of fortune illustrates the same home truth. Economics leads to a rhetorical idea of wealth. Competition leads to cooperation—or at least can.

Plenitude

Sixteen flavors of Eggo waffles is not the kind of triumph celebrated in the best circles nowadays. The curse of plenitude! I'm not sure why but I've always rejoiced in this plenitude. So does the economist Tyler Cowen, in two recent books, *In Praise of Commercial Culture* and *Creative Destruction: How Globalization Is Changing the World's Cultures.* Cowan's voice is so original, his knowledge of contemporary art and music so broad, his way with the doomsayers of contemporary culture so brisk, that you rejoice in the pure intelligence that shines on every page. An example:

> Many cultural pessimists, such as Allan Bloom, insist on linking contemporary music to depravity and disorder—Bloom refers to "hymns to the joys of onanism or the killing of parents." He also tells us that, in rock and roll, "these are the three great lyrical themes: sex, hate, and a smarmy hypocritical version of brotherly love." This description represents the lack of familiarity with contemporary music shown by most cultural pessimists.
>
> Contemporary music offers a startling diversity of directions. Chuck Berry sings about the pleasures and freedom of commercialized society, the Byrds

uphold Apollonian ideals with the motif of flight, Bruce Springsteen has moved from romantic yearnings to postmodern bleakness and resignation. Van Morrison is a Celtic mystic, James Brown flaunts pride and self-assertion, the Louvin Brothers sing "Tragic Songs of Life," David Bowie portrays a glittering androgynous world, and Hole offers a fully realized feminist rock mini-opera. The Beatles, with their amazing versatility, offer a miniature worldview in each song, focusing on nostalgia, longing, and the richness of the past. Techno music promulgates a cyberpunk aesthetic, and bebop jazz is based on freedom and spontaneity. The range of available aesthetics and visions is vast, corresponding to our conception of a liberal capitalist society.

My knowledge of the world he describes doesn't run much beyond Chuck Berry and the Beatles, but if you are going to lament modern culture you should first know something about it, as Cowan does. And you should, as you do with all art, approach it with generosity of spirit, lending yourself to its illusion before you condemn it. Generosity of spirit springs off every page in Cowan's books.

He continually walks the line between economic thinking and the arts and letters, pulling wisdom from both sides. He brings the two together as few— well, I can think of only one other, Deirdre McCloskey—economists do and even fewer humanists. He shows you what you can learn when you think about the arts and letters, and the complex human motives they reflect, from an economic point of view, rather than trying to exclude it from economics. Example:

> By placing conservative culture at the top of their political agenda, the neo-conservatives risk losing their skepticism about big government. Many neo-conservatives, such as Irving Kristol, pay lip service to the free market but do not accept the artistic revolutions that markets inevitably bring; market-based art often overturns conservative social conventions and morals. Daniel Bell takes a more consistent attitude by calling himself a conservative in matters of culture and socialist in matters economic.
>
> Bell started as a left-wing socialist and Kristol was a Trotskyite in his early years. Both have since rejected central planning but they retain their suspicion of the values that result from a purely voluntary civil society.

This sort of thinking leads somewhere, unlike the tiresome "the dollar rules all" whining so common in the world of arts and letters.

James B. Twitchell's *Lead Us into Temptation: The Triumph of American Materialism* provides a lively introduction to the languages of our new plenitude: advertising, branding, design. The book has an odd satiric posture though, half description and half implied condemnation. We are forever hearing that while the rich are getting richer, the poor are getting poorer—the curse of plenitude strikes again. W. Michael Cox and Richard Alm take a detailed and convincing exception to this commonplace plaint in *Myths of Rich and Poor.* The subtitle tells it all: *Why We're Better Off Than We Think.* Another curse of plentitude is developed in Robert H. Frank and Philip J. Cook's *The Winner-Take-All Society.* Again the subtitle tells all: *How More and More Americans Compete for Ever Fewer and Bigger Prizes, Encouraging Economic Waste, Income Inequality, and an Impoverished Cultural Life.* Here the view is totally dismal. For a different view of plentitude, try the current IKEA catalog, a living proof that mass-produced products can be beautifully designed, effectively advertised, richly varied, environmentally sensitive, easy to transport, and sold for prices affordable by all. IKEA makes an interesting contrast to Twitchell's argument, too. A random walk through one of their stores can teach you a lot.

Let me conclude with a word about the current quarrels between economists about the nature of "rational man" and his decisions. An article in the *Economist* several years ago outlined attempts to widen the view that economists take of the psychology of human choice. If you make the assumption, not one hard to make in the light of human history, that people are sometimes irrational, you get what Richard Thaler of Cornell University calls "quasi-rational economics." Peter Monaghan, in a more recent article in the *Chronicle of Higher Education,* has described this quarrel as the efforts of a dissident group to start a fire under the "wet blanket" of conventional economists. I'm not competent to take part in this street fight even if I wanted to. What interests me is the economist's habit of thinking in terms of constraints and trade-offs. Rhetoric has always dealt with thought under constraint and the purposes mistook to which such thought often leads. I've been pursuing some similarities between the two. If this puts me in the world of "wackonomics," as Lowell Taylor of Carnegie-Mellon has styled it, I'll abide that prospect with equanimity. I do think, though, that an ability to move from an economics of stuff to an economics of attention comes in handy if you are trying to understand the present scene.

CHAPTER TWO   {ECONOMISTS OF
                       ATTENTION}

O ur recently ended twentieth
century overflows with monuments to artistic outrageousness.
Never have so many artists flung so

In the *spontaneous* unfoldings of history, the
imaginative expression of a trend precedes its
conceptual-critical counterpart.

Kenneth Burke

many paint pots and puzzles in the face of so many publics: urinals turned
upside down and exhibited as art, Rube Goldberg machines that do abstract
drawings, canvases that are all white or all black, paintings of Campbell's
soup cans, sculptures of the boxes the soup came in, trenches dug in the
desert where nobody can see them, the Pont Neuf in Paris wrapped up in gold
cloth for a few days and then unwrapped again. One strand of this outrageousness isn't outrageous at all, once we see the lesson it teaches: During
the twentieth century, art was undergoing the same reversal from stuff to
attention described in chapter 1. Art's center of gravity henceforth would lie
not in objects that artists create but in the attention that the beholder brings
to them. Some examples.

In 1917, the French artist Marcel Duchamp got together with two friends,
the painter Joseph Stella and the connoisseur Walter Arensberg, to play a joke
on the Independents' art exhibition. They bought from the J. L. Mott Iron
Works a urinal on which Duchamp, after turning it upside down, painted the
nom de plume R. Mutt. They then sent it into the show under Mutt's name,
with the $6 registration fee. Since, under the rules of the show, any artist
could submit any piece of work, it had to be shown. But the committee refused to show it. Nevertheless, none has engendered more comment than
this *Fountain*. In 1989, an entire museum show and book were built around

it. The usual explanation of the joke has been that it illustrated the premise of the show: art was what an artist decided it was. This ipse dixit definition of art, though, however much it may elevate the artistic ego to godlike stature, doesn't help much unless you take it a step further. Art is whatever the artist wishes to call to our attention. Art is an act of attention the artist wishes to invoke in the beholder.

Duchamp had developed this theme a few years earlier with his "Readymades." The first, apparently, was a bicycle wheel mounted on a kitchen stool. You could spin it around when you felt like it. Early "interactivity." Later came a kitchen bottle rack, less user interactive but equally stimulating to serious interpretation. You could say, for example, that there was a great deal of beauty hidden in a bicycle wheel, but so long as it was attached to the bicycle, its utility obscured its beauty. Likewise with the bottle rack. From such efforts descended the long list of "found objects" littering the museums of the last century. The lesson was simple and, once learned, tedious. Art is not stuff made out of stuff taken from the earth's crust. Art is the attention that makes that stuff meaningful. The more commonplace and physical the objects teaching the lesson, the more they taught the final insignificance of physical objects.

But Duchamp himself repudiated this interpretation. He said he did not think his Readymades had any hidden beauties to reveal. Furthermore, as he said on more than one occasion, he despised the high seriousness the beholder brought to art. Art, he thought, was a worse religion even than God. He made his feelings clear when he annotated a postcard of the Mona Lisa by drawing a mustache on it. Art not only was a way of paying attention to the physical world, it was a pompous and overblown one as well. His oeuvre since then, indeed over his lifetime, is slender. Yet his recent biographer Calvin Tomkins argues that he is the most important artist of the twentieth century. How could this be?

Duchamp said that he wanted to deflate the seriousness of art. He wanted to make a game out of it, a game with the beholder. We might, thus, consider his career as fabricating a series of attention games with the art-loving public. Consider the famous urinal. It illustrated the premise of the Independents' Exhibition and so constituted a serious statement. It mocked the premise of the Independents' Exhibition ("See, art is a real pisser, isn't it?") and so mocked the serious statement, and the conception of the artistic ego that the exhibition stood for. The art historians and interpreters have fallen into this ironic bear trap every time they've walked over it.

Inquiry of all sorts has to be serious. That is its organizing premise. But if you subtract the object of that seriousness by putting a urinal in its place, that seriousness is turned into a game. To understand it, you must then write a serious treatise on games and play, wondering all the while what you are about. The critic, like a bull bemused by the toreador's flashing cape, starts pawing the ground, angry and confused. Such confusion has made Duchamp famous. The urinal proved to be an extraordinarily efficient generator of fame because other people—the critics and historians—did all of Duchamp's work for him.

Likewise with the Readymades. Duchamp said he made the first one, the bicycle wheel, just because it was fun to spin the wheel around. But when you exhibit it, when you put it into an attention field called "art," it becomes a catalyst. You must look at it differently. Yes, we should indeed pay more attention to the utilitarian world, savor its beauty as beauty. But when you find yourself gazing at it worshipfully, Duchamp turns around and says, "It's just a bicycle wheel, you silly jerk." The final result is to make us oscillate back and forth between the physical world, stuff, and how we think about stuff. It makes us look at our own patterns of attention and the varieties of "seriousness" we construct atop them.

That oscillation constitutes a serious lesson about seriousness. But it does not constitute great art, if we think of art as composed of stuff shaped into beauty, as forming part of a goods economy. In this industrial framework, Duchamp is the charlatan some have taken him for. But if you are willing to put him into an attention economy rather than a goods economy, let him work in attention, not in stuff, then things look different. Duchamp, as few before him, knew how to catalyze human attention in the most economical way possible. The disproportion between his oeuvre, the physical stuff he left behind, and his reputation can be explained in no other way. If we are looking for economists of attention, he provides a good place to start, an excellent lesson in efficiency.

When we consider the twentieth century from this point of view, we are reminded that futurists not only ushered us out of it but into it as well. These first futurists were led, and often financed, by Filippo Tommaso Marinetti, a wealthy Italian intellectual who wanted to catapult Italy into the future, or at least into the sophisticated present of Paris, where Marinetti lived in spirit and often in the flesh. He announced his utopian vision in an advertisement, a "Futurist Manifesto," that appeared on the front page of the Parisian journal *Le Figaro* on 20 February 1909. Marinetti would have made a stupendous ad man in our time but, more remarkably, he already was one in his own, before blitz ad campaigns had been invented. He was, above all, an economist of attention. "Italian Futurism was the first cultural movement of the twentieth century to aim directly and deliberately at a mass audience." He ran his intellectual campaign at the beginning of the century exactly as spin doctors would conduct political campaigns at its end. To reach this audience, Marinetti generated a torrent of manifestos and position statements. And, like an Internet company trying to buy "eyeballs" by giving away its product, he gave his products away to purchase attention: "It is believed that two thirds of the books, magazines and broadsheets that the futurists published were distributed free of charge as 'propaganda' material."

The platform of this campaign for Italian cultural leadership, the famous "Manifesto," might have come right out of the sixties. Here's a sample: "It is from Italy that we are launching throughout the world this manifesto, charged with overwhelming incendiary violence. We are founding *Futurism* here today because we want to free this land from its foul gangrene of professors, archaeologists, guides and antiquarians. For too long Italy has been a market-place for second-hand dealers. We mean to free her from the innumerable museums that cover her like so many graveyards." Get rid of everyone over thirty, especially those gangrenous professors. Forget the past. Fearlessly mount the *Star Trek* holodeck. Marinetti's friendship with Mussolini and his association with Italian Fascism and its glorification of war have brought futurism into well-deserved discredit. But in a later manifesto, from 1913, he points to a less horrific future, one that Marshall McLuhan was to describe later at greater length: "Futurism is grounded in the complete renewal of human sensibility brought about by the great discoveries of science. People today make use of the telegraph, the telephone, the phonograph, the train, the bicycle, the motorcycle, the automobile, the ocean liner, the dirigible, the aeroplane, the cinema, the great newspaper (synthesis of a day in the world's life) without realizing that these various forms of communication, transformation, and information have a decisive effect on their psyches." Later on he speaks of an earth shrunk by speed and of the global awareness thus engendered. Like futurists today, Marinetti had no use for the past but rather tried to glimpse the operating system of the global village to come: "The earth shrunk by speed. New sense of the world. To be precise: one after the other, man gained the sense of his home, of the district where he lived, of his region, and finally of his continent. Today he is aware of the whole world. He hardly needs to know what his ancestors did, but he has a constant need to know what his contemporaries are doing all over the world."

We're not so far here, in the preceding, from the Internet-based paradise of perfect information prophesied by digital seers like George Gilder. And not far, either, from Peter Drucker's conviction that information is the new property, the new stuff. Marinetti's cultural campaign, in fact, makes sense only if we assume that such a world already exists. Assume that, in an information economy, the real scarce commodity will always be human attention and that attracting that attention will be the necessary precondition of social change. And the real source of wealth. Marinetti's conviction that attention was the vital stuff ran so deep that it went without saying. Everything he did implied it.

Look at how this worked out on a small scale, in his declaration of war on conventional typography. One favorite battleground of this war was the journal *Lacerba*, a revolutionary Italian journal published between 1913 and 1915. A page from it can be seen in figure 2.1.

Why would anyone want to construct such a ransom-note pastiche? The usual explanation—conventional typography symbolizes bourgeois convention, which the avant garde exists to *épater*—works well enough here. That's what the journal was all about, after all, and what Marinetti certainly yearned to do. He called it "spitting on the altar of art." But might there be another lesson lurking here? Who, or what, is actually getting spat upon?

It helps if you don't know Italian and look only at the visual pattern. Conventional printed typography aims to create a particular economy of attention, but, since this economy is so ubiquitous, the basic reality of reading, we have long ago ceased to notice it. Print wants us to concentrate on the content, to enhance and protect conceptual thought. It does this by filtering out all the signals that might interfere with such thinking. By nature a silent medium and, for people of my generation at least, best read in a silent environment, print filters out any auditory signal. It also filters out color, prints only black on white. By choosing a single font and a single size, it filters out visual distraction as well. Typographical design aims not to be seen or more accurately, since true invisibility is hard to read, to seem not to be seen, not to be noticed. We don't notice the verbal surface at all, plunge without typographical self-consciousness right into the meaning.

Print, that is, constructs a particular economy of attention, an economy of sensory denial. It economizes on most of the things we use to orient ourselves in the world we've evolved in—three-dimensional spatial signals, sounds, colors, movement—in order to spend all our attention on abstract thinking. The "abstraction" can be abstruse philosophy, but it can also be a particolored landscape description. Doesn't matter. They both work within the same econ-

Figure 2.1. Carlo Carra, "Words-in-Freedom." From *Lacerba*, 1914.

omy, one that foregrounds "meaning" in the same way that a goods economy foregrounds stuff you can drop on your foot.

The *Lacerba* typographical manifesto makes us aware of that "invisible" convention, forces us to notice it as a convention. By breaking all the established rules, it makes us notice them, look at them rather than through them. It makes an economic observation that is an attack not on a particular economic class but on a particular economy of attention. It aims to make us economists of expression.

In conventional typographical text, meaning is created through syntactical and grammatical relationships. In figure 2.1, "meaning," such as it is, is created by visual relationships that pun on the meaning of the words. One example: on the right side, halfway down, "Gravitare" (to gravitate, tend toward) "of perpendicular masses onto the horizontal plane of my little table." But little table gets a big bold font and an even bigger *T,* which is a letter and a table at the same time. We read the words for meaning—we can't help doing that—but we are made to "read" them for shape as well, and in an uneasy combination. The print economy of attention has been destabilized. It is still there, but it toggles back and forth with a new one.

Marinetti's spiritual successor was Andy Warhol. Warhol the commercial artist, Warhol the painter, Warhol the filmmaker, Warhol the writer, Warhol the collector, Warhol the philosopher, and, superlatively and climactically, Warhol the celebrity: all these roles float on a sea of commentary, nowadays mostly hagiographical. Let's try, as a perspective by incongruity, to describe Andy Warhol as an economist, an economist of attention. And perhaps the perspective would not in fact seem so incongruous to him. Here's what he said about the relation of art to business: "Business art is the step that comes after Art. I started as a commercial artist, and I want to finish as a business artist. . . . Being good in business is the most fascinating kind of art . . . making money is art and working is art and good business is the best art."

Warhol was an avid collector of stuff. His last house was so stuffed with his collected stuff, from cookie jars to diamonds, that there was no room left for the people. He would have been delighted, had he been able to attend Sotheby's auction of it all after his death, to see it knocked down for nearly $27 million dollars, far more than the pre-auction estimates. And to see his silk-screen painting of *Marilyn Monroe Twenty Times* (the actress's face, taken from a publicity photo, silk-screened onto canvas twenty times) fetch nearly $4 million. He did not share the conventional liberal intellectual's distaste for stuff and the advertising of stuff. It was his life's work to illustrate the paradoxical relationship of stuff and attention.

Warhol used to ask his friends what he should paint. One friend suggested that he should paint what he liked best in the world. So he began to paint money. This wasn't what he truly liked best in the world, however. That was attention. But you couldn't paint attention, at least not directly. So he went about it indirectly.

He began, in 1960, to paint pictures of Campbell's soup cans. Never has a single source of inspiration been so commercially exploited. People usually remember him as the painter of a can of tomato soup but he developed the product far beyond this simple notion. His soup cans "had legs." He painted pictures of the different kinds of soup—vegetable beef, beef noodle, black bean—in single portraits and in a group of two hundred that seemed, at least, to run through all the flavors. He painted them half-opened, crushed, in the act of being opened, with torn labels, without a label (you know it is a soup can because the caption tells you so), stuffed with money, and so on. Most were photorealistic in technique but a few were sketches. He then made exact models in wood of the boxes that the soup cans came in, along with the now-famous Brillo and Heinz ketchup boxes. These boxes then made wonderful gallery shows, stacked in various new and exciting ways. How's that for brand name exploitation?

When he began, the New York galleries would not show him. You can't blame them. The great pop explosion of the 1960s, the style that took the attention economy as its central subject, had not yet occurred, and nobody knew what to make of this new genre of mass-produced commercial still life. And so it was left to the Ferus Gallery in Los Angeles to mount the first Campbell soup can show in 1962. Let that show stand for many to follow. What happened there? Like Duchamp with his urinal, Warhol put a banal object in an alien attention structure. An art gallery, public or private, is a place to which we come with a definite set of expectations. Duchamp mocked these expectations; like Marinetti, he was spitting on the altar of art. Not young Andy. No disrespect intended either for the soup or the public who looked at it. No meaning, in fact, at all. What you saw was what you got. He never pretended otherwise.

The surface, he said, was all there was. He sung not of the soup but the can it came in. Obviously no art critic could be content with this dead-end candor. Those soup cans had to mean *something*. You could repeat the mantra of "art for art's sake" but no critic can actually accept this as truth because it leaves the critic no function. There had to be *some* reason why the soup cans were put into an art gallery, why we were asked to admire their beauty, even take one home and hang it over the mantelpiece. There had to be *some* soup in the can. And so all the interpretive machinery, professional and amateur, went into action. The soup cans represented the detritus of consumerist capitalism, its vacuous tastelessness, etc. Or the tastelessness of modern mass-prepared foods. Or they represented the signage with which we are surrounded these days, no less fitting a subject for a still life than a dish of pears was for Renoir. Or, since the paintings were all the same, they represented the sterility of mass production. Or they allegorized the bankruptcy of the masterpiece tradition in Western art, a tradition based on skill of hand and beauty of form. Or, quite to the contrary, because formal decisions were required to transform the soup can labels to canvas, they represented an exquisite case of ever-so-slight formal transformations that elicited the beauty implicit in the Campbell's label, lent it a tailor-made beauty the store-bought can did not possess.

It took time for this flood of commentary to flow downstream. Meanwhile, when the show was still up in the Ferus Gallery, another gallery close by put some real soup cans on display, suggesting that you could get the real McCoy for much less. Nice comparison. What did the exhibit do that a local grocery store could not? It created a powerful yet economical attention trap. A maximum of commentary was created by a minimum of effort. Subject? Off the shelf. Basic design? Off the shelf. Technique? Ditto. Replication? Silk screen, off the shelf too. Thought, allegory, philosophy, iconography, meaning? Nothing in that line required at all. Drafting ability: *de minimis*. The meaning, since this was an attention trap, would be supplied by all the interpreters waiting out there to make sense of such artifacts. For them, the more puzzling or outrageous the artifact, the better. Altogether, a dynamite niche product at a bargain basement cost.

But hasn't it always been so? No. Attention traps had been tried before—Rabelais set them for his humanist explicators all the time—but they could come into their own only when there was a powerful and established Interpretive Bureaucracy of Attention Economists waiting there to be used. The Interpretive Bureaucracy was what made pop art such a success. Made it possible, in fact. The right cultural judo expert could make use of all that established power to get talked about, to get famous. And if asked about the meaning of it all, as Warhol repeatedly was, he could make up the meanings expected (I was raised on Campbell's soup. I had it for lunch every day. I love it.). Or he could shrug and say that there wasn't any meaning. What you saw was what you got. The surface *was* the meaning. Once the Interpretive Bureaucracy got started, it didn't matter. With the bureaucracy's relentless seriousness, it could philosophize surface as well as depth. And so what if Andy did say one thing one day and contradict himself the next? More grist for the mill. That's how an attention artist works.

So there was a way to paint "attention." You had only to add the right enzyme to a preexistent mixture. Then that enzyme—and a soup can would do as well as anything else—could represent the subsequent interpretive conversation. It would, as time passed, embody a complex attention structure, an entire cultural moment in the same way that, say, Barbie dolls do.

Once the attention-trap formula was worked out, it was easy to apply it elsewhere, to the celebrity portraits, for example. The day after the Ferus Gallery closed, Marilyn Monroe died. David Bourdon describes what happened next: "Within a few days of Monroe's death, Warhol purchased a 1950s publicity photograph of her and, after cropping it below her chin, had it converted without any alteration into a silkscreen. The silkscreen enabled him to imprint her portrait hundreds of times onto various canvases. He screened her face one time only on small, individual canvases, and repeated it—twice, four times, six times, twenty times—on larger canvasses, positioning the heads in rows to create an allover pattern."

Marilyn was already a cultural icon, and her death ensured that the golden hair would never gray. Here was an attention trap already made, waiting to be exploited. Its power could, in a simple judo throw, be harnessed for mass production. Some of the silk screenings were out of register, blurring the image, but that only individuated the various iterations. Again, it was such an economical, such a profitable and efficient, way to paint attention. A 1950s publicity shot, silk-screen technology, and you were ready for mass production. Vary the size, the number of iterations, the color, actually induce the off-register blurring, all these were the signs of real artistic creation and cried out for interpretation. The next step? Obvious. Extend the franchise to other celebrities. Get them into a contest to have their faces replicated.

Thus was attention converted into money by instantiating the attention in physical objects, stuff. The ingeniousness of the solution should not blind us to the difficulty of the problem. The Internet dot-coms have not yet solved it, and this indeed may be what shortened their life. Information, digital or otherwise, is not like stuff. You can eat your cake, let somebody else eat it too, and you both still have it. Books are a great way to bring information down to earth in a salable product. Warhol found a way to bring a certain category of information—somebody else's celebrity, maybe even celebrity itself—down to earth in salable products. And no one sued him for copyright infringement, or unauthorized use of personal image, or trademark violation. All these starlets lined up to be violated. An amazing business coup.

The celebrity portraits, like the celebrities themselves, drew their power from *Homo sapiens'* fondness for the centripetal gaze. We love looking at movie stars, sports stars, royalty. We simply cannot get enough of it. Louis XIV based the plan of Versailles on this centripetal gaze (all the alleyways radiated out from the king's bedroom) and palace plans ever since have striven for the same visible ego enhancement.

The centripetal gaze, the flow of energy from the margins of a society to its center of attention, creates by its nature the winner-take-all society. To be one of the winners who took all, Andy knew, he had to create a public personality that would function as an attention trap as efficient as his artwork. As he himself said of his endless party-going and art-going: "But then, we weren't just *at* the art exhibit—we *were* the art exhibit, we were the art incarnate and the sixties were really about people, not about what they did." Such self-dramatization is as familiar as Douglas MacArthur's corncob pipe or General Patton's ivory-handled six-shooters. Andy's social self stood out from the crowd, however. The celebrity press is built on trying to find out about the private selves of the social selves, the celebs' scintillating inner lives. Andy preempted this effort. He had, he kept saying, no central self, no private self to peer into. As with the soup cans, he was pure *wysiwyg* (what you see is what you get). He aimed to impersonate a purely social, two-dimensional self with no central interiority other than the ambition to be rich and famous.

A more resonant incarnation of his time would be hard to contrive. And, apparently, he didn't need to contrive it. He was naturally shallow, selfish, and unreflective, a person who would let his kind old mom take care of him for much of his life and then not bother to go to her funeral. Like Henry VIII, he was a genius at playing off the members of his entourage (and what a gallery of grotesques the Warhol entourage comprised) against one another. True enough. But he was unusual, truly unusual, in not pretending otherwise. Each time when asked about his early life, he sketched a new one. He even sent an impersonator on a college lecture tour for him, explaining when the imposture was exposed that the impersonator was much better at saying the kinds of things college audiences expected to hear. The customer is never wrong! The colleges asked for their money back or a visit by the real Warhol. When the real Warhol did come and was asked if he was the real Warhol, he answered no. He was a creature of the surface and happy to be so. "If you want to know all about Andy Warhol, just look at the surface of my paintings and films and me, and there I am. There's nothing behind it." The question of a "real" Andy, like the question of meaning in his painting, simply didn't arise. In a pure economics of attention, one of his college-attuned impostors might have replied for him, such questions simply make no sense.

In Andy Warhol, then, our perpetual hunger for sincerity was finally given a rest. If you looked only at the surface, and if the surface was all there was, you did not need to peer beneath it. He was all package. That's why he knew a genuine celebrity like Judy Garland when he met her: "To meet a person like Judy [Garland] whose real was so unreal was a thrilling thing. She could turn everything on and off in a second; she was the greatest actress you could imagine every minute of her life." But what was such candor but another attention trap? The more he confessed that he had no central self, except hunger for the centripetal gaze, the more the celebrity-interpreting bureaucracy would try to pry out, or synthesize, a central self. There had to be one, just as there had to be soup in the can. Otherwise they would be out of a job. So also with the celebrity writers who perpetually searched for the "real Marilyn" or the "real Princess Diana."

Warhol once remarked, "That's what so many people never understood about us. They expected us to take the things we believed in seriously, which we never did—we weren't intellectuals." He was not lying but he was not telling the truth either. He did take the economics of attention seriously. That seriousness, however, differed from the kind the "intellectuals" operated under. They were always looking through the self-conscious surface of things to find the meaning hidden there. He was always looking at the surface instead.

We can see, too, that he understood the paradox of stuff. The stuff you dig out of the earth's crust becomes, in an information economy, less important than the information that informs it, what you think about the stuff. Yet the more you ponder that information, the more you understand about that stuff, the more real the stuff becomes. To put it in terms of the art world Andy lived in, the more you see that style matters more than substance, the more you see the vital role, the vitality, of substance. So, like Andy, you pursue your twin hungers: for the spotlight and for collecting stuff, knowing that each needs the other to make it real.

Let's summarize the rules of attention-economy art as Andy practiced them:

- Build attention traps. Create value by manipulating the ruling attention structures. Judo, not brute force, gets the best results. Duchamp did this for a joke. Do it for a business.
- Understand the logic of the centripetal gaze and how to profit from it.
- Draw your inspiration from your audience not your muse. And keep in touch with that audience. The customer is always right. No Olympian artistic ego need apply.

- Turn the "masterpiece psychology" of conventional art upside down:
  - ~ Mass production not skilled handwork
  - ~ Mass audience not connoisseurship
  - ~ Trendiness not timelessness
  - ~ Repetition not rarity
- Objects do matter. Don't leave the world of stuff behind while you float off in cyberspace. Conceptual art gets you nowhere. Create stuff you can sell.
- Live in the present. That's where the value is added. Don't build your house in eternity. "My work has no future at all. I know that. A few years. Of course my things will mean nothing."

Now for a different kind of attention economist. Once upon a time, long ago, in the early 1970s, there dwelt in New York an artist named Christo Javacheff. Born in Bulgaria, he came of age in the perpetually avant-garde artistic atmosphere of Paris. From his Paris beginnings in the early sixties, Christo was a wrapper. He wrapped magazines, flowers, mailing boxes, and on occasion and temporarily, naked young women. Later he scaled up and wrapped a portion of the Great Barrier Reef, the Pont Neuf in Paris, and the Berlin Reichstag.

We can look at a 1966 project, *Wrapped Boxes*, as representing the early small-scale wrapping. A design class he taught at Macalester College in St. Paul, Minnesota, wrapped a hundred boxes in plain kraft paper and tied them with ordinary string. These were then mailed out to members of the Walker Art Center's Contemporary Arts Group. Twenty of the members fell into the attention trap and opened the boxes. Inside was a note from Christo: "The package you destroyed was wrapped according to my instructions in a limited edition of a hundred copies for members of Walker Art Center's Contemporary Arts Group. It was issued to commemorate my '14130 Cubic Feet Empaquetage 1966' at the Minneapolis School of Art, a project co-sponsored by the Contemporary Arts Group."

What had these unwitting desecrators (unacquainted with the game? simply curious? determined to find the "soup"?) desecrated? Not a beautifully wrapped parcel in, say, the Japanese manner but only a tidily wrapped ordinary one. No aesthetic offense. They had destroyed not a thing of beauty but Christo's economics lesson and, in the process, they taught it to themselves. The lesson could not have been simpler. Wrappings matter. You should pay attention to them. They are more important than the content. And, in extreme cases, such as this exemplary one, they may be the content. If, in your zeal to get at the content, you destroy the container, you've missed the fundamental reversal of our time, the reversal between stuff and what we think about stuff. The wrapping is the attitude surrounding the contents, the spirit in which it has been sent or given. If all you can think of is the stuff contained, if you keep looking for the soup in the can, you'll overlook where the real value lies. You've failed to see that style and substance have traded places.

Nowadays, when a product's design has become a powerful, often the dominant, attribute of the product; when brands and brand recognition are acknowledged as attention assets often worth far more than the physical assets of a company (the last I knew, the Coca-Cola brand was reckoned to be worth $70 billion plus); when the publicity campaign for a book is designed before the book is finished, or in some cases before it is written, we may well claim to have learned this lesson. Thirty-five years ago, much less so. We were so accustomed to looking through the package to the contents that it took an auctioneer's sealed box trick like Christo's to make us pause and look at it and, thus, finally to restore the balance between inner and outer, to think of "stuff" as a complex toggling between the physical object and what we think of it.

Christo is often, for lack of a better pigeonhole, called an "earth artist." But the term is more properly applied to artists like Michael Heizer and Robert Smithson who move around a lot of earth, dig gigantic holes in the desert, or build spirals in the Great Salt Lake. Christo himself liked to talk about "public art," and for good reasons. But it is clear from the simple example of his *Wrapped Boxes*, and true I think throughout his career, that the material he worked in, as against the material he worked with, was human attention. He has always been an "attention artist."

His large-scale wrappings, of which we may take the Pont Neuf project as exemplary, teach a lesson that is both less extreme and more inclusive than the one we've examined. The main difference is not, as we might think, in the scale of the enterprise, vast as that difference is. The difference is that the outsized wrappings—the Great Barrier Reef, the Surrounded Islands in Miami, the Pont Neuf—were all beautiful. In the case of the Pont Neuf, with its golden fabric, breathtakingly so. The Macalester boxes taught their lesson entirely within an economics of attention. It was purely didactic, a classroom lesson. The wrapping was not beautiful and did not need to be. The box contained only the note explaining the attention trap that had been fallen into. The Pont Neuf lesson is altogether more complex. There is content, for a start, the best-known bridge in Paris. Real stuff. Substance. And the wrapping was extraordinarily beautiful, as the many photographs of it document. By way of contrast, once you learned the lesson of the Macalester boxes, that game was over. There was no aftereffect, no resonance, no point in looking at it any more. As with Duchamp's R. Mutt urinal, and its immense artistic progeny, once you get the point, learn the lesson, the experience evaporates. But the large-scale Christo wrappings still inhabit the traditional "masterpiece" conception of art where beauty matters. There is more to them than the didacticism.

All this is by way of introduction to the Christo project that illustrates most richly how he shapes attention: the *Running Fence*, which stood in Marin and Sonoma Counties in northern California for two weeks in September of 1976. In 1973, Christo and Jeanne-Claude—his wife and chief executive officer—scouted sites for the fence in California and Oregon, settled on the Marin-Sonoma site for the twenty-four-mile long fence, formed the Running Fence Corporation to create and dismantle it, and ordered the 165,000 yards of eighteen-foot nylon that would constitute its twenty-four-mile wide sail. Carrying the 2,100 eighteen-foot by sixty-eight-foot sail panels would be 2,050 twenty-one-foot steel poles, 312,000 steel hooks, and ninety miles of steel cable. The project employed twenty vehicles, some of them specially designed. From April to September 1976, sixty employees installed the steel poles, and then at the end of August and the beginning of September 360 employees were hired to install the fence. Some stayed on after the fence was built to direct traffic and then, two weeks later, disassemble it. All of them had to be trained and fed, managed, transported, and paid. It was an immense civil engineering project. It was an even more immense social engineering project. The fence was to run through fifty-five parcels of private land. It required easement agreements from each. It also required building permits, removal bonds, seventeen public hearings, several court sessions, an Environmental Impact Report, the input of fifteen governmental agencies, and the services of nine lawyers.

It cost $3 million. Christo and his wife, as in all their projects, paid for it themselves.

It stood for two weeks.

What did they have in mind in constructing this extraordinary temporary monument? What economic lessons, in the framework of our discussion here, did they propose to teach?

Easiest to start where the fence ended—beauty. The fence was extraordinarily beautiful. I was not privileged to see it in person but I have always found the many photographs of it haunting. It created a generous beauty, one that moved outward to transform everything around it. Its extraordinary ribbon of sails made us see the invisible. As Christo said when he looked at it: "See how it describes the wind." We could, with the fence, look at the wind rather than through it—and, as the film by David Maysles et al. illustrates, hear the wind as well. Perhaps most magical of all its transformations was how it (let me phrase it as a pun) caught the light. It allowed the viewer to see what the light looked like by refracting it back in a million ways. It allowed the beholder to see what before was only seen through. It measured where the sun was and what density the air had at that particular time and place. It created new ways to pay attention to the world. It calibrated our attention.

We perceive the world around us according to different scales: the regular 3D world we walk around in; the minute world of the microscope; the unimaginable light-year measurements of astronomy. By its very nature a scale of perception is not something we can see. We look through it, not at it. It is our means of perceiving the world. To view *Running Fence*, its participants had to become self-conscious about spatial scale. The sheer size of it required a view 24,000 feet up to see it entire. Walking alongside it meant seeing an altogether different object. And an infinite number of focal lengths in between created an equal number of *Running Fences*. Its participants were able to see, to look *at*, how they paid attention to the world, how they saw. And it calibrated timescale as well. No monument lasts forever, as Ozymandias taught us in another famous lesson. But to restrict deliberately the life of an immense and expensive piece of sculpture to fourteen days is to make us see timescale as well. You can't hold in your mind's eye the life of the Parthenon. But two weeks? Anyone can do it. You are allowed to see the scale of time, look at it as you pass through it.

Beauty, however, was not Christo's avowed central purpose. Instead, it was to work, as in the small-scale wrappings, in human attention. This work of art, as he said repeatedly, was composed of the human behavior that was required to create it, not only the building of the fence but also the hearings, lawsuits, rulings, reports, meetings, and pleadings that were necessitated by the project. To create the fence he needed a myriad of permissions and to obtain those permissions he needed to persuade a myriad of people to grant them. The fence was created as an attention structure that dramatized how persuasion works in human society. It was not only a thing of beauty that did not last forever, it was, as well, a model of how persuasion works in human society, which is to say a model of rhetoric, which should last, if not forever, at least as long as such things can last. He persuaded people of what? What rhetoric has always persuaded people of: to share a beautiful attention structure. To cherish eloquence.

Vital to the fence's artistic integrity, Christo felt, was continuing it right down into the sea. The fence was to end in a long, downward-sweeping plunge from cliff to sea; full height at the top of the cliff, it would taper off to nothing as it married the sea. Certainly the dramatic photographs of this section show the climactic visual drama this plunge created. They also show why Christo was willing to risk a climactic bureaucratic drama by building it without the Coastal Commission's approval. After he had decided to do this, he offered to release the contractor from responsibility to protect him from legal action. If someone went to jail, it would be Christo himself. The primary construction contractor was A&H Builders, Inc., of Broomfield, Colorado, and its president was Theodore Dougherty. Dougherty declined to hide behind Christo's coattails. He then remarked, "The amazing thing is how one man, with his idea, can get so many people so involved."

That involvement, as Christo frequently pointed out, was why he built the fence, why he pursued all his projects. His business as an artist was to create attention structures, structures that would teach particular lessons. The fence has always been considered, and has been richly annotated, as a work of avant-garde art. Let's consider it, instead, as a series of lessons.

Suppose you wanted to teach a civics lesson. Suppose you wanted people to become aware of how they form collective purposes, how they resolve their differences to complete grand endeavors. Suppose you wanted to teach them how leaders, entrepreneurs, worked in this drama of social purpose. Suppose you wanted to show how ideas get built in a highly regulated society. How would you do it? Well, I can give the conventional answer by telling you what I would do. I'm a school teacher, and I would invent a nifty course and try to persuade people to take it. With what success, however engagingly I might teach it, who could predict? I have, in fact, spent a substantial part of a long career trying to do precisely this, to do what Christo was trying to do with the *Running Fence:* teach about rhetoric, usually defined as the "art of persuasion" but in our framework as "the economics of attention." Rhetoric has, since Plato first calumniated the Sophists, been synonymous with the art of deception. In democracies, we always call the methods by which we come to common purpose "politics" and scorn them, as if there were some other way to decide business in a democracy. Nowadays, we've come to call it "spin." The flipside of this definition is the art of cooperation. That is the fundamental lesson Christo sought to teach. How to create social cooperation from the bottom up. How to persuade people to reflect on the social machinery of persuasion and thus to understand its necessity. To redeem the "rhetoric" in daily life.

Dictating from the top down is much easier. That is the conventional direction of the magisterial artistic ego. In our time, you get a government grant to make a large sculpture and then you place it where a builder needs one to fulfill a government mandate. If your sculpture interferes with what people see or where people walk, tough. Philistines must be made to recognize the primacy of artistic purpose. Let them walk around it every day and learn this vital lesson of humility before art. (I am instancing here the lesson taught by Richard Serra's *Tilted Arc*, in Jacob Javits Plaza in New York.) Christo went about the job differently. If attention is the prime economic asset, as Christo's creative universe assumes, how do you raise this new species of money? How do you provide the attention financing? How do you "get so many people so involved"? You start with a grand idea, dramatic in the making, beautiful in the execution. This is what beauty is for in an economics of attention, not to be gazed on for its own sake but to focus social purpose. (It may work the same way in other species too, but that is another story.) Such a focus does not mean that the beauty need be of the "Seven Brave Tractor Drivers" socialist sort. Far from it. The more absolute it is, the less connected it is with social purpose, the better it works in leading social purpose.

Then you take your grand idea and you persuade people to share its grandeur. You do this in all those hearings and applications. This plunges you deeply into the paradox of stuff. You are trying to build something—the stuff is vital—but the attention structure the stuff creates, both in the making and the standing, is what finally matters. You create, as persuasion must, a participative drama. It must include, if it is to have dramatic vitality, a vociferous opposition. This was supplied by the local artists. They hated this foreigner coming in and hogging all the attention and redefining art in a way that left them clerks of a forgotten mood. And so they organized the opposition. But this was the part they were cast for in Christo's drama anyway, and the madder they got, the better they played their parts. When Christo pointed their roles out to them, they got madder still.

Participatory drama of this sort does what drama always does: it makes us see ourselves acting. It makes us look at our behavior rather than through it. But here, no proscenium arch, no theater, no suspension of disbelief. Christo always stressed that he, and his art, "lived the real life." No artistic isolation.

His enterprise was as real as that of the sheep ranchers through whose land his fence must pass. *Running Fence* was far more like a startup company (was in literal fact a startup company) than like the *Mona Lisa* or the self-satisfied little joke Duchamp played on her by giving her a mustache.

Christo kept his enterprise in the real world by his method of financing it. He neither sought nor accepted outside support. The project was entirely self-financed. The financing constitutes a vital and original part of the story. When the project was fully conceived, a number of museums were offered a chance to share in its sponsorship. They would receive, in return, credit as coproducers. In token whereof, they would also receive, as a stock certificate issued in a corporation that made attention, sketches of the fence signed by Christo. Something you could collect, put on the wall, buy and sell. And something that, as when you back the right stock, would increase in value. It was joint-venture capitalism, but in a new breed of enterprise and with a new breed of capital: attention. The money was derivative—a theme often heard in venture-capital halls today: Money isn't the problem—it is finding good ideas to back.

To this new kind of joint-stock company he added a medieval means of finance, the sale of relics. The two big Christo books I own, the *Running Fence* one and the Pont Neuf one, both contain relics, actual pieces of the fence's silver and the Pont Neuf's golden cloth. In addition, these books and many others like them are photographic reliquaries for the photos taken of the projects, both by the public and by professional photographers. Each creates relics. And relics, as the medieval Church knew so well, walk off the shelf. The spirit can be made flesh with a big markup to the maker. The paradox of stuff in a well-documented theological manifestation.

The local artists accused Christo of seeking only profit and notoriety, not creating "art for art's sake." It was an accusation that, as we've seen, would have fit Andy Warhol perfectly, but it was perfectly wrong for Christo. Both Christo and Jeanne-Claude stressed that a central part of their project was the financial risk, and this risk they assumed themselves. They put all their assets into the project. All the money they raised by their distinctive fundraising techniques was plowed back into the company. They bet their company and stood behind it in their private persons. The financial risk was real and ever-present. The fence nearly did not get built. It was one cliffhanging hearing after another. If they had not been willing to go ahead and build the last segment without Coastal Commission approval, and assume the legal risk for that, the project would have lacked its artistic climax. Risk stood at the center of the project. And the risk conferred genuine daring on those who assumed it. This bravery was not lost on the ranchers through whose property the fence had to run. It was the artists who never understood.

I once had occasion to talk about the *Running Fence* to a group of distinguished media moguls, a group that included their then-favorite prophet, George Gilder. The two gospels that Gilder has preached from the beginning have been the power and importance of the individual entrepreneur and the new rules of the information paradigm for wealth. In my naïveté, I thought he might find my remarks interesting and see how they agreed with his thinking. I was right about the interesting but wrong about the agreement. Christo was, according to Gilder's outraged postlecture comment, part of a postmodern plot of anarchistic God knows what, etcetera, etcetera. He responded the way the local artists did to the project. He was still thinking in their box, he who prides himself in having escaped all boxes whatsoever. Why, I wondered, the knee-jerk response from such an informed commentator on the present scene? He bought, I think, the interpretation that the art critics had handed out, the avant-garde artist doing one of those strange things: digging holes in the desert, piling up bricks on the gallery floor, painting paintings that did nothing but reflect the light of the room that hung them. The fundamentally economic focus of *Running Fence*, and Christo's work in general, had simply not occurred to him, and he did not expect to find a friend for entrepreneurship in the artistic community. Yet no greater monument to business entrepreneurship has ever been erected. I wonder how many of the many courses in entrepreneurship that have sprouted up like mushrooms include *Running Fence* in their case studies?

No wonder Gilder couldn't understand what Christo was about. The artistic community has always stressed the need for separation, for protection, and above all, for governmental and philanthropic financing. The artist is a top-down Platonic lawgiver and the society should have enough sense to understand this and to pay generously for the ex cathedra pronouncements, and the works of art, however insulting they might be to their audience, created by such a system. Artists are the priests, after all, in the religion of art.

Christo's modus operandi stood opposite to this. He raised the money by his own labors, by reinventing the joint-stock corporation on a medieval attention model. He took the risk. Courted the risk because risk was part of the lesson he wanted to teach. It was to its core a lesson in entrepreneurship. Here was a development team, Christo and Jeanne-Claude, who bet the company on every new project they undertook. How's that for lessons in entrepreneurship? This commitment was part of the persuasive argument Christo offered to the community whose support he needed. This was a private enterprise, a startup business, and this guy might well fail and was willing to take the rap if he did. He didn't take the pulpit and preach the gospel of art. Instead, he said, "Look, this is what I want to do and how I propose to do it. I don't ask for any money from you, or from your state humanities council, or your National Endowment for the Arts either. The financial system is one of the systems I'm trying to teach you how to work. My economics lesson won't work if I suspend the ordinary rules."

Because he sought to teach a lesson in pure attention entrepreneurship, he subtracted the conventional purpose from the project: permanence and profit. The corporation created to create the project was self-liquidating. It spent the money it raised to raise the fence. And the fence would be taken down after two weeks. Two powerful objections were dealt with thereby, the two knee-jerk objections of the local artists, in fact. The local artists argued that Christo was an Andy Warhol, motivated by ego and profit. No ego involvement in a project that was going to disappear in two weeks. And no profit either. The lesson was pure: How do you bring an idea to fruition in an economics of attention?

One of the amazing things about the public response was its understanding of the temporality of the fence, the deliberate choice to put it into time rather than trying to stand it outside time, constitute a "timeless" masterpiece. As one supporter of the fence said at one of the many hearings: "My husband is a farmer and I am a housewife. Some of the meals I prepare aren't much. But sometimes I go to a lot of work to prepare a meal that I think is 'art.' It is a masterpiece. And what happens to it? It gets eaten up."

One opponent of the fence, objecting to Christo's redefinition of art as an attention structure rather than a physical object meant to endure through the ages, pointed out that by such a definition "every land developer is an artist and every land development is a work of art." Lesson learned, or at least half-learned. Christo made land development into a work of art by subtracting the practical purpose and the lasting physical entity. The lasting monument, the Environmental Impact Report pointed out, was not going to be environmental damage but the changed thinking and feeling of the community that debated the project at such length. Land development was, and is, a big issue in places like Sonoma and Marin Counties. The *Running Fence* offered a different way to pay attention to that development. We return thus to the paradox of stuff in a society that transfers its center of gravity from stuff to information. The stuff becomes more important, not less, than before. What changes is the relationship between stuff and what we think about stuff. What is learned is how to move from the one to the other, hold both in mind at once. This ability was Christo's target in *Running Fence*. Talking about an artist's intention has been forbidden in aesthetic circles for a long time, and more recently, the very idea of a creating artist has been dismissed as a Romantic delusion. But economists, so far as I know, are still permitted to have intentions and purposes. They are still permitted to teach lessons about human behavior, and Christo teaches an unmistakable one here.

It is instructive to compare these two economists we've just considered, Andy Warhol and Christo Javacheff. Christo insists on living "the real life," as he puts it. His projects are built at real risk. Andy admired Judy Garland because "her real was so unreal" and wanted (at least according to one anecdote told at his funeral) to be reincarnated as a ring on Elizabeth Taylor's finger. Christo is a planner, a builder, a responsible bill payer; he knows what he wants to do and why. Andy was a drifter, schemer, and opportunist who asked his friends to suggest subjects for his painting so he wouldn't lose touch with current trends. Christo is deadly serious about his artistic entrepreneurship and what it intends to teach. Warhol kept insisting that he was not serious about anything except making money and being famous. They embodied two antithetical conceptions of self and society. Christo has a clear central self and lives, and wants to live, in "the real world." Andy said, and nothing in his life contradicts it, that he was entirely a creature of the social surface, that what you saw was what there was, and that his ideal society was the hyperventilated self-consciousness of the New York art scene.

And yet both of them made their art from the same substance: attention. Not stuff but what we think about stuff. They were both rhetoricians, economists of attention. Rhetoric has always, in its long history, seemed to divide into two parties: those who created attention structures to form and strengthen social purposes and those who sought only to serve themselves. The division was reenacted in this pair of attention economists.

Artists are supposed to be, as our epigraph from Kenneth Burke reminds us, prophets of things to come. To an uncanny degree, the artists we've been considering here, and a great many more, have done just that for an information society. From Marinetti onward, they have singled out attention as the central asset in a new economy and tried to "paint" it. They have, in the process, sketched out a new expressive field, a new means of cultural notation, one that has moved, with little change, from artistic prophecy to reality on the digital screen. That electronic expressive field finds its home no longer in the printing house but in the computer graphics studio, and to it we now turn.

Background Conversations

Dada: Creating "The Brand of the Century"

From a middle distance, it is hard to distinguish between Dada, the futurism that preceded it, and the surrealism that followed. Hans Richter, one of the original Zurich Dada group and, to my mind, its best explicator, explains the relationship to futurism this way: "In 1909 the Italian futurists were publishing manifestos that were as like Dada as two peas in a pod—typography à la Dada and public hell-raising in Dada style."

> Like all newborn movements we were convinced that the world began anew in us; but in fact we had swallowed Futurism—bones, feathers and all. . . . The youthful élan, the aggressively direct approach to the public, the provocations, were products of Futurism, as were the literary forms in which they were clothed: the manifesto and its visual format. The free use of typography, in which the compositor moves over the page vertically, horizontally and diagonally, jumbles his typefaces and makes liberal use of his stock of pictorial blocks—all this can be found in Futurism years before Dada. . . . But here the influence of Futurism more or less stops. . . . Here is the fundamental difference: Futurism had a programme and produced works designed to "fulfill" this programme. . . . Dada not only had *no* programme, it was against all programmes. Dada's only programme was to have no programme . . . and at that moment in history, it was just this that gave the movement its explosive power to unfold *in all directions,* free of aesthetic or social constraints. This absolute freedom from preconceptions was something quite new in the history of art. The frailty of human nature guaranteed that such a paradisal situation could not last. But there was to be a brief moment in which absolute freedom was asserted for the first time.

Here is how Richter describes what came after Dada, surrealism. "In its beginnings, Surrealism seems to me to be as like Dada as two peas in a pod." He goes on to quote Salvador Dalí: "Surrealism is the systematization of confusion. Surrealism appears to create an Order, but the purpose of this is to render the idea of system suspect by association. Surrealism is destructive, but it destroys only what it considers to be shackles limiting our vision." This, Richter says, "could not possibly be more precise as a description of Dada." But then surrealism "codified the Dada revolt into a strict intellectual discipline. . . . It is this theoretical and methodical infrastructure that distinguishes Surrealism from Dada." But the two movements belong together: "They cannot be separated. . . . They are basically a single coherent experience reaching like a great arch from 1916 until about the middle of the Second World War, a renaissance of meaning in art, a change in our field of vision that corresponds to a revolutionary change in the nature of our civilization."

So, a futurism program precedes Dada, and a surrealism program follows it. Dada stands at the center of this cultural revolution, but what was it, if it had no "program"? What did it do? As Richter, who was present almost from the creation, tells the tale, it began at a café in Zurich during the First World War. Hugo Ball and his mistress, Emmy, founded the Café Voltaire, on 1 February 1916. It was a great artistic success; people have been quarreling about the authorship and ownership of "Dada" as a brand name ever since. But it was also, it seems worth observing, an economic success as well: "[Ball] had come to an arrangement with Herr Ephraim, the owner of the *Meierei,* a bar in Niederdorf, a slightly disreputable quarter of the highly reputable town of Zurich. He promised Herr Ephraim that he would increase his sales of beer, sausage and rolls by means of a literary cabaret. Emmy Hennings sang *chansons,* accompanied by Ball at the piano. Ball's personality soon attracted a group of artists and kindred spirits who fulfilled all the expectations of the owner of the *Meierei.*" Sausage sales aside, the café's sole purpose, according to Ball, was "to draw attention, across the barriers of war and nationalism, to the few independent spirits who live for other ideas." Its real economics was an economics of attention, and the economics worked. The movement spread from Switzerland to Europe and to New York. No cultural movement has ever had a brand name to compare with Dada.

What went on at the Café Voltaire? Imagine a hip coffeehouse in San Francisco and you are halfway there. The format was "World Arts and Cultures." Emmy sang popular and folksongs in a fey style. People recited poetry. Performers put on masks and improvised theatrical happenings. Noises of various kinds were generated in the name of music. The audience was interactive, as we might say now, often being taunted and responding with jeers. Richter describes the music and drama and illustrates the alphabetic experiments. The visual art is amply reproduced in William S. Rubin's *Dada and Surrealist Art,* Robert Short's *Dada and Surrealism,* and Malcolm Haslam's *The Real World of the Surrealists.* The futurist predecessors are illustrated in Caroline Tisdall and Angelo Bozzolla's *Futurism* and in Marianne W. Martin's *Futurist Art and Theory, 1909-1915.* The best collection of futurist manifestos I've found is *Marinetti e il Futurismo,* edited by Luciano de Maria.

What did this all add up to? What was the Café Voltaire trying to call people's attention to and how was it trying to do it? Robert Short gives the standard explanation:

> According to the stereotype, it stands for a movement of radical, cultural revolt: the disgusted response of artists to the debacle of Western civilization and its values in the First World War. Dada represents a revolt against art by artists themselves who, appalled by developments in contemporary society, recognized that art was bound to be a product, reflection and even support of that society and was therefore criminally implicated. Dada stands for exacerbated individualism, universal doubt and aggressive iconoclasm. Debunking the canons of reason, taste and hierarchy, of order and discipline in society, of rationally controlled inspiration in imaginative expression, Dada resorted to the arbitrary, to chance, the unconscious and the primitive, where man is at the behest of nature and gives up pretending to be its master.

So, at the center of this central movement in twentieth-century Western culture stood a series of negatives. Renounce conceptual thought. Repudiate hierarchical order. Reject planning. Embrace chance. Above all, embrace guilt. Everything we do, or can do, is complicit in the general guilt of a hopelessly corrupt society. The only logical response to such a world—if "logic" be permitted to enter it—is, like a medieval hermit, to leave the world in disgust. This, in fact, is what Hugo Ball did, retiring to the small village of Ticino "to live the religious life in voluntary poverty." Sure sounds like a "program" to me, and one that has seen a lot of service in avant-garde programs in art and literature ever since.

How was this repudiation of the world accomplished? First, the art and music created would have no meaning; they would be all surface. The repudiation of ordinary typographical design was an obvious way to do this. Hugo Ball's "abstract poetry" was another. Ball explained it this way: "The human figure is progressively disappearing from pictorial art . . . The next step is for poetry to discard language as painting has discarded the object." What was left was pure sound: "zimzim urallala zimzim urallala zimzim zanzibar zimsalla zam." Music was reduced, as John Cage was later to reduce it, to pure sounds, randomly collected or generated. Seriousness of all kinds was to be discarded, and the way to do this was to concentrate only on the expressive surface. The only attention permitted was *at* attention; looking *through* was abolished.

What happens when you do this? Two things, and the audience at the Café Voltaire demonstrated both right away. You get mad and you start to laugh. Both the anger and the laughter remind you that human respiration means both breathing out and breathing in; you have to do both, as the baby finds out by holding its breath in a temper tantrum. So seriously has Dada's repudiation of seriousness been taken that the laughter has been left out. But if seriousness was repudiated, play certainly was not. The play that was liberated by the invocation of chance became the new seriousness. Play and seriousness traded places, just as design and chance had traded places. It was meant to be, at least at the beginning, a one-time trade. But the baby can't hold its breath forever. Soon these sets of opposites began to switch back and forth.

For the object of chance creation was still creation. Richter tells this story without, it seems, understanding its moral. One day Jean Arp was discontented with a drawing and tore it up and threw it on the floor. He then noticed that the pieces of paper had, by chance, assumed the creative pattern he had sought in vain. Aha! "The conclusion that Dada drew from all this was that chance must be recognized as a new stimulus to artistic creation. This may well be regarded as the central experience of Dada, that which marks it off from all preceding artistic movements." But you still had to recognize an expressive pattern when chance delivered it to you. Artistic intention walked right in the back door when kicked out the front. So with meaning in Ball's meaningless *zimzim* poem. He was standing up on stage in an immovable cardboard costume, trying to remain serious ("and this I wanted above all things") and what happened? "I noticed that my voice, which had no other way out, was taking on the age-old cadence of priestly lamentation, the liturgical chanting that wails through all the Catholic churches of East and West." Back comes the impulse to find meaning, to create meaning. *At* vision automatically starts creating *through* vision. So, too, when the performers put on masks that had been created purely as visual designs. They immediately felt that they had to make the masks mean something, take their place in a gestural vocabulary. You can start with looking *at* the masks, but you can't stop there.

So the Dada brand represented not only repudiation and condemnation, as much fun as that was. It also represented the same oscillation that we require when we hold in our mind an economics of stuff and an economics of attention at the same time. Chance and planning, conceptual thought and pure play, had to be held in a fruitful oscillation. And the Dadaists saw this themselves. As Richter says: "We were all fated to live with the paradoxical necessity of entrusting ourselves to chance while at the same time remembering that we were conscious beings working toward conscious goals. This contradiction between rational and irrational opened a bottomless pit over which we had to walk. There was no turning back; gradually this became clear to each of us in his own secret way." "The realization that reason and anti-reason, sense and nonsense, design and chance, consciousness and unconsciousness, belong together as necessary parts of a whole—this was the central message of Dada."

Aha! A program! A program of breathing out *and* breathing in! A program built on oscillation between opposites. A program that sought to teach how this oscillation could be created and sustained. "We were looking for a way to make art a meaningful instrument of life"—back to Christo! The stereotype of point-less nihilism, attractive as it has been to avant-garde thinkers ever since, told only half the story, and that was worse than half a truth. Once we see the Dada program for what it was, we can invert the judgment with which we began about the relationship of Dada to its predecessor and its successor. Futurism did not, finally, have a "program" but only half a one, and the same was true of surreal-ism. If either was to work in the world, they would finally have to adopt the Dada program.

Dada did have a program, and its program was our central trope: *oscillatio*. Once it got people's attention, this bi-stable poise is what it was trying to teach them. This is what the Dada brand was all about. It did not mean unifying oppo-sites. That was not in the cards of the world. It was about holding opposites alternately in the mind, about the need to train the human imagination to do this. You can fairly argue that Dada was the central cultural brand of the twenti-eth century. By being so manifestly a brand, it suggested that the opposition of art and commerce was a false opposite from the beginning. In an attention econ-omy, the Dada brand shows, the opposition—on which so much artistic com-mentary has been built—simply dissolves.

Two Unlikely Dadaists

Two quite different people taught this same Dada lesson about breathing out and breathing in, the anthropologist Gregory Bateson and the economist Friedrich Hayek, though neither, I fancy, would acknowledge Dada as inspira-tional. Let me start with Bateson. He was, like the Dadaists during World War I, trying to break the pattern of thinking that had led up to the war. You can see it most clearly in a talk called "From Versailles to Cybernetics," which he gave at Sacramento State College in 1966 and which was subsequently published in his retrospective collection *Steps to an Ecology of Mind*. Like the Dada experiment, it departs from the madness of World War I: "The question is, '*What* is going to count as important in the history of the last sixty years? I am sixty-two, and, as I began to think about what I have seen of history in my lifetime, it seemed to me that I had really only seen two moments that would rate as really important from an anthropologist's point of view. One was the events leading up to the

Treaty of Versailles, and the other was the cybernetic breakthrough." An odd pairing; here's how he explained it: "My criterion of historical importance: Mammals in general, and we among them, care extremely, not about episodes, but about the patterns of their relationships. . . . This is crucial. This is what mammals are about. They are concerned with patterns of relationship, with where they stand in love, hate, respect, dependency, trust, and similar abstractions, vis-à-vis somebody else. This is where it hurts us to be put in the wrong." Significant moments in history are when these relationships (he calls them "attitudes") change. The treaty that concluded World War I was remarkable for relationships that did not change. The Treaty of Versailles, many have argued besides Bateson, imposed a vengeful peace on Germany that led to the impoverishment and inflation that led to Hitler. The madness that the Café Voltaire was fleeing, the pattern of relationships where hate and vengeance lead to more hate and vengeance, was thus extended through another generation and through another, even worse, war. A way was needed to break this pattern. Christianity has long suggested the path of forgiveness; Bateson chose to construe it as a problem in the economics of attention.

He argued, in a way not so different from the performers at the Café Voltaire, that "mere purposive rationality unaided by such phenomena as art, religion, dream, and the like, is necessarily pathogenic and destructive of life; and that its virulence springs specifically from the circumstance that life depends on interlocking *circuits* of contingency, while consciousness can see only such short arcs of such circuits as human purpose may direct. . . . Unaided consciousness must always tend toward hate." Toward hate and war and the Treaty of Versailles. So the counterstating balance is something that, in the Versailles essay, he confusingly calls "cybernetics" but that he, and the twentieth century, has found not in the gospel of forgiveness but in the gospel of art. So he argues: "But if art . . . has a positive function in maintaining what I called 'wisdom,' *i.e.,* in correcting a too purposive view of life and making the view more systemic, then the question to be asked of the given work of art becomes: What sorts of correction in the direction of wisdom would be achieved by creating or viewing this work of art? The question becomes dynamic rather than static." The Café Voltaire existed to suggest these sorts of correction. Correct a too-purposive view of life by disavowing purpose and embracing chance. Invoke the subconscious mind directly and consciously (a paradox the café-goers themselves felt!). Disrupt the protected play space so that the psychology of play leaches out into ordinary life. Invigorate the oscillation between play and purpose by aggressively denying a purpose that had become overweening.

Consciousness, for Bateson, was only part, and a small part, in the human economy of attention, an economy he called "systemic awareness." The trick was to toggle back and forth between scarce consciousness and the rest of the human mind, and the way you did this was—as the Café Voltaire argued— through art:

> Our life is such that its unconscious components are continuously present in all their multiple forms. It follows that in our relationships we continuously exchange messages about these unconscious materials, and it becomes important also to exchange metamessages by which we tell each other what order and species of unconsciousness (or consciousness) attaches to our messages. In a merely pragmatic way, this is important because the orders of truth are different for different sorts of messages. . . . Art becomes, in this sense, an exercise in communicating about the species of unconsciousness. Or, if you prefer it, a sort of play behavior whose function is, amongst other things, to practice and make more perfect communication of this kind.

The metamessages are what we ordinarily call style. Bateson, to make his argument a little clearer than he makes it himself, thinks of style as the "cybernetic" corrective to a human purpose run out of control. Again, if not exactly the Café Voltaire, only a couple of storefronts from it. So, for him, at the center of the human economy of attention stands the need for an oscillation between purpose and play, between substance and style. The "ecology of mind" requires the Dada brand as much as the economy of the larger society.

Bateson contended that the human mind cannot bring more than a small percentage of what it knows into consciousness. We should then be wary of conscious purpose and try to balance it "cybernetically," with game and play. This was a balance congenial to the spirit of the sixties, when Bateson came to popular notice. The Vienna school, and later Chicago school, economist Friedrich August von Hayek (1899-1992) argued the same case on a larger scale. We "must use our reason intelligently and . . . in order to do so, we must preserve that indispensable matrix of the uncontrolled and non-rational which is the only environment wherein reason can grow and operate effectively." Like Bateson, Hayek argued "that the knowledge which any individual mind consciously manipulates is only a small part of the knowledge which at one time contributes to the success of his action." Hayek distrusted utopias. We don't know enough to plan our future in detail: "The mind can never foresee its own advance."

Like the performers at the Café Voltaire, he argued that we must leave a great deal to chance, that we must collaborate with chance to bring about unexpected outcomes. Like the Dadaists, he built chance into the center of his nonsystemic system. And, like the Dadaists, he put his faith in emergence. If you let enough unpredictable things happen, something desirable will emerge. What is needed, Hayek argued, as did the Café Voltaire Dadaists, is the atmosphere of freedom that such emergence requires: "Liberty is essential in order to leave room for the unforeseeable and unpredictable. . . . It is because every individual knows so little and, in particular, because we rarely know which of us knows best that we trust the independent and competitive efforts of many to induce *the emergence of what we shall want when we see it.* Humiliating to human pride as it may be, we must recognize that the advance and even the preservation of civilization are dependent on a maximum of opportunity for accidents to happen" (my emphasis). The Dadaists reduced art to artistic surfaces for their own sake—the sound of words, the clashes of color and shape, noise, drumming, gesture—because they wanted to subtract the overweening conscious purpose that, like Bateson, they saw as creating the Versailles pattern of vengeance and retribution. "Progress" had to be left to the chance collision of word, sound, color. So, too, for Hayek: "Progress by its very nature cannot be planned. Progress is movement for movement's sake."

An interesting illustration of Hayek's argument comes from an unexpected source. In June of 1987, an unusual ship was launched by the Greek navy. It was called the *Olympias* and it was a historical reconstruction of a Greek trireme, a ship with three decks of rowers, such as was used by the Greeks when they defeated the Persians in the battle of Salamis in 480 B.C. The construction of the *Olympias,* a fascinating tale of collaborative effort by archaeologists, rowers, and the Greek Navy, is told by J. S. Morrison, J. F. Coates, and N. B. Rankov in *The Athenian Trireme: The History and Reconstruction of an Ancient Greek War- ship.* In the course of it, they make a point that precisely illustrates Hayek's emphasis on the importance of social institutions that evolve over time, and how they differ from those social planners create ab ovo. "A reconstruction of an original whose design and whose techniques for building, operation, and main- tenance have been lost has to be redesigned. This is a process of deduction, calculation and spatial organization utterly different from the slow step-by-step process by which the original was developed over a time-span running to de- cades, even centuries . . . our ability to design at will devices of practical use in wide variety does little, of itself, to help us to work back to deduce the 'design' of ancient artifacts."

This coaxing of chance, when it occurred at the Café Voltaire, seems silly and pointless, a surreal "chance meeting on a dissecting table of a sewing machine and an umbrella." But the pointlessness gains point when you add in the power of endless iteration, as the digital computer has done in our own time. Put together a random pattern with a couple of general rules, and you can evolve an orderly system, as the "artificial life" evolutionary biologists have done. Hayek, because he was thinking of an entire economy operating over time, built in this endless power of iteration, of repeated small choices. This was precisely what free markets were all about, the cumulative force of iterative choice and random juxtaposition. The Café Voltaire menu started out with randomness, trusting that a spontaneous order would emerge. The Dadaists were, amid all the posing, political and social, feeling their way toward a bottom-up, evolutionary method of creation. But they lacked the computer's ability to fructify chance by amplifying time.

The artistic arguments at the Café Voltaire were, then, like those of Warhol and Christo, economic arguments as well. The economic system of "serious art" against which Dada rebelled was an economy directed from above by a "masterpiece" tradition and "masterpiece" rules. The rule of conscious purpose and top-down design needed to be balanced, as Bateson and Hayek argued, by countervailing bottom-up forces driven by chance juxtaposition in an environment of freedom.

The argument of the twentieth-century artistic avant-garde took its structure from Dada. It is remarkable, then, that the politics that went with the avant-garde were the politics of the Left, of central planning. Free markets, and certainly advocates of them like Hayek, were anathema. (When Hayek won the Nobel Prize for Economics in 1974, the cowinner was Gunnar Myrdahl, a perfect representative of the planned society. Myrdahl would hardly speak to Hayek, such was his indignation at Hayek's election.) This disjunction is part of a larger one; the advocates of a free market of ideas have often at the same time advocated a centrally planned economy of stuff. The disjunction, as we've already seen, becomes uncomfortable when you must consider a stuff economy and an attention economy in the same frame.

So the Dada brand combined the political discussions about top-down/bottom-up social direction and the same discussions in the world of art. They are both economic discussions, about the scarcity of human attention. Both of these positions have, to be sure, been argued by many other voices. The futurist/Dada/surrealism cluster of arguments informed the rest of the century. The Dada brand was the brand of the century—not Coca-Cola. These arguments aimed at restoration of balance not through synthesis but, as I have been arguing, through an oscillation between opposites. As both Bateson and Hayek show, the arguments were in fact about a scarcity of human attention. They were economic arguments but about an economics of attention, not of stuff. They were concerned to reassert the claims of bottom-up systems of attention in the face of overweening top-down systems. The method for doing this was in both cases *oscillatio.* For Bateson, the top-down message was conscious information and behavior, the bottom-up, all the messages from the unconscious and the subconscious about what kind of message a message is—about style. For Hayek, the top-down force was the state planning of socialism, the bottom-up force was the market and its pricing system. The market, like the subconscious, moved in mysterious ways. The problem for Bateson was that the mind could not pay attention to everything at once. Its central dilemma was an economic one: scarcity of conscious attention. The problem was an economics of attention problem for Hayek, too. The central planners could not pay attention to all the details. There were too many facts to pay attention to them all. The market was a way, subconsciously, to pay attention to them all while reserving the conscious attention for other things. So Hayek was arguing for society the case Bateson was arguing for the mind. Bateson was a voice of the 1960s' Left; Hayek the inspiration for the 1970s' Thatcher Right. But both were working out the implications of that plea for attention that emanated from the Café Voltaire in 1916.

Pop: Exploiting the Brand

I first came to ponder the progeny of Dada by reading Calvin Tomkins's books on them, starting out with *The Scene: Reports on Post-Modern Art,* which introduced me to Andy Warhol and to Christo. I encountered Jean Tinguely in Tomkins's *The Bride and the Bachelors: Five Masters of the Avant-Garde.* His *Off the Wall: Robert Rauschenberg and the Art World of Our Time* first got me thinking about Duchamp, and I followed up with his *Duchamp: A Biography.*

The book that first posed for me postmodern art as an economics of attention was Lawrence Weschler's *Seeing Is Forgetting the Name of the Thing One Sees: A Life of Contemporary Artist Robert Irwin.* Irwin is a Southern California artist, and I felt the impress of his way of thinking about light from the moment I moved to Los Angeles in 1965, but I couldn't codify what I felt about it until I read about Irwin's long contemplation of how we attend to light, learn to look at it as well as through it, and move with agility from one way of seeing to another. Irwin was interested in hot rods when he was a teenager, and the classic worship of pure form that was the 1950s' California hot rod culture led me to think about other cultures that loved form for its own sake, notably Bali. Here is where Gregory Bateson reentered my conversation, and Clifford Geertz's discussion of game motive and Bali in *The Interpretation of Cultures* and *Local Knowledge.* Further tracking of Dada's descendants took me to Adrian Henri's *Total Art: Environments, Happenings, and Performance,* Edward Lucie-Smith's *Late Modern: The Visual Arts since 1945,* and Corinne Robins's useful *The Pluralist Era: American Art, 1968-1981.* Everywhere I looked, I saw an attention economy trying to break out of the egg.

As we've seen with Andy Warhol, pop art embodies the paradoxical relationship in an attention economy between stuff and what we think about stuff. On the one hand, stuff: Warhol's soup cans, Oldenburg's billiard balls, soft toilets, baseball bats, Kitaj's pictures of book covers. (I've taken these examples from the exhibition catalog of Henry Geldzahler's famous show, documented in the catalog *Pop Art, 1955-70.*) The pop figures, Lucy Lippard reminds us, were all commercial artists as well as "fine" artists. "Warhol was a successful fashion illustrator of shoes; Rosenquist learned billboard painting as a trade; Lichtenstein worked in design and display; Oldenburg in magazine illustration and design; and Wesselmann studied to be a cartoonist." "Yet," she continues, "all of them were artists first and foremost, devoting their energies to serious painting." They were painting, that is, not only stuff but information—advertising and popular iconography. Advertising, not something we look through as persuasion, but look at as pattern for its own sakes. "The central novelty and perhaps most fruitful aspect of Pop Art," Nancy Marmer writes, "obviously consists not in its concentration on common objects . . . not in its popular culture subjects . . . nor in its 'questioning' of the nature of the relationship between depiction and reality . . . but in its sanctions of advertising, illustration, and commercial art conventions as well as techniques for the presentation of these, or any other figurative subjects, in a context of 'high art.'" The pop artists toggled between the two in a series of variations on Hayek's central thesis, that the mind can never foresee its own advances and that it must collaborate with chance to find its future.

John Cage devised compositional formulas based on Zen texts and a host of "aleatory compositions" followed, pieces that could be played in many different ways, depending on the choices of the performers. Cage also collected the junk sounds of everyday life and framed them in compositions in much the same way that many artists collected junk objects and framed them in collages. They were redeemed by being put into a different attention field.

"Happenings," the pop version of theater, inverted the traditional relationship of play and prop: "Instead of the character-context matrices of traditional theater, the focus in Happenings was on the props, costumes, and sets. Where words were used they functioned as sounds, independent of meaning. The primary concern was the creation of vivid and arresting 'pictures' whose potential for superimposed and constantly changing imagery offered a degree of invention far greater than that in more static art forms." The audience, seeing the "props, costumes, and sets" was then asked to supply the dramatic imitation to go with them. The audience was converted into an assemblage of playwrights. The final result, the creative innovation, was to be found in the oscillation between play and prop.

Roy Lichtenstein performed the reversal in his comic book paintings. The best survey of the world from which these paintings come, at least that I have found, is the "Comics" section in Kirk Varnedoe and Adam Gopnik's *High and Low: Modern Art and Popular Culture*. Comic books, of the kind Lichtenstein imitated, are action narratives. You follow the action, you don't comment on the draftsmanship. Lictenstein reversed background and foreground. He painted paintings about the genre of painting that comic-strip frames created. The power of the painting comes from looking at what the genre asks us to look through. Try this with any of his comic book paintings and you'll see what I mean. I'm looking right now at a series of three in Lawrence Alloway's *Lichtenstein,* but Diane Waldman's catalog of the Guggenheim Lichtenstein exhibition, *Roy Lichtenstein,* provides examples of this at/through oscillation on practically every page. The "brushstroke" paintings, where the means of the painting becomes the subject of the painting, provide the most extreme examples of this oscillation. See, for example, *Yellow Brushstroke II* in the Waldman catalog.

The brushstroke paintings work by changing scale. *Yellow Brushstroke II,* for example, is thirty-six inches by 108 inches. Claes Oldenburg made a career out of such scale changes. Changing scale forces us to look at what we usually look through. Gigantic baseball bats, saws, light switches, lipsticks, flashlights, binoculars (see R. H. Fuchs, *Claes Oldenburg: Large-Scale Projects, 1977-1980,* for examples) make us self-conscious about how scaling decisions determine the physical reality that we see. When we observe one of the large public monuments, our eyes are forever moving back and forward from the scale of the monument to the scale of its setting. The aim is to cultivate a way of seeing that can hold two kinds of reality in the mind's eye at one time. The means are pretty simple— scale up everyday objects—but the program is more complex: "His approach to popular art was not to create it but to use it 'for something more serious.'"

This was the program that James Rosenquist followed as well. I was overpowered by it when I saw the Rosenquist show at the Denver Art Museum in 1985. Rosenquist started out as a commercial artist on a gigantic scale: he painted billboards. His enfranchising decision was to bring these billboards into the art gallery, as happened in Denver. (The show is illustrated in Judith Goldman's *James Rosenquist.*) As you walked through the show, you were continually pulled back and forth from ordinary scale to billboard scale. It was not only the immense paintings that did this (*F-111* is eighty-six feet long and ten feet high). Judith Goldman feels that "these pictures are about doubt: the doubt that has always concerned Rosenquist about living in twentieth-century America, with too much noise and too much information and too many things on one's mind." This certainly fits the standard litany provoked by an information economy and its concomitant short supply of attention. It is possible, though, to feel precisely the opposite response to the paintings that caught me up in their environment. They celebrated the energy of modern information flow, they didn't denigrate it. They are trying to depict information flow at its most dynamic, its most bewildering. The scale has to be big because the information flow is big. The paintings themselves do not move, but we must move, both literally and emotionally, when we see them. No artist illustrates better than Rosenquist what it means to paint information.

Maturity of the Brand

At the center of Hayek's argument about how markets and pricing mechanisms work (and I suppose we could say Adam Smith's as well) was time. A great many small, individual decisions, over time, create an emergent order. The genius of central planning works the other way. You figure out how everything should work out before you do it, out of time and the changes time brings. Markets, in contrast, start something in motion and see what happens. Happenings did this, but the main developer of this theme was the Swiss sculptor Jean Tinguely. Again, I was entranced by a museum exhibit, this time at the Tate Gallery in 1982 (*Tinguely at the Tate*). Tinguely makes moving sculptures out of junk welded together in what look like entirely random designs. The resulting machines move, jiggle, clang, wiggle, rotate, and in some cases self-destruct in spectacular ways. (For those unfortunate enough not to see one of these machines in action, the best illustrations can be found in Pontus Hulten's *Jean Tinguely: A Magic Stronger Than Death.*) When I saw them in the Tate, banging and clanging and tossing out balls that children then picked up and put back in the machine, I felt as if I was seeing a hidden agenda suddenly come to life, a history of frustrated motion, of comic-frame paintings that wanted to be films, suddenly allowed to move. It was not unlike the argument I make in chapter 3 for kinetic text as liberating stylistic patterns that are frozen in place in printed texts. Here is how, I found when I read Hulten's book, Tinguely had expressed this sense of liberation:

I am an artist of movement. Initially I did painting but I got blocked there, I found myself stuck. I was handicapped by the whole history of art and the Ecole des Beaux-Arts. I got hung up in the pictures, on the pictures—finally all I could do was to wait until they were tired; I could never find their end. So I decided to introduce movement. . . . I began to use movement simply to make a re-creation. It was a way of re-doing a painting so that it would become infinite—it would go on making new compositions with the help of the physical and mechanical movements I gave it. . . . I wanted something ephemeral, that would pass like a falling star and, most importantly, be impossible for museums to reabsorb. I didn't want to be "museumized."

So, as with Christo, the ideal of the timeless masterpiece is turned on its head, is reinserted into time. Christo's projects were, like Tinguely's sculptures, planned to be temporary. In both cases, the physical stuff of the accomplishment, the built work, was subtracted so that only the volumes describing it would remain. The abiding structures were to be the attention structures created by the physical structures and not the structures themselves.

Tinguely once remarked, "With Dada . . . I have in common a certain mistrust toward power. We don't like authority, we don't like power." The power of art had to flow from the particular response upward, like individual market decisions, not viewed through a grid of greatness sent down from above. Christo's work illustrates this fear of power; it could endanger what Hayek meant by "liberty," the freedom to create new enterprises where none could have been planned. No central planner would have thought to include wrapping the Great Barrier Reef or the Pont Neuf or building a curtain over Rifle Canyon or a twenty-six-mile fence in California. Ideas like this emerged from the Café Voltaire; they have that kind of radical individualism written all over them. They courted risk.

And yet Christo, unlike the Dadaists, is willing to work the system instead of repudiating it. Is willing, in fact, to make the system part of the work. Look at the big archival books for the *Running Fence* and other projects. Full of the plans, specifications, environmental impact reports, and other documentation the projects required, they are textbooks for the top-down planning, the meticulous purpose, that the Café Voltaire repudiated and that Bateson and Hayek feared. Built into all his projects is a rocking rhythm between the radical individualism needed for entrepreneurial enterprise and the design skills that it also requires, toggling bottom-up design with top-down planning. These projects model (to use an economist's favorite word) the need for a mixed economy and how such a mixture might be created. They constitute the final development of the Dada brand as an economic model, its full maturity.

CHAPTER THREE

This chapter began life as a series of illustrated lectures, and that's what it should be still. The argument takes its natural form only when the images that illustrate the argument are allowed to move, and that is precisely what the printed page does not allow. So the argument, set down on a page, always strains against itself. What seems perfectly natural and easily understood in its natural form as digital expression seems artificial and a little kooky in the alien world of print. Can't be helped in a printed book. The electronic version of this chapter includes the illustrations in their natural dynamic form. It can be found at www.rhetoricainc.com/eofa. But while we are in the print world, I ask print readers to piece out my imperfections with their thoughts.

{WHAT'S NEXT FOR TEXT?}

In 1932, the famous English ty-
pographer Beatrice Warde designed a type-display poster "to
show off Perpetua Titling to good advantage." A reproduction of it by the
Monotype Corporation hangs in my office.

Letters are the greatest beginning of understanding.

Byzantine school tablet, fifth century A.D.

THIS IS

A PRINTING OFFICE

CROSSROADS OF CIVILIZATION
REFUGE OF ALL THE ARTS
AGAINST THE RAVAGES OF TIME

ARMOURY OF FEARLESS TRUTH
AGAINST WHISPERING RUMOUR

INCESSANT TRUMPET OF TRADE

FROM THIS PLACE WORDS MAY FLY ABROAD
NOT TO PERISH ON WAVES OF SOUND
NOT TO VARY WITH THE WRITER'S HAND
BUT FIXED IN TIME HAVING BEEN VERIFIED IN PROOF

FRIEND, YOU STAND ON SACRED GROUND
THIS IS A PRINTING OFFICE

In the present cornucopia of print, this splendid declaration still rings
true. It cheers me every time I walk by it. But my copy of the poster includes

a small footnote: "In keeping with the look and feel of the original, this version integrates electronic publishing technologies with letterpress printing methods. The type was set on a Windows™ system. Film output was produced on a PostScript™ imagesetter." Beatrice Warde's printing house now stands on a digital foundation. The generative substructure is electronic; only the final display mechanism remains: the printed page. The notational field has moved from the printing house and the book to the computer graphics lab and the electronic screen.

Casting the present day as a titanic struggle between the forces of print and the digital raiders no longer makes sense. All text is digital in origin. Fixed print has become printout, one substrate of expression for a preexisting digital code. And it is no longer the only game in town. Other, digital, displays— regular cathode-ray tube computer screens, liquid crystal display flat screens, plasma screens, book-sized electronic display devices, smaller electronic date/ address books, digital screen projectors, heads-up displays, goggles, helmets, immersive virtual reality environments—now compete with the printed page for final display. These digital displays can re-create the full electronic expressive space, a three-dimensional, dynamic world, as the flat, fixed world of print cannot. Text will find its future as the various ways we can now display it compete for our attention.

Fixity stands at the center of Beatrice Warde's brave declaration: "not to perish on waves of sound, not to vary with the writer's hand, but fixed in time." Fixed in time because fixed in stuff, print on paper. A theory of typography came with Warde's fixity. Print should be like a crystal goblet that contains a fine wine: transparent but containing; metaphysically invisible. You do not see the print but look through it to the heady meaning swirling within. And a theory of style came with the theory of typography; the ideal style, like the ideal print, is a style never noticed. Fixed and invisible. That fixity comes unglued in digital expression, and in the process we come to see the expressive surface, typography and style, to look at it rather than through it.

But wait a minute. The poster, we are told, was designed "to show off Perpetua Titling to good advantage." It wants us to look at it, as well as through it. Two responses are solicited. First, "Yes, Perpetua Titling *is* a spiffy typeface. Notice how well it looks." We respond to the printed surface. Second, "Yes, print enshrines, fixes, the best in human culture." We look through the printed surface to the meaning beneath. Our whole response must be an oscillation between these two ways of seeing, between typographical surface and symbolic notation, between image and meaning. The poster offers a more comprehensive illustration of how we read print than Ms. Warde's theory about it.

The competing substrates for textual display find themselves surrounded by a larger sphere in which text must compete against image and sound in all kinds of mixtures, many of them much newer, more complex, and more adroit than our familiar family villain, broadcast TV. I am not thinking of films here, or video games or theme parks either, though they may stand for a yet larger circumambience of competitive attention structures. I am thinking of new ways to express what text has traditionally expressed.

In the world of fixed print, writers had to decide which genres and which styles answered their expressive desires. A decision about genre (we might call it the macroeconomics of style) implied a decision about sentence structure (its microeconomics). The typographical conventions and metaphorical densities that separated prose from poetry were also decisions about how to compete for a reader's attention. So were the basic decisions about verbal style—high/middle/low, running/periodic, and so on. So were the rhetorical figures of sound and arrangement that the Greeks invented to smuggle oral power back into written utterance. Now those expressive decisions encompass a much wider domain. Superimposed on the traditional choices of style, a new layer of stylistic choice faces anyone who would communicate in text. What display device do I choose? And what stylistic rules come with it?

Above this, yet another layer. Since digital information exists in a code that can be displayed in words, sounds, or images, these three modes constitute yet another level of stylistic decision. Text itself is a self-conscious expressive choice as it has never been before. How, when you are "writing" in the electronic space, do you decide when to use words, when images, and when sounds? Or in what combination? It all makes for a much more self-conscious mixture for both writer and reader. The crystal goblet becomes opaque. You have to be governed by the poster's bi-stable logic instead.

"Fixed in time." Let's begin our examination of digital expression by unfixing it. Here is a student exercise submitted in a class at Carnegie-Mellon University's School of Design (fig. 3.1). It fulfills the venerable composition-class assignment: Describe the most exciting thing that happened to you last summer. Bear in mind that these are still frames from a short movie. Since we're considering a dynamic text in the print world, I'll have to ask you to fill in the "in-betweens."

What is happening here? For one thing, the linearity of print is discarded. In a printed text, words come a line at a time, left to right and then down one. You can skip around a little if you must, but the order of presentation does not. You are not aware of the order of presentation at all. It is part of "reading" and completely transparent. All your attention goes to the meaning of

(a)

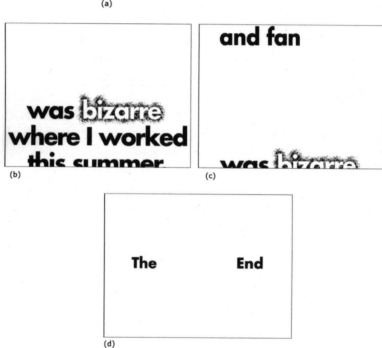

(b)

(c)

(d)

Figure 3.1. Patrick Hong, "The Elevator." School assignment, Carnegie-Mellon School of Design. By permission of the author.

the text. Here the text moves, and the eye is always attracted to movement. The movement constructs a moving picture of an elevator in operation, doors opening and shutting (figs. 3.1*a* and 3.1*d*), an elevator getting stuck and vibrating a little on its cables as they so disconcertingly do at such times, an elevator again enduring its customary ups and downs (figs. 3.1*b* and 3.1*c*).

When you look at images, still or moving, you apprehend them not element by element, as you read words, but all at once, as a single entity. So two timescales operate here: sequential for the alphabetic text, instantaneous for the elevator movie. Our apprehension of the text oscillates between image and writing, first the one then the other. The result is a short short story built on a pun. A pun is a word or phrase that carries simultaneously two separate and often opposite meanings. Here the story is carried by both the image and the words. The image is not an illustration in the margin of the alphabetic text but part of it. Two kinds of apprehension are multiplexed together.

Would it be stretching things to call the moving text—the "kinetic text," as it has come to be called—more efficient? Or might it, at least, model how a greater compression of meaning, a greater efficiency, might be constructed? Two ways of telling a story reinforce one another. Classical rhetoric had a special term for efforts at such compression: it was *ekphrasis*. An *ekphrasis* was a "speaking picture," a descriptive passage so immediately suggestive of visual imagery that it seemed to yoke together the power of words and images. Here such a yoking literally takes place. When I show this short short story to live audiences, they always laugh. Their laughter applauds the clever artistic balance between image and word, the pleasure conveyed by condensed yet immediately available information. No decoding needed.

Linear prose notation can say only one thing at a time. The history of literature, considered in one way, is a long struggle to overcome this limitation. On a small scale, the pun represents such a two-for-one meaning; on a larger scale, literary figures like irony work the same way, manage to say both X and non-X in the same words at the same time. If you cannot say everything at once, you can at least say two things at once. Such figures—though to my knowledge no one has ever thought to construe them in this way—strive for greater productivity. When writing moves from the printing house to the computer graphics lab, kinetic typography can be used for the same purpose.

What happens, in such an expressive field, to the workaday distinction between prose (writing that goes to the end of the right margin) and poetry (writing that doesn't)? It collapses. Neither category fits. Instead, a notation emerges that tries to stretch across the gulf between the abstract notational space of conventional print and the animated life of movement and gesture that characterizes the everyday world we live in. Poetry tries to do this, too, and so we must call it poetry. An efficient compression operates here too. Stimulus and response are, punlike, made part of the same utterance. Writer and reader become part of the same perceptual sensibility. The piece is a process, and processes don't stay still, fixed in time. They move.

Western notation had been trying to create this compression for a long time. It fulfills a traditional genre called "shape poetry." Shape poems, or pattern poems, are poems whose shape refers to their subject: a poem about an altar in the shape of an altar, a poem about an ax in the shape of one, a poem about an umbrella that outlines a raised umbrella. It is an old genre. The earliest shape poem we know of is by the Greek poet Simias of Rhodes, who flourished about 300 B.C. He wrote a poem, in the shape of an ax, "probably meant to be inscribed on a votive copy of the ax with which Epeius made the Wooden Horse, in which the Greeks finally penetrated Troy and ended the war." And he wrote a famous poem, meant to be written on an egg and in the shape of one. In both poems, you must read first the top line, then the last, then next-to-top, then next-to-last, and so on. The usual pattern of reading, a line at a time, is inverted, so that we become self-conscious about putting the lines together into sensible meaning. And in both poems, the usual inscriptional substrate (papyrus, presumably, for Simias) is discarded in favor of mapping the words onto the actual objects to which they refer. Computer graphics now does such "texture mapping" routinely, wrapping objects, or text, in whatever surface pattern is required.

Since Simias, shape poems have been written at many times, in many languages, and in all kinds of shapes. One of my favorites is the contemporary poet John Hollander's "Idea: Old Mazda Lamp, 50–100–150 W" (fig. 3.2). Here, the light bulb shape, so familiar to us as the shape that keeps the dark at bay, becomes a visual focus for a meditation on the ideas that light the mind, on visual seeing as intellectual seeing.

Why contrive poems like this? Why combine an abstract alphabetical signal with a visual image? Why did people continue to find it of interest for two and a half millennia? Because we want to heal the pains of abstraction. We want to insert the text into the three-dimensional physical world, to engrave it onto the three-dimensional world of stuff, just as we do with tombstones and public monuments. We want to bring the world of literacy, and all that literacy carries with it, into the world of objects and of oral conversation. We want to breach the gulf between letters and the world of objects: our old friends stuff and fluff. An utterance like this makes us toggle between the text, an abstract world, and a familiar three-dimensional object from our everyday world. When our eye, top-to-bottom, maps the text onto its object, we are made to feel self-conscious about how we see. We are asked to ponder, to keep ever in mind, the uneasy relationship between words and the objects to which they refer.

But this effort, though of long standing, has never gotten much respect. It isn't "serious," however cleverly it may puzzle about the relationship between words and things. We might profitably ask ourselves why. Words create one

```
                    On or
                 off Either darkness
              unlocked again or feigned
           daylight perhaps graded only by
        stepped intensities fifty watts apart
       In any event no continuities like those
       of flickering no nor even of fading Flick
     Click and there it is suddenly Oh yes I see
     Indeed A mind hung brilliantly upon filaments
     stung by some untongued brightness opening up
     also encloses and the dark unbounded room lit
     by bare bulbs collapses into an unhurting box
     occupied by furniture now avoidable The dot
       of closure menaces the attention which in
        the flutter of eyelids can only tremble
         like a nervous child lying awake lest
           he be aware of the moment a closing
             shutter of sleep claps to But a
                snapped-off dream disperses
                 into darkness like gold
                   becoming mere motes
                    becoming light If
                    the eye lies open
                     to such dust as
                     sunlight brings
                     it will never
                     burn But that
                     creation make
                     a visible big
                     difference in
                     the way minds
                     look a shaper
                      will burn
                      outwardly
                      first and
                      thus once
                      there was
                        light
```

Figure 3.2. John Hollander, "Idea: Old Mazda Lamp, 50-100-150 W." From *Types of Shape*, no. 3. Copyright 1967, 1968, 1969, 1991 by John Hollander. By permission of Yale University Press.

order of meaning, images another, and we don't want them too close together. Our alphabetic habit of mind rejects pictographs and ideographs, notations that use a picture of the object to denote the object. Writing systems like these, which use images rather than an abstract alphabet, assume the punning compression that kinetic text often reenacts. The great victory of the alphabet was to separate thought from image, and we don't want to compromise that victory. But, as the long tradition of pattern poetry attests, we also want to bring the alphabetic world back into the behavioral one.

And so we have two kinds of "seriousness." In alphabetic seriousness, we concentrate on looking through the notational system to the abstract reasoning beneath it. We build a monopolistic attention economy. In pattern-poetry seriousness, we accept a bi-stable seriousness that allows us to toggle from word to image, from at to through and back again. Digital expression, the familiar computer screen, creates, and assumes, a bi-stable seriousness. Perhaps that is why it often seems, to all of us print readers, distinctly unsettling.

Under the influence of digital graphics, the shape impulse is now showing up all over the print landscape, and not only in ads but in workaday prose as well. One example can be found in an advertisement for an investment firm that appeared in the *Economist* (fig. 3.3). Shrewd business persons, when they come to invest for themselves, are often "all thumbs." Leave such decisions to Paine Webber, skilled in prestidigitation. They know that your investment portfolio should be as unique to you as your fingerprints. Another example is a celebrity profile located in a magazine called *Mondo 2000* printed as a "profile" (fig. 3.4). What does such an outburst of shaped prose tell us about the current environment for text? Clearly, a new pattern of attention is being elicited from the reader, the bi-stable attention that pattern poetry has so long incarnated. Shaped prose deliberately cultivates a competitive market economy in which words and images, and the different worlds they represent, compete for our attention.

It is useful to remember, at the present juncture of our argument, that a craving for shape and motion has always lurked beneath the frozen surface of Western alphabetic notation. Its fossils are the rhetorical patterns that in the classic rhetorical terminology are called "figures of arrangement." Look, for instance, at an example that has always had popular currency, an *abba* pattern called chiasmus. It is called that because it wants to be shaped like an X and the Greek word for X is "chi." You will have come across the figure in your daily reading. Here's an example I noticed recently: "You don't stop playing because you get old, you get old because you stop playing." Or a more venerable example from President Kennedy's inaugural address: "Ask not what your country can do for you. Ask what you can do for your country." See how the suppressed X design wants to break free from the linear bounds of print (fig. 3.5)? We want words to move for the same reason we want everything else to move, because movement means life, and the space and time in which life exists.

Now let me illustrate how electronic text can liberate a shape and motion buried deep in a text designed to marmorealize fixity, a legal statute. (Again, I'm using here stills to imply motion; please try to imagine the motion back into them.) Legal writing loves long sentences and this single one takes up an entire page. The warning, in plain language, means "Don't pick the flowers

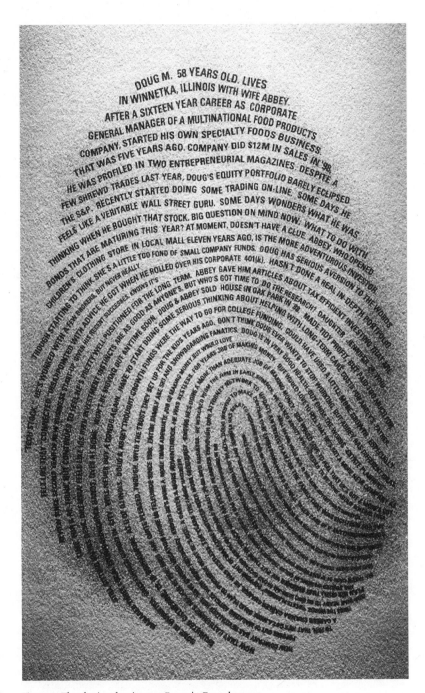

Figure 3.3. Thumbprint advertisement, *Economist*, December 1999.

You,

my dear,

can have a

toaster

that

thinks, that's

sentient and aware

and wants to

make toast

the way you

like it

M2: *Galen Does Lassie.*

CO: Right. And then we could composite that digitally into any scene you can imagine. We could have you doing that on the surface of Mars and it would be completely believable.

M2: To whom, I'd like to know.

CO: Depends on the imagination profile of the user. But the technology exists today to do that—we could present a film that would include that content.

M2: My mother's worst nightmare.

CO: No doubt. And the next step would be to translate that technology to actual, dynamic entities that would act independently of our paying attention to them, and then play back their behavioral processes before an audience. I suppose, theoretically there is that possibility... but let me reiterate. An avatar is nothing more than a data set.

M2: But if it's connected to—

CO: Yes, if it's connected to a sentient entity, it becomes an independent creature of sorts.

M2: Connect me to the brain of Bob Gurcione and we've got *Galen Does Lassie On Mars,* coming, as it were, to a theater near you.

CO: The mind reels. In fact, the behaviors of an artificial personality would not be confined to those originally assigned to it. The human creator of the virtual personality would have a decreasing mantle of control over the behavior of his or her avatar-organism. Does the potential for rebellion exist? Maybe. But how much more stimulating might a virtual experience become if the avatars, including your own, were independent, argumentative and changed with experience? This is the true boundary of emotional sentience.

M2: And where there's rebellion, there's censorship?

CO: I personally was queried directly by a client who represented a country which shall remain nameless—but the nation itself wanted to have their entire backbone insulated with a prophylactic content-addressable recognition filter that would look for certain sexual and religious content that they could screen from any image files that might be coming through the line.

M2: Porn avatars meet censor avatars.

CO: By today's standards, they are very primitive, but the fact is that somebody might court me as a client and ask me: "By the way, could you design a process by which we could screen all images that might be fetched up through our system to look for an exposed nipple or a pubic hair or a religious symbol that doesn't agree with our cultural whatever?" And the answer is yes, I know how to do this; the technology's been around for years, but would I *want* to do this? The fact that there are governments and other institutions looking to do this now suggests that in the future there will be even more stratified kinds of access procedures.

M2: Controlled by humans... or machines? Just how real is synthetic "emotional sentience" today?

CO: The most stunning example I've seen is the work of Professor Daniel Thalmann and his wife Nadia Thalmann from the Swiss Federal Institute of Technology. Already, you can mimic or model emotive communications. At the first annual Virtual Humans Conference held this year, Thalmann showed a tape of one of his synthetic environments which used his virtual human simulation system, MARILYN (an in-joke nod to Chatterbot, one of the first ever biokinetic studies which used a virtual Marilyn Monroe). It had twenty hominids in it, ten males and ten females.

The hominids would wander around randomly in a virtual garden setting, and if two or more got within a certain proximity of one another, they would emote: use facial expressions, certain hand and body gestures, as a way of conveying whether they were in a pleasant, receptive mood or a not-so-pleasant, not-so-receptive mood—

M2: Did they do the macarena?

CO: No, but I'm sure we could toss a macarena algorithm in there somewhere. The point is that in very subtle ways really, if the two emotive creatures had a positive interchange they would decide to acknowledge the interchange. They would clasp hands or even embrace. And if a third entity approached, they could collectively decide whether they liked each other as a group, or whether the original two wanted to remain private. This whole process was an entirely synthetic environment, populated by avatar entities driven by synthetic sentience components.

M2: So this was not virtual me hugging virtual you; this was machines hugging machines.

CO: Yes, via their avatar representations. It was a very compelling modeling scheme that showed emotive communication as a process on the fly.

M2: Are you saying these creatures had hearts—and

Figure 3.4. Profile shape prose from *Mondo* 2000.

along the freeway." First, read the text in its original California Highway Code form. (For fun, try reading it aloud.)

Every person who within the State of California willfully or negligently cuts, destroys, mutilates, or removes any tree or shrub, or fern or herb or bulb or cactus or flower, or huckleberry or redwood greens, or portion of any tree or shrub, or fern or herb or bulb or cactus or flower, or huckleberry or redwood greens, growing upon state or county highway rights-of-way,

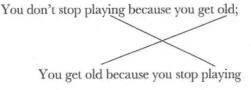

You don't stop playing because you get old;

You get old because you stop playing

Figure 3.5. Chiasmus diagram.

or who removes leaf mold thereon; provided, however, that the provisions
of this section shall not be construed to apply to any employee of the state
or of any political subdivision thereof engaged in work upon any state,
county or public road or highway while performing such work under the
supervision of the state or of any political subdivision thereof, and every
person who willfully or negligently cuts, destroys, mutilates, or removes
any tree or shrub, or fern or herb or bulb or cactus or flower, or huckleberry
or redwood greens, or portion of any tree or shrub, or fern or herb or bulb
or cactus or flower, or huckleberry or redwood greens, growing upon
public land or upon land not his own, or leaf mold on the surface of public
land, or upon land not his own, without a written permit from the owner
of the land signed by such owner or his authorized agent, and every person who knowingly sells, offers, or exposes for sale, or transports for sale,
any tree or shrub, or fern or herb or bulb or cactus or flower, or huckleberry
or redwood greens, or portion of any tree or shrub, or fern or herb or bulb
or cactus or flower, or huckleberry or redwood greens, or leaf mold, so cut
or removed from state or county highway rights-of-way, or removed from
public land or from land not owned by the person who cut or removed the
same without written permit from the owner of the land, signed by such
owner or his authorized agent, shall be guilty of a misdemeanor and upon
conviction thereof shall be punished by a fine of not more than five hundred dollars ($500) or by imprisonment in a county jail for not more than
six months or by both such fine and imprisonment.

If you read this aloud with any emphasis or vigor, you soon break up in
laughter. And as for sense, you are lost almost from the first boilerplate repetition of shrubs and ferns. It is a pathless wood, on the other side of which,
somehow, lie fines and jail. Yet if only you could see the shapes within the bog
yearning to be free, you could understand the statute at a glance. Let's let
them loose (fig. 3.6). We'll use space and typographical variation (both free

Every person who

within the State of California

willfully or negligently
  cuts,
    destroys,
      mutilates, or
        removes

(a)

(provided, however, that

the provisions of this section shall not be construed to apply
to any employee **of the state**
or of any political subdivision thereof
engaged in work **upon any state,**
county or public road or highway while performing such work
under the supervision **of the state**
or of any political subdivision thereof **),**

(c)

[chorus]

any tree or shrub, or fern or herb or bulb or cactus or
flower, or huckleberry or redwood greens,
or portion of
any tree or shrub, or fern or herb or bulb or cactus or
flower, or huckleberry or redwood greens,

growing upon public **land** or
upon **land** not his **own,**
or leaf mold on the surface
of public **land,** or
upon **land** not his **own,**

(e)

[chorus]

any tree or shrub, or fern or herb or bulb or cactus or
flower, or huckleberry or redwood greens,
or portion of
any tree or shrub, or fern or herb or bulb or cactus or
flower, or huckleberry or redwood greens,
or leaf mold,

so cut or **removed** from state or county highway rights-of-way,
or **removed** from public **land**
or from **land** not owned by the person
who cut or **removed** the same without the written permit
from the **owner** of the **land**
signed by such **owner** or his authorized agent,

(g)

Figure 3.6. California Highway Code with its implicit shape made explicit.

[chorus]

any tree or shrub, or fern or herb or bulb or cactus or
flower, or huckleberry or redwood greens,
or portion of
any tree or shrub, or fern or herb or bulb or cactus or
flower, or huckleberry or redwood greens,

growing upon state or county highway rights-of-way, or
who removes leaf mold thereon;

(b)

and **every person who**

willfully or negligently
cuts,
destroys,
mutilates, or
removes

(d)

without a written permit from the **owner**
of the **land**
signed by such **owner**
or his authorized agent,

and **every person who** knowingly

sells,
offers, or
exposes for sale, or
transports for sale,

(f)

shall be guilty of a misdemeanor
and upon conviction thereof

shall be punished

by a fine of not more than five hundred dollars ($500) or
by imprisonment in a county jail for not more than six months
or **by** both such fine and imprisonment.

(h)

in the electronic writing space, remember) to make the structure clear. Start with figure 3.6*a*. And now, we focus the boilerplate repetition as what it is, the chorus of an incipient poem (fig. 3.6*b*). Next, we separate out as a parenthesis the parenthetical "provided, however that" (fig. 3.6*c*).

Notice what happens here? A repetitive pattern ("of the state," "upon the state," "of the state") begins to make a vertical visual pattern that shows us how the parenthesis is arranged and can be understood. Next the opening pattern is repeated (fig. 3.6*d*). Then the chorus is repeated, again with vertical patterns repeated (fig. 3.6*e*). Then the third repetition of the "every person who" opening (fig. 3.6*f*). Then the chorus once more, with a more emphatic vertical boldface emphasis to lend visual order to the repetitions (fig. 3.6g). And finally the core utterance, subject and verb united over the boilerplate repetitions by the same dominant typeface: "every person who . . . shall be guilty" (fig. 3.6*h*).

It works much more effectively in dynamic text form, but you can see what finally happens even in this series of still frames. The marmoreal prose melts into poetry. It wants, in fact, to be Homeric epic poetry, with its ritual repetitions of fixed phrases and its pronounced oral rhythms. And when we rearrange it, vertical patterns emerge from the linear horizontality. A visual imagination is at work here, albeit unawares.

Legal texts are notoriously hard to understand. Might we find, in this new pattern of attention, an increase in efficiency in how knowledge is communicated? The kinetic typographical design seeks to help the reader by separating the main argument, carried in a gothic type, from its endless qualifications and subdivisions. Like all good layouts, it strives to lend to the mind the powers of the eye.

Legal writing has come under pressure from a "plain language movement" that seeks to make legal texts more available to the common understanding. Imagine, then, if large areas of legal writing, the kinds that ordinary people need to know about, were accessible in a format that could toggle from the linear to the diagrammatic arrangement. If we consider the enormous amount of time spent trying to make sense out of legal prose like this, not only by laypeople but by the lawyers themselves, we can glimpse the enormous saving in time and effort such dynamic texts might bring. Our eyes are programmed to detect motion. We like it. When we see text move, we are drawn into the movement. And when the movement takes us to a land where meaning has a visual embodiment, we pay attention to it.

In digital expression, text not only moves, it often moves in three-dimensional space. Again, we've had warnings about what was coming. The

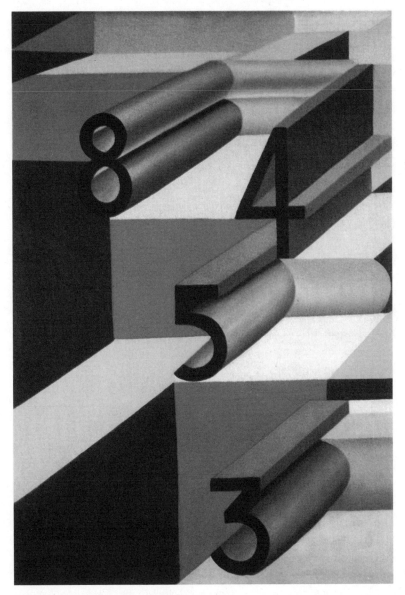

Figure 3.7. Giacomo Balla, *Numbers in Love* (1923).

last century abounded in visual exhortation to consider letters as images rather than alphabetic code, to look at them rather than through them. The futurist painter Giacomo Balla took a series of numbers and broke the two-dimensional print convention by extruding them into three-dimensional space (fig. 3.7).

Another futurist painter, Francesco Cangiullo, in a complex pun, animated

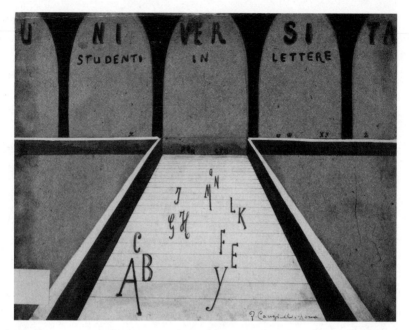

Figure 3.8. Francesco Cangiullo, *Università* (1914–15).

letters into students climbing the steps of the Faculty of Letters, the stairs becoming the classical stairs of learning, the *gradus ad Parnassum* (fig. 3.8). The letters, now stick-figure students, struggle up the steep steps of learning, and the "studenti in lettere" written on the back panels repeats in words the visual pun: the students have been put inside the physical letter forms, as well as being depicted as students who study the arts and letters.

Claes Oldenburg took a series of letters and numbers and inflated the hard-edged symbols into fat, squishy inner tubes (fig. 3.9). Jenny Holzer bent a dynamic alphabet around the spiral curves of the Guggenheim Museum so that we read the letters as writing and as spatial design in equal parts (fig. 3.10).

There have been many other flotations of letters into the foreground and into three-dimensional space. Whatever other aesthetic or political purposes such designs had in mind, they shared a central didacticism: pay attention to letters as three-dimensional figures, as material objects. An experimental field called dimensional typography has been doing precisely this. Here are two examples. The first is an ABC from a font called Univers Revolved, by Ji Lee, created in 1996 (fig. 3.11). It takes as its inspiration a well-known font, the 1957 Univers font designed by Adrian Frutiger, and injects it into three-

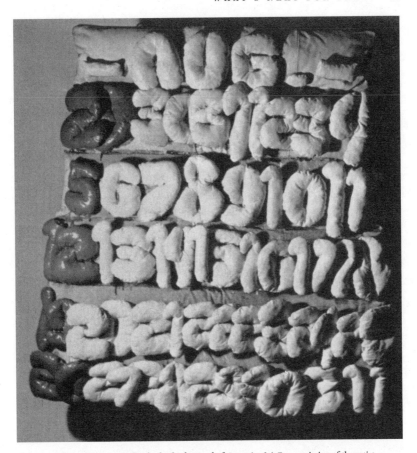

Figure 3.9. Claes Oldenburg, *Soft Calendar for the Month of August* (1962). By permission of the artist.

dimensional space. You would hardly recognize the letters if the regular form were not given below them. A text printed in them would be hard to read. No increase in perceptual efficiency here. Why then such an endeavor? It comes from a desire to put letters back into the three-dimensional space where we all live and breathe and have our being. We want to think of a letter as a physical object, a piece of stuff, which we can pick up in our hands and rotate on an axis, as we do with objects in the ordinary world. We want to put letters back into the world of stuff. But we still want them to be letters.

Here's another example of "dimensional typography." Ligature, designed by Bart Overly in 1995 (fig. 3.12), welds the traditional specimen letters *A* and *B* into a single 3-D form, one that yields alternate readings—first *A* then *B* then *A* again—as you turn it around in your mind. Again, a visual pun.

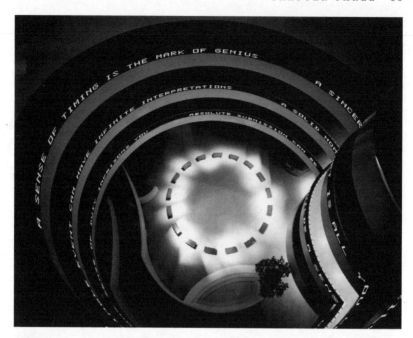

Figure 3.10. Jenny Holzer, *Untitled (Selections from Truisms, Inflammatory Essays, The Living Series, The Survival Series, Under a Rock, Laments, and Child Text)*, Guggenheim installation, December 1989–February 1990. Extended helical tricolor L.E.D. electronic-display signboard. Site-specific dimensions: 41.9 cm × 49 m × 37.8 m (16½ inches × 162 feet × 6 inches). Solomon R. Guggenheim Museum, New York. Partial gift of the artist, 1989. 89.3626. © 2005 Jenny Holzer/Artists Rights Society (ARS), New York. Photograph by David Heald © The Solomon R. Guggenheim Foundation, New York.

Such a jeu d'esprit exudes maximal alphabetic self-consciousness but at a high level of granularity, the individual letter form. It reveals a yearning for three-dimensional space and for compression of meaning that merges letters as symbols and letters as objects.

Such letter-scale self-consciousness has formed a part of our common expressive universe ever since the computer graphics labs started making TV commercials. Letters in broadcast TV commercials want to be three-dimensional like Oldenburg's puffy integers and to move around on the page like the Marinetti typographical explosions discussed in chapter 2. They often seem like buildings that we fly around. Then we see that we've zoomed up preternaturally close to the letters, changed scale drastically, as we do with one of James Rosenquist's gigantic paintings when we look at it up close. The letter space has become a three-dimensional cityscape.

Here are three stills from an early dynamic logo for CBS-TV New York (fig. 3.13). In the dynamic version, we zoom into the text and then fly around it.

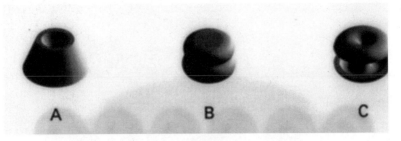

Figure 3.11. Ji Lee, *Univers Revolved* (1996). By permission of the artist.

Electronic text of this sort answers a question that simply cannot arise in conventional printed text. What does the other side of a letter look like? After we see it from the front (fig. 3.13*a*) we start our circumnavigation. Next we are halfway around the letters, which now hang in three-dimensional space (fig. 3.13*b*). Then we are on the back side of the text (fig. 3.13*c*), an area that, in print, is as invisible as the back side of the moon.

Once after I showed this segment to a group of academics, one came up to me and introduced himself as a professor of accounting. He said I had illustrated his fundamental principle in teaching accounting: "Always ask what's behind the numbers!" Three-dimensional dynamic text can literalize many of the metaphors we use to describe what happens in a flat printed text. Not only do we strive to see "what's behind" an argument, but "what's at the bottom" of it, where its "center" is, where you can "get your bearings" in it or "clarify your position on this issue," or "take a stand," or "draw back from a conclusion," because we yearn to use the orienting powers our species evolved to deal with the three-dimensional world. These venerable metaphors betray an unsatisfied hunger for spatial orientation in conceptual notation and thought. They suggest that a dynamic imagination has stood behind fixed text from the beginning.

Let me illustrate one of these ancient hungers, the desire that word and thing become one, that the abstract symbol and the physical object it describes present the same image. The final still from a sequence that does this, a visual pun of a "table," can be seen in figure 3.14. Let me describe the sequence. The letters are first extruded into three-dimensional space, then metamorphose, as a flower and vase is created on top of them, into a conventional flower-and-fruit still life in which the *word* table has become the *thing* table. We read the letters both as abstract alphabetical notation and as stuff. A major strand of Western philosophy, the debate between things and the

Figure 3.12. Bart Overly, *Ligature* (1995). By permission of the artist.

words we use to name them, has been rolled up into a clever and lighthearted pun. Again, two kinds of expression, alphabet and image, form the same letters into a visual pun. Alphabetic expression yearns to recapture the imagistic notations that preceded it.

When you put writing back into time and space you have animated it, and animation is proving the central expressive power of computer graphics. Not surprisingly, letters have begun to dance on the screen. But, like shape poetry, animated letters have been around for a long time. Consider a sample from an alphabet developed at Bergamo in the late fourteenth century by Giovanni

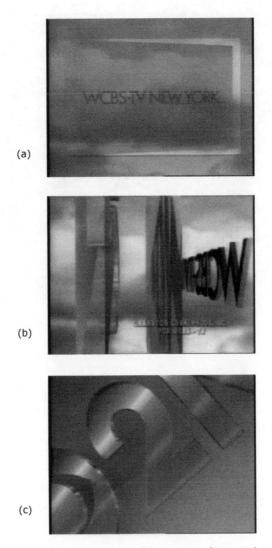

Figure 3.13. *WCBS-TV Logo* (Cranston Csuri Prods., Inc.). By permission of Wayne Carlson.

dei Grassi (fig. 3.15). The letter forms strive to hold in the life trying to burst out of their alphabetical boundaries. Chivalric human figures intricate themselves with animal life, all of them writhing with motion. Again we see symbolic notation and the world of life, of physical body, sharing the same notational space. Typographical life struggles with flesh and blood. First we read the letters as printouts from an animation, and then and, with a little difficulty, as letters.

Figure 3.14. *Table* (Wavefront Technologies/Alias Designs), 1987.

We see the same choreographic power at a higher level of magnification in an *R* from an early twentieth-century French "circus" alphabet (fig. 3.16). The contorted bodies that form the upper and lower elements of the letter seem imprisoned by the letter form and struggling against its confines. The physical world of kinesthetic movement struggles with the fixed world of print. A different frequency of oscillation between the two worlds can be seen in the *C* from a seventeenth-century French alphabet (fig. 3.17). The letter form floats above the ceremonial scene behind it as if mounted on a transparent glass surface. We see the alphabetic surface when we look at the letter and the world of three-dimensional physical reality when we look through it.

The dance these letters have wanted to dance all along is now danced in TV commercials. Let me tell you the story of one such, a commercial for a Scottish nonalcoholic ale, and then reproduce one still frame to represent, inadequately, the whole. "Walk in a Straight Line" tells a forty-second moral fable about the letter *A* (Adam? Alcohol? Ale?) who has learned how to walk a straight line home from the pub by laying off the sauce. Adam-A gets up out of a letter bed and goes on his perilous way through a scaled-up letter landscape. Figure 3.18 shows a still frame of one of the perils through which he makes his way. As he makes his way along, either the letters have grown

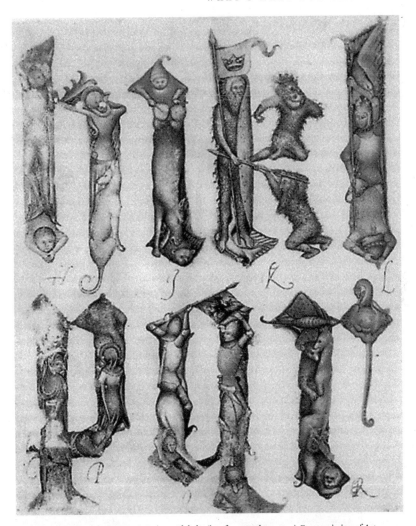

Figure 3.15. Giovannino dei Grassi, *Bergamo Alphabet* (late fourteenth century). By permission of Art Resource, New York.

into buildings or we have shrunk into ants. When finally the can is popped open, out foams another visual pun, an ale composed of 1% signs that tell us about the 1% alcohol stuff that is foaming. Surely this is what Cangiullo, what all the animated alphabets, would have done if they could. Motion, and emotion, suppressed and contorted for a couple of millennia, have suddenly found a release.

Why animate letters? Why force the alphabet into a series of graphic puns with the body? Again, to heal the breach between ordinary human kines-

Figure 3.16. Circus *R* (early twentieth century).

thetic motion and the abstract motions of conceptual thought, between dance and philosophy. Western notation has grown more and more remote from the felt realities of the world we evolved in, culminating in the symbolic logic notation pioneered by George Boole and Gottlob Frege in the nineteenth century. The digital expressive space moves back in the opposite direction, toward a more energetic oscillation between conceptual thought and behavior. Homer was doing the same thing when, instead of talking about courage,

Figure 3.17. French *C* (seventeenth century).

he put Achilles into action and when, wanting to describe Odysseus's crafti-
ness and guile, he used a phrase that meant both "well-traveled" and "a man
of many turnings." His imagination worked, like that of a modern computer
graphics artist, in a world of actions rather than abstract thoughts. The fast
cutting now so common in film and TV tries to do the same thing, to "think"
through a hundred images of "Achilles" rather than by saying "courage" or
"anger" caused X or Y. We may object to this distracting technique, think image is slaying word, but we cannot say it represents an abandonment of Western literary values. It returns to them.

If you were to ask, in a metaphorical way, what talent you need to deal with
complex printed texts, you might do worse than say that you need to cultivate
a sense of where you are in an argument or a story. In digital expression, that
metaphor becomes literalized. The central literate talent in electronic space

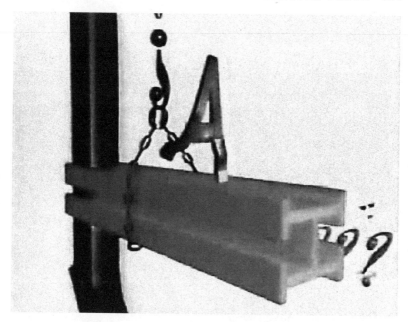

Figure 3.18. McEwan's L.A., "Walk in a Straight Line," still. Producer David Botterell. By permission of Snapper Films, *Siggraph Video Review*, no. 53 (1989).

is the pilot's gift for "positional awareness." In the print world, both print and the reader's distance from it are fixed. In digital space, both come into play as you fly over the informational landscape. We move in simulacra of such a sign field every day, of course. Ever since the poster first entered Paris's cityscape in the nineteenth century, we have navigated a three-dimensional city of layered words. Las Vegas at night must represent the climax of this development. The pop artists in the sixties pointed out this new landscape of words and signs and stressed its three-dimensionality. James Rosenquist, for example, painted huge billboard-sized canvases before which we stood, art gallery–wise, close-up, as if we had flown through the air from the street to the billboard soaring overhead. He imagined a beholder who flew through a three-dimensional expressive field as you do in a computer graphic landscape. Claes Oldenburg's overstuffed numbers seat us in the same position, suddenly, through magical scale change, able to shrink and walk among them as equals.

Simulation of aircraft flight was an early computer graphics triumph, thanks to Defense Department backing. But the expressive machinery seemed to have a natural talent for such simulations anyway. The characteristic motion of a low-flying aircraft has become the standard path into three-dimensional textual space, analogous to the left-to-right, down one line, motion of the eye reading a fixed text. And the position of the pilot becomes the generic posture for all of us, flying over complex informational typography at great speed and having, somehow, to take it all in. The cockpit of a jet fighter has served, in fact, as an experimental laboratory for new techniques in "speed reading" an informational landscape. "Heads-up" displays superimpose alphanumeric information on the cockpit windshield in an exact embodiment of the oscillation between looking at an inscriptional surface and looking through it that we experience as we move from stuff to attitude about it and back. A host of other electronic displays make available to the pilot compressed information that must be absorbed and acted on immediately. Not a bad image for how we all feel about the information pouring at us from all sides in the "information economy."

The uninterrupted linear text you are reading right now evolved to maximize a scarce resource: the expressive substrate. Papyrus and parchment cost a lot. Two hundred and fifty calves donated their skins to make a big church Bible like the Winchester Bible. Even paper, while it was still made by hand, was expensive. Writing by hand on any of these surfaces was laborious and time consuming. As white space became cheaper, designers arranged type on the page's two dimensions so that our visual cortex could correlate abstract subdivisions of matter with physical subdivisions of space. What more logical extension of conventional layout than to step into three dimensions when, as now, we can do it?

Let's turn now to a different variety of animation and a larger-scale alternation between the flatland of print and the three-dimensional world of human behavior. "Animation" is not a word that usually comes to mind when we think about a scholarly book by a university professor, but here is one that certainly offers it. Professor Marvin Minsky, the MIT mathematician, published his *Society of Mind* as a conventional codex book, but it was later issued in electronic format. The "e-book" version was designed by the Voyager Co., its publisher, to be as close as possible in concept and feeling to a printed book. And yet notice the differences. Here are a series of vignettes from it, with comments on each. First, look at the title page (fig. 3.19*a*). Color, with a Bach harpsichord accompaniment. Animated three-dimensional letters. A Kilroy-type figure who peeks up from the bottom of the page, and who turns out, like the harpsichordist, to be the author, Professor Minsky. A new presentation of academic self starts fast.

On the right, in the next image, conventional text, right out of the book. In

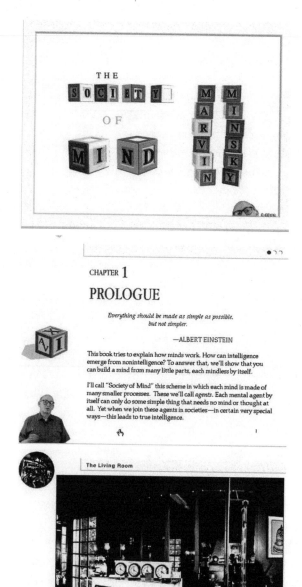

(a)

(b)

(c)

Figure 3.19. Screens from *First Person: Marvin Minsky: The Society of Mind* (Voyager, 1996). By permission of Robert Stein.

the left margin, a magic box. Click it and out pops the author, to give you an informal commentary on his book (fig. 3.19*b*). We can also follow this author into his living room and, with the aid of a magical arm, pan around the room (fig. 3.19*c*). Various crucial items will light up as we pass over them, indicating a special commentary attached to them. This living room panorama constitutes what, in classical rhetoric, was called a "memory theater." An orator, when he had to memorize a complex argument, would associate its basic parts with various elements in a well-known physical location, often the room or forum in which he was to speak. The visual memory thus aided the conceptual memory. Concepts were equated with specific physical locations. So here, the living room is turned into a domestic memory theater, with various parts of it coming alive with the "arguments" stored beneath it.

What's going on in this new reading experience? To begin with, nothing goes on that alters the printed text. It is there just as in the book. But some vital things have been added, and they counterpoint the printed text where they, we now notice in a new way, do not occur.

First, soundtrack. A musical greeting from the author's harpsichord welcomes the reader. And the title page puts letters into a three-dimensional dynamic space, making us notice the regular printed space as what, after all, it always is, flat and fixed.

Second, two elements vital to live human communication but absent in print, voice and gesture, return. The author walks around in the margin, waving his arms like a typical professor in full lecture mode. Gesture is fundamental to how we communicate, a continual counterpoint to how we speak. Gestures come in a stylized repertoire, culture specific in many cases but not in all (the well-known "universal gestures"). They also declare our personality, some of us waving a lot and others a little, some dynamically, some anemically. Classical rhetoric had already in ancient Greece codified these gestures and taught them as a fundamental part of a public speaker's education. This repertoire lasted, as a recognized learnable code, for both professional speaker and professional actor, through the eighteenth century.

When written text left out this element of communication, a significant act of expressive self-denial was passed. When text was regularly read aloud, performed rather than read silently, as it was until after the Middle Ages, this omission could be rectified. But ever since reading fell silent, composition teachers like me have had to talk about things like "shape," "rhythm," and "emphasis" in printed prose to try somehow to create in the printed text a pale simulacrum of gesture.

Voice is yet more vital than gesture. We make a series of rapid stylistic judgments about people, most of them unreflective, when we hear them speak. We may recognize a Brooklyn accent, a maddening adenoidal whine, or repetition of "like" after every third word, but we always make appraising judgments about character from voice. Likewise from costume. So Professor Minsky, by how he talks and what he wears, tells us something about himself. He does not appear often or at length. He does not read the full book to us, or indeed any part of it. He does not need to. Once we have his voice and gestural vocabulary in mind and eye, we can supply it ourselves for the rest of the text. If you want to spotlight how important a stylistic clue this is, imagine how much we could learn if we had the same animated marginal presence of Plato in one of his dialogues or Chaucer beside a famous passage in *The Canterbury Tales*. Authorial voice and gesture would flow back over the entire text like the Nile flood fertilizing Egypt. Suppose Plato turned out to have a high-pitched funky little voice or Chaucer talked with a deep bass-baritone?

But Plato would not have done such a thing and neither would Chaucer. Such a "backstage" presentation was not part of a formal written document. It seldom has been. It would have been a relic of the oral world that writing sought to supplant. A fortiori for books. Printed books, certainly scholarly books, because the text is unchangeable, almost always present an authoritative presence. If there are any muffed lines, they are emphatically not included as humorous outtakes. "Editing" a book means getting rid of such embarrassing intimations of oral mortality. If you are an author, you are, as the saying goes, a person standing up to be shot at. You want, before you stand up, to make yourself as bulletproof as you can.

Here, the "backstage" authorial presence contrasts with the "front-stage" presentation of the printed book and thus gives us two ways to read it. An august author—Minsky is one of the founding fathers of the field of artificial intelligence—lets us into his living room both literally and symbolically.

We see a lot of such bifocal presentations around us in the current presentational landscape. *Famous Movie* is swiftly followed by a TV special, "The Making of *Famous Movie*." The offstage life of movie stars is, for many people, more enthralling than their on-camera work. And when we tune into a TV news program, we don't immediately see the famous duo of newscasters at their desk (the front stage) but first dolly through the studio (the backstage) before we finally get to the talking heads. We like this backstage/front-stage alternation, especially in the English-speaking world, where Shakespeare created the immortal examples of it. So here with Minsky. It is as if we were given a binocular vision onto the text, able to see and read it with a new depth.

We might also notice that Minsky plays a different role in the margin and on the page. Marginal Minsky is a literary critic, commenting on his text and paraphrasing it. Textual Minsky is a neuroscientist, telling us how he thinks the brain works. Such a pairing resides in every authorial self. We write something, and that uses one part of our brain and talent. But we also revise what we write, and that editorial self reads and thinks differently from the creative one. Any full cycle of creation comprises an oscillation, usually repeated ones, between the two authorial postures. Here they are put side by side in the same visual frame, both working at the same time but in different stylistic registers.

Add all these differences up and we get a complex and detailed reenactment of the oscillation between the flat and fixed expressive field of printed text and the fluid animated world of three-dimensional human behavior. This oscillation becomes a fundamental one: the difference between an oral and a literate culture.

The marginal Minsky impersonates an oral culture. Voice and gesture provide a vital accompaniment to word. Both invite us to reply in kind, to start a conversation. Oral cultures are interactive. Interactivity is what creates them. Since in an oral culture, a culture without writing, there is no written cultural record, when the talking stops the culture vanishes. Oral cultures thus tend, as we see in the speeches of third world politicians, to be long-winded. The most convincing interpretation of the Homeric poems in our time suggests that they were the cultural repository of an oral culture and that their stylistic habits (oral formulas like "rosy-fingered dawn," for example) were driven by the need for memorability in an oral culture. "Poetry," in such a world, was not writing that did not run to the margin but a series of techniques for making cultural wisdom memorizable and hence memorable. In a culture where speaking is fundamental, not writing, the self is necessarily a dramatic self, an actor, and the conversation a drama. The expressive surface is not a "see-through" in such a culture. It is all there is.

How different the textual Minsky. Voiceless, gestureless, a frozen one-sided drama. The "rhetoric" of human communication is strained out in favor of a fixed conceptual "meaning." The late Walter Ong, an acute student of the orality/literacy contrast, puts this fundamental dichotomy in a historical context.

> In this economy [of print] where everything having to do with speech tends to be in one way or another metamorphosed in terms of structure and vision, the rhetorical approach to life—the way of Isocrates and Cicero and Quintilian and Erasmus, and of the Old and New Testaments—

is sealed off into a cul-de-sac. The attitude toward speech has changed. Speech is no longer a medium in which the human mind and sensibility lives. It is resented, rather, as an accretion to thought, hereupon imagined as ranging noiseless concepts or "ideas" in a silent field of mental space. Here the perfect rhetoric would be to have no rhetoric at all. Thought becomes a private, or even an antisocial enterprise.

The fault line between orality and literacy constitutes the fundamental plate tectonic in Western expression. On the literate side, the neutral theory of communication in which "noiseless concepts or 'ideas'" are exchanged in a "silent field of mental space." On the oral side, ideas exchanged in the emotionally charged field of attitude and design, of voice and gesture. From classical Greece onward, these two ways of communicating have existed in perpetually shifting combinations. From the collision of these two tectonic plates—orality and literacy—the great earthquakes of Western creativity have erupted. The written versions of Homer's epics and Plato's oral *Dialogues,* Chaucer's juxtaposition of the two states of mind in his great love epic *Troilus and Cressida,* Shakespeare's double plots, all testify to this expressive geology.

From the contrast, the oscillation, between the two kinds of culture flows the power that has dynamized Western expression. It does so because all of us continue to dwell in both oral and literate universes. We all possess both the central self generated by literate expression and the social self that exists only in company. We need company in order to feel real, yet we feel equally strongly that the most real part of us is the "sincere self" created in our private reading space. We want to hold together these two dichotomous ways of being in the world because that uneasy combination makes for the deepest humanity. When print triumphs, becomes wholly "literate," when it manages to become truly voiceless and without gestural animation, when human utterance ceases to try, in its infinitely various ways, to hold together both kinds of self and both kinds of society, the life goes out of expression. Read a paragraph in the bureaucratic official style and you'll see what I mean.

It is along this fault line of expression where oral and literate casts of mind and habits of expression continually rub up against one another that digital expression is now working. Print no longer enjoys a monopoly of serious expression. The economy of digital expression is a truly mixed oral/literate one, with new mixtures emerging every day. It seeks at its best (and like all human expression it is not always at its best) to heal the separation of powers between oral and literature cultures and put them into dynamic interchange.

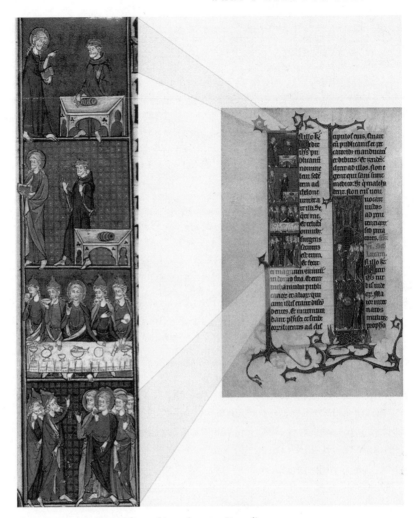

Figure 3.20. Historiated initial from a thirteenth-century Evangeliary.

The history of Western expression is full of these dynamic interchanges. The filtered and stabilized text, though present from the Greek beginnings, has not always had its own way. Medieval illuminated manuscripts provide a salutary instance of this continual counterstatement and an interesting comment on the Minsky electronic book. Again and again, medieval manuscript illuminations look like stills from an animation in progress. Consider a historiated initial (the *I* in "In illo tempore") in a thirteenth-century Evangeliary from the Sainte-Chapelle in Paris (fig. 3.20). I have no doubt that the illuminator would have had Christ walking around in the margin arguing

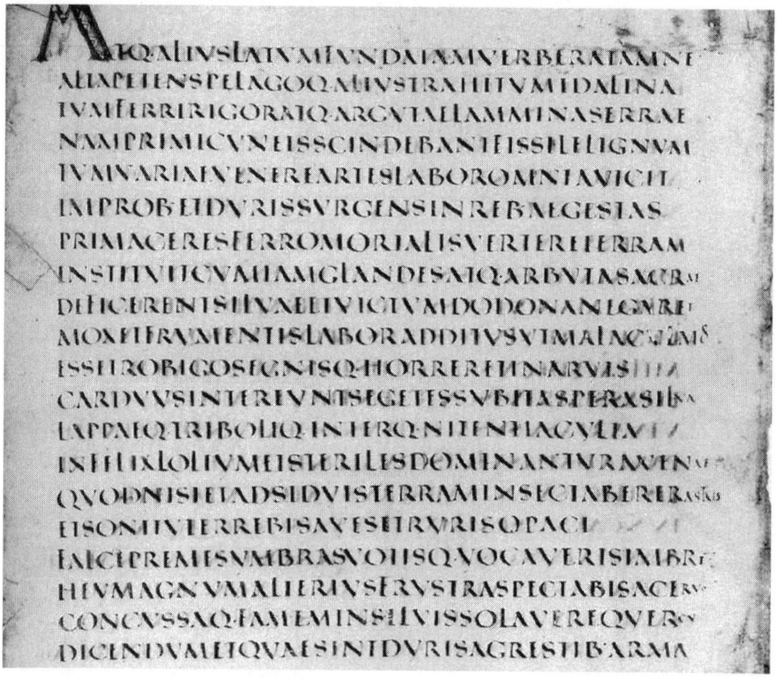
ATQ·ALIVSLATVMFVNDAIAMVERBERATAMNE
ALTAPETENSPELAGOQ·ALIVSTRAHITVMIDALINA
TVMFERRIRIGORATQ·ARGVTAELAMMINASERRAE
NAMPRIMICVNEISSCINDEBANTFISSILELIGNVM
TVMVARIAEVENEREARTESLABOROMNIAVICIT
IMPROBETDVRISVRGENSINREBEGESTAS
PRIMACERESFERROMORTALISVERTERETERRAM
INSTITVITCVMIAMGLANDESATQ·ARBVTASACRAE
DEFICERENTSILVAEETVICTVMDODONANEGARET
MOXETFRVMENTISLABORADDITVSVTMALACVLMOS
ESSETROBIGOSEGNISQ·HORRERETINARVIS
CARDVVSINTEREVNTSEGETESSVBITASPERASILVA
LAPPAEQ·TRIBOLIQ·INTERQ·NITENTIACVLTA
INFELIXLOLIVMETSTERILESDOMINANTVRAVENAE
QVODNISIETADSIDVISTERRAMINSECTABERERASTRIS
ETSONITVTERREBISAVESETRVRISOPACI
FALCEPREMESVMBRASVOTISQ·VOCAVERISIMBREM
HEVMAGNVMALTERIVSFRVSTRASPECTABISACERVVM
CONCVSSAQ·FAMEMINSILVISSOLABEREQVERCV
DICENDVMETQVAESINTDVRISAGRESTIBARMA

Figure 3.21. Virgil's *Georgics* written in square capitals, fourth century.

with Levi the tax collector (as he does in Luke 5) if he could have contrived it. The expanded palette of textual display offered by digital expression pulls us back into the history of Western notation. These alternative display modes recapture this history instead of repudiating it. We have always craved rich, mixed, competitive, antiphonal signals.

Discussions of digital expression usually take the invention of printing as their starting point. The current digital revolution is the new "Gutenberg revolution." We might enrich the discussion, though, if we looked back farther than Gutenberg, to a notational revolution in some ways more analogous to our present one, the development of space between words. From the first extant Greek texts until somewhere around the year A.D. 1000, plus or minus a couple of hundred years, alphabetic texts were written without space between words and, mostly, without punctuation either. At the beginning, too, all in capital letters. A striking example of a Latin text of this sort is a passage from Virgil's *Georgics,* preserved in the Codex Augusteus. It is written in square capitals without punctuation (fig. 3.21). This text is inscribed on parchment. Text, in classical Greek and Latin times, more usually came in rolls, not the codex "book" we are familiar with. The text itself came in narrow columns of

```
MARGARETAREYOUGRIEVI
NGOVERGOLDENGROVEU
NLEAVINGLEAVESLIKETH
ETHINGSOFMANYOUWIT
HYOURFRESHTHOUGHTS
CAREFORCANYOUAHASTH
EHEARTGROWSOLDERITW
ILLCOMETOSUCHSIGHTSC
OLDERBYANDBYNORSPAR
EASIGHTHOUGHWORLDS
OFWANWOODLEAFMEALL
IEANDYETYOUWILLWEEPA
NDKNOWWHYNOWNOMA
TTERCHILDTHENAMESOR
ROWSSPRINGSARETHESAM
ENORMOUTHHADNONOR
MINDEXPRESSEDWHATHE
ARTHEARDOFGHOSTGUES
SEDITISTHEBLIGHTMANW
ASBORNFORITISMARGARE
TYOUMOURNFOR
```

Figure 3.22. *Spring and Fall* (1880), Gerard Manley Hopkins, in *scriptio continua*.

uninterrupted letters. Such texts were hard to read. If you look at a familiar poem written out in this way, you'll see what I mean (fig. 3.22).

Yes, sure, you can finally make it out but look how much easier Gerard Manley Hopkins's wonderful sonnet is to read when space is left between words and punctuation lends a hand (fig. 3.23). Space between words, with capital letters and punctuation to signal its component parts, does not seem so far-fetched a scheme that it would take the best part of two millennia to invent. The increase in reading efficiency seems so plain that we wonder why it wasn't adopted earlier.

For an answer, we must look to the reading and writing practices represented by *scriptio continua,* as such continuous alphabetic notation is called.

SPRING AND FALL:
to a young child

Márgarét, are you gríeving
Over Goldengrove unleaving?
Leáves, líke the things of man, you
With your fresh thoughts care for, can you?
Áh! ás the heart grows older
It will come to such sights colder
By and by, nor spare a sigh
Though worlds of wanwood leafmeal lie;
And yet you wíll weep and know why.
Now no matter, child, the name:
Sórrows spríngs áre the same.
Nor mouth had, no nor mind, expressed
What heart heard of, ghost guessed:
It ís the blight man was born for,
It is Margaret you mourn for.

Figure 3.23. *Spring and Fall* (1880), Gerard Manley Hopkins, with spacing and punctuation.

Reading continuous script in Greek and Latin was much more like reading a musical score today than reading a text. The reader was familiar with the text. He (they were usually men) had prepared it as a conductor prepares a performance. He separated its parts in advance and memorized the separations. He read it aloud. It was a dramatic performance and considered as such. It took time and the reader had plenty of time to take. Rapid ingestion of information was not possible in such a method, but neither was it required.

Gradually, however, it became required. There was more to know and less time in which to learn it. Our present system of silent rapid reading for information replaced the older slow performance declaimed aloud for dramatic effect. The propulsive force was reading efficiency, and the technique was increased speed. Moreover, readers came from more diverse backgrounds and needed more performance clues. A different literacy emerged from these changes.

Surely a similar process is occurring in our time. We are all piloting that informational fighter plane as it flies low over an ever-changing informational landscape. Long on information and short on time to absorb it, we need, and have created, a new way to economize our attention, another revolution like the earlier one of leaving space between words. Global trade, mass migrations of one linguistic community into another, the geometric growth of knowledge—all have generated a need to depict, in order to imagine, how information flows. We need as never before to bring abstract reasoning down to earth because more people than ever before need to learn how to reason abstractly. We need new spaces between words, and spaces for words, in order to depict this new and more complex information flow. We've reviewed what some of those spaces look like. They are as yet mostly terra incognita, but as we continue to explore them, their stylistic repertoire will become clearer. If we don't develop these new spaces for words, we will have thrown away an immense opportunity.

The present fear in the bookish classes that formal reasoning is a thing of the past comes not from its imagined eclipse but from our halting efforts to democratize it. We need to process information faster and to express it in a more immediately intuitive way. What else can the wide pattern of puns we have discussed reflect but an intense pressure to compress meaning, multiplex its signal so as to deliver it faster and more powerfully? We need to use the human brain more efficiently. We need to find new shapes for traditional arguments and shapes for new kinds of arguments. We need to develop a notation that allows us to move from stuff to what we think about stuff more easily than print permits. To develop it, we will have to embrace a traditional enemy, stylistic self-consciousness.

The great Hellenist Eric Havelock, in a series of essays on the Greek alphabet, isolated this enemy. He argued that the Greek alphabet was simple enough to learn in early youth and totally internalize. It became transparent; you looked right through it to the conceptual arguments it could be employed to set forth. The letters had no visual content themselves. They did not give you pause for a moment, have any calligraphic power, make you think about them as shapes. "It is a sign of the arrival of modern scientific and socialized man that calligraphy as an art form has largely expired. This is a welcome development. . . . A successful or developed writing system is one that does not think at all. It should be the purely passive instrument of the spoken word even if, to use a paradox, the word is spoken silently." Kinetic text does what Havelock deplored. It creates *an alphabet that thinks*. It has resurrected a new and complex form of calligraphy, of notation that is to be noticed for surface form as well as content beneath. It brings back together the world of stuff and what we think about stuff.

There has always been, as we've seen, an alphabet that thinks. It was there from the beginning as hieroglyphics, cuneiform, shape poems, and, more recently, shaped prose. It appears as animated alphabets. It appears in medieval manuscript illumination and, earlier, as fiendishly complex Latin verbal and imagistic poetic puns called *technopaegnia,* and in "art prose" of all kinds, prose that is meant to be noticed as such, *Kunstprosa* as the Germans call it. It appears in later forms, as *poésie concrète,* and French *lettrisme* and as *livres d'artiste,* books designed by artists that grant primacy to image rather than letter.

We have long thought this mixed operatic writing an inconsequential vagary, an unfortunate remnant of primitive notation. What suppressed the agenda of these "alphabets that think" was the triumph of black-and-white print. Everything that did not build toward this triumph—not fully realized, we might remember, until the invention of the rotary press in the nineteenth century—had no real part in the story of human expressivity. Now an alphabet that can think has returned as a genuine alternative to the transparent medium of print. Only now can we see how accurate Havelock was in describing it as a threat to that transparent medium.

Print has striven for purely *through* vision. So Beatrice Warde's argument for a crystal goblet. So we have all been taught that the best style, for anything from writing to clothes and cars, is the style that is never noticed. A potent showcase but never the show. Since electronic expression invites us to look both at and through and in continual oscillation, since it writes in an alphabet that thinks, it requires a more capacious theory of communication than we operate under at present. To that theory we now turn.

Background Conversations

Healing the Pains of Abstraction

"Natural selection didn't build our brains to write or to read, that's for sure, because we didn't do those things for so long." So the anthropologist Stephen Jay Gould reminds us of the gulf between alphabetical notation and the world we evolved in. The alphabet gains its abstractive powers by breaking with the evolved world of behavior, but then it immediately tries to heal this break. It does so in two fundamental ways. It tries to heal the break within sequential alphabetic notation by using rhetorical figures, metaphors, similes, puns, and so on—all the resources of verbal style. Or it works beyond alphabetic notation by pouring the alphabetical notation into an image, into shape poetry of all kinds. These shapes can sometimes work—as in experimental book designs—in three-dimensional space. And there is a third healing strategy, too, though one needs to be a specialist to discuss it, the world of mixed notations: hieroglyphics, Greek Linear B inscriptions, and the Asian language scripts.

Stylistic devices first. These reenact for us basic emotional rhythms: climax and anticlimax, repetition for emphasis, balance and antithesis, parenthetical enclosures to establish special spaces, and puns to compress dissimilar worlds of meaning. The book that introduced many literary scholars, at least of my generation, to this world is Sister Miriam Joseph's *Shakespeare's Use of the Arts of Language*. It tells the full story, through Shakespearean example, of how alphabetic notation heals the pains of its own abstraction. If you want to know something about the educational system that made Shakespeare Shakespeare, this wonderful book is the place to begin. Willard Espy has built an alphabetical listing of the basic rhetorical figures on the base of a famous Renaissance treatise by Henry Peacham and called it *The Garden of Eloquence: A Rhetorical Bestiary*. Lee Sonnino's *A Handbook to Sixteenth-Century Rhetoric* gives examples from a variety of Renaissance English rhetoricians. There are several more general listings. Arthur Quinn's *Figures of Speech: Sixty Ways to Turn a Phrase* provides a good beginner's introduction to how rhetorical figures work. Robert Fogelin's *Figuratively Speaking* can stand for the many advanced discussions of particular figures. My favorite discussion of a single figure, the *chiasmus* I illustrate in the text of this chapter, is Mardy Grothe's *Never Let a Fool Kiss You or a Kiss Fool You*. Walter Redfern has written *Puns,* a thorough analysis of this vital figure. Punning is a way to orchestrate different signals, harmonize them. If punning, visual, verbal, or both, happens a lot, then it is a sign that a lot of harmonization is going on or that it's felt to be needed. At the center of the pun is oscillation, bi-stability. The reader might want to see if Redfern's discussion bears out this argument. As for general lists of rhetorical figures, Bernard Dupriez has compiled a full collection in French (*Gradus: Les procédés littéraires*), including many general terms that illustrate how rhetorical figures infuse alphabetic notation with behavioral implication. My own *Handlist of Rhetorical Terms* includes, in its alphabetical list, a number of longer entries, for example, "Figures of Rhetoric," which have a similar aim. As for larger discussions of verbal style, they are far too many to discuss here. I've written an introduction, *Analyzing Prose,* which shows how prose style, through our eyes and ears, aims to pull alphabetic text into closer proximity to the behavioral world we evolved in.

The art historian Michael Baxandall has argued, in *Giotto and the Orators,* that Renaissance painters conceived of painting within a system of thought based on rhetorical figures. "Quite a high proportion of the terms of ancient rhetoric were metaphors from visual experience, metaphors sometimes half-dead it is true, but which the humanists necessarily re-activated simply in the course of learning them from the outside." This repertoire of figures kept the abstract alphabetical world saturated with concrete physicality.

We might build a larger point here. For the Renaissance, "rhetoric" meant, as

Baxandall argues earlier, "a systematic study of verbal stylishness." Rhetoric, that is, was for them the study of ways to connect the world of abstract alphabetical notation with the world of behavior. That was what the study of verbal style was all about—efforts to keep the two worlds connected. As we have lost the discipline of, and interest in, verbal style we have lost the ligatures that connect alphabetic notation with the world of behavior. The more these ligatures are lost, the more distant and strange the world of text becomes. Perhaps this is where our present "literacy crisis" comes from.

The most direct way to bring alphabetic text into the world of behavior, the oral world, is to read it aloud, to perform it. Such performance was the norm in classical times. Now, after a long period of silent reading, reading aloud is returning, via books on tape, courtesy of the long automobile commute. Although we think of punctuation today as providing a system of syntactic clues for silent reading, it began as a system of performance clues. But, as M. B. Parkes makes clear in his nicely titled *Pause and Effect: Punctuation in the West,*

> By the ninth century readers and scribes had come to perceive the written medium as an autonomous manifestation of language, which was apprehended as much by the eye as by the ear. Since punctuation had ceased to be solely a form of direction for the oral performance of the written text, more emphasis was placed instead on the identification of marks with pauses in the process of reading silently as well as aloud; such marks enabled readers to recognize the constituent grammatical structures of a Latin text, and to evaluate the rôles which these structures played in communicating the message of that text.

In other words, punctuation migrated from providing clues for the ear to providing clues for the eye. But in both cases, it was putting the text back into the world of the senses, of our intuitive responses to the world around us.

As reading fell silent, the role of gesture in textual performance faded away. But we ought not to forget that for much of its history alphabetical notation was meant to be read aloud and performed. The gestures that would normally accompany public performance had early been codified, and rhetorical study preserved this study right up through the eighteenth century. We know a lot about these gestures. John Bulwer published, in 1644, a treatise on hand gestures (*Chirologia; or, The Natural Language of the Hand and Chironomia or the Art of Manual Rhetoric*) so involved that it taxes the credulity of the modern reader. Gilbert Austin's 1806 *Chironomia; or, A Treatise on Rhetorical Delivery,* begins with charts of hand, arm, and body gestures, with their emotional equivalents, which shows that the behavioral repertoire survived intact a century and a half later. Andrea de Jorio, in a now-classic investigation published in 1832 in Naples, *La mimica degli antichi investigata nel gestire napoletano*, investigated what the title indicated, how classical gestures survived in the popular culture of Naples in his own time. If you read it (and there is, at long last, a modern English translation by Adam Kendon), you will find many gestures still in current use. Just check it against a modern compilation like Desmond Morris et al.'s modern compendium *Gestures*. But it is hard to believe that this repertoire of gestures, so wide and yet so long-standing, has not been used by textual performers throughout their long history. The alphabetic text would be reintroduced into the oral world by reading aloud and, then, enhanced there by a rich vocabulary of corresponding gesture. One scholar of classical Greek, Alan Boegehold, has attempted a reconstruction of how this might have been done, trying to isolate "ellipses in sense or grammar that could easily have been filled with a nod or a motion of hand or body." Meticulous and subtle as his study is, surely he has only touched the surface of this phenomenon. Wherever we can, we want to draw alphabetical notation back into the world of behavioral communication. And the explosion of animation created by computer graphics draws, albeit without knowing, on this repertoire of nonverbal communication. Look at Frank Thomas and Ollie Johnston's *Disney Animation: The Illusion of Life* and see if you don't agree with me.

So much, then, for a sketch of how we have tried to heal the pains of alphabetic abstraction while remaining within the framework of conventional notation. What do you do when you step beyond it? For a start, animate the letters themselves. In the text of this chapter, I've cited examples from Hugues Demeude's collection *The Animated Alphabet*. It illustrates animal energies in many forms, struggling within the confines of alphabetic notation. But the body of animated letters is vast, starting with medieval illuminated manuscripts. This desire has reappeared again in our own time. As Laura Kendrick says in introducing her *Animating the Letter: The Figurative Embodiment of Writing from Late Antiquity to the Renaissance*, "The late twentieth century seems to share with the seventh through ninth centuries a desire to animate the letter by giving it the appearance of liveliness or of being, a desire provoked by the introduction of a more abstract, disembodied, 'cold' way of communicating and saving knowledge. In the early Middle Ages, handwriting in codices was introduced into oral cultures whose sacred 'texts' had always been conserved in people's memories and communicated in live performances; in the late twentieth century, the support of writing, the codex itself, is being replaced by the video screen." Kendrick explores in detail the relationships created by medieval scribes between the alphabetic meanings of a text and the animations that took possession of the body of the letters. The oscillation between the two kinds of notation created political or religious meanings not expressible by either method of notation alone. Take the "authority" of the text, for example: "From the medieval point of view, the most authoritative of the Gospels was not necessarily the most correct or scholarly, but it was the one perceived to be a relic imbued with divine presence, for such a text inspired viewers with fear of transgressing against divine or saintly powers if they presumed to change its letters or words." You imbued the text with the divine presence by awesome animation.

Johanna Drucker has explored this same interface working at the beginning of the twentieth century in *The Visible Word: Experimental Typography and Modern Art, 1909–1923*. She is especially good on Marinetti but also explores typographical experiments by Mallarmé, Apollinaire, and many others. Letters have had, from the beginning of alphabets, all kinds of significances—mystical, alchemical, religious, political—attached to them and complex allegories built atop the attachment. Drucker has explored these associations in her fascinating, and wonderfully illustrated, *The Alphabetic Labyrinth: The Letters in History and Imagination*.

Many books illustrate the animated letters that such studies as these analyze. J. J. G. Alexander has collected some striking examples in his *The Decorated Letter,* and Christopher de Hamel has described and illustrated how the illuminations were created. Barbara Shailor describes, with illustrations, how the books were created that held these illuminations in *The Medieval Book*. Many, many books describe and illustrate medieval manuscripts. Three that I find myself repeatedly consulting are Robert Calkins's *Illuminated Books of the Middle Ages,* Janet Backhouse's *The Illuminated Page: Ten Centuries of Manuscript Painting,* and Giulia Bologna's *Illuminated Manuscripts*. The world illustrated in these volumes makes an instructive comparison with the current world of computer graphics and the hungers it reveals.

What animated letters have always wanted to do is be themselves, actually move. That, in digital computer graphics, they can now do. Jeff Bellantoni and Matt Woolman show how in *Type in Motion: Innovation in Digital Graphics*. It is a most instructive book to read juxtaposed to Kendrick's and Drucker's. What happens to fixed type design under the digital metamorphic pressures is illustrated in Steven Heller and Anne Fink's *Faces on the Edge: Type in the Digital Age* and in J. Abbot Miller's *Dimensional Typography,* from which I've drawn a couple of examples. The urge to move, and the painful constraints that predigital technology imposed on this urge, is illustrated in Robert Russett and Cecile Starr's *Experimental Animation: Origins of a New Art*. If you want to understand the exhilaration with sheer technique often displayed in the current computer animation scene, this book is the place to begin.

The next step, after the animated letter, is the animated text, that is to say, shape poetry and shape prose. Dick Higgins, in his now classic *Pattern Poetry: Guide to an Unknown Literature*, catalogs and illustrates shape poetry from around the world. Higgins demonstrates how strongly the urge to heal alphabetic abstraction has operated across world cultures. After his encyclopedic survey, he devotes a chapter ("Analogues of Pattern Poems") to what are sometimes called *technopaegnia*, or *carmina figurata* (figured poems), texts that weave elaborate patterns from alphabetic notation. He sees three categories: "Acrostics are texts, not necessarily poems, in which the initial letters, read vertically, form a word or inscription. Telestics are texts in which the last letters of the lines, read vertically, form a word or inscription. Mesostics are texts in which there is an alignment of letters in the interior of a text, so that the aligned letters form a word or inscription, sometimes called an 'intextus' or 'intertext.'" These correspond to three common rhetorical figures, though Higgins does not draw the parallel. Acrostics make us look at the pattern formed by the beginning letters of a series of lines or phrases, as the rhetorical figure *anaphora* does. Telestics do the same for ending patterns, as the rhetorical figure *epanaphora* does. And the mesostics point, although the alignment is not so clear here, to rhetorical figures of internal pattern like *chiasmus*. Higgins cites the medieval monk Hrabanus Maurus (784–856) as the archetypal author in this regard. Hrabanus's poems *In Honorem Sanctae Crucis* have been published, with notes and French translation, in the Corpus Christianorum Continuatio Mediaevalis series. The main volume presents the texts in a normal typographical format; the second volume, a packet of color plates, reproduces them in their shaped form. The comparison illustrates more than Hrabanus's diabolical ingenuity and originality, great though those are. It shows how much is lost when texts of this sort, and all the impulses they represent, are filtered out by modern typographical convention. In their shaped form, a violent oscillation between the surface pattern and the alphabetical meaning draws us, as in a vortex, into the complex paradoxes of the Christian faith. This oscillation is stopped dead in the printed form, and thus the central meaning, the central kind of meaning, is destroyed. The same problem can be observed in some of the leaves from early manuscripts of Cassiodorus's *Institutiones*.

Complicated as these relationships are, they seem simple beside the poems of the fourth-century Roman poet Publilius Optatianus Porfyrius. Let me hasten to confess that I know these poems only as they are discussed in W. Levitan's dazzling article, "Dancing at the End of the Rope." Here is how Levitan begins the explication: "Frankly, the poems make entirely unremarkable, even banal reading—competent verse for the most part but repetitive and very tired. But it is not *reading,* as the word is commonly understood, that the poems invite; rather *wonder,* to say the least, at the appalling genius responsible for them." In one poem (no. 15), "the first line is composed entirely of disyllables, the second of trisyllables, the third of tetrasyllables, and the fourth of pentasyllables. The fifth line reconsiders this progression with a sequence of one-, two-, three-, four-, and five-syllable words. . . . If, in the sixth line of Optatian's poem, the final word maintains its position, the rest of the verse can be inverted without affecting its rhythm or sense." It gets more complicated after this—much. Just staying with poem number 15, "in none of the lines does the wit depend on the reference of its words. This is true of all technopaegnia: Writing no longer functions primarily as the record of speech but as the medium of a linguistic artifact whose interest lies in an aspect of language extrinsic to its reference, usually a sensory aspect. The poems of course make sense, but the impulse to verbal mimesis is conspicuously weak." Optatian breaks down the "flow of speech into its elemental constituents—the appositional phrase, the syllable, the metrical unit, the finite parts of speech." When language is broken down into these discrete units, "it suggests that the generation of new statements, new linguistic possibilities, will rest solely on the mechanical re-combination of the same particles." And, "his poems demand just such re-combination. Lines must be read backward; metrical elements transposed; nouns considered in grammatical cases other than those in which they appear; individual elements of one line isolated and . . . re-combined with isolated elements of another to form new patterns." Yes, I know this is not altogether clear. You'll have to read the article for yourself to understand how this poem works, and the poem which reads as Latin one way and Greek another, and other such effects. It is not puzzles that Optatian is after. Nothing is hidden. It is maximum self-consciousness about words and how they interact with the visual field. He is trying to make us *see* the visual field in which words work. Ji Lee has published a worthy successor to the technopaegnia of Optatian and Hrabanus Marus, his *Univers Revolved: A Three-Dimensional Alphabet.* It puts into his three-dimensional alphabet a collection of visual puns, proverbs, a verse by Emily Dickinson, and a three-dimensional chess set-up. The three-dimensional letters are also used as an erector set to create droll cartoon-like characters that, like Optatian's poems, still make some kind of alphabetical sense. A beautiful, and beautifully clever, book that creates a new form of visual poetry that is possible, or at least feasible, only in a computer-based world. Happily for flatland readers, a normal alphabet translation is included.

After these agonies, it is a relief to return to a plain and direct short discussion of shape poetry, that which prefaces the expanded edition of John Hollander's shape poems, *Types of Shape*. Hollander describes how he went about composing his shape poems: "The composition itself was frequently done on graph paper, with a box allowed for each letter . . . no typography was involved in shaping these, in that they were composed with one em per character." Not so far, in principle, from the grids that Optatian sometimes used, but far away in practice, and much closer to looking through the verbal surface to the meaning beneath. Hollander closes his brief discussion with some references to further discussions of shape poetry that you might find useful, if Optatian hasn't made you too dizzy.

Not everybody has been enthusiastic about the technopaegnian impulse. H. T. Kirby-Smith, toward the end of a fine study, *The Origins of Free Verse*, quotes advice given to the crown prince of dullness in Dryden's *MacFlecknoe*:

Leave writing plays, and choose for thy command
Some peaceful province in acrostic land.
There may thou wings display and altars raise,
And torture one poor word ten thousand ways.

Kirby-Smith himself offers, in a chapter called "Ideogrammatology," some bracing criticism of the typographical games played in modern poetry. And in a concluding chapter, "The Prose Poem," he calls that chapter's subject "the ultimate refuge of bankrupt talent." "The great majority of such pieces [prose poems] published in the last fifty years are pretentious and presumptuous bits of writing that fail to make use either of the discursive generosity of prose or the compressed energies of good poetry." His critique raises a useful red flag about the prose/poetry blending that I argue, in the text of this chapter, is invited by electronic text.

The next stage after shape poetry is to interpenetrate the typographical and the behavioral space in a more radical way, by superimposing word on image. As chance would have it, a book has been published recently on the subject of the book you are holding in your hands, the information revolution and the economics of attention that follows from it, and that attempts not only to discuss the metamorphosis of the book but to illustrate it. It is called *The Information*

Inferno, and it was "written and designed by Whodini" and published by Designer Books, "an imprint of Cybercity Press, LLC" in 2001. So, don't say you haven't been warned. It breaks up text into a series of epigraphs and imposes them on striking images. Quotations from the Bible, Plato, Dante, and many lesser lights are floated above images of flames, circuit boards, running classic Greek warriors, close-ups of insects, Dantean grotesques, Rembrandt and Raphael paintings, petri dishes, color panels, what I think are infrared images of the cosmos and many more. The chapters are called "gigabytes," and the images of the book, various as they are, are unified by the computer graphics style into which they are all cast. The book shows, in radical form, an influence that we can now see all around us, the feedback from dynamic display onto the conventions of fixed print. Letters swell and shrink, bend, catch on fire, and metamorphose from one font to another, just as they do on an electronic screen.

Like Hrabanus Maurus and Optatian, the author breaks up the text into small units of meaning and then places them in imagistic environments that set off an oscillation between denotative meaning and imagistic power. And, like Optatian, the book invites the reader to pass through it in more than one way. Naturally, we start from the front, as we normally do, but after a twenty-four-page opening Dantean preface about the information inferno, the book is not paginated but divided, rather, into gigabyte and megabyte subdivisions. It soon occurs to you that the customary sequential reading practices of a printed text don't apply to such a book, and you start to move around in it as the spirit takes you. Speedily thereafter, it occurs to you that perhaps the book was intended to be read backward, and you start at the back. Such a book, composed largely of visual quotations, poses a copyright and permissions nightmare and, if you start reading from the back, the first page you come to is a conventional printed text describing these difficulties. If I had been writing this book as a conventional book, that page would indeed have come first. Then follows a black-and-white two-page opening about "Whodini" that, since the book argues for a movement from black-and-white to color presentation, serves as a good starting point for the book's argument. Then, as you come to ads, I think, for forthcoming books by Whodini, that particular proposition breaks down. The book is not a palindrome. But it is full of palindromic patterns, visual isocolons. Since there are no page numbers, it is hard to direct you to an example but twenty-two pages from the end, if I have counted correctly, there is a two-page opening with "forgive me friends" on the left and "for i have grinned" on the right, which is as good a visual isocolon as I have ever seen. In fact, the book is full of invitations to describe its visual strategy using the terms of rhetorical figuration, as

Michael Baxandall does in a book discussed earlier in this background conversation.

In its presentation, the book both illustrates and argues for a maximum interfoliation of word and image. In its prose argument, it develops many of the principles I have been presenting in the more conventional book you hold in your hand. It depicts the information revolution as an inferno (Dante provides an umbrella structure for the book's quotation strategy), a hell of plenitude from which we strive to escape. In gigabyte 8, it presents another isocolon pairing of a Medusa face screaming, with "Attention" in lightning script. All the letters are red, printed on a background of white flame, with a quotation from Herbert Simon, "A wealth of information creates a poverty of attention," and the argument that I develop in chapter 1: "Information used to be the scarce resource. Now attention is the scarce resource." Toward the end of the book appears "Rhapsody on Color Writing," which makes the same arguments for color that I've presented in the text of this chapter. It argues for color as a more efficient means of communication not, or at least not only, a more elegant one. You can, then, have some fun by comparing the conventional presentation of the book you hold in your hand with Whodini's effort—a successful one in my eyes—to embody the arguments he advances. Among many other things, he has illustrated, on almost every page, the at/through oscillation that, I've been arguing, lies at the heart of our expressive revolution. Thus, I think I might legitimately claim that Whodini has provided empirical support for *oscillatio* as a central contemporary trope.

It would be a mistake to think that Whodini, or the expressive world he describes, has devalued the word or its alphabetic denotation, much less abolished it. The codex book is not abolished or diminished but redefined and energized. And we can suggest this as a general argument: May it not be the case that digital expression will redefine the fixed codex book, backlight its traditional powers and create new ones?

The typographical experiments of David Carson in *The End of Print: The Graphic Design of David Carson* do seem, in most of their manifestations, to diminish the word into a visual motif like any other. They certainly transfer the powers and conventions of computer graphics onto the printed page. David Carson is a graphic designer who first came to notice in a magazine called *Beach Culture* and after that publication disappeared, in another called *Ray Gun*. As David Byrne points out in the introduction, Carson's revolutionary design seemed to appear "in the wrong place, directed at the wrong audience." The avant-garde on a surfboard? "Well," as Byrne continues, "Southern California was the home of Kustom Kars and Low Riders, both examples of beautiful, radical, impractical design of and by the people. Maybe this was another step along those lines?" Clearly it is, but hot rod design was a purely visual phenomenon and, in Carson's work, the alphabetic word moves decisively into the visual world. The oscillation between the two is much less vibrant than in *The Information Inferno*. The two books thus make a revealing comparison.

A more conventional relationship between word and image has long been available in what are called "Artist's Books," books not only illustrated by a visual artist but created and designed by the same person. A recent (2001–2) show at the California Palace of the Legion of Honor exhibited the Logan Collection of these books and demonstrated their wide range. Here is how Donna Stein describes them in the catalog of the exhibition: "The term *livre d'artiste,* a distinctively French creation, is a limited edition, handmade book that typically combines words with original graphic art, executed and printed under the artist's supervision. . . . For a *livre d'artiste,* the artist, author, publisher, and printer must often work together designing the relationship of text to image, selecting typography, paper, printing, and binding in order to achieve a high standard of workmanship." Such books aim at harmony, however, rather than the disjunction and oscillation between image and word engendered in *The Information Inferno* and the work of David Carson and the designers who have followed him. Again, an interesting contrast between a high-frequency oscillation between word and image and a low-frequency one.

If you take the book one last step into the three-dimensional world, you take leave of the codex format and enter the world of pop-ups and pop-outs and books that are made into sculptures. Keith Smith anatomizes this world in his *Structure of the Visual Book*. This world, viewed in one way at least, would seem to be an early attempt at the plasticity that comes into its own on the digital screen.

If anyone wants to explore the relationship of alphabetic inscription to the ideographic systems of notation used in some Asian languages, an excellent place to begin is Wm. C. Hannas's *Asia's Orthographic Dilemma*. Hannas analyzes the "unique systems of writing shared by China, Japan, Korea, and until recently Vietnam." He attacks the idea that the Chinese system of writing, and those derived from it, confer any advantage of imagistic understanding, arguing instead for the uniform superiority of alphabetic notation. I'm far from being qualified to express an opinion about the book, but Hannas's learning is immense, his analysis precise and detailed, his prose open to common understanding, and his arguments persuasive. Against such a background, one reads the histories of writing systems with a renewed respect for the power of alphabetic notation. The best of these histories that I've found is Albertine Gaur's *A History of Writing*, comprehensive in scope and amply illustrated. More encyclopedic in detail and organization is Peter T. Daniels and William Bright's collection of essays *The World's Writing Systems*. I also profited from three of the slender volumes in the University of California/British Museum Reading the Past series: John F. Healey's *The Early Alphabet*, W. V. Davies's *Egyptian Hieroglyphs*, and C. B. F. Walker's *Cuneiform*. For a short survey of these areas, Michelle P. Brown's *The British Library Guide to Writing and Scripts: History and Techniques* serves well. One sees in all of these books repeated examples of alphabetic abstraction, at all stages of its history, under continual pressure from the visual imagination and the need for behavioral context. The struggle that seems to have reached a climax of sorts in digital expression, and in the unique *The Information Inferno*, has a long history.

I know of no book like *The Information Inferno*, but the same impulse can be observed in Heather Child et al.'s *More Than Fine Writing: The Life and Calligraphy of Irene Wellington*. Look, for example, at "Upon Being Given a Norfolk Turkey for Christmas," and you'll see the same impulses at work.

Against the background of the studies I've cited, the ordinary history of typography began to look different to me. Its imagistic elements loomed much larger; its alphabetic components less so. The history of typography came to seem the history of an effort to preserve the abstract power of alphabetic notation as it felt enormous pressures to push it back into the three-dimensional world of ordinary life. I noticed this with Friedrich Friedl, Nicolaus Ott, and Bernard Stein's enormous *Typography: An Encyclopedic Survey of Type Design and Techniques throughout History*. I started leafing through this book soon on in my multimedia lecturing and each time I returned to it I read it in an increasingly visual way. The letters all began to look as if they wanted to take off, to pop into motion, to twirl around, or in some other manner to shoulder their way into three-dimensional space. Take a look at it and see what you think.

The development of punctuation and space between words is, of course, more complicated than I have indicated. The story has been told brilliantly by Paul Saenger in *Space between Words: The Origins of Silent Reading*. Complexities aside, the fundamental change in notation most comparable to electronic text is not the Gutenberg revolution, as we are usually told, but the earlier spatial and punctuation changes that made rapid silent reading possible. "Stated summarily," Saenger writes, "the ancient world did not possess the desire, characteristic of the modern age, to make reading easier and swifter because the advantages that modern readers perceive as accruing from ease of reading were seldom viewed as advantages by the ancients. These include the effective retrieval of information in reference consultation, the ability to read with minimum difficulty a great many technical, logical, and scientific texts, and the greater diffusion of literacy throughout all social strata of the population." All of these goals have been reasserted in our attention economy with renewed vigor and, however it develops, the digital expressive space will answer to them.

The best discussion of digital expression I know of is Lev Manovich's *The Language of New Media*. He summarizes his argument in the prologue: "A hundred years after cinema's birth, cinematic ways of seeing the world, of structuring time, of narrating a story, of linking one experience to the next, have become the basic means by which computer users access and interact with all cultural data. In this respect, the computer fulfills the promise of cinema as a visual Esperanto—a goal that preoccupied many film artists and critics in the 1920's." But Manovich fails to include one element that has remained surprisingly persistent on the digital screen: the written word. He just doesn't consider it. We are to suppose that it doesn't matter any more.

But perhaps there is something to be said for text after all, something that would fit between writing it off and digging one's heels in around the printed and bound book. After all, do we seriously think we are going to communicate entirely in terms of cinematically presented images? Or spoken language? Have we come to the end of three-thousand-odd years of alphabet notation? If we have, how might we design a strategy for words for the intermediate period until the cinematic paradise comes totally to pass? And what about all those old books? How, in the cinematic future, will we teach the past human record, contained as it is in books? Will readers become like classical scholars, clerks of a forgotten discourse, a now-obsolete mood of Western culture before the invention of the movies? If we find in the past evidence that alphabetic text had "multimedia" ambitions, then perhaps we find in this past a clue to a digital future, one that we might construct, rather than one that will inevitably come about. If there is evidence in the past that letters wanted to cooperate with images and sounds, perhaps they can still successfully do so in the future.

Manovich argues that rhetoric itself expires along with text. So human persuasion will give way, presumably, to purely neutral communication. And so he returns to the Edenic dream. Or, if he does not mean this, he must mean that persuasion through text will vanish as text itself vanishes. What will remain, presumably, will be persuasion through image and sound.

Manovich argues that the multimedia signal began with film and thus is an affair of, at best, the past hundred years. But, as we have seen already, this is not so. Manovich argues that digital expression represents the triumph of film, but one might also argue that it is the return of orality after the long three-thousand-year alphabetic interlude. This is a different stage of orality, what Father Walter Ong called "secondary orality," since based on a system of alphabetic notation. There is no reason, though, why this system of notation cannot take on a new relationship to our behavioral world without basing itself entirely on the history of film. What that relationship will be, remains to be seen—and heard.

CHAPTER FOUR

{AN ALPHABET THAT THINKS}

E lectronic text provides powerful new ways to allocate human attention. It puts words on a screen in ways that make complex arguments easier and quicker to understand; ways that democratize verbal expression; ways that promise to economize the time and effort we spend in reading words and trying to understand them; ways that provide new and rich mixtures of word, image, and sound. We have an expressive field, which has created new "spaces between words" and filled them with image and sound. We have available to us, once again after all these centuries, "an alphabet that thinks." Yet, except recently in TV advertising, and in experimental ways elsewhere, none of them has been explored. Business and government have ignored them, though these worlds manufacture billions of words a day (in an attention economy, remember, words are stuff). The business world has pushed its cost-containment efforts down to the paperclip level, and some governments have even begun to make half-hearted gestures in this direction. And yet no equivalent of the "lean manufacturing" enzyme has appeared in the word factories of the world. Quite the opposite. The bureaucratic official style rolls on like the Mississippi. Amid the feeding frenzy inspired by digital technology, the new technology of textual expression has been ignored. Why?

Why have we not embraced these new expressive opportunities? The current "e-books" offered to the public, and the debate about them, ignore the fundamental changes electronic text brings with it. Why have we left these new expressive powers to advertising or simply to languish in the corner of experimental fiction? In the graphic domain, they have been embraced with a vengeance. Computer-assisted design and manufacturing programs, architectural drafting and modeling systems, and scientific visualization of every kind, all of these often shared between computers worlds apart, have revolutionized how information is handled and shared. But the same revolution has not occurred in communication using the word, written and spoken. Business people and economists have turned themselves inside out evaluating what productivity gains, if any, computers have brought to the world's business. They have not considered how, when print moves from book to screen, changes in the logic of expression might affect that productivity.

All we've done is to imagine how word processors might make us longwinded or how computers are destroying books or how images are driving out words. Those who think about the evolution of imagery have pondered how digital multimedia carries on the history of film. Those who defend books have told us that the sky is falling on text. Neither group has much considered what happens to text in digital expression. They have framed the debate around the form of the printed codex book, not about its contents. They have defended, or discarded, the binding, not the book.

Electronic books have a short history. They started out, in the mid-1970s, as electronic databases. "Project Gutenberg" was the pioneer. Classic texts in the public domain were offered in electronic form. This means of reproduction and distribution has continued to the present day, with the University of Virginia E-Book Web site perhaps the outstanding example. Then the Voyager Company took a step forward and created a format called expanded books. We have already seen an example of this format, the electronic edition of Minsky's *The Society of Mind*, in the previous chapter. These books were designed to be read on a portable computer screen. They included a "print" text with moving images and sound added. A subsequent version, TK3, allows you to create an e-book in which text can quote sound and moving images. Other formats that permit such quotation have appeared. But this is not the direction in which electronic book publication has gone.

Instead, most e-books have chosen to mimic printed books as closely as possible. They transport to the screen all the expressive limitations of printed books: no color, no motion, no sound. Those who develop them have striven to make them as much like a printed book as possible.

The third stage of e-books has been the migration from desktop or laptop to personal digital assistant, the Palm Pilot and its ilk. You might not think that many people would want to read extended texts, especially literary texts, on such a small screen, but if so, several million people have proved you wrong by doing just this from the University of Virginia's E-Book Library for the MS Reader and Palm devices. Not so long ago, when I had to spend a lot of time lying on my painful back, I tried reading Jane Austen's *Persuasion* on a Palm Pilot. It wasn't as bad as I anticipated. It was like reading the novel in a tiny one-handed edition, a couple of sentences per page. But here, too, the advance—if advance it was—in expressive technology aimed to preserve the printed format in a new expressive substrate. A new kind of binding, not a new kind of book.

So we have an expressive space that expands what a "book" can mean. Text can move in two and three dimensions, creating new relationships with the space around it. Complex texts can thus be clarified by spatial clues; the visual cortex can enhance conceptual argument. Moving images and sound can be quoted as easily as text. Yet the electronic book wants to mimic the limitations of a printed codex. Why such a disinclination to use the mental, as well as the electronic, equipment? There are many explanations. Let me review some, concluding with what I think is the fundamental reason: We have been thinking about human communication in an incomplete and inadequate way, a way based on stuff, not attention.

First: the CD-ROM failure. This first attempt to create texts that used the new expressive space was a commercial failure. They were more expensive to produce than a printed book. By nature and by custom, word people and image people do not speak the same language and getting them working together to create a genuine electronic book was often difficult. And when the product was ready for sale, the distribution channels had not yet been created. The production schedule of a digital text differs from that of a printed text in fundamental ways. Further, before this new medium had a chance to succeed or fail on its merits, it was swept away by the Internet. A lot of people lost money on the CD-ROM gamble. Once bitten, twice shy. Nothing makes you lose face faster than losing money.

The CD-ROM failure was the first manifestation of a much larger problem: antique and incompatible software and hardware. Compatibility has been a problem from the beginning, but it is only in comparison with the codex book that we see how acute it has always been. The codex format for alphabetical text has remained constant for the best part of 2000 years. You can pick up a tenth-century manuscript of Virgil and, after some paleographical training, read it. The volatility of electronic text and the machines that display it has reminded us of a virtue in books we had taken for granted. Here, as elsewhere, the librarians have led our thinking. Some archivists even see a gap in history opening up, as the documents of our time slowly become unreadable. Since I was so blind to the original problem, I won't opine as to the probability of such a catastrophe.

Second: screen resolution. "No one," the litany goes, "wants to read extended text on a computer screen." There are, however, some exceptions to this powerful argument. Some people do want to read extended text electronically, else why do they download millions of texts from the free Web sites? Why do people spend hours in online discussion groups and artificial worlds created by words? Why do people, when they want to look something up, try Google first? A mountain of extended text is available, and read, on screen: articles, reports, newspapers, and magazines, both current and archived. Scholars create Web sites to anthologize the latest work on a particular topic. Why do people pursue all this extended textual reading on screen if they hate to read extended text on screen? Because it is more convenient, obviously, and that convenience trumps the screen-reading problem. Make it easier to read on screen, and people no longer find it so hard to read on screen.

Screen resolution used to be the problem but surely not now. The ability to increase the size of text on a screen benefits many readers. Small print in a book is often harder to read than large print on a screen. People get used to reading text even on a small screen, much more so on a larger one. Incurable readers like me have found that, in many lighting situations, a self-illuminated backlit surface like a computer screen is easier to read than a book. And, sooner or later, commercial electronic publishers are going to discover that a common format for the reading machine must be adopted and that the reading machine itself must be giveaway cheap. They will learn, as Kodak did, to give away the camera and make your money on the film. Instead, the public has been offered high-priced and incompatible electronic reading boxes and sensibly left them alone.

But in spite of all these arguments, printed books do, *consideratis considerandis*, have better resolution. And they will be read as long as they do. Or at least as long as electronic text is not substantially easier to create, distribute, store, and carry around with you. When the Voyager Company first published the Jane Austen novels in electronic form, I bought them and put them on my laptop. It was an early laptop with poor resolution, but it sure beat carrying around the *Complete Novels of Jane Austen* for those inevitable afternoons you spend hung out to dry at O'Hare airport. And when you finally get on the plane and the passenger in front of you reclines fully, leaving you no space to use a computer, or even hold a book, your Palm Pilot will come to your rescue. Readability varies with text, reading machine, and occasion, and these equations will continue to change. Screen resolutions will continue to improve. Some of the experiments in "electronic paper" (flexible sheets that display an electronic image) may come to fruition. Resolution is not an insuperable problem.

Third: Books are not only reading machines, they are talismans. They bring with them the profound penumbra of all that books have represented to all of us who value them. Here touch and feel and binding do matter. The physical stuff of the book carries a profound electrical charge. The walls of my house are covered with books and looking at them gives me a profound pleasure. A life's reading paints a mural on every wall. I look at the bookshelves and reread my reading life. I sometimes use as a lecture prop a late sixteenth-century vellum-bound pocket-sized edition of the *Epistolae obscurorum virorum*, the *Letters of Obscure Men*. The *Epistolae* is a humanist parody of the long-winded humanist conversation of the time. My edition is a worm-eaten volume of no cash value, but I bought it as a graduate student, when I wanted to make a physical connection between a text I was reading and the time it came from. I wanted the *stuff* of the text. This talismanic charge evaporates on the screen. Naturally enough, we regret losing it. We should; it is a big loss.

Books, especially for those of us whose lives are built around them, usher us into a magic land. We lose ourselves, as we say, in a book, but we have found something too, that magic land inside the book. It is built from the interweaving of the two kinds of alphabet. On the one hand, we have the flat, silent, and colorless world of classic print. It works by shutting out the continually distracting world of behavior. But this always proves too great a deprival. We hunger to find again our natural ground of sight and sound. To regain it, verbal styles have always tried to build sight and sound back into themselves. They have always tried to heal the split between the flat two-dimensional world of denotation and the rich three-dimensional world of behavior. They create wonderful passages of sensory description, vivid "speaking pictures." All kinds of rhymes and sound patterns recall the voice that is missing.

Here again, we can find precedent in the teachings of classical rhetoric. Rhetorical training preserved and categorized a storehouse of decorative patterns, called figures. Among them were the figures of sight and sound. These verbal pictures and sounds invited us to recall the sights and sounds of the behavioral world that fixed text banishes. The reader thus became the bridge between the alphabet and the world. Together, these verbal patterns constitute the world of verbal styles. In turn, these styles have created a particular world, the world of books, partly the product of the writer and partly the creation of the reader, a world that floats somewhere between the flat world of writing and the three-dimensional world of behavior. The reader is invited to think by oscillating between these two kinds of alphabetic information. Style and substance, they are sometimes called.

Oddly enough, the institution of the library, which preserves these talismans and magic worlds for us, has always operated with a digital, not a fixed print, logic. Books, the physical books themselves, were incidental to the real library mission, which was the dispersion of knowledge. Fond as librarians are of books, and dedicated as they are to preserving them, their native generosity of spirit comes from their zeal to make knowledge available to whoever needs it. Their final loyalty is to knowledge, to the free marketing of ideas, to the cultural conversation. Libraries have always tried to make documents of all sorts circulate with the freedom natural to electronic notation. The elaborate indexical apparatus that they have built around printed books amounts, in a broad view, to an early model of the "global search" that digital expression makes possible. It is not surprising that the ever-shifting interface between books and screen came to them first. Nor is it surprising that the most fruitful thinking about digital expression has come from the library world.

Fourth: The strongest barriers to a full use of electronic text's "alphabet that thinks" comes from copyright claims. Sales and distribution of e-books that are simulacra of printed books have been constrained at every point by rights holders' fears that someone will steal their texts. So copy protections are added that make e-books hard to use in a normal book-like way. So, too, constraints are invoked against electronic distribution and print-on-demand at the point of sale. And when you try to create a genuine multimedia text, the issues of intellectual property loom larger still. It is harder to get permission to quote images or film segments than to quote text, and when permission is granted, the fees for it are higher. The polite conventions of "fair use" that authors writing nonfiction depend on have not been extended to images and sounds and are being threatened for words themselves. Beyond this, in an economics of attention expression of any sort, the sum total of the cultural conversation is where the value lies and copyright is being extended over increasingly large areas of it. As a result, authors who want to contribute to this conversation soon come upon new No Trespassing signs. And these signs turn up increasingly for simple print-publishing projects as well. Behind such a preemption of the cultural commons stands, for electronic text, a conceptual difficulty. Copyright thinking, as it has developed around print, does not fit alphabets that think and efforts to make it do so will always hamstring its logical expression.

Fifth: Alphabets that think create texts that mix words, images, and sound in dynamic ways. Such mixtures do not seem, to many people, and especially to scholarly audiences, as "serious" as a fixed printed book. Thus they do not make adequate career tokens. Even texts that are "printed" in everything but name—that is, print on a screen—do not seem serious to an academic audience until they are printed out in a codex book. Back again to our paradox of stuff. Nobody would say that the binding is more important than the contents, but in fact it often is, because the binding authenticates the package—as Christo so well knew. The binding makes the talisman.

Sixth: Alphabets that think make us suspicious in another way, too. They hark back to prealphabetic scripts, and these are bound to seem primitive and inexpressive. It is this iconic notation, as Eric Havelock argued, which conceptual thinking must discard if it is to advance. Here, as so often, such a prejudice will affect the old more than the young, but it is there for all of us. A competitive attention economy does not seem as serious as the monopolistic one of the printed book.

Beyond the "touch and smell" nostalgia for the printed book, electronic text elicits deeper and more serious fears. For nonfictional prose, the central fear is the blurring of conceptual thought that comes with a thinking alphabet. Just as Havelock argues, only by transcending the alphabet that thinks can conceptual thought find a condign notation. Only the aesthetics of subtraction that alphabetic notation creates can allow us to ignore the expressive surface, filter out extraneous signals, and concentrate on the conceptual meaning. Look through rather than at. It is a legitimate fear. We don't want coffee-shop chatter in the library of our mind. We feel we must preserve the unselfconscious transparency of the medium if we are truly to "lose ourselves in a book." A bi-stable form of notation, like a bi-stable economics, that switches periodically from at to through and back, from stuff to nonstuff and back, makes us queasy.

Readers of prose fiction especially have felt these fears. People often argue that the book leaves much to our private visual imagination that a moving image violates. But you could say the same for a movie, and yet movies prompt as many individual interpretations as novels. What is the rich interiority that we fear to lose as we move from book to screen? Clearly, the loss must be real because so many sensitive readers feel it. Do we object to voice because we are so long used to a voiceless notation? If the visual imagination undermines fictive illusion, why does fiction include so many vivid descriptions? Why has the "speaking picture" been a part of rhetorical training since the Greeks? Do we lose the privacy of a book, the one-to-one relationship? But why should a reader-to-screen relationship seem less private? Some critics have lamented the passing of eloquence, the love of ornate language or of language itself. But formal eloquence has not prospered well in either the world of the high-speed rotary press or the sound bite. If we have forsaken it, we can blame neither the alphabet that thinks nor the digital screen on which it thinks. Only the passage of time will specify this loss or ameliorate it.

Surely poetry cannot complain when it regains its voice. And, as we have seen, there is a long tradition of poetry written in a thinking alphabet—shape poetry—in Western expression, which testifies to a continuing hunger for the rich signal digital expression permits. If we think for a moment of the kinetic alphabet examples of the last chapter, we see poetry extending its domain, not shrinking it.

Even more fundamental than the fear for lost interiority, however, lies a deeper misapprehension. The standard model we use for human communication is one I have called the clarity-brevity-sincerity, or "C-B-S," model. It is one based on the exchange of goods, of physical stuff. Words are like things and ideally should *be* things. You have a message that you want to send to someone else. It must be clear: you don't want the wrapping to obscure the stuff. It must be brief. You don't want to waste anybody's time. That's why UPS delivery persons run from the truck to your door. And you must be sincere. You must not, that is, have any designs on anybody, try to persuade them of anything. You must say exactly what you mean, neither more nor less. You owe the whole truth to everybody.

The inadequacies of this model have been widely observed. In oral cultures, people talk for the sake of keeping the human conversation going, to remind themselves that they are still alive. There is no written repository for reality so, to maintain the culture, the conversation must be continual. And since much of our cultural reality remains oral, we continue to do the same even though we can write and record and photograph. "Symbolic human interchange has very little to do with the passage of information. . . . It has to do with keeping up the interaction," as behavioral biologists have made clear.

We also talk because we like to play around with language. We love slang, the special terms of art we use in our work, word games like pig Latin, or cockney rhyming slang. And we have always loved formal eloquence, too, the special languages we invent to mark special occasions. All these are the domain of rhetoric. But "rhetoric" we also know as the familiar antonym of "reality," as the synonym for deception. We distrust self-conscious ornament, artifice that shows. This war with ourselves about what we want words to do has been waged since Plato's day. It was relaunched by the Royal Society in seventeenth-century England as a plea for scientific clarity against rhetorical obfuscation: "They have therefore been most rigorous in putting in execution, the only Remedy, that can be found for this *extravagance: and* that has been, a constant Resolution, to reject all the amplifications, digressions, and swellings of style: to return back to the primitive purity, and shortness, when men deliver'd so many *things,* almost in an equal number of *words.* They have exacted from all their members, a close, naked, natural way of speaking; positive expressions; clear senses; a native easiness: bringing all things as near the Mathematical plainness, as they can."

This theory of communication has dominated our thinking to the present day. Words should be as much like things as possible, ideally *are* the things they represent. The word "table" should look like a table. If you try to wrap words up in emotion, in design, you are only masking the naked truth with fallacious glosses. You are trying to persuade somebody of something. The truth, like Adam and Eve before the Fall, is naturally naked. And the heart that delivers it should always be naked as well. These assumptions are so fundamental to how we think about communication that they inhere in the terminology we use to describe it: rhetoric versus reality; style versus substance. They have been strongly reinforced by the hyperventilated romanticism of our own age, where we spend so much time, defenses down and conventions aside, in telling each other how we really feel.

The C-B-S model of communication has, then, an economic basis—the economics of stuff. It fit perfectly the industrial revolution that followed speedily upon it. The advent of printed text only reinforced this stuff-based conception of human communication. Print came in books, and books were undeniably stuff. You could drop them on your foot. More to the point, in daily life you could put them on store shelves and sell them, store them in a bookcase at home, hoard them or lend them as you liked. And after the details were worked out, you could copyright and publish them and thus own what was inside them as well. All good, sound stuff. But what happens when the economy is not based on stuff but on information and the attention that makes sense of it? And what happens when we move from the fixity of print to the volatility of digital expression?

The C-B-S theory of communication comes with a powerful moral charge.

If loyalty to stuff is communicative virtue, then an interest in the wrapping, or the person doing the wrapping, or the effect on the wrappee is communicative vice. No wonder Christo, the archetypal modern wrapper, has taken so much flak. The moral basis for this suspicion may be even older than the economic one. "Rhetoric," the general term of abuse we now use for everything not conforming to C-B-S code (that is to say, all the expressive devices used by our opponents, as against those that we use ourselves), has from early Greek times been portrayed as a woman. To start with, she was a goddess named Peitho, but by Christian times she had metamorphosed into a temptress. She it was who tarted up the plain truth in fancy clothes, put on the glossy lipstick and seductive eye shadow of a "rhetorical mask," and led us down the primrose path.

Plain language is thus nearly allied to plain living. No fancy clothes. No cosmetics. No fancy food. No fancy cars. Thoreau's cabin on Walden Pond. From plain living, we can take a step deeper into the argument. When you do away with "fancy" things of all sorts, you are declaring war on ornament. On style. Neither, in the plain world, should exist at all. And beneath the hatred of ornament we find the deepest level of all, the hatred of theater. In *The Anti-Theatrical Prejudice*, Jonas Barish traces this prejudice from Plato's hatred of poetry through its reincarnation in the hysterical Christian Church father Tertullian, through the Puritan closing of the theaters in England during Cromwell's time right through to Jane Austen's suspicion of playacting (in *Mansfield Park*) as something respectable people did not do. And so into the current raging among puritanical religions on the dangers of beauty, human and artistic, and the need to destroy it and the people who create it.

The iconoclastic drive runs deep. It reflects a fear for our sense of self and society. Our self should be our soul, permanent, self-standing, unique. Something halfway between the ears and preeminently real. Our society should be equally self-standing, equally preexisting. Nothing artificial or temporary or "theatrical" about it. The theater, by its generic appeal, suggests that life itself is theatrical. The advent of print reinforced this moral charge, too, as well as the economics of stuff, for it is a puritanical medium. Print abjures sensory stimulation of all sorts to concentrate on presenting propositional thought. It seeks, like the silence of a library, to isolate us from distractions, to put utterance in an ideally plain frame.

The rhetorical view of life has always departed from premises opposite to these. It sees the self as a social fabrication, created by the many dramas we pass through in our lives. It is formed from the outside in, not vice versa. In this view, we accrete a self by playing a series of roles as we pass through life, rather than being born with one. A self like this can exist only in society, a society that is an ongoing drama, which evolves and changes. Such is the world we saw Andy Warhol creating and living in, a world dominated by self-conscious role-playing. In a world like this, Christo's wrapping is a legitimate part of the scene, not an aberration to be ignored or described in dyslogistic epithets. Such a "rhetorical" world has always seemed, to one part of our minds at least, the incarnation of falsity, everything we don't want the world to be.

So. We have a theory of communication that is based on a theory of economics that is based on a theory of morality that is based on a theory of self and society. It goes all the way down to bedrock. How can you possibly argue with this perpetual dream of native innocence and simplicity? Argue for hypocrisy? More narrowly, how can you argue against clarity? Or brevity? Or, above all, sincerity?

Well, sometimes you have to. There are, as we all know once we think about it, big problems with the C-B-S theory, and at all levels. It is a wonderful theory to avow but less useful in practice. Imagine what would happen if you lived your life according to such precepts, stripping away the rhetorical mask and "fallacious gloss" of ordinary life in a disinterested zeal for the naked truth. After a day or two of this you'd lose your job and your family, and the next day your mind, too.

The tact and forbearance, the sense of decorum that tells us what may be said when and where, all are stripped away by the C-B-S theory. As a way to live with others, it is unworkable. It suffers from the worst fault a theory can suffer from. It leaves out much of what it sets out to explain—human behavior. And if it does not work as a theory of behavior, still less does it work as a theory of expression. You don't, as Sarah Churchill once said, owe the whole truth to everybody. You adjust what you say to time and place. A message is not an inert package of lead shot. It is intended for a particular recipient, with particular abilities and sensibilities. The C-B-S ideal of communication, while great for moral exhortation, proves of limited use in analyzing actual acts of communication. Powerful and important, but limited. Consider clarity, for example. An air controller's transmission will be clear to the pilot of the plane (at least we hope so) but not always to the passenger listening in on the conversation back in the cabin. What will be clear to the physician may not be to the patient. A message is not a lump of coal, either delivered or not. It is not a message at all, in fact, unless it reaches the recipient and changes that person's view of the world.

Or we might consider brevity as an expressive ideal. Keep it short. Cut the cackle. No one can argue with that. But how short? Well, no longer than it needs to be. Well, but how long is that? Well, it depends. But it always depends. Depends on time and place, on human situation. When a navy pilot on patrol in the Pacific during World War II radios back to his carrier, "Sighted sub; sunk same," he is about as brief as he can be. But he is conveying a far longer signal, one full of emotional overtones that tell us what he thinks about what he has done, the insouciance with which he views his triumph. He is not being brief to be brief, but as a short way of being long. Just saying, "Ah, good, I am being brief," doesn't tell us anything about the communication. Or take an even shorter famous military message, that returned by General McAuliffe of the 101st Airborne Division when surrounded by German forces at Bastogne. To the German demand for surrender he replied famously, "Nuts." Such a communication depends for its power not on its length but on how that length works in a particular context. It is an informal reply on a formal occasion, one that expresses not simply an answer to the demand, "No," but contempt for the enemy and defiance of his strength.

Still, you must admire it. What sincerity! Yes, except that famous generals have been, with rare exceptions, poseurs, self-conscious actors on the killing fields. Douglas MacArthur, with his endless photo ops and press releases, provides the defining case, but rough, tough, down-to-earth heroes from Patton to Montgomery and Rommel took great care to present a particular image to the public. So, it does him no disservice to think, it must have been with McAuliffe. He was writing to posterity as well as to the German commander opposite him.

The C-B-S theory of communication, then, doesn't always work, powerful and powerfully needed though it is. It doesn't fully explain what it purports to explain. It doesn't describe accurately what is happening. As a theory of written expression it substitutes for accurate description only vague moral exhortations, satisfying in the saying but hard in the doing. And it is an unteachable theory. It argues that all expression should be transparent, not noticed, existing only to showcase the meaning. But how do you teach transparency? You can't hit what you can't see. You can, as sometimes happens in prose composition courses, correct a little grammar and then give up and talk about something else, current events, race-gender-class oppression, or whatever is fashionable in the current conversation. If you try to describe the "C-B-S" pattern, then you must look at it not through it. You must deny its fundamental premises in order to think about it. Serious inquiry into such a theory is thus intrinsically self-confounding. Time, again, for some "of courses."

Of course we should always get the lard out of our prose. I have written two textbooks and two videos that show how to do this. Of course we should make ourselves clear instead of writing pretentious hokum. Here is where the revisionist thinking I discuss in the final chapter begins, and it is a vital beginning. Of course we should tell the truth, as it has been given us to understand it. Of course we should try to be candid as well as kind, as truthful as the bounds of civility permit. Of course we should, in every way we can, temper the wind to the shorn lamb, aware that our own shearing-time cometh apace.

But these laudable goals often don't offer much help in understanding how human communication works. They have never worked well even in the goods economy they are based on (as economists sometimes find out) and they lead us hopelessly astray when we leave the comforting world of stuff. For an attention economy, we need a richer and more inclusive theory of expression, one that defines clarity, brevity, and sincerity formally and descriptively rather than with moral platitudes. Recall Walter Wriston's request quoted in the first chapter: "The world desperately needs a model of economics of information that will schematize its forms and functions." The matrix of style sketched out in the next chapter tries to supply such a model. I cannot think it is the model Wriston might have had in mind, but he was, after all, asking for a new way to think about the problem.

In the Western conversation about human expression, spoken or written, the great villain has always been self-consciousness. As soon as our audience thinks we are considering how we are speaking, paying attention to style instead of substance, they start feeling their pockets to make sure their wallets are safe. Every time we open our mouths, then, or put our fingers on the computer keyboard, we should cast contrivance aside and be spontaneous and sincere. Every rhetorician since the Greeks invented the craft has been taught this as a first operating principle. But, since any training in speaking and writing is a training in precisely these arts and contrivances of insincerity, such advice has always been fraudulent. Whether it applies to writing, or to the fine arts where artists are always taught that the best art is the art that conceals art, it always finally amounts to the advice the English comedy team of Flanders and Swann gave in one of their satiric sketches: "Always be sincere, whether you mean it or not." Thus if we accept self-consciousness in human expression as a vice, as has been universally the case, we end up by recommending hypocrisy as the way to save our souls.

But self-consciousness about behavior of all sorts, not only communication, has been a part of human life from the beginning. And in an information society it can only increase. The more we are deluged with information, the more we notice the different ways it comes to us, the more we have—in pure self-defense—to become connoisseurs of it. The torrent of information makes us more self-conscious about it, about all the different packages it comes in, about the different ways we interpret it, and about how we should express our responses to it. It is more counterproductive than ever to demonize stylistic awareness. Stylistic self-consciousness should be the first line of defense for a child swimming in the information flood.

The need for a new way of thinking runs deeper still. Stylistic self-consciousness, the habit of looking at an expressive surface as well as through it, emerges logically from the nature of digital expression. The center of the computer revolution, as a new system of human expression, lies in its central polyvalent digital code. The same code that expresses words can generate images or sounds. Information can be moved from one sensory modality to another while still being driven by the same data. This choice of expressive means naturally generates stylistic self-consciousness.

Digital expression has heightened our expressive self-consciousness both of words and of images and sounds. We've seen in the previous chapter how this heightened consciousness of expressive medium has worked for words and the letters that compose them. Desktop publishing has made typographical layout and font selection matters of everyday expressive concern. We no longer take them as givens; we can make the choices ourselves, and thus we become more conscious that they *are* choices and that other choices might be made. Or consider still images. Image-processing programs allow us to perform all kinds of permutations on digital images, and we are used to seeing such permutations in print and on television. Such editing of images as used to be possible was the province of professional specialists. Now anyone can do it. We edit our snapshots while they are still in the digital camera. Perhaps most powerful of all, the editing of moving images, of home videos, has become a consumer-level phenomenon. When you use a simple film-editing program like Apple's iMovie you become self-conscious about how moving images work in a way that no other means of engagement can equal. You can snip and clip and reassemble with a few mouse clicks, and the more you become a video editor, the more conscious you become of the medium you work in. You have become used to looking at rather than through. That is what editing of any sort is all about, but it seems especially dramatic when you can edit movies that until recently you could only look at.

A few years ago, the idea of "sound design" as a concomitant to image design was restricted to special effects people and a few acousticians. Now anyone can take sounds from alien contexts, translate them on the screen into their visual equivalents, and stretch and bend them at will. Such bending and sampling, long a staple of electronic musical composition, is rapidly becoming part of everyday expression. A flourishing industry caters to people interested in high-level musical reproduction, the so-called high-end audio world. People in this world become extremely conscious of recording techniques, the basic rules of acoustics, listening-room design, the nature of human hearing. As a result, the act of listening becomes acutely self-conscious. People become connoisseurs of sound. Their listening habits always oscillate between the sound and the music.

Wherever we look in the current landscape of expression, then, we find people increasingly self-conscious about what they see and hear. The *at* pattern of attention has been democratized. In a matrix with these requirements, stylistic self-consciousness, *at* attention, must be considered not as a sin but as a fundamental variable in human expression. We should seek to chart it, not to condemn it. Only thus can we come up with a means of description that will comprehend the full range of human expression, plot the full range of design, rather than dismissing half of it as sinful or mistaken. And only thus can we calibrate style with behavior.

So where do we stand with the electronic book? It has not yet been created. The alphabet that thinks has not yet found its condign format. It would be easy enough to say that the Internet provides this format, but it doesn't. It is a gigantic library, not a limited expressive format like a codex book. Certainly electronic texts that mix word, image, and sound are usually more expensive to produce than printed books. At the deepest level, though, our failure to use digital expression in a fruitful and efficient way comes from a theoretical misunderstanding. We are thinking about it using an incomplete set of templates for thought. Just when our expressive horizons have been expanded, we want to narrow them. We have been thinking about electronic text as the wrong type of revolution. We have confused an extension of the Gutenberg revolution in replication and distribution with a revolution in expressive logic. We have now a new expressive alphabet, an alphabet that thinks. It creates new spaces for words and between words. We can use these new spaces, this new alphabet, alongside our present fixed-print one. We have a choice between the two. This choice unifies the two great strands of notation in Western culture, the neutral, transparent alphabet that the Greeks created and the older imagistic notation of Egyptian hieroglyph and Sumerian cuneiform.

We have, that is, at last unified the history of Western cultural notation. We have two kinds of alphabets and thus two kinds of reading. We are free to choose whichever notation suits our purpose. The real electronic book, when it appears, will be a rich and fruitful combination of the two.

The Latin rhetorician Quintilian gave this advice about how reading should be taught: "It is impossible, except by actual practice, to make it clear how a boy is to learn when to take a fresh breath, where to make a pause in a verse, where the sense ends or begins, when the voice is to be raised or lowered, what inflection should be given to each phrase, and what should be spoken slowly or quickly, excitedly or calmly." Such a reading world was full of sound and gesture; it existed in the world of ordinary behavior. It was itself a social behavior that performed a text in the way a pianist performs a score. Readers had spent a millennium and a half perfecting such performance. It was "literacy" as it presented itself in a world still profoundly oral, still dependent on the live spoken word.

But when you need to absorb more information more quickly, when a performer is not readily to hand, you want to subtract the behavioral context. You want to filter out the reading voice and dramatic gesture and pregnant pause and careful change in pitch. You want to filter out orality entirely. It took us another millennium to perfect this new manner of reading. We see its perfected state, a state happily not reached until recent times, in courses in speed reading, in business writing that consists of bullet points, and in bureaucratic prose that has lost its voice and become literally unreadable. Such text aims to be transparent and unselfconscious.

Now, electronic text has made it possible for us to have both kinds of "book" and to choose between them, or mix and match as needed. Both kinds of reading are "efficient," but they maximize different variables. The expressive powers of oral culture and literate culture can now be put into synergistic relationships with one another. We do not yet know how these new synergies will work themselves out. One thing, however, is clear. The new spaces for words will be competitive and self-conscious. They will require a new conception of rhetoric, a new doctrine for teaching expression in an electronic attention economy.

At present we have no such educational program. Because we still think that stuff is more important than nonstuff, educational programs that teach communications skills have always been secondary to the main enterprise. Freshman Composition has always lived in the basement. It will remain there until we understand the new economy in which we dwell. Meanwhile, here and there programs in electronic expression, in using an alphabet that thinks, are beginning to develop. The modern educational enterprise being as compartmentalized as it is, those who teach the old alphabet rarely make common cause with those who teach the new.

If we are to bring these two alphabets together into a common universe, we must have a common way to think about them. That common theory the following chapter seeks to provide.

Background Conversations

Technology and Values

I've been arguing, in this chapter, that electronic books, "e-books," change how conventional books are produced and distributed but do not change their fundamental structure. They try, in fact, to preserve it in every way they can. They have pages, and you can turn them over; they have "print" and it doesn't dance about; they have margins and other visual clues taken over from the codex book. They even, in some versions, impose restrictions greater than those of a codex printed book. If I buy a book at the bookstore, I can take it home and read it wherever I want to, and loan it to whomever I want. Some electronic books allow you to download your e-book onto only one computer, so that if you want to read it on another computer in another room, you have to buy another copy. We return to the pre-Gutenberg convention of the monastic library, where the manuscript book was chained to the stand. You can't get more zealous about denying the logic of digital expression than returning to a time when the printed book had not been invented yet.

I've also been arguing that the rich signal that will animate truly electronic books, whatever shapes they ultimately take, does not represent the end of Western culture or the repudiation of its essential values. Such a multiplexed signal represents, as I've tried to suggest, a return to the "traditional" Western means of communication, if by that we mean the conventions that have been employed since written history began. It does not repudiate this tradition, a tradition that has not always been built on the printed book and yet has somehow preserved the "values" supposedly endangered by electronic expression. In the first place, the oral culture that preceded the invention of writing was not replaced by writing but existed side by side with it. Wherever we place Homer on the oral/literate spectrum, no one denies that The Iliad and The Odyssey were meant to be recited aloud. So was Virgil's Aeneid and every major literary work at least up through Chaucer's Canterbury Tales. Plato thought writing itself represented an impoverishment of conceptual thought, and Chaucer would certainly have thought that his poetry, read silently and in isolation, had suffered a diminution. Shakespeare wrote for the stage not the book. And surely the aristocratic owners of those splendidly illuminated medieval books of hours would not have preferred a text without distracting pictures.

So, if we are afraid that the values, intellectual or moral, that come with the printed codex book are now in peril, we can't contend that we are turning our back on Western culture. Quite the opposite; we are turning back to it and examining it afresh in ways that digital expression now allows. But, nevertheless, Western culture may have been wrong before 1453, and only got its head on straight when printed books became the dominant communications technology. That has, in fact, been the dominant humanist argument about electronic text, and I ought to take it into account. It is conveniently expressed in two widely divergent books, Sven Birkerts's *The Gutenberg Elegies* and Jane M. Healy's *Failure to Connect: How Computers Affect Our Children's Minds—and What We Can Do about It.*

Birkerts's book has two parts. In the first, he reflects on what reading has meant to him in his life and on what he feels to be the current shallowness of American life, a shallowness that he feels comes from a proliferation of texts and of other claims on our attention. When there were many fewer texts to read, people read them more intensively, "vertically," as he calls it. Now we read more texts but "horizontally," without dedicated attention. It is the standard argument: too many claims on our attention. He expands this argument into a general condemnation of shallowness in our current life. We lack depth, the depth that we find in authentic works of art and literature. "Resonance—there is no wisdom without it. Resonance is a natural phenomenon, the shadow of import alongside the body of fact, and it cannot flourish except in deep time. Where time has been commodified, flattened, turned into yet another thing measured, there is no chance that any piece of information can unfold its potential significance. We are destroying this deep time." What's the villain? The electronic communications revolution, of course. "When the electronic impulse rules, and where the psyche is conditioned to work with data, the experience of deep time is impossible. No deep time, no resonance; no resonance, no wisdom."

A central cliché floats clear of the muddled metaphors: The lives we live are too busy for reflection. More precisely, reading printed text now has a number of competitors for our attention. This competition is a bad thing. But monopolists have always thought this way. Allow competition and where will it lead?

The beginning of competition in this attention field has always been resisted.

Plato's Socrates had harsh things to say about writing, as against speaking. The written word is mute and unchangeable, not a suitable vehicle for the advancement of wisdom, which requires the lively interchange of human conversation. Socrates' argument for orality as against literacy precisely reverses the argument Birkerts advances, but Socrates felt it led to the same result: superficiality of thought and feeling. When printing was invented, and texts made available to a wider audience—the first revolution in duplication and distribution of books—the authorities of church and state thought their communications monopoly threatened. Where would such irresponsible dispersal of knowledge lead? A bunch of shallow "horizontal" thinkers dealing with "vertical" subjects? Impossible! Alexander Pope had a similar response when, at the beginning of the eighteenth century, the franchise of literacy was extended beyond those with a proper classical education. Deprived of this background, what could people be but dunces, suitably described in his *Dunciad*? But if the response to changes in communication technologies has always been the same—superficiality!—even though the changes themselves differed, might the response come from some other source?

Birkerts seeks to defend what he calls "the real heart of reading." The kind of reading he is thinking about becomes apparent a little later. "When we enter a novel, no matter what novel, we step into the whole world anew." Throughout, he has in mind novels. All the other kinds of reading—biography, history, political science, economics, business writing, scientific writing—none of these participate in this breathless metaphysics of reading. Surely these other kinds of reading do not involve the sublime self-transformation he is talking about. So his argument comes down to the willing suspension of disbelief that any great work of art demands, novels included. This is not precisely a new idea, but it is as close as he gets to "the heart of reading." And we can get "lost in a book" in other kinds of books besides novels, and in lots of novels, popular romances of all kinds, that do not claim to be soul transforming.

As it happens, a great literary critic, C. S. Lewis, inquired into the same subject, the heart of literary reading. In *Experiment in Criticism* he explores "how far it might be plausible to define a good book as a book which is read in one way, and a bad book as a book which is read in another." Art, once again, defined as attention. He divides readers into two classes, the "few" who are literary readers and the "many" who are not. This division, he contends, is not invidious. "I have a notion that these 'many' include certain people who are equal or superior to some of the few in psychological health, in moral virtue, practical prudence, good manners, and general adaptability. And we all know very well that we, the literary, include no small percentage of the ignorant, the caddish, the stunted, the warped, and the truculent. With the hasty and wholesale *apartheid* of those who ignore this we must have nothing to do." He includes art and music in his inquiry. The many use art for other purposes, the few "receive" it. Here is what "receiving" means: "We must look and go on looking till we have certainly seen exactly what is there. We sit down before the picture in order to have something done to us, not that we may do things with it. The first demand any work of art makes upon us is surrender. Look. Listen. Receive. Get yourself out of the way. (There is no good asking first whether the work before you deserves such a surrender, for until you have surrendered you cannot possibly find out.)" Don't worry, as Birkerts does, about what it does to your soul. Get the self out of the way.

The many read only for the story, never for the style. "They have no ears. They read exclusively by eye." In the terms I use in this book, they are all *through* readers. But readers who look only *at* are part of the many, too. They are the "stylemongers." We are here talking, in either case, about literary reading. He makes clear that "scientific or otherwise informative reading" is different from literary reading; there we need not "believe or approve the Logos." No suspension of disbelief required.

What do the few read for? "The nearest I have yet got to an answer is that we seek an enlargement of our being. We want to be more than ourselves. . . . We want to see with other eyes, to imagine with other imaginations, to feel with other hearts, as well as with our own. . . . One of the things we feel after reading a great work is 'I have got out.' . . . Not only nor chiefly in order to see what they are like but in order to see what they see, to occupy, for a while, their seat in the great theatre." Here, for Lewis, is the vital center of reading: "Literary experience heals the wound, without undermining the privilege, of individuality. There are mass emotions which heal the wound; but they destroy the privilege . . . But in reading great literature I become a thousand men, and yet remain myself." Here is what Birkerts was, I think, trying to say. "Those of us who have been true readers all our life seldom fully realize the enormous extension of our being which we owe to authors. We realize it best when we talk to an unliterary friend. He may be full of goodness and good sense but he inhabits a tiny world. In it, we should be suffocated."

Experiment in Criticism was published in 1961. At that time, computers were still data-management tools run by a priestly programming guild. The profile of the many had nothing to do with supposed pernicious effects of digital expression. It was a perennial way of reading, not a crisis or failure that had to be blamed on someone or some technology. Lewis argues finally, I think, for something like what I've called oscillation. We should not ignore style but not read entirely for it (*at* vision). We should not read only for the plot (*through* vision) but we can hardly ignore it. The few are the people most skillful in preserving the bi-stable reading. The many become many because they shut that bi-stability down, read only one way or the other. We may, then, want to say that what we are trying to preserve, as the reading of printed text comes under so much new competition, is precisely the bi-stable pattern of attention that separates the few from the many. And we might argue that we can judge the new means of digital expression by asking whether they enable the many to become the few in ways not formerly possible. I have been contending that digital expression does precisely this.

Birkerts argues that digital expression flattens our historical perspective. Here's his argument: "The depth of field that is our sense of the past is not only a linguistic construct, but is in some essential way represented by the book and the physical accumulation of books in library spaces." But this is to confuse codex books with what is in them. It is a natural mistake for someone who works in a bookstore to make, but a mistake nonetheless. How can the accessibility, replicability, and transportability of historical information flatten our historical perspective? It can only enhance it. Books were stored in libraries because knowledge was in books and someplace was needed to organize and store them. But books don't, any more than bookstores, create historical perspective by their very existence.

It is Birkerts's own lack of historical perspective that informs his argument about "the waning of the private self." The perennially uneasy relationship between the private and the social self is as old as Western culture. It has ebbed and flowed for many reasons. Orality depends on a public self; literacy creates or, depending on who you read, reinforces a private self. The two kinds of self have varied as the oral/literate interface shifts. It is a fundamental dichotomy. I've argued, in *The Motives of Eloquence,* that the fundamental structure of Western literature comes from this relationship. It may be that the ratio has tipped in favor of the social self, but to argue that electronic communication has been the prime mover in the alteration, if there has been one, requires more than just regretting that "our slight solitudes are transected by codes, wires, and pulsations." The crucial issue here is making sure that the oscillation between the two kinds of self remains dynamic; there are many reasons for thinking that it has never been more so than today. That, perhaps, is why we fuss so much about it. We feel the strain. That is as it should be.

What really troubles Birkerts is that "a terrible prestige-drop has afflicted books themselves." Here lies the main offense of electronic information. It provides a competitor to books for our attention. For such a devotee of books, he has surprisingly little faith in the object of his devotion. Are books so weak that they cannot survive competition? Might they not be improved by it, as occurs whenever we see competition in any other sphere of life? We'll see, but as of now it doesn't look as if books are going out of style. There are too many of them, not too few, too many to buy, read, understand, shelve. Birkerts's view is so narrow and mean-minded a bundle of mercantilist fears amid an emerging global market that he won't raise his head and look around him.

Jane Healy's critique of digital expression (*Failure to Connect: How Computers Affect Our Children's Minds—and What We Can Do about It*) goes deeper, and is better informed, than Birkerts's fears for the future of novels. She was an early enthusiast for the personal computer as an aid to learning but has come to think it a disastrous waste of time at best and an unfortunate misprogramming of the growing child's brain in "that precious interval when brain, body, and spirit are still at their most formative stages." But, like Birkerts, she takes arms against the entire communications revolution.

Healy is a "language arts specialist," and that means that she is concerned with the same issues that concern me. What happens to words, and the teaching of words, when they move from page to screen? Words on the page, she feels, generate a richer interiority than they do on screen. Or certainly than do images on a screen. Furthermore, they use the eyes in a different way: "The rapid, rhythmic eye movements used when reading printed text are called 'saccades,' and they differ from those demanded by electronic transfer from one medium to another. These differences make it hard to transfer from one medium to another. Whether or not children's eyes will successfully adapt to electronic text is unknown, but the new technology places more demands on the eyes at any age." Just so, just as reading did, when literacy became common. As for moving from one medium to another, we are back to our standard villain, competition for our attention.

About digital multimedia, Healy quotes with approval another authority, Richard E. Mayer, who argues that "Technological advances in computer-based graphics . . . have not been matched by corresponding scientific advances in understanding how people learn from pictures and words." I certainly agree that, so far as words are concerned anyway, computer graphics have not been used with anything like the imagination and bravery they should have exhibited. The fault, however, is not lack of research but lack of creative enterprise in how electronic text works. And lack of interest in text. Before we study how people learn from pictures and words and sounds in new combinations, we ought to have some imaginative and original examples of how they work together in the electronic expressive space. First you do something and then you study it.

Rhetoric has thought about how words and images and sounds go together for several thousand years now, but it has always proceeded on the basis of practice. The real villain here is lack of understanding about how alphabetic notation works, and how it has worked in the past, in manuscript or print. During much of this history, the "reader" was a "listener" and had to move, and often suddenly, from the world of orality to the very different one of literacy. He or she had to re-create in the literate world simulacra of the gestures and images and voices that play such a fundamental part in the oral world. What a difficult job to do. It seemed, in fact, as we have seen, an impossible one to Plato's Socrates. (Plato himself, as his own prose style shows, was a master at this fundamental oscillation.) And yet, somehow, we have managed to do it, to become readers who can create a simulacrum of three-dimensional vibrant reality inside our heads. The creative imagination has been fed.

Healy is concerned with what we all seem to be concerned with, in one way or another, the economics of attention. Information is bombarding young children from all sides and bemusing them. "In fact, teachers believe that increased 'tuning out' by media-blunted brains is one factor in the growing 'epidemic' of attention problems." But we always "tune out" something when we "tune in" something else. We confront a plenitude of signals to be sure, but is this utterly new? Would we truly want to return to the good old days when information was sparse indeed and the world was therefore, since it was based largely on inherited ignorance, much easier to make sense of? Alas, the historical record does not suggest that people in those less informed days found the world any easier to understand. Healy would have us, presumably, ration these signals according to patterns of which, informed by the latest educational research, she approves. We should be clear about the issue here. It is not whether the brains of young children are being formed in one way or the other. It is, by explication as well as implication, about the rationing of attention. That rationing is what a great deal of this media doom-prophesy is all about. The free market of attention, and of the technologies that compete for it, is too dangerous. Think of all the things that might go wrong. Better, as with markets in stuff, to know thoroughly what we are doing before we do it. But nobody can ever have this proleptic wisdom. Much of the time, perhaps most, we don't know what will happen until it happens.

Like Birkerts, Healy is concerned with the damage electronic media may be doing to the human soul: "We turn now, finally, to 'soul-making.' Instead of merely asking what our children will *learn* with computers, we also need to ask what they will *become*." This concern about what children will become is a real one, perhaps the fundamental one, as it has been since Plato posed it in the *Republic*. And it is as central if we believe that we arrive in the world already equipped with an immortal soul as it is if we think we are issued one in school. Healy worries that the computer will become an avatar of authority and that children will treat it as human, with emotions, and that those who program it will thus mislead youth, just as Plato's Socrates feared rhetoric would do. Here's how she puts it: "Our children will be confronted by never-imagined problems of what it means to be human. Already advertisers are on deck . . . How should we prepare them for such challenges? Let me respectfully suggest that a thorough grounding in values, empathy, and a core sense of self should be our primary goals." Clearly. How could anyone disagree with this? But it is hardly a new problem. The future has always been new and unforeseen and dangerous. As Alfred North Whitehead reminded us in *The Aims of Education,* it is the business of the future to be dangerous. It has always posed "never-imagined problems of what it means to be human." The enemy is feigning, simulation. Plato characterized it as "rhetoric" and its villains were called "sophists." Tertullian characterized it as the theater, and its villains were all those who supplied theatrical illusion to mankind. Now Healy characterizes it as the computer, and the villains the "advertisers" (that all-purpose villain) who use it to mislead youth. Simulation is something that computers are indeed good at. It may be that the computer's fundamental powers will turn out to be theatrical rather than computational. I think it may work out that way. She has certainly picked the right villain. Computer graphics have indeed called up all the variations of the antitheatrical prejudice that Jonas Barish, in his book of that name, has chronicled.

Now that she has selected her villain, she moves on to her critique, the standard one since Socrates. Our age lacks "values." And, as with Birkerts, and Neil Postman, and a host of other commentators, the villain is—you guessed it—technology! "Yet it is hard to teach 'values' in a culture that fails to respect them. What has gone wrong? I would suggest that our passion for the fruits of technology has caused us to separate intellectual and moral values, mind and soul. We seem to care more about how fast our children can learn than how deeply they can feel."

The standard complaint first. We no longer respect "values." But what have we been learning to do this past fifty years? Ethnic values, religious values, the values of social justice—most of the legislation since the New Deal has striven to teach us new respect for values and with some success. If we have failed, it certainly has not been for lack of trying. Values and our supposed lack of them are constantly in our mouths and in our minds. Are we less principled than those in earlier times? I can only say, "Lady, open a history book, any history book." Never, for better or worse, has there been a time of more delicate feelings, of a more relentless pursuit of values in all their anfractuosities. We are all the children of Laurence Sterne's Uncle Toby. Far from neglecting how "deeply we feel," we seem often to debate nothing else, from talk shows to an educational system that has made "facts" into a dirty word. Whether or not our world turns out better or worse than earlier times (I would take my stand on better) it will not be for lack of debate about values and deep feelings. As for the state of our souls, I'm not so brave as Healy is, either to debate about them or to try to straighten them out. Like the first Queen Elizabeth, "I would make no windows into men's souls." That, as the good Queen so well knew, leads to the rack and the stake. Healy's social critique, then, is not new or profound or, so far as we can determine, any truer of our time than of any earlier one.

Now her critique of technology. As so often with humanist critiques, a standard satirical load is simply dump-trucked onto technology as a general-purpose villain. Again, this is not a new coupling. The relationship between virtue ("morals," "values") and the means of human communication, full as it has always been of "feigning" of one sort or another, has always been problematic. Humanist teaching since the Renaissance has argued that it was a good relationship, and the "humanities" curriculum has been relying on this unproved relationship ever since Quintilian made it in his compendium on classical education, the *Institutes*. The humanities, unlike the sciences, teach us values and moral depth. Quintilian at least posed the argument honestly: Is the orator always a good man? Does rhetorical training, the training in the word that has always stood at the center of the humanities, always by its nature, produce good men or only good orators? Quintilian answered good men. C. S. Lewis gave a less facile answer. The few, the really good readers, are by no means always good men, nor the many always bad ones. Two different kinds of talent, and neither dependent on reading.

Healy has turned the Quintilian assertion on its head. We can make a direct causal connection between a communications technology and moral virtue, and in the case of the digital computer, it is a negative one. Computers corrupt the mind and soul. It is a pretty big assertion. A gigantic one, in fact. Each reader will have to decide whether the many educational studies that Healy cites prove the causal relationship or only assert it. But we ought not to forget that it is a causal relationship that has been asserted about every big change in communications technology, as well as about social changes of all sorts, and that it makes assumptions about the nature of the self and of society that have, likewise, been debated at least since Plato maligned the sophists.

As with Birkerts, the real issue is whether the central self, the rich human interiority that both he and Healy seek to defend, is to be conceived, and sustained, as existing on its own or only in alternation with the social self. If the center lies in vital and vibrant movement from the one to the other, then the real question about computers as a communications technology is whether they enhance this vital oscillation or try to shut it down.

I argue that they encourage it; if so, perhaps the sky will not fall as words migrate from page to screen. Mitchell Stephens, in *The Rise of the Image, the Fall of the Word,* thinks that the sky of conceptual thought may stay up after all. His thinking about television comes as a great relief after the prophets of doom. He points out that television to date has been an imitative medium: "There is only one sight this audience has not seen much of during this first era of video: original uses of moving images."

Stephens is arguing that the vast resources of the moving image can create a new dimension of creativity and human expression, one with expressive powers equal to that of the written word. "We live, however, in a culture that, despite the proliferation of images, not only has little faith in their ability but has at times been actively antagonistic toward them." His argument for images is not ecstatic or simple-minded ("For certain important purposes, a picture may actually be worth *less* than a single, relatively narrow, well-placed word") and it is an argument for moving images, for what video excels at. He believes that "once we move beyond simply aiming cameras at stage plays, conversations or sporting events and perfect original uses of moving images, video can help us gain new slants on the world, new ways of seeing. It can capture more of the tumult and confusions of contemporary life than tend to fit in lines of type. Through its ability to step back from scenes and jump easily between scenes, video can also facilitate new, or at least previously underused, ways of thinking." I think he is right, and I think that we can learn a lot about the hidden dynamic of text, what we call style, by pondering these powers and using them to examine fixed text. But, whatever the powers of textual expression as against those of "complex seeing," as Stephens puts it, we'll learn about these powers only by exploring them. Allowing them to compete with one another.

I remain enamored of reading text. Maybe "addicted" is not too strong a word. Piles of unread books are piles of hidden gold. I want to get at them. I also have faith in written alphabetic text. It will continue to do what it does best, what it has always done best. If other forms of expression relieve it of some duties that they can better perform, why should we lament? "Paraventure," as Chaucer said, "thou has cause to singe." It is the competitive economics of attention that will tell us which medium does what best. We should not be surprised that this competition, like other kinds, disturbs as well as refines.

CHAPTER FIVE

{STYLE/SUBSTANCE MATRIX}

S tyle and substance, fluff and stuff are loose and baggy categories but useful ones even so. Important versus peripheral, planned versus spontaneous, natural versus mannered, appearance versus reality, inside versus outside, why versus how, manner versus matter: we must make such distinctions every day. Confusingly enough, though, such pairings describe both the world and what we think is important in it, so the opposites in each pair can change places in a wink.

Rationality is only an instrumental concept: it refers to how people go about achieving their goals. Where do goals come from? In traditional "narrow economics" we do not ask this question.

Jack Hirshleifer and David Hirshleifer, *Price Theory and Applications*

In the inanimate action of matter upon matter, the motion produced can be but equal to the force of the moving power; but the operations of life, whether private or public, admit no such laws. The *caprices of voluntary agents laugh at calculation.*

Samuel Johnson, *Thoughts on the Late Transactions respecting Falkland's Islands* (my emphasis)

If you are a car designer, for you the style of the car will be the substance. If you are a philosopher, "what you think about things" will be the "things" of your world.

Such loose but handy categories do not endear themselves to the scientific mind, either physical or social, and rightly so. What good are terms if they can change places with their opposites just by how you look at them? Worse still, if you can't define the one without the other, if you can't define "backstage" without defining "front stage." Such definition by oscillation causes the poets no problem. So Wallace Stevens:

Two things of opposite natures seem to depend

On one another, as a man depends

On a woman, day on night, the imagined

On the real. This is the origin of change.

But origin of change though it may be, such bi-polarity will cause those driving without a poetic license some difficulty. Let me try now to define the style-substance pairing more richly. If you are to understand how it does originate change, you must show it in action. I've chosen to do so in a set of spectra that I call a matrix. I use the term not in the mathematical or modern movie sense but in a simple dictionary definition: "A place or enveloping element within which something originates, takes form, or develops." The "something" here is the style/substance judgment we make every day.

Let me put the matrix before you (fig. 5.1); then we'll examine it a spectrum at a time.

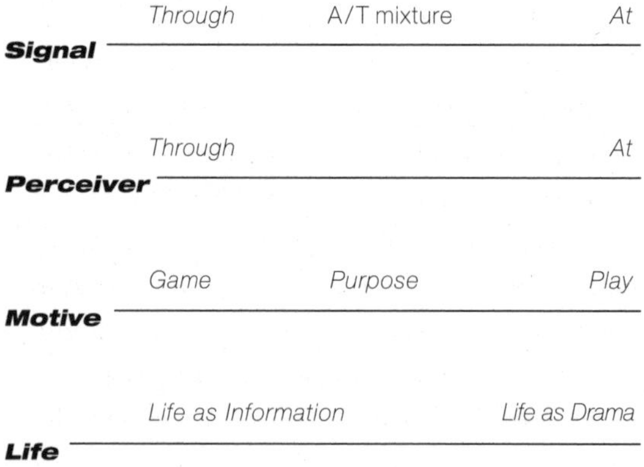

	Through	A/T mixture	At
Signal			

	Through		At
Perceiver			

	Game	Purpose	Play
Motive			

	Life as Information		Life as Drama
Life			

Figure 5.1. Style/substance matrix

The Signal Spectrum

Let's start by considering the means of expression. I'm going to call it the signal and use it to refer to text, image, or sound. We first notice that it is a variable. Some signals are naturally more artful, more self-conscious than others. Some ask you to notice the magnificence of their going, others not. Some players only try to hit a home run; others point to center field first. We call a magnificent painting a "masterpiece," meaning a work of surpassing, but unassuming, genius. But a "masterpiece" originally meant a deliberate show-off piece, the piece of work every apprentice made to prove that he was a "master." It deliberately displayed all of the talents required for his craft. (Every scholar revising a Ph.D. dissertation into a first book is trying to move from a "masterpiece" in the original sense to one in the second.) Some movie celebrities are famous for their acting, others for being famous. A Honda sedan driven to work projects one kind of signal. A Honda coupe "slammed" by lowering the suspension, fitting a loud flow-through exhaust system, an even louder stereo system, and special wheels with inverted rims, projects quite another. You're reading these words in a transparent typeface but *suppose I change to a more ornate one?* Still easy to read but more attention is called to the form. We are asked to look at as well as through. And if I really want to show off? *How about this?*

How might we measure this variable without condemning any particular degree of it? Suppose we sought to plot expression on a spectrum that looked like this.

	Through	A / T mixture	*At*
Signal			

At one end, the *through* ideal. Minimal awareness of an expressive medium. At the other end, the *at* ideal. Maximal awareness of how we say what we do, or paint it, or sound it out. In the middle, all the daily mixtures. Please note: no point on the spectrum is intrinsically evil or virtuous; it seeks to describe rather than to proscribe, to analyze rather than to condemn. Our natural impulse is to condemn self-conscious form. Fonts made to be noticed are called display fonts. Hot-rodded cars are for "show" as often as for "go." Doctoral dissertations that parade your learning to prove you've done it are, often, a terrific soporific. But at that stage in the game you are obliged to display your learning. When you are an adolescent the temptation to display vehicular courtship splendor is irresistible. You want to celebrate the style of your going. Why, if all you need is American Typewriter, were the hundreds of other fonts invented? Why are there now Web sites devoted to inventing and selling, or giving away, new font designs? It is stylistic self-consciousness that drives much of human invention. We condemn it at our peril. Can't we bring to all these efforts a more capacious understanding? The human imagination wants to use the entire range of stylistic self-consciousness, not merely one point on it. And each point on it brings with it a characteristic mixture of powers.

Look again at the AB visual pun we examined in chapter 3 (fig. 5.2). Here,

Figure 5.2. Bart Overly, *Ligature* (1995). By permission of the artist.

the designer has deliberately invoked a particular kind of attention, one that oscillates between perception in two dimensions and perception in three, between letters as flat symbols and as three-dimensional objects. They are transparent as symbols, opaque as three-dimensional objects. The designer attempts to yoke together the two extremes of the signal spectrum, to bend it around into a circle. As with all puns, the aim is compression of meaning. Here again, the paradoxical connection is between stuff and what we think about stuff. Between two ways of thinking about (among other things) eco-

Figure 5.3. Mies van der Rohe, architect, Farnsworth House. Photograph by author (1999).

nomics. To dismiss such an effort as "unclear" dismisses such an experiment before we can understand what it is trying to accomplish.

Designs, in the real world, are often more complex than they seem. Consider, for example, a famous architectural design, Mies van der Rohe's Farnsworth House (fig. 5.3). An example of *through* design if ever there was one—you can see straight through it into the garden beyond. Every detail has been pared away to reveal the genus "house" and nothing else: foundation, four walls, roof. Pure unornamented use. The glass walls provide a transparent window into a domestic dwelling space pared to its essentials.

When you walk around and in it, though, as you can now do since it has been opened to the public, you feel the spareness of it as you do, say, in Shaker designs. Mies's career was one long attempt to get rid of architectural decoration of every sort, but, as with Shaker design, the resulting aesthetic paradoxically brings formal self-consciousness, the basis of decoration, flooding in by the back door. Never has there been a structure more self-conscious about its form. Mies was compulsive about it, grinding the rough edges off the structural steel to make decoration out of its abolition, agonizing about what part of the utilities stack should show beneath the house, refusing to fit screens even though the mosquitoes in this river bottom land eat you alive in the summer.

The attention we bestow on the house is fundamentally paradoxical: our stuff/nonstuff paradox again. We feel its absence of ornamentation as intensely ornamental. It occupies, at the same time, the through and at extremes on our spectrum. The two ends of the spectrum seem to be pulled together into a style/substance pun. The house, in this way, seems almost a statement about the spectrum of design itself. The pun between the two kinds of vision makes us self-conscious about how we are seeing. This paradoxical placement at both extremes suggests a second spectrum, one that plots the same range of self-consciousness but in the beholder not in the signal.

The Perceiver Spectrum

Signals of all sorts bring with them their own suggestions, then, about where they might be placed on a spectrum of formal self-consciousness. But we can choose, if we like, to ignore these indications and bring a different kind of attention to the experience. A simple example: an art gallery is a place to which we bring an *at* expectation. We expect to be looking at paintings as paintings. We don't usually look at a Brueghel harvest landscape as an agronomist might, trying to decipher what kind of grain is being cut and what the probable yield per acre might be. That's not what art galleries are for. Yet we could do this, if we happened to be an agronomist. We can for our own purposes bring a kind of attention that falls on the *through* side of the spectrum. Sailors do this when they look at a picture of sailboats at sea and check to make sure that wind and sails form a consistent and realistic relationship. I do exactly the opposite when the spirit moves me by going to granite yards to look at the stone. I'm not planning to build anything more from these huge sheets of polished stone. They simply embody beautiful patterns, these slices of geologic history. Masquerading as a customer, I visit these slabs of dirty rock exactly as I would go to an art gallery.

A literary critic does the same thing when she reads a work of literature. Ordinary readers read for pleasure, to "get lost in a book," live other lives and see through other eyes. Reading this way, we don't, as a critic does, chart, measure, analyze, count, because such murder by dissection spoils the fun. I'm an addicted reader of detective fiction, thrillers, war stories, and tales of the sea, and as I read I sometimes start locating them on an analytical grid of literary romance, starting with the Greek romances that come to us from several centuries before Christ. But when I do, I'm switching modes of attention, changing selves, working a different part of the brain. And the same thing happens when I notice Patrick O'Brian's prose style instead of wondering whether the ship will sink.

So here is a second spectrum, which plots the perceiver, not the signal perceived.

	Through	*At*
Perceiver		

We can choose any point on this spectrum as a way to look at the world, to pay attention, to distinguish style from substance. Some people endure difficult lives by learning to look at them, consider them as dramas to which they have a free ticket. Jane Austen's Mr. Bennet, the father in *Pride and Prejudice*, learns to live this way as an alternative to strangling his wife and drowning one, or perhaps two, of his daughters. Other people come across as hysterical because they can never detach themselves from any scene, always seeking immersion in its drama. They live at the other end of the spectrum. Life is for them one emotional thunderstorm after another.

A great deal of money is spent in the business world on retreats and seminars of various sorts that aim to move the seminarians from the left side of the spectrum to the right, at least for a day or a week. People immersed in absorbing and demanding daily tasks are asked to step back and reflect on these tasks and on their place in the larger enterprise. They are being asked to look at the business as an art, to look *at* what they spend exhausting days working *through*. Because they have, mostly, had no training in throwing this switch, it is always hard for them to throw it. A consultant must be hired who specializes in this toggling. *At* vision looks impossibly theoretical and arty to someone hardened into one shape by daily tasks. Yet, obviously, employees who can range across the spectrum are the most adroit, in a larger sense the most efficient, employees. One might almost define managerial skill as the ability to understand and work at any point on the spectrum of perception. And the higher up you go on the management tree, the more this is so. The Japanese practice of rotating workers among the different jobs in a large corporation aims to cultivate just such awareness, as does the American military's conception of a tour of duty at a particular location for a definite time. Human talents, these training procedures assume, are best cultivated by learning how to look at the world from many viewpoints on the perceiver's spectrum. This is the "practicality" that, in an economics of attention, replaces the "stick to your last," "keep your head down and work," and "don't go wandering off into academic theorizing," which defines "practicality" in a goods economy. You should certainly stick to your stuff, but the stuff you stick to is different, and always shifting. Style is always turning into substance and back again.

The same problem occurs in the world of university teaching and scholarship. People absorbed in a particular research agenda can teach that agenda quite well, sometimes at least, but find it awkward, or even repugnant, to step back and try to place it in the broader context of a survey course. And people good at teaching survey courses often don't triumph as researchers. The professional schizophrenia endemic in American higher education comes from its insistence that, at least in theory, professors successfully span the entire perceiver spectrum.

You can see this choice of an *at* perspective in all kinds of hobbies. A devotee of audio equipment will listen to music alert not to how well the Emerson String Quartet is playing Mozart but to how well they have been recorded, how clearly the separation of the instruments is rendered, how wide the soundstage is. A film director looking at Branagh's film of *Hamlet* will remark not on the quality of the acting but on how garishly the picture is lit. The experimental American composer John Cage made a career of asking us to listen *at* the sounds that surround us, rather than through them. If you notice ambient sounds as sounds, they become—at least to Cage—"musical" by that act of attention.

There is nothing wrong with any of this; you are free to choose what you pay attention to, and other people should be free to recommend one place on the perceiver spectrum rather than another. Sometimes, however, having chosen a particular way to look at the world, we cast a jaundiced eye on those who have chosen another way. There is a reason for this.

The great American rhetorician Kenneth Burke was fond of saying, "Every way of seeing is a way of not seeing." He meant that paying attention in one way means you cannot pay attention in another. And the manner of attention changes the object. A lawyer accustomed to reading legal prose will find there a transparent clarity that seems opaque to the lay reader. Translating the legal prose into plain English, as plain language laws now sometimes require, seems to many lawyers to be making it more obscure, not plainer. It undoes everything they were taught in law school.

The same rule governs moving from one sensory modality to another. Designers of multimedia texts, Web sites, for example, or educational texts that involve a real mixture of media, find that their first problem is getting the design team to see the problem in the same way. What is clear to one sense is opaque to another; what seems substance to one seems style to the other. Graphic designers construe the world differently from writers or musicians. One way to harmonize them might be along the perceiver spectrum. It provides a common ground on which to plot inevitable differences. It is thus the backbone, in the largest sense, of interdisciplinary effort of any sort. It provides a place to start useful conversations.

To bring this argument home, ask yourself, as an exercise, what part of your job requires *at* attention and what part requires *through* and which part you enjoy more and why. I asked the same question, although in a different way, when I recently visited a class in rhetoric at a large urban university. The class met at night, and the students all worked during the day in jobs involving, almost to a person, digital design work using words and images. I asked them to suppose that their company had given them six months off with full pay to study whatever it was they thought would help them do their jobs better. What would they study? Almost every reply fell on the right-hand side of the perceiver spectrum, involved a broader background, a more thorough theoretical grounding, training of all sorts that would allow them to look at their jobs rather than through them. Job training of the sort most companies provide falls emphatically on the left side of the spectrum. Practical training is required for jobs that need to be done. Maybe a broader definition of "practicality" might improve productivity fully as much. In a goods economy, the case is hard to make. If you have to run a lathe, you want to learn how to make it turn. In an attention economy, the case for the other side of the spectrum, for the "poetry" of work, may be a stronger one.

I've been developing a justification here for the utility of art. It is by no means an original one. To take only one example, a body of critical thinking in the twentieth century argued that art's job was to defamiliarize experience, to make it new by making us see it in a new way. The technique employed was to make us look at what we usually look through. The power resident in a polyvalent digital code may end up operating in precisely this way, allowing us to renew our experience and enrich it by displacing expression from one sensory mode into another, printing out a message in sound, say, rather than word, or "printing out" in real space the rapid prototype specified in a series of numbers. This defamiliarization has already happened across a broad range of scientific thinking through the visualization techniques developed by computer graphics. One striking example is the translation of mathematical formulas into their visual equivalents. To people like me, whose gift for mathematics must be reckoned in the minus numbers, such translation offers a miraculous democratization. Here's a window into a world that I otherwise simply could not see.

Surely this point is generalizable. Digital expression allows an ease of movement across the perceiver spectrum that was impossible in two-dimensional fixed media of expression. If it is important that we learn to see the world through others' eyes, digital expression offers powerful new tools to do so. As we saw in chapter 3, the characteristic way to enter the digital expressive field is to fly over it. Here is defamiliarization with a vengeance. All of the now myriad techniques for manipulating images and sounds fall into the same category. They allow us to work at various places along the perceiver spectrum in new ways. Doing so tells us a good deal about human motive.

The Motive Spectrum

Eric Hoffer, the American popular philosopher, once said that a vigorous society is a society that has set its heart on toys. What can he have meant by this? It contravenes all that we think about human seriousness. Toys are frivolous by definition. Fluff! A vigorous society is a society that has gone back to primitive and simple virtues, "russet yeas and honest kersey noes," seeks to live on Walden Pond, or at least join a volunteer simplicity group that reads Thoreau in the evening instead of going to the mall. No fluff! A vigorous society distinguishes genuine needs from "conspicuous consumption." Toys, except for children, are waste. Grownups should grow up out of them. Stop playing around. A people that has set its heart on toys, so conventional wisdom holds, is a corrupt people, in the last stage of cultural decline. Materialist! Consumerist! Style has replaced substance. The society has lost its moral center, a center that must reside in seriousness, restraint, good sense, and genuine need.

Toys are the behavioral equivalent of an ornate and affected prose style, of a fussy overdecorated Victorian parlor, of an SUV with rhinoceros-guard grille and backseat TV. And just as, when artistic and verbal styles become self-conscious and mannered, we know we have arrived at a "decadent" period, so we know that when toys begin to outnumber tools we have become a decadent people. Thus the formal judgments of art and the moral theories of behavior come together in the C-B-S theory of expression.

But, as we have seen, this theory excludes most of human expression and, in its moral branch, nine-tenths of human behavior as well. Leave out the toys and you leave out a lot. Let's try to recover them by building a third spectrum for our matrix, one on which we can plot human motive. It will allow us to think about style and substance in a more satisfactory way, to connect formal judgments about expression and moral judgments about behavior.

	Game	Purpose	Play	
Motive				

This time let's start in the center and work outward to both sides. In the middle, we find the practical motives of daily life. Plain purpose, let's call it. Here in the middle we buy a car not to flaunt our income, or our good taste, but to get to work and to the grocery store. We buy a house not to feed a hunger for Mies-like simplicity or Victorian clutter, or to shoulder up to the curb a little larger than the house next door, but to give each of the kids a bedroom and mom and dad a little insulation from the rap music. We pay attention to things that architects ignore, like roofs that don't leak, floors that don't cup or squeak, and enough light so you can read a book. And we factor in our ability to pay the mortgage. Here reside good sensible people like us, and if the vigor of a society does not reside here, where are we to look for it?

At the left, or "game," extreme of our behavioral spectrum, we locate the competitive side of human nature. It is immense, if not always predominant. The struggle for dominance and reproductive advantage animates the animate world. We humans are hierarchical primates, concerned above everything else about where we stand on the social ladder. If we are born on the bottom, we fight our way to the top, or try to, thereby providing novelists with rich material. Or, if we are born at the top, we often lose our balance and fall off, thereby providing medieval storytellers with rich material about the wheel of fortune and the fall of kings. If we get to the top and stay there, we are likely to have a midlife crisis in which we feel sorry for ourselves because we did not spend more time sniffing the roses on the way up, providing yet more material for novelists and for social scientists who study the stages of life.

We dramatize this struggle in every way we know how because it is, after all, the fundamental human one, the struggle to survive and to prevail. The ancient Greeks calibrated it in fame, in the everlasting honor of always being first, *aien aristeuein,* as Homer puts it. We calibrate it in money, and business magazines obligingly provide rankings of the richest among us, so the next richest and next-next richest can eat their hearts out. The game is the best metaphor for this sort of human motive. We want to win the game. Which game is irrelevant. Winning is everything. The games themselves are like an expressive surface; you look through them to the vital struggle beneath. It doesn't matter whether you are a football captain, or an army captain, or a captain of industry, so long as you are a captain of something.

If this kind of motive stands at the bedrock of our nature—and human history seems to permit no other conclusion—it is often a pretty bleak rock. Ambition denatures experience, the day-to-day living of life, makes life so transparent that we no longer see it. We look through it to the vital scoring of points that lies beneath. We are held prisoner by our hierarchical hungers. (When Homer gives Achilles a choice of a short famous life or a long obscure one, he had in mind something deeper than death as the alternative. When you live the life of ambition, a part of you dies even if you live long.) Yet here, I think many people would agree, is where the real dynamic power, the true vigor, of a society resides. Ambition drives the intellectual as well as the economic engine. We must then reconsider our conclusion that social vigor, the real substance of life, lies in the careful center of practical purpose. Enterprises are not created by nine-to-fivers who go home and have dinner with their families, who work to live rather than live to work.

If we can all agree on anything, it seems to be that the other extreme of the motivational spectrum, which I have called play, saps social vigor rather than energizing it. Here clusters all the scorn contained in terms like "ornament" instead of "meaning," and "decoration" instead of "essence," "rhetoric" instead of "truth"—"style" instead of "substance." Fluff! Here we find the refined aesthetics of art rather than the firm realities of stuff. Here we find connoisseurs and students of the struggle rather than participants in it. Here we find scientists and scholars with paltry career skills who pursue inquiry for the pleasure of knowledge rather than the pursuit of a Nobel prize, a Barbara McClintock, for example, as against a James Watson. Here we find mountaineers who climb mountains simply because they are there to climb, as opposed to the rescue teams who climb them for the purpose of rescuing the climbers who climb them simply because they are there. In the valleys below, dedicated fishermen, having traveled far and expensively, take great pains to catch fish that they then release to bite again another day while, a pond away, naive natives catch the fish in order to eat them.

Kipling caught the essence of such motives in "When Earth's Last Picture Is Painted" (1892):

When Earth's last picture is painted and the tubes are twisted and dried,
When the oldest colours have faded, and the youngest critic has died,
We shall rest, and, faith, we shall need it—lie down for an aeon or two,
Till the Master of All Good Workmen shall put us to work anew.
And those that were good shall be happy: they shall sit in a golden chair;
They shall splash at a ten-league canvas with brushes of comets' hair.
They shall find real saints to draw from—Magdalene, Peter, and Paul;
They shall work for an age at a sitting and never be tired at all!
And only The Master shall praise us, and only The Master shall blame;

And no one shall work for money, and no one shall work for fame,
But each for the joy of the working, and each, in his separate star,
Shall draw the Thing as he sees It for the God of Things as They are!

"The joy of the working." Here we find the amateur as against the professional, the player who plays the game for the pleasure of the playing, not of
the winning. Occasionally this contrast finds dramatic representation. In a recent Olympics, one of the ice-skaters, a young Japanese woman, gave a performance so tense and wound up, so concentrated on the technical acrobatics that she had to perform, that it was painful to watch. She was skating out
the cold terrors of ambition before your very eyes. The skating was good
enough, however, to win the competition and relieve her of the pressures
of losing the game and, as she must have felt, disgracing her country. After-
ward, the specter of shame banished, there was a skating exhibition by the
medal winners, just for the pleasure of the skating. Here her performance was
transformed into a beauty and grace and ease that brought tears to your eyes.
Here, I said to myself, is what all the commentators were talking about when
they talked about her transcendent talent. But it was allowed expression only
when she moved from the game extreme of the spectrum to the play extreme.

If the game extreme has a biogrammatical underpinning in hierarchical
primate hungers, so one occurs at the play extreme, too. Konrad Lorenz, the
great student of animal behavior, coined the term "vacuum behavior" for acts
that a species just wants to do, has inherited a genetic hunger to perform. Performance brings its own satisfaction. It doesn't have to accomplish anything
else. We are born, it seems, with hungers to behave in certain ways. Dancers
are born wanting to dance, musicians to play, artists to draw. They do so because, in some deep way, they must. Something inside craves expression. The
circuits want to fire. For the rest of us, although perhaps we feel such pressures, we don't find the opportunity (or, usually, the talent) to express them
in practical daily life. From this genetic kernel springs one of the great, and
greatly undervalued, domains of daily life, the world of hobbies.

Every activity on earth, it seems, can give pleasure in the enactment, from
acting out deadly Civil War battles happily on a Saturday afternoon to jump-
ing out of an airplane and doing group acrobatics before you open your para-
chute. This love of form for its own sake we see everywhere in Western culture, from Egyptian tomb decorations that would never be seen by the living,
to gargoyles on Gothic cathedrals that the living could see only from airplanes not yet invented, to hot-rodders chrome-plating parts of the engine that

no one will ever see. (But wait a minute; haven't style and substance changed places here, too? The tomb decorations were intended to serve a purpose in the afterlife; the gargoyles, as the art historian Ruth Mellinkoff has recently demonstrated in *Averting Demons*, were intended to scare away demons; chrome-plating, in its origins, was intended to preserve a metal surface.)

In play lie the pleasures of theater purely conceived, of amateur theater, whether it takes place on stage or in life. We might include here, for example, Louis XIV, who lived his life as a series of staged rituals, the *métier du roi*. Or closer to home, we might locate at this end of the spectrum people whose manners seem to us affected or needlessly refined, all the people who over-play their roles. All the behavior in life that is not sincere, and not likely to be brief or clear, either—"stylized" in fact.

We view this cluster of motives with an ambivalent and paradoxical eye. On the one hand, these are the motives that the clarity-brevity-sincerity theory of communication and behavior teaches us to despise. Behavior of this sort stands outside our normal range of causality and so, outside any productivity formula. It is a wild card, and bean counters don't like wild cards. Neither do scholars. If people often do things for the hell of it then much of intellectual history is devoted to finding motives and causes where there were none. If people write poetry or music simply because they were born to do so, then what becomes of copyright law, which argues that artistic creation must be motivated by profit or artists will down tools and sell insurance instead?

On the other hand, such motives seem to have an admirable purity. We admire the amateur playing the game for its own sake rather than the pampered shortstop whining because he makes a few million a year less than the man playing second base next to him. We admire a fisherman who will go to the antipodes to find rare fishing and then release the catch. A selfless dedication to what you do, a desire to do the best job you know how to do, whether it be restoring an old car or teaching a class or conducting a sales campaign or trying to find the answer to a scholarly question, brings out the best in us. We are not trying to serve ourselves and we are not trying to serve our fellows; we are serving a formal ideal. We act out of disinterested generosity of spirit, for the pure love of form. We pursue the goal for its own sake. We are drawing the Thing as we see it for the God of Things as They are.

Most of us act this way once in a while. Some people, however, characteristically act in this way. They are the pure researchers, the mechanics who love machinery, the workers who work for the joy of the working. They love their activity for its own sake, whether it is exploring the genetics of corn or the location of the magneto in a classic Isotta-Fraschini motor car. In a world of danger and chance, they find moral guidance in a loyalty to form. Hamlet says, of such guidance, "Rightly to be great is ... to find quarrel in a straw, when honor's at the stake." They have chosen to live in the domain of pure play. They have "set their heart on toys." In more than a manner of speaking, style has become their substance.

Our paradoxical attitude toward this kind of motive has played itself out in contemporary society in two opposing directions. On the one hand, many of our basic activities have been displaced into the play sphere. Sex is for reproduction only occasionally, the rest of the time for play. The cheaper food becomes, the more we flock to the gourmet club and the wine cellar. The cheaper computers become, the more popular the collection of antique fountain pens. We might consider the sixties one long displacement of human behavior from competition to play. That is what "dropping out and turning on" meant, after all. Even the ultimate trips, the power trips, are moving in this direction. The more we write about the lives of tycoons of industry, the more we see the pattern coalesce into a genre (upward struggle hand-in-hand with partner no. 1, arrival and discontent with partner no. 1 as insufficient for present greatness, exchange for partner no. 2, high-maintenance but gorgeous, etc.), the more self-conscious we become about it, the more we see it as a role, as displaced to the right side of the spectrum from the left. "Oh, haven't had your midlife crisis *yet?*" And the richer we get, the more our behavior moves into the play sphere. We no longer have to work so hard for a living and we can play more.

At the same time, we intensify the competitive side of our lives at every stage of its living. Six-year-old children are put into football leagues, basketball and hockey and baseball leagues, with all the photo albums and awards and other panoply of the professionals. Executives become busier and busier, lawyers bill more and more hours. At every stage and in every occupation, the delights of the work for its own sake are eviscerated in the name of ambition. We become so accustomed to looking through life to the success that lies beyond it that we forget how to look at it. We boast that we not only "work hard" but "play hard" as well.

A regular development flows in the opposite direction, too, from play to game. Poetry has from its earliest days in Greece moved from pure playful creation to struggle for first prize in that year's drama competition. Today there is something called a National Poetry Slam where poets come together to compete. Activities like drag racing, which began as pure play at making a car accelerate faster, immediately became a game and then moved back to the center of the motive spectrum as a big business. The most dramatic of these changes in motivational flow, in our time, has been in the invention of the computer. The early computer inventors, Zuse, Aiken, Atanasoff, Eckert, and Mauchly, all had practical purposes in mind; they lived in the middle of the motive spectrum. But the theoretical basis for their efforts had been laid by Alan Turing, working isolated in his own thoughts, and developed by John von Neumann, whose central intellectual focus began in game theory. The personal computer, by way of contrast, began in the domain of pure play, a product of the first generation of hackers. The continual dynamic interchange between play and game motives has characterized Western enterprise since World War II. Perhaps this continual flow and reflow characterizes dynamic societies of all sorts.

As in the signal spectrum, the opposites exhibit a strong attraction to one another. A newspaper article about the Tour de France offers a striking instance. "When Lance Armstrong was dropped to the pavement by the wayward handle of a fan's yellow bag, his closest pursuers, even Jan Ullrich, who had trailed Armstrong by only 15 seconds at the day's start, slowed to wait for Armstrong to pick himself up, dust himself off and get back in the race." About this act of gentlemanly courtesy, so strange in today's world of athletic competition, Ullrich replied: "Of course, I would wait. If I would have won this race by taking advantage of someone's bad luck, then the race was not worth winning." Competition in the Tour de France is about as competitive as competition can be. Pure game. Yet insisting that the game be played in such a way that pure performance, not chance, determined the outcome showed an equal loyalty to pure form, the form of the game. Such behavior bends the two extremes of the spectrum back toward one another as if with a piece of spring steel. This tension, in the literature of chivalry, was called "honor." When you take the tension off the spring, disconnect "winning is everything" at one end of the spectrum from, at the other, the amateur's "it's not who wins but how you play the game," honor evaporates. The title of the article? "In Cycling, Winning with Honor Means Everything."

If there has been an intensification in American life of the middle position between these two extremes, however, I'm not aware of it. Play and game are self-motivating. They spring up spontaneously in human behavior. Not so with calm good sense in the center. Fondness for the ordinary moderate pleasures of ordinary moderate life, what the Greeks called *Sophrosyne*, has not threatened to run out of control. Why not? Isn't ordinary purpose where the generative force of human behavior originates? Doesn't human effort originate in the immediate purposes of ordinary life? Shelter, transportation, food? Shouldn't we, that is, chart the generative power of human behavior this way?

But suppose it works the other way, flows from the extremes inward rather than vice versa? Suppose it looks like this:

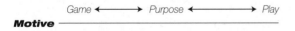

Practical purpose is driven and sustained, if not created, by the goadings of ambition on one side and play on the other. The economic history of the twentieth century would seem to bear this out. Economies driven by the collective dreams of practical purpose, economies where each gives what she can and takes what she needs, have proved gigantic failures. If you abolish hierarchies, they are either re-created or labor turns rancid. The dynamic of ordinary work vanishes. If you abolish nice clothes in favor of Peking uni-smocks or Fidel fatigues, if you outlaw cosmetics, if you proscribe the free play not only of ideas but of anything else, the joyful heart of human life—the joy of the working—shrivels up inside us. When we invert the common proverb by saying that "Invention is the mother of necessity" we try to describe this galvanizing of central ordinary purpose by game and play. Eric Hoffer was pointing to the same movement, but since the dynamics of ambition were so omnipresent, he wanted to stress the corresponding extreme.

But necessity does mother invention, too. A balanced chart of motivational dynamic would look like this:

Game ←——→ Purpose ←——→ Play
Motive ——————————————————————

We should bear this fundamental dynamic flow in mind for the other spectra on the matrix. It provides a fundamental, rather than simply a metaphorical, way to connect them. It shows how the style/substance pairing "originates, takes form, and develops."

Considered in this way, the motive spectrum might well be called the productivity spectrum. Whatever managers may think they are doing, they are trying to orchestrate these two flows. The dominant one seems at first to be

from the center outward, but the larger lessons of collective versus free economies argue for the opposite flow. The inventor may work in the play sphere,
and the entrepreneur in the game sphere, but the manager, who by definition
works in the middle ground of practical purpose, finds his task in balancing
the flow from the extremes without inhibiting it. No wonder good managing
is such hard work.

We might for a moment reflect on markets in the light of this chart. We
think of markets as created to exchange goods. And so they do, and in a goods
economy that would seem to be the end of it. But in an economics of attention, markets trade motives rather than goods. Their great virtue is making
human motive fungible. Motives can be mixed and traded. "Attention goods"
carry a stylistic charge, and that charge can be competitive (putting down the
Joneses) or playful (watching a Alexander Calder mobile detect the ambient
air currents) or deceitful (selling a fake Calder as a real one). You can buy into
a range of motives as wide as the range of goods. Imagine buying a new car:
you don't want it to break down (Honda); you may want it to tell people
where you are in the world (Mercedes, BMW, Ford Explorer, generic plain
van); you may want it to be fun to drive (Miata). You buy a package of satis-
fied mixed motives. The attention economy that has always hovered over cars
lets you pick and choose among motive packages.

Friedrich Hayek regarded this fungibility of motive as the purpose of
money:

> . . . the erroneous belief that there are purely economic ends separate from
> the other ends of life.
>
> Yet, apart from the pathological case of the miser, there is no such thing.
> The ultimate ends of the activities of reasonable beings are never eco-
> nomic. . . . What in ordinary language is misleadingly called the "economic
> motive" means merely the desire for general opportunity, the desire for
> power to achieve unspecified ends. If we strive for money, it is because it
> offers us the widest choice in enjoying the fruits of our efforts. . . . Money
> is one of the greatest instruments of freedom ever invented by man.

Here you can see the interface between the stuff economy and the attention
economy.

If managing is an affair of motive mixing, then productivity is a matter
of motive mixing, too, of encouraging the flow in both directions, from the
extremes inward and from the center outward. To clarify the argument, let
me cite two extreme examples from World War II, the Bletchley Park code-

breaking establishment in England and the Manhattan Project, which made the atom bomb in the United States.

Work at Bletchley Park was exhausting, nonstop, and intellectually demanding to a surpassing degree. Both generative flows that we've been describing operated at full force. The practical purpose could hardly have been more exigent. Break the German codes and win the war; don't break them and lose it. Immense power flowed from the center outward. But code breaking depends on formal problem solving or playing with a code until it comes clear. The people good at it were people who liked to solve problems for their own sake: chess players, crossword puzzle players, scholars of dead languages, rarified mathematicians—people good at intellectual play. All the powers of play had to be invoked. And the struggle to win the game was equally strong. They had to come in first. Beat the Germans. Both motives operated equally strongly and in a rich roiling mixture. The people who worked there look back on it as the most exciting time of their lives, the time when they felt most engaged, most fulfilled, worked most to purpose.

The Manhattan Project evoked the same powerful mixture and the same sense of landmark labor, of productivity, but the management lesson played itself out more clearly. Physics was, and is, a discipline full of macho competition. A Nobel game. Ambition was the air universally breathed. Yet the play mentality was equally needed for the task in hand. And that task, the practical purpose, was momentous. Get the bomb before the Germans did or lose the war. A manager was needed who could orchestrate both directions of the flow. Normally, someone like General Leslie Groves would have been appointed. A creature of the center with the many talents of the center, he could understand neither the career game of physics nor the mentality of play. But, almost miraculously, Robert Oppenheimer was appointed, General Groves being added as business manager, as balancing liaison with the outside world. Oppenheimer understood both extremes and knew how to orchestrate them. That is what makes the Manhattan Project such a good lesson in management, in how to mix human motives for maximum yield.

I don't mean to suggest by these examples that such rich mixtures of motive occur only in war. Working at Apple Computer in the beginning, or at Microsoft, must have provided the same kind of intense mixture. And the world of ordinary work offers continual examples. But the crucible of war paints the mixture in exemplary colors.

If toys don't provide the sole dynamic, Hoffer was certainly right to single them out as the great neglected power. The play motive has from the begin-

nings of Western culture been denigrated. Its very name, like style and ornament, is tainted. Play is always opposed to purpose just as style is always opposed to substance. Purpose is serious; play is not. The genre that has always
stigmatized the play motive and despised toys is satire. The satirist's enemy
is excess, excess in diet, behavior, clothes, pomp. But the common ground for
all these kinds of sin is stylistic self-consciousness. Against the mountain of
human folly created by stylistic hungers is juxtaposed good sense, plain purpose, useful clothes, pewter instead of gold. The locus classicus, the prime example, of this genre is Sir Thomas More's *Utopia*. There everything that More
despised in the world around him, all the examples of excess, all the toys,
all the style is abolished in favor of a regime of rigorous plain purpose and
pure substance that has supplied both the model and the name for collective
enterprise ever since. More's mantle has been worn most notably in our time
by Thorstein Veblen, whose condemnation of "conspicuous consumption"
has formed part of our guilt portfolio about stuff ever since. More taught us
how and why to hate stuff and Veblen brought the argument up to date.

We might focus these three places on the motive spectrum by using the
word "serious" to define them. What do we mean when we say someone is a
serious person? Well, a serious doll collector is fully committed to the hobby
of doll collecting, spending far too much time and money serving this enthusiasm. A serious lawyer is one who bills ninety hours a week. But if that
lawyer should be elevated to the bench, the serious judge who results must
consider the whole spectrum of motive in trying to adjudicate human behavior. Seriousness is to behavior as clarity is to writing. It sanctifies whatever
position on the spectrum one wishes to make central.

The Reality Spectrum

The simplification of stylistic judgments is like the simplification of motivational judgments. If you are to give a rich description of style and substance,
you must link these two kinds of judgment, consider style and behavior in the
same universe. Plotting motive in the same matrix as signal and perceiver
does just this. But we need one more spectrum to round out our periodic table
for communication, our matrix for style and substance. We've created locations to plot the variables for signal, for perceiver, and for motive. But we need
one more, one that plots the reality to which all the others refer. Much of
Western intellectual history has been concerned with making reality an in-
variable. It is simply out there, the reference point for all we do and think. But
the reference has varied. For Plato and the many philosophers who followed
him, it was a world of ideal forms; for the Middle Ages, it was the mind of

God; for Newtonian science, it was the laws of physics. In such worlds, we have felt equally rocklike about our selves. They were actually there inside us, whether immortal souls or a confident if disbelieving me.

But from classical Greece onward, there has always been an alternative conception of human reality: *O kosmos skene,* the world as theater. The play of the world might be God's great play or humankind's smaller ones, but the dramatic metaphor was more than a metaphor. The world was an essentially theatrical one, essentially self-conscious. That is how we experienced it. Twentieth-century social science has elaborated subplots of the *kosmos skene,* talking about social roles, presentation of self, front stage and backstage, stages of life, and so on. Theatrical thinking is as much with us as ever, though it forms part of the insincere world of artifice that we ritually condemn. So we have now a spectrum with two extremes.

> *Life as Information*   *Life as Drama*
> **Life** ————————————————————

At the left, extreme unselfconsciousness, we might consider "life as information." Here information provides the stuff of life, not stuff. Plato's world of ideal forms has been reincarnated as a world of genes, of biological forms. It is the genes that provide the templates of life, not abstract forms of human invention. We might just as easily consider the genetic basis of life as the mind of God, manifesting itself in life. However we choose to construe it, though, it provides human life at its most unselfconscious. If we are only a gene machine, the device genes have created to replicate themselves, then the self has become an epiphenomenon, part of a much larger design with which it may have vague feelings of unity but from which it has not emerged as an independent consciousness. We border here on all the arguments from Eastern religions to Emersonian transcendentalism that think of us as all part of one vast oversoul, one great organism of life. Here, too, we might locate the world of dreams and the Freudian argument for human subconsciousness.

We have now to reckon with not only a genetic substrate but with a behavioral one as well. Behavioral biology has argued that behaviors form part of our evolutionary heritage as well as genes, that indeed the behavior is regulated by the genes. Both the genetic and the behavioral worlds preexist our social one and govern its development.

And so we have a full spectrum that looks like this:

> *Life as Information*   *Life as Stuff*   *Life as Drama*
> **Life** ————————————————————

Both extremes have been focused and reinforced by digital technology. The left-hand extreme has been reinforced by the arguments of formal communications theory invented by Claude Shannon and by the metamorphic powers of a polyvalent digital code. There, as we have seen, the information precedes the printout we choose, the way we choose to incarnate the information in the world of stuff. The world as theater has intensified all the techniques of digital representation. Simulation, the conversion of conceptual thought into a theatrical equivalent, has become a dominant form of expression. Virtual reality, its real-time equivalent, imposes an omnipresent theatrical self-consciousness on the synthetic reality it creates. Perhaps the most revolutionary reinforcement of life as theater has come, however, from the new discipline of artificial life. Artificial life is the name given to the creation of new forms of life entirely within digital computers, life that evolves according to Darwinian principles but entirely within silicon, not in carbon-based matter, stuff. Life as purely information turns out to be essentially theatrical, radically self-conscious. Again, as with the Tour de France, the extremes attract one another.

Both of these extremes, then, are flooding the troubled middle ground of commonsense stuff-based reality with a confusing and disorienting self-consciousness. If we have to treat self-consciousness as a sin, in the way we have been accustomed to, there won't be much life left in which to be virtuous. Manifestly, our way of thinking about communication, and about how it works in human life, requires the expanded matrix we have constructed here.

OK. What have we constructed?

We started by redeeming the central villain in how we pay attention to the world: self-consciousness. In a textual signal, it need not be a sin. Objects in the world can be constructed to call attention to themselves in all kinds of ways, none intrinsically superior to the other. The long established cliché that the best art is the art that conceals art is a half truth. It supplies no general rule because it omits much of what it claims to have generated the rule from. As with Mies van der Rohe's Farnsworth House, you do notice the art that is concealed. The better the art, the more it is concealed, the more you notice it. That's why we call it better.

But we can consider art not as objects but as ways of seeing objects, as argued in chapter 2. If objects can invite us to look through them or at them, or alternate from at to through using a particular frequency of oscillation between them, then our attention can operate in the same way. Our attention is richest and most powerful when it oscillates between everything that *at* vision does and everything that *through* vision does. And this variation will operate concomitantly with the variation in the signal itself. A particular act of attention will connect a point on one spectrum with a point on another. Together they will constitute knowledge.

"Wisdom," Whitehead tells us in *The Aims of Education*, is "how knowledge is held." The central villainy in the diagram of attention constructed here is not self-consciousness but shutting the at/through oscillation down. When this fruitful oscillation, at a particular point on one spectrum or between spectra, shuts down, then atrophy begins. Francis Bacon saw this in the seventeenth century, when he was pondering how knowledge should be held: "Surely, like as many substances in nature that are solid do putrefy and corrupt into worms, so it is the property of good and sound knowledge to putrefy and dissolve into a number of subtle, idle, unwholesome, and (as I may term them) vermiculate questions, which have indeed a kind of quickness and life of spirit, but no soundness of matter or goodness of quality." Good and sound knowledge requires that questions be always submitted to testing in the world, that the play of theory be immersed in the game of practice. Good and sound knowledge requires, too, that soundness of matter and goodness of quality be continually leavened with the quickness and life of spirit. How we look, and how what we look at asks to be seen, exist in continually changing combinations. If we rule out our stylistic self-consciousness, we rule out the powers of mind that allow us to oscillate between the combinations.

We can, here, avail ourselves of an analogy from the world of electronic music. The Russian scientist and musician Lev Theremin invented a musical instrument that generated a sine wave between two electrical poles. The performer then made music by moving her hands between these two poles, thereby altering the frequency and amplitude of the audio signal. Exactly so do we act in the world, taking a basic oscillation in how we view the world and varying its frequency and amplitude in infinite ways. Game, play, and the central purpose created by their collaboration is always, as we make our way in the world, being mixed in different proportions. Energy flows only when we are waving our hands about!

By now we have moved to the bottom two spectrums of behavior. Let me here invoke an observation from Peter Drucker's first book, *The End of Economic Man*. "Economics as a social or 'moral' science dealing with the social behavior of man and with institutions devised by him, can only claim to be a science if the economic sphere is regarded as autonomous, if not as supreme, and economic aims as desirable over and above all others. Otherwise economics can offer only a historical or classifying description or technical rules for realizing certain economic intentions. But it can supply no 'laws' of economic cause and effect—the criterion of a science." I've been arguing that, in an economics of attention, the economic sphere is not autonomous. The "buying decision" that allocates the scarce commodity of attention is a complex one. It cannot be resolved into a simple choice between selfishness and altruism. The caprices of voluntary agents do indeed laugh at calculation. Information purchases must assess the informational signal, the category of information the perceiver is prepared to perceive, the motivational structure that animates the communication, and the global assumptions about the human world within which human communication takes place. In an economics of attention, we must ask not only how people go about achieving their goals but where the goals come from. Economics in an information economy is about how choices of attention are made and, thus, about human motive. That is what the matrix analyzes into its constituent parts.

To the degree that style and substance change places in an attention economy, it is vital that we be able to relate judgments of the one sort to judgments of the other, to put style and substance into relationships that are as complex as human reality. Only thus can we define either one. We can no longer afford to trivialize the one and reify the other by the words we use to describe them. If, as I've been arguing here, both can be plotted on a common matrix of self-consciousness, we have an integral, and not simply a metaphorical, way of relating them. Any time we discriminate between style and substance, we have made a fixation on all four spectra in the matrix. That self-consciousness should turn out to be a vital, perhaps the vital, variable, should not surprise us. Western culture has been confronting a crisis of self-consciousness ever since the Renaissance, doubly so since Darwin, and triply so since the invention of the new cultural notation, the new literacy, created by the digital expressive field. Coming to terms with self-consciousness means coming to terms with the kind of being we are. We have been sedulously dodging this audit since the Renaissance. The stigmatizing of stylistic self-consciousness is important not least because it points so directly to the similar and larger stigma attached to human motive and human reality. A single matrix, a "place or enveloping element," that aligns these similar variables will help us more candidly and capaciously to confront and understand them and, hence, ourselves.

In chapter I, I quoted Walter Wriston's plea for "a model of economics of information that will schematize its form and functions." The first step in schematizing the form and functions of an information economy is to establish what "style" and "substance" mean and how they are related. It is a complex and dynamic relationship, the one that the matrix of expression I've set forth aspires to model.

Background Conversations

The Quarrel between Style and Substance

A quarrel as old as human life, surely, but Plato's dismissal of art in *The Republic* can serve as a starting point. This earthly paradise of central planning requires that style, and the stylistic motive that drives social and economic change, be banished along with the human family and other frivolities. Eric Havelock's *A Preface to Plato* discusses the logic of this repudiation and makes of his inquiry a detective story. Plato's argument was restated archetypally in Sir Thomas More's *Utopia,* and I tried, in an article called "The Choice of Utopias," to contrast it with Baldesar Castiglione's *The Book of the Courtier,* a utopia embracing rather than repudiating style. Most utopias from then until now, when Bin Laden trains his cannon on religious sculpture in Afghanistan, have repudiated style, seeing in it the sources of social change that they most want to banish. The hatred of style has often surfaced in religious disputation as hatred of the theater, or cosmetics, or all adornment. Jonas Barish provides a rich chronicle of this hatred in *The Anti-Theatrical Prejudice.*

Cultures based on style rather than substance illuminate this debate. The anthropologist Clifford Geertz describes Balinese culture in two elegantly written essays, "Person, Time, and Conduct in Bali" and "Deep Play: Notes on the Balinese Cockfight," in *The Interpretation of Cultures.* And Luigi Barzini's classic, *The Italians,* portrays a more familiar Western civilization, one notoriously—at least for northern Europeans—based on style as substance.

Recently, people have begun to awaken to stylistic innovation as an economic driver. Virginia Postrel, in an article called "The Aesthetic Economy," quotes Mark Dziersk, president of the Industrial Designers Society of America: "When you're selling computers based on their personality and color choices, these are new rules." They are rules in which style and substance change places. Dziersk again: "We're seeing design creep into everything, *everything.*" In her recent *Substance of Style,* Postrel develops this argument at length. Such an economic force, one the American literary critic Morse Peckham called "nonfunctional stylistic dynamism," is not one currently taught in business schools but it requires no particular perspicacity to see that it should be.

The Farnsworth House

If you'd like to know more about this masterpiece of reductionist domestic ar-
chitecture, the place to start is Franz Schulze's *Mies van der Rohe: A Critical Biography.* If you'd like to see the house in person, and it is a rare treat, you're in
luck. The house was up for sale but the National Trust for Historic Preservation,
with the aid of other groups, has now bought it and will keep it in its original location and open to the public.

Vacuum Behavior

I first began to think about vacuum behavior, behavior that occurs spontaneously, without an external cause, with Konrad Lorenz's famous anecdote in
On Aggression.

> A hand-reared starling that I owned many years ago had never in its life
> caught flies nor seen any other bird do so. All his life he had taken his food
> from a dish, filled daily. One day I saw him sitting on the head of a bronze
> statue in my parents' Viennese flat, and behaving most remarkably. With his
> head on one side, he seemed to be examining the white ceiling, then his head
> and eye movements gave unmistakable signs that he was following moving
> objects. Finally he flew off the statue and up to the ceiling, snapped at some-
> thing invisible to me, returned to his post, and performed the prey-killing
> movements peculiar to all insect-eating birds. Then he swallowed, shook him-
> self, as many birds do at the moment of inner relaxation, and settled down
> quietly.

But there was no insect there. The circuits for this behavior wanted to fire and,
absent a stimulus, fired anyway, in a vacuum.

Scale this argument up, and it calls into question our effort to make sense
of past or present. "The ever-recurrent phenomena of history do not have reasonable causes. . . . Unreasoning and unreasonable human nature causes two
nations to compete, though no economic necessity compels them to do so; it in-
duces two political parties or religions with amazingly similar programs of salvation to fight each other bitterly, and it impels an Alexander or a Napoleon to
sacrifice millions of lives in his attempt to unite the world under his scepter."
Why do we behave this way? Our inherited evolutionary baggage. But no historian can leave it at that. There have to be "reasonable" explanations for the unreasonable behavior, economic competition, religious animosity, demographic
imbalance. Thus we can argue that, using the terms of our motive spectrum,
both play and game are vacuum behaviors, just waiting to happen. If this is
so, it is odd that, in our efforts to manage our affairs, we readily acknowledge

the power of competition, of game, as a motivator, but we rarely reckon the powers of play, of the myriad things we want to do because we want to do them. They seem an unpredictable factor in the equation and so we tacitly agree to ignore them.

Lorenz is arguing for the origin of style and stylistic behavior in play. "The human who has at his command many different kinds of skillful movements is simply incapable of not putting them into action, of not playing with them—and through a combination of such skill and play *art* emerges." And play has to remain pure: "Expressed in another way: play and exploratory behavior have their own motivations; neither playing nor exploring, as activities, ever appears in the service of another specific motivation."

So Lorenz argued for the play sphere as outside the sphere of purpose. Geoffrey Miller, in *The Mating Mind,* argues the opposite case. The ornamental frivolities that we usually group under the loose label of "style" actually evolved to further sexual selection. They thus are essentially purposive, could not be more so. Style is part of, the creation of, sexual selection. And so sexual selection provides the fullest explanation of the relationship of style and substance. Style evolved to fulfill the sexual selection that creates human substance. They are linked at the deepest level of human evolution, and profoundly linked, one might say entangled, in the structure of the human mind. If this is so, then the paradoxical relationships that we've been considering here seem less paradoxical. They are, in fact, just what we would expect. Miller's argument is a complex one, though presented in sparkling prose aimed at the general reader. Its weakness, to this same general reader, may be not that it does not explain enough but that, by the time Miller has finished, it seems to have explained almost everything.

One thing that it does seem to explain, though Miller does not couch it in these terms, is the origins of rhetoric. Here's what he says about his explanatory metaphors: "My metaphors for explaining this theory will come more from marketing, advertising, and the entertainment industry than from physics or genetics." From, that is, aspects of rhetoric as currently practiced. He seems to argue—I hope I'm summarizing and paraphrasing him correctly—that the human mind evolved to create the rhetoric necessary for sexual selection. If so, might we not consider his argument as an evolutionary explanation of the economics of attention? Read *The Mating Mind* and see what you think.

The Joy of the Working

I've always wondered about the argument that humanists make for their work, that it is pursued "for its own sake." It is a useful justification, for it stops dead any inquiry into what the humanities are about, or how well they are being pursued. But there is a large kernel of truth at the heart of the argument—"the joy of the working." And it is not limited to humanist inquiry. Walter Bagehot once cautioned—I am quoting from memory—that "to illustrate a principle you must exaggerate much and you must omit much." To flesh out my argument for the play motive, soften the exaggerations, and fill in the omissions, let me give some instances.

You see it when the champion steeplechase jockey and champion thriller writer, Dick Francis, explains why he rode horses:

> The real reason for my being a jockey, however, was not to be found in the freedom, the friendships or the traveling that I enjoyed, or even in the great satisfaction of winning races: and it was not in the means it gave me of earning a living either, for if I had been a millionaire I would still have been a jockey. The simple fact is that I liked riding horses, and I liked the speed and challenge of racing.
>
> I cannot explain why all jockeys, amateurs as well as professionals, are happy to take pain, cold and disappointment in their stride as long as there are horses for them to race on. Why do people climb mountains, or swim the Channel? Why do people swing on trapezes or explore [caves]? Because they can, they want to and, in some obscure way, they feel they must.

Or, he might have added, train for years to compete in Olympic single-scull rowing, as David Halberstam describes it in *The Amateurs: The Story of Four Young Men and Their Quest for an Olympic Gold Medal*. Rowing as a sport attracts neither attention nor money. Single-scull rowing is a classic case of how complex the joy of the working can be, how the motive spectrum can bend itself into a circle, with game and play drawn together. You might think that it is a case of pure competition, where "winning is everything." The more you learn about it, however, the more simple-minded this seems. Winning a race is a measure of efficiency in effort, and in rowing this efficiency is a complex affair. The game impulse drives it, but so does the intense formal loyalty to form and self-discipline. It is a hard, lonely game to play. The training is brutal; you row until it hurts, and it keeps on hurting, and you keep on rowing. When you see a gold medalist rowing at dawn, her perfect strokes floating her boat on the rising mist, as I did one morning while I was trying to extricate my shell from a mud bank, it seems magical. But there is nothing magical in the living of it. As Halberstam points out, amateur rowers usually come from well-to-do families. "One could understand the son of a ghetto family playing in the school yard for six hours a day hoping that basketball was a ticket out of the slum; it was harder to understand the son of Beacon Hill spending so much time and subjecting himself to so much pain to attain an honor that no one else even understood. Perhaps in our society the true madness in the search for excellence is left for the amateur." Beyond excellence, though, there seems to lurk a goal less easy to admit: purity. Rowing does seem to be something you do, finally, "for its own sake." Amid all the competition, finally pure play.

Scholars often wish that the world would leave them alone, so they could go about their work in library or laboratory without interruption. The scholarly paradise in the classical world was a shady grove of trees in springtime and a group of congenial spirits talking together. In the past century, it was a more solitary affair, an isolated cabin in New Hampshire where you could, like Eric Havelock writing his masterful *The Liberal Temper in Greek Politics,* sit beside a wood stove and compose "the entire first draft in a sort of sustained fury of composition." For most American scholars, such periods of pure concentration have come seldom, amid all the other legitimate activities (I had first written "distractions") of university life.

Barbara McClintock, a classical geneticist who studied maize, spent her entire career in such pure dedication. Evelyn Fox Keller describes her extraordinary life and work in *A Feeling for the Organism: The Life and Work of Barbara McClintock.* Her cabin in New Hampshire was the Long Island Biological Laboratories at Cold Spring Harbor, and there she did work that, initially unfashionable, later brought her wide recognition. But the recognition was not sought and left her uncomfortable and wishing for the isolation of her laboratory. At one time she worked for two years on a problem without result. A colleague asked her how she could "have worked for two years without knowing what was going to come out." She replied: "It never occurred to me that there was going to be any stumbling block. Not that I had the answer but [I had] *the joy of going at it. When you have that joy you do the right experiments."* The pure "joy of the working." McClintock was a natural solitary, needing no companionship. ("There was not that strong necessity for a personal attachment to anybody. I just didn't feel it. And I could never understand marriage.") Her life provides a remarkable instance of scholarship as total concentration, as pure play.

A different version of this concentration, less alembicated, can be found in the life and career of the British electronics engineer Alan Dower Blumlein. Never heard of him? You've got company. He was so uninterested in fame that, though he registered his work in patents, he almost never wrote it up. It was the "joy of going at it" that led him on. His accomplishments were great, and they have been set out in great detail in a recent biography, Robert Charles Alexander's *The Inventor of Stereo: The Life and Works of Alan Dower Blumlein*. Blumlein seems the opposite of McClintock. He lived in the world, married, had children, worked as engineers do, in groups. And his work all went toward applications, again as engineers do. He invented the high-quality microphones and the lateral cutting system that made possible LP records. And he arguably did "invent stereo." And that was not all: "Telegraphic networks that linked countries and continents; submarine cables; much of the infrastructure of the 405-line high definition television systems." He was doing important work in radar when, in 1942, the Halifax bomber in which he was working crashed and he was killed at the age of thirty-nine. Each reader can assess the importance and originality of Blumlein's work, for Alexander gives detailed descriptions of it and reproduces the crucial patents. Blumlein did not "stage himself to men's eyes" as some scientists and engineers soon learn to do and he needed a meticulous biographer to do it for him. He was, like McClintock, too busy with "the joy of going at it." Play motive in the pure state does not need isolation, as his career proves. But, for other people to share it, you do need to publish your work—or have a good biographer.

Hiding your light under a bushel was not James Watson's problem when he and Francis Crick were pursuing the structure of DNA. He and Crick were in a race with Linus Pauling to find the structure and win the Nobel Prize. Watson's *The Double Helix: A Personal Account of the Discovery of the Structure of DNA*, tells the story. The way to read it now is in Gunther S. Stent's edition, which includes not only the text of the book but Stent's "Review of the reviews," of the book, the reviews themselves, and a selection of the original scientific papers, including the famous 25 April 1953, "A Structure for Deoxyribose Nucleic Acid." As for the book itself, Robert Merton's review gets it about right: "This is a wonderfully candid self-portrait of the scientist as a young man in a hurry. Chattily written with pungent and ironic wit and yet with an almost clinical detachment, it provides for the scientist and the general reader alike a fascinating case-history in the psychology and sociology of science as it describes the events that led up to one of the great biological discoveries of our time."

I am not competent to comment on who deserved credit for what or on whether Rosalind Franklin was wrongfully deprived the credit that, had she lived, would have gained her a Nobel. I do want to comment on the "joy of the working" that emerges from Watson's account. The scientific community found much to take umbrage at in Watson's account when it was published. It was written in a colloquial style, and as Merton noted, "with pungent and ironic wit,"

virtues hard to forgive in scientific writing. Watson was honest about his ambitions. And, worst of all, he attained them at the age of twenty-five. Soaring
ambition he certainly had—finding "the secret of life" being about as high as
hopes can fly—but it doesn't seem to have squeezed the joy of the working out
of him, or of Crick. They found the structure of DNA, after all, by playing around
with models. Scientists, well, scholars of all sorts, would like us to think that
they are all as motivated by pure play as Barbara McClintock. Watson blows the
whistle on that. But his account is not of a man consumed by ambition, slaving
at the lab bench as the seasons pass unnoticed, or continually conniving at the
career game. The joy had not been squeezed out of his work. Perhaps that is what
some scholars found hardest of all to forgive.

There's not much joy in Carlo Rubbia's struggle for the Nobel Prize in Physics,
at least in Gary Taubes's account in *Nobel Dreams*. Rubbia did not sit on the stage
in Stockholm until he was fifty, and his career up to that time illustrates Marty
Perl's remark: "This generation of high-energy physicists could also have done
very well in the retail garment trade." In this world winning is indeed everything.

There is no joy whatever in the tale Nicholas Wade tells in *The Nobel Duel*.
It begins on the stage in Stockholm, where the two scientists who fought the
twenty-one-year duel, Roger Guillemin and Andrew Schally, sit graceless and
cross waiting for the award that has shaped their lives. The award, for "discoveries of the peptide hormones of the brain," has been spoiled for each by their
having to share it with the other. For them, science is not a collaborative effort
to explore the unknown. As Schally says: "No two laboratories working in the
same field have ever collaborated. Did Pauling collaborate with Watson and
Crick? You just simply don't collaborate—it's a race." The two men had started
out working in the same laboratory and then became bitter rivals. To the race
for the Nobel was added the race against the other. The opposite extreme to Barbara McClintock, then: pure game not pure play. One colleague of Schally remarked that "Guillemin and Schally are both militarists, they have turned themselves into warriors." Their scholarly lives were shaped by how it would play in
Stockholm. What a joyless struggle to a stage where they sat, their joyless game
ended in a tie.

As an instance of optimal flow from the middle to the extremes, and extremes
to the middle, we could hardly do better than the extraordinary life of Henry J.
Kaiser. The adventures that Albert P. Heiner recounts in *Henry J. Kaiser, Western
Colossus* were infused with the things the Nobel Prize seems to drain out of
people: joy and generosity. He left school at thirteen, became a road builder, and

then left that for larger construction projects. He was a prime actor in building Boulder Dam, Bonneville Dam, and Grand Coulee Dam. When he lost the bid for Shasta Dam, he illustrated his motto that every difficulty is an opportunity by going into the cement business and supplying the cement for Shasta. In November 1940, he offered to build thirty cargo ships for the British. He had no experience in shipbuilding and no shipyards. He built the shipyards, then the ships, then went on to revolutionize the shipbuilding business by introducing assembly line techniques. He ended up building seven shipyards, and from them 1,383 merchant ships and 107 warships emerged. He made a minor success in the steel business and a major one in the aluminum one, and a nice try attempting to break the big-three monopoly in the automobile business. His lasting monument, however, came with the Kaiser Permanente Medical Care Program, which pioneered the idea of prepaid healthcare and, thus, we might say, of the modern practice of medicine. It is a complex story, which Heiner tells in detail. The idea came from Dr. Sidney R. Garfield, and first took shape on the Coulee Dam project. Garfield was having a tough sell getting doctors interested in his ideas. Here's how he describes his first meeting with Kaiser: "I was amazed that in three hours he had grasped the essence of my plan, and had seen a wider application than I had ever dreamed of. He never lost that vision. For the nearly thirty years after that meeting, until he died, Henry Kaiser had a missionary zeal in his efforts to strengthen and broaden the health program."

Perhaps this vision came from his equally generous vision of labor relations. With the exception of one long steel strike, the labor relations of Kaiser enterprises were a model of harmony. He went out of his way to make friends with union leaders, and they reciprocated his friendship. When he was eighty-three, he was given the Murray-Green Award, "the labor movement's highest humanitarian citation."

What do we make of this extraordinary entrepreneurial career? There was plenty of competition, but he rejoiced in it and befriended his competitors. The enormous stage on which he created his projects was so much more joyful a place than the stage in Stockholm, and he romped through it like a playground. His immensely productive life drew energy in equal parts from both extremes of motive, game and play. He got extraordinary work from his employees by believing that they could do it and making them believe that they could do it. Yet the common pairing of "hard-driving" and "ruthless" didn't apply to him at all. He knew "human resources" were the primary resources before an economist got his Nobel for telling us so. And he knew theatrical presentation of self formed part of great enterprises. If you want to study human motive, the life and work of this master promoter have much to teach.

Mount Everest

The classic activity animated by the joy of the working has always been mountain climbing. Jon Krakauer has described a striking, indeed fatal, instance of the etiolation of such joy in his book about climbing Mount Everest, *Into Thin Air*. Krakauer was a recording journalist/climber accompanying an expedition in which several climbers were killed. The larger theme that emerges from this fascinating book is more general: what happens to mountain climbing when it becomes a business. Everest is climbed so often now that you need a reservation, and must pay a stiff fee, to try the ascent, and the room at the summit is often crowded. Mountain climbing used to represent the perfect instance of the magnetic attraction of pure play and pure competition, the natural magnetism of the two ends of the spectrum to bend into a circle. When guides run unqualified people to the top, and guides and climbers dramatize their ascent for television, the nobility of the climb evaporates into thin air. An extraordinary book about the spoiling not only of a mountain but of the efforts to climb it. One could think of it as an allegory of exploration as it turns into tourism.

Bletchley Park

These case histories are examples of what Justice Holmes called "the *dureté* of nature to get our work out of us." ("So I accept the motives of vanity, ambition, altruism, or whatever moves us as fact, only reserving the right to smile on half-holidays at the obvious *dureté* of nature to get our work out of us.") The motives nature employs to get our work out of us are endlessly varied and mixed, and they act always in concert with the other variables I've plotted on the matrix.

I've instanced the British code-breaking establishment at Bletchley Park as an illustration of complex motive working to great effect. Although I doubt if it has ever been used as such, it would make a wonderful case study in successful management under difficult circumstances. The breaking of the German codes enciphered using the Enigma machine forms the center of the story. Its beginnings are told in Jozef Garlinski's *The Enigma War*. David Kahn describes the breaking of the U-boat codes in *Seizing the Enigma*. F. H. Hinsley and Alan Stripp have edited a series of memoirs by people working at Bletchley: *Code Breakers: The Inside Story of Bletchley Park*. The most remarkable part of the story was how the information from the decrypts was relayed to the military commanders who could make use of it, without revealing the source or the fact that the Enigma codes were being broken in a massive and systematic way. F. W. Winterbotham tells this story in *The Ultra Secret,* and the system he describes constitutes perhaps the extreme case of an economics of attention, of allocating a scarce information source in the most adroit way possible. Winterbotham's account gets bad marks from John Keegan in his recent *Intelligence in War*—itself a series of studies of crucial battles as economies of attention—but Winterbotham makes clear the crucial role of allocating scarce information as well as anybody I've read on the Ultra secret.

The United States mounted an effort to break the Japanese codes similar to the British one at Bletchley Park, and it provides a similar lesson in motivation and management. Ronald Lewin tells this tale in *The American Magic: Codes, Ciphers and the Defeat of Japan*. The real American counterpart to Bletchley Park, as a study in motivation, was the Manhattan Project. Richard Rhodes has written the definitive history, *The Making of the Atomic Bomb*.

When I was doing cryptography in the military, I never thought of code making and breaking as an economy of attention, a series of lessons in how information can be best put to use. But it can be thought of in this way. Read David Kahn's *The Code Breakers: The Comprehensive History of Secret Communication from Ancient Times to the Internet* and see if you think such an argument can be sustained about cryptography over its long history.

No discussion of cryptography in World War II should fail to mention a wonderful and wise book that appeared in 1998, Leo Marks's *Between Silk and Cyanide: A Codemaker's War, 1941–45*. It is so funny, so sad, so profound about the ironies of information flow in a secret bureaucracy (and secret bureaucracies are the most bureaucratic of all) that it defies summary. But it teaches powerful lessons about an economics of attention when it became a life-and-death matter. Read it and laugh, and weep.

CHAPTER SIX

Let me tell you how this oddly framed article came to exist. I'll then leave it, since my argument plays a little with the legal format, just as it was published in the Houston Law Review.

My friend David Nimmer sent me a long article—in humanistic circles we'd call it a book—on a copyright action emerging from the Dead Sea Scrolls controversy. Vexed to desperation by the failure of the scholars to whom the texts were originally assigned for editing and publication, actually to publish them, other scholars obtained copies of the crucial texts and published them. Among these was the editor of the Biblical Archaeological Review, and he was in due course sued by one of the text-hoarding editors. I read David's piece with great interest, twice, and sent him a commentary on it. He, in response, asked me if I would write an essay along these lines for inclusion in a collection of essays responding to his piece. I said, as scholars usually do, "Of course."

Then, when the time came to produce the essay, I had to face the music. I wasn't a copyright scholar (all my activities in this line were in

*the practical business of expert witnessing)
and, although I knew the Dead Sea Scrolls had
created one of the longest-running and most
vicious scholarly controversies of modern times,
that was about all I knew. I poked around a bit,
read through the back numbers of the* Biblical
Archaeological Review, *and in desperation
put my fingers on the keyboard. This is what
came out.*

*P.S. In the lingo of show biz contracts, "above
the line" is where all the real money is made.
"Below the line" is profits less expenses, the expenses usually being manipulated so as to eliminate the profits.*

CHAPTER SIX {BARBIE AND THE
TEACHER OF
RIGHTEOUSNESS}

Two Lessons in the Economics of Attention

conversations about the law
CUTTING CONTINUITY—SHOW #27
BROADCAST 15 JANUARY 2001

CONVERSANTS

Boffin Pundit, J.D. Pundit is Mabel Brady Frumpkin Professor of Law, Economics, and
General Moral Goodness at the Chicago School. Broadcast television's importu-
nate demands for the legal mind have, however, enticed him onto a broader public
stage. He now hosts a series called Conversations about the Law, of which this is
one. His blue pinstripe law suit struggles to contain a telegenic floral tie.

Barbie. A life-size living doll. She wears, to start, a plain dungarees-and-blouse outfit
dating from her 1959 debut days on the American scene.

The Teacher of Righteousness. A spiritual leader of uncertain authority and provenance
but unmistakable statutory penumbra. He may be, or at least is alleged to have been,
the author of *MMT*,[1] the vital document at bar. Perhaps we'll find out more about
this later. The beard made mandatory for biblical prophets by Cecil B. DeMille
does not entirely mask a bone structure surprised, mid-morph, between Bill Moy-
ers and Pat Robertson. He wears a vermiculated robe of coarse brown homespun.

---

1. REFERENCE FOOTNOTE. *MMT* is the commonly used abbreviation for *miqsat ma'ase ha-Torah*,
meaning "some precepts of the Torah." Six copies of *MMT* were found in Cave 4 of Khirbet Qumran
and are part of the Dead Sea Scrolls. David Nimmer, *Copyright in the Dead Sea Scrolls: Authorship and
Originality*, 38 HOUS. L. REV. 1, 55–56 (2001).

The Author. The voice of the abolished, or at least marginalized, or at very least dis-
credited, writer of a text. He is an emeritus professor of English and wears the standard costume for a male academic: faded chinos and wrinkled sport shirt from the
Goodwill.

A Chorus of Footnotes. Solo or "above-the-line" footnotes rise between the sofa cushions
to speak. Choral footnotes remain marginalized "below-the-line" but may speak
in their individual voices. They are a small group but, as we shall see, feisty.

SETTING

The Conversations about the Law are set in a virtual reality where the constraints of
time and space have long since ceased to matter. The participants are seated on a
semicircular sofa composed of very large marshmallow cushions spaced out pre-
cariously on a stainless steel frame.[2] The design allows room for, and shows off to
a marvel, Barbie's sudden costume changes. It also permits solo Footnotes to appear, like the ghost of Hamlet's father, from beneath the platform.
The sofa sits on a stage that floats on a stream of hot air.

TIME

The time is the Interminable Present of a TV talk show.

THE CONVERSATION

Boffin Pundit: The text we have been reading this week is David Nimmer's long article—well, book, really—in the *Houston Law Review* on the *Qimron v. Shanks* case.[3]
And Author here [*he makes a slightly dismissive gesture toward Author*] has been asked
to comment on it by Mr. Nimmer. Right, Author?

Author: Yes, and I . . .

Boffin Pundit: And you thought that Miss Mattel here could somehow clarify the issue
of Professor Qimron's textual agonies and the . . .

Barbie: That's OK, Boffo. You can just call me Barbie. Everyone does.

Boffin Pundit: . . . resulting lawsuit. Yes, well, we'll see what she has to say for herself.

Author: Yes, and I thought that the Teacher of Righteousness . . .

Boffin Pundit: Of course, of course, he had to be here. And we are certainly looking
forward to what *he* has to say for himself. Especially since those funkstick editors

---

2. STYLISTIC FOOTNOTE. Because this conversation is about scholarly credit, Author ought to have
confessed here that he had in mind a sofa produced by George Nelson for Herman Miller, but—such
are the vagaries of who gets credit for what—actually designed by Irving Harper. There's a good picture of it in Leslie Piña's *Fifties Furniture* (LESLIE PIÑA, FIFTIES FURNITURE 108 [1996]).

3. See, generally, Nimmer, *supra*, n. 1.

he's saddled with keep playing career games and won't tell us what he said, if indeed he said it. We are, as I mentioned to you all earlier, the first legal conversation show to discuss Nimmer's work. We are thus breaking new ground here, and I expect fine lines from all of you during the course of the show. Do you want to start things off, Teacher?

Teacher of Righteousness: Thank you, Professor Pundit. I am, of course, delighted to be here and to finally say a few words for myself. Though I will admit to being a little jet-lagged from a very long flight, it did give me time to read Professor Nimmer's admirable essay carefully.

Boffin Pundit: And what did you think? He certainly writes well, doesn't he? What a relief from the usual law and economics stuff I have to wade through. Jokes, too.

Barbie: I'll say. It's written for people with a sense of style.

Teacher of Righteousness: Jokes? Where? I didn't notice those.

Boffin Pundit: Well, no, not jokes, really—this is a serious legal argument—more like plays on words, verbal wit, that sort of thing. Our Stylistic Footnote can give some examples while we get on with the main discussion.[4]

---

4. STYLISTIC FOOTNOTE: I'm usually gagged and bound in a legal environment, if not banished altogether, so it is a pleasure to comment on Nimmer's style here. First of all, I want to praise the way he moves from the easy manner of a middle style to the more formal manner of the law. He does not shrink from a plain colloquial phrase when it fits—a claim "functions as the ultimate wedding party-pooper"—but nor does he hesitate to call up the suitable term of art when another claim "seriously overreaches" (Nimmer, *supra*, n. 1, at 89). And his fondness for word play—"dexterous or sinister, gauche or adroit," and "To the Middle East from West"—continually focuses attention on the central issue in this case, the precise meaning of words (*id.* at 6, 43). He is even willing to verge on a joke, as in the humorous *periphrasis*, "the Admiral whose name eventually became eponymous with Columbia Pictures" (*id.* at 16). He is not only precise in his choice of metaphors, he allows his style to be a little self-conscious about them. To wit:

"Peeling further layers off the onion yields more tears" (*id.* at 116).

"[T]he works of authorship that she has brought to term in her womb" (*id.* at 136).

"In other words, for Qimron to turn a phrase nicely to achieve a pleasing esthetic effect would be for him to leave the realm of history, for which his visa was stamped, and to enter the realm of literature, in which he is an illegal alien" (*id.* at 125 [footnote omitted]).

"[H]ow copyright protection should be titrated in order to produce the most potent mixture benefiting future authorship" (*id.* at 135).

I'm even going to charge Nimmer with *felicitous phrasing.* When he told us, of Judge Jacobs's approach to an argument, that he "alighted on it independently," one sees the judge coming to rest on his point like an eagle settling delicately on a suitable branch from which to dive down on his victim (*id.* at 47). And the wonderful names he invents for his fictional (whoops! his *hypothetical*) cases—M. C. A. *Wasserman* is my favorite but *Sy Kadique* comes in a strong second—must not go unremarked (*id.* at 16–17 [discussing the hypothetical case of whether M.C.A. Wassermann has a copyright in a flowing fountain], and *id.* at 30–31 [detailing the hypothetical case of whether Dr. Kefalos has a copyright in Kadique's character]).

Don't we see, throughout, a creative writer peeping out from between the case citations? Nimmer seems, in fact, to exhibit a disturbing kind of professional schizophrenia in this essay, the lawyer always threatening to morph into a biblical commentator or, worse, a literary critic. I am not our Psy-

Teacher of Righteousness: I hope I appreciated Professor Nimmer's lighter side as well as anyone, but I was deeply troubled by one assumption that he made throughout. He says, you'll remember, that "[c]opyright protection requires the subjective choice of an author in order for protection to lie."[5] And he argues, proceeding from here, that the author of *MMT* has a copyright lasting at least until 2002.

Boffin Pundit: Yes, of course. Clever argument, don't you think?

Teacher of Righteousness: Well, Mr. Pundit, I'm not a lawyer, only a lawgiver, philosopher really, but the author of *MMT*—I knew him well, of course, the Cave Men called him their Spiritual Leader—wasn't *creating* anything when he wrote the documents (there were at least half a dozen) from which the now-famous *MMT* document has been assembled by Professors Strugnell and Qimron. He was simply transcribing the Word of God, as it had been given him to understand it. This was not Creation but Fact; not Aesthetic but Scientific Truth. Especially the part about the calendar . . .

Author: Yes, that's why I thought he should . . .

Barbie: For the rest of us, though, it's just another opinion, isn't it? Maybe even the invention of a deranged prophet, and so entirely fictional.

Teacher of Righteousness: No, no, the whole Cave Man community where he dwelt believed that it was the Word of . . .

Boffin Pundit: Wait a minute, Teacher. Do you mean you *didn't write MMT*?

Teacher of Righteousness: No, No. Of course I didn't. Does it sound like the work of a philosopher?

Barbie: Tell me, Teacher, reading Nimmer's article made me wonder, when you live in a cave, where do you keep your *clothes*?

Teacher of Righteousness: Clothes? The Cave Men didn't wear clothes. Well, I mean, not in your sense of the word, vulgar adornments of the person, the invitation to pride and . . .

Barbie: . . . and, much later of course, after Marx, to the crassest kind of late Capitalistic fetishist consumerist commodification. Yes, yes, we know all about that. But are you sure that you spiritual leaders don't flatter yourselves sometimes that your robe is just a little bit more worm-eaten than the others?

---

chological Footnote but, as the Stylistic Footnote, I ought to say this: I am sure that Nimmer understands how dangerous an entertaining prose style can be in a legal career, but I hope he understands that it is the kiss of death if he aspires to be a literary critic. It would be a pity if he damaged his career for want of a kind word in his ear. Although, on second thought, someone who has worked in the Dead Sea Scrolls disputes must know as much about humorlessness as is possible to learn.

5. REFERENCE FOOTNOTE. Nimmer, *supra*, n. 1, at 22 & n.75.

Teacher of Righteousness: Of course I'm sure. That would be style, not substance. And even down in the Health Spa where I lived, style was suspect.[6] Ornament was thought to be a creature of . . .

Barbie: How well I know it. The hatred of style has haunted me all my life. You can do a lot with it, though. Even the angels use it. Watch. [*She metamorphoses into Harp-Angel Barbie.*]

Author: Not surprising, really, because that's what you represent. That's why I invited . . . My God . . . [*noticing the metamorphosis*]

Boffin Pundit: Let's get back on the beam, Teacher. What about Barbie's question? How do *we* know that you are taking dictation from God? Nimmer's whole argument about *MMT*'s still being in copyright falls to the ground if the author was just taking dictation from God about How Things Are.

Teacher of Righteousness: Copyright in Divine Writ? Nonsense. How could he do that? Why . . .

Boffin Pundit: You'd have to find His agent first.

   [*Humor Footnote pops up between the cushions.* Honestly, Boffin. There's a limit to stale Hollywood jokes. *Footnote disappears.*]

Teacher of Righteousness: I *started to say* that, why, that would be like Saint Paul syndicating his letters to the Corinthians.

Barbie: OK, OK, but what were you going to say about the "whole community"?

Teacher of Righteousness: Only that they all agreed that the Spiritual Leader's writings were Holy Writ. They were too important to the whole civilization for the question of private ownership to arise. That's where Nimmer begins his essay, after all, isn't it? Pondering how a vital cultural document like *MMT* could be owned by, well, by somebody like Professor Qimron. Inconceivable, he thought, before *Qimron v. Shanks* forced him to conceive it.[7]

---

6. ARCHAEOLOGICAL FOOTNOTE. This is not the place to enter into the heated debate (in the world of the Dead Sea Scrolls, there are no cool debates) about the relationship between the caves and the excavated Qumran site below. The heated debate about the excavated site turns on what it was. A monastery? A Roman-type *villa rustica*, where rich Jerusalemites came to cool down and off? A ritual cleansing center for the Essene sect? For a full discussion, see Hershel Shanks, *The Qumran Settlement—Monastery, Villa or Fortress?* BIBLICAL ARCHAEOLOGY REV., May/June 1993, at 62. The Teacher of Righteousness's description of it as a *spa* would seem to make sense of all three suggestions. The delicate glass unguentaria found on the site, for example, would make perfect sense for massage oil, but not much for religious contemplation.

   AUTHOR'S FOOTNOTE. While we are on the subject of the *Biblical Archaeology Review*, the Author would like to thank his good friend Jay Blum for the loan of a full run of *Biblical Archaeology Review* so that the *MMT* story could be read as breaking news.

   7. Nimmer, *supra*, n. 1, 69(iii) P.M. 10.

Boffin Pundit: Interesting you should bring up this subject, Teacher. A book came out just last year talking about this very subject—it was called *Playing Darts with a Rembrandt*—and we discussed it on the program.[8]

Barbie: But did they *all* agree that the *MMT* material was canonical? Didn't one little apple of discord drop into the scene? [*At this point, Harp-Angel Barbie metamorphoses into the original 1959 striped swimsuit Barbie, an apple of discord if ever you saw one.*]

Teacher of Righteousness: Of course they all . . . [*He stops, stricken dumb with Barbie's transformation*] they all . . .

Boffin Pundit: Honestly, Barbie, give the Teacher a break. Up in the caves, the women didn't wear swimsuits.

Barbie: Of course. [*She metamorphoses into Archaeologist Barbie, sweaty bush jacket, sunbleached hat, smudged face.*]

Teacher of Righteousness: Wait a minute. Let's get one thing perfectly clear. I *did not* live up in the caves. I lived *down below* in the Qumran Spiritual Health Spa. And there weren't any women in the caves. They didn't believe in them.

Boffin Pundit: Huh? You've got to tell us about this.

Teacher of Righteousness: Well, I worked at the *spa*. The Spiritual Health Spa. I was the resident Spiritual Philosopher. Our clients were busy people from Jerusalem who were overcome with the pressures of city life and with, well, spiritual doubts. Was the race worth it? What did it all finally amount to? That sort of thing. They came to us to decompress, relax in the baths, talk about something besides money, for a change. Spiritual enrichment.

Boffin Pundit: Wait a minute . . . so you didn't write *MMT*?

Teacher of Righteousness: No, no, of course not. It was written by the Spiritual Leader of the Cave Men. They used to live down in the flats ages ago, but when the Spirit of Zeal came among them, they moved up into the caves to escape the pollution of their fellow persons. They'd been in the caves for donkey's years when I was offered the *Righteousness* job in the spa. These guys were, not to put too fine a point on it, a little wacko. No women, nothing but ritual cleanliness and virtue.[9] So when they "went up," as they called it, the women left behind remodeled the whole area into the Spiritual Health spa. The ritual baths were expanded to real spa stan-

---

8. REFERENCE FOOTNOTE. JOSEPH L. SAX, PLAYING DARTS WITH A REMBRANDT: PUBLIC AND PRIVATE RIGHTS IN CULTURAL TREASURES (1999). Someone should option that dynamite title!

9. REFERENCE FOOTNOTE. Pliny the Elder talks about them as follows: "On the west side of the Dead Sea, away from the coast, . . . lives the solitary tribe of the Essenes. This tribe is remarkable beyond all the others in the whole world, because it has no women, has rejected sexual desires, is without money and has only the company of palm-trees" (PLINY THE ELDER, NATURAL HISTORY: A SELECTION 61 [John F. Healy trans., 1991] [footnote omitted]).

dards, and of course there was still that terrific view of the mountains from every room and . . .[10]

Author: Could we get back to *MMT*? The Cave Men all agreed on its canonicity. But when they didn't, who would decide . . .

Barbie: Exactly. Who would decide what is canonical and thus exempt from ownership? Sax—I read his book because of the discussion about antiquities at the end—all but says that it should be some agency of the government.[11] But what would *they* do? Appoint a bunch of experts like the Israel Antiquities Authority. And what would *they* do? Appoint . . .

Boffin Pundit: . . . appoint the collection of pompous, constipated, scroll-hoarders whom they did appoint. Some improvement. . . . But wait a minute, Barbie. You seem to have changed shape when you changed into your Barbie Archaeologist outfit.

Barbie: Yes, courtesy of my chaperones at Mattel. I'm here as the new inoffensive, plain Jane, make everybody feel good, flatter-chested Barbie.

Boffin Pundit: Well, what's wrong with that? Now all those envious women won't be eating their hearts out that. . . .[12]

Barbie: What's wrong with that? I'll tell you what's wrong with it. A more hegemonical violation of my personhood would be hard to imagine. I mean, suppose someone had come along to you, Boffo, and proposed to cut a couple of inches off your . . .

Boffin Pundit: That's enough, Barb.

Barbie: . . . so that you ended up looking like poor Ken with his shrunken little funsack.[13]

---

10. Our ARCHAEOLOGY FOOTNOTE comments: It has been suggested that all the oversized water-handling capacity was there to provide for the heavy-duty purification ceremonies the Essenes required, but we may take the Teacher's comment as finally putting that rather contrived conjecture to bed.

11. *See* SAX, *supra*, n. 8, at 179 (discussing how an authority decides if an item should be acquired in the public interest).

12. REFERENCE FOOTNOTE. The reader may need some help here about this *really* heated controversy. In 1997, Mattel announced that they were going to sell a new Barbie with a more "realistic" figure: broader hips and smaller breasts. It was front page news. Whether this effort to meet political-correctness critics by making the *femme* less *fatale* will succeed only time will tell. It is no wonder, in the meanwhile, that Barbie is indignant at what has been done to her by this reverse plastic surgery.

13. REFERENCE FOOTNOTE. The common reader needs more help here, too. The debate about the origin and nature of Ken's "genital bulge," as it is chastely referred to, has been as heated as the debate about the origin and nature of *MMT*. Ken was of course Barbie's boyfriend, but he came out of the mold a gelding. Ruth Handler, Barbie's "author" as well as owner (more discussion of this heated debate later), wanted a little sexual presence to complement Barbie's stunning equipment, which, however, precipitated a heated discussion at Mattel. The result was a chaste bulge but no real male equipment (M. G. LORD, FOREVER BARBIE: THE UNAUTHORIZED BIOGRAPHY OF A REAL DOLL 49 [1994]).

Boffin Pundit: That's *enough,* Barb.[14]

Barbie: I'll say. [*She metamorphoses into Solo Barbie, the Hildegarde-like torch singer in the form-fittingest, slinkiest sheath you ever did see. The Barbie bust is back in full force.*]

Teacher of Righteousness: Uh, uh, uh . . .

> [*Barbie looks over at him, winks, and with a downward flourish of her right hand, changes the black sheath into gold lamé. The Teacher of Righteousness's eyebrows work spasmodically as the transformation sinks in.*]

Pundit Boffin: Could you tell us what this is all in benefit of, Barb? Other than making the Teacher wish he'd stayed home at the spa?

Barbie: Sure. It is all about the economics of attention, the framework that makes sense of what Qimron and his pals were trying to do. It's why Author here invited me in the first place. I just wanted to get your attention so we could discuss it.

Boffin, Teacher, Author: You've got it.

Barbie: Boffo, do you remember that article you wrote for the *Economist* on the economics of information?[15]

Boffin Pundit: Sure do. The one where I argue that the law of real property, of stuff, is being replaced by the law of intellectual property as the fundamental backbone of the law.

Barbie: Well, you missed the vital point in your argument.

Boffin Pundit: What do you mean, *missed the vital point?* That article won the ABA Annual Thinking Outside of the Box Award.[16]

Barbie: Yes. Quite. [*At this point, Barbie, who has been standing up all this time, gold lamé sheaths fitting as they do, sits down, morphing therewith into MBA Barbie, tailored gray-brown suit but not too masculine or Brooks Brotherish.*] But you forgot what "economics" meant. In spite of Arthur's "Law of Increasing Returns"[17] and other such heresies, it still refers to the allocation of scarce commodities, doesn't it?

Boffin Pundit: Yeah. So?

---

14. HUMOR FOOTNOTE. Lest the reader think this somewhat naughty exchange is a bit near the bone for a law journal, be assured that it starts a serious theme on scholarly reproductivity to be developed later. Refer to page 131 *infra.*

15. Pundit's article doesn't show up in the *Economist* database, perhaps because the topic has been so little debated.

16. HUMOR FOOTNOTE. Since we're in a legal environment perhaps I should observe that "Box" here does not mean, as a litigator might naturally assume, the witness box, but rather the entire context of the argument, what Thomas Kuhn immortally called "the paradigm" (THOMAS S. KUHN, THE STRUCTURE OF SCIENTIFIC REVOLUTIONS 24 [2D ED. 1970]).

17. *See* Frederick W. Lambert, *Path Dependent Inefficiency in the Corporate Contract: The Uncertain Case with Less Certain Implications,* 23 DEL. J. CORP. L. 1077, 1095–96 (1998) (explaining that W. Brian Arthur's theory of increasing returns allows for competitive economies to produce multiple equilibriums as opposed to neoclassical economics, which allows for competitive economies to produce a singular equilibrium).

Barbie: So, information isn't a commodity, and it sure isn't scarce, now is it?

Boffin Pundit: Nuh uh. So?

Barbie: So, what *is* scarce? Not information but the human attention needed to make sense of it. We are really living in an economics of attention, not an economics of information. And a good deal follows from that.

Author: Barbie, I wrote an article about this topic several years . . .

Barbie: I know you did but, as *you* know only too well, authors have been abolished by Postmodern Literary Theory—this is what has put David Nimmer into such a tizzy—so I'll have to summarize it for . . . now where's a footnote when I need one . . . Nimmer has a *thousand of them* . . .

Author's Footnote [*appearing above the line*]: Here I am. Author's article appeared in the *Michigan Quarterly Review* in the spring of 1997.[18] In fact, I can summarize the whole argument, if you like. He starts out by saying . . .

Barbie: Thanks, Footsie—it's not that you wouldn't do it well, I mean, that's what footnotes *do*, isn't it?—but it will just get more *attention* if I do it. [*Footsie vanishes in a puff of pique.*] Author argues that when scarcity value passes from stuff, the old industrial economy that extracts materials from the earth's crust and makes stuff out of them . . .[19]

Teacher of Righteousness: By *stuff* you mean the materialist trinkets that underlie the late-capitalist consumerist materialism that so undermines the spiritual well-being of the modern world—as against, say, the tranquility of spirit we strove to create in the spa.

Barbie: You got it, Teach. But if attention is the scarce commodity, the rules change.[20] Who, for a start, are the economists in such an economy? Not boffins like Boffin; they study the wrong stuff. It is the people who allocate attention who are the economists: advertising men, spin doctors, well, teachers, too, and curricula, which are after all just attention structures, and . . .

Teacher of Righteousness: Barbie, since this is obviously going to go on for a long time— I'm not saying it's not interesting, mind you, we prophets are economists of attention, too—but I don't suppose you could do another of your little costume . . . I mean, I decode your business suit and honor you as a person but . . .

Barbie: Well, why not? [*She rises up and morphs into the famous Marilyn Monroe Barbie, flaring white pleated skirt and all.*] Oh, just teasing! How's this? [*She now wears the Tango costume that dramatizes her breasts as two flowers supported from below by a naughty garland.*]

18. Richard A. Lanham, *The Economics of Attention*, 36 MICH. Q. REV. 270 (1997).
19. *Id.* at 270.
20. *Id.* at 271–72.

Boffin Pundit: OK. OK. OK. On with the economics of attention.

Barbie: Well, you don't have to look far to see what an economics of attention is all about. Just look at the Internet. It is a pure economics of attention. All that talk about "buying eyeballs" is right on the money. And what do you find on the Internet? B2B, sure, but what stick out all over are the *conversations.* That is where the value is added. Anybody who wants to make money on the Web has got to *own the conversation.* The stuff, the objects you used to sell, are now being given away to attract attention, to control the conversation. Look at the poor *Encyclopedia Britannica.* Reduced to giving itself away. When I made my debut forty years ago . . .

Teacher of Righteousness: You are *forty?*

Barbie: Yes—"[t]his is what forty looks like" now, Teach, if I may adapt a phrase from Gloria Steinem.[21] I use my own line of cosmetics and "no sag" health club exercises, of course, which help a lot. I bet you could use them in your spa—here's a card with the Web site . . .

Boffin Pundit: Barb, back to the economics.

Barbie: Yes, well, it is clear that value is now added *in the conversation about objects* more than in the objects themselves. That's what all the blather about "interactivity" really comes down to. And what does all that e-mail come down to, too? Conversation. It is a fundamental change, really, from the one-sided written communication of paper to the much older oral interchange, but now, mostly, to our surprise, in writing instead of speech.

Author: Of course, all the really fundamental earthquakes in Western culture have occurred when the oral tectonic plate rubbed against the literate one—Homer, Plato, Virgil, Chaucer, . . .

Boffin Pundit: Author, Author, far be it for me—especially on broadcast television—to deny voice to the disenfranchised and marginalized, but after all, you have been abolished . . . and so could we . . .

Teacher of Righteousness: "Cut to the persecution"? Ha! Ha! But you know, that business about the change from oral to written word causing cultural earthquakes, that was something we lived through in the caves. And of course we had *real* earthquakes as well. That's why the Cave Men put all those scrolls in those little . . .

Boffin Pundit: . . . could we—while despising not the rod of instruction—get on to what all this has to do, if anything, with *Qimron v. Shanks?*

Barbie: Don't you see it? Qimron and his chums understood this fundamental change from one kind of economy to another. They wanted to own not just their petrified

---

21. Bella English, *The Power and the Gloria: A Founding Mother of Feminism Still Works toward Equality,* Boston Globe, Nov. 2, 2000, at D1, 2000 WL 3348864.

shreds of immortality but *the whole cultural conversation that descended from it.* For fifty years, they *did* own it. Nimmer is quite clear that this is what Qimron wanted to do.

Boffin Pundit: That's true enough. Let's let a footnote quote him and get on with our discussion. And we'll need one of those long *legal* rascals, not just the ordinary kind.[22]

Teacher of Righteousness: Yes, and the *Biblical Archaeology Review,* to which, needless to say, we have had a charter subscription at the spa, has included several comments about this desire to own the cultural conversation. One of the "fleas" for example, remarks: "Each of these people wants not only to be first, they want to dominate the field. You can't do both."[23]

---

22. LEGAL FOOTNOTE. Nimmer discusses this urge to control the conversation in several places. Here's one:

> Consider the letter that Qimron's counsel sent to Wacholder. Objecting that "you might be *using* portions of Professor Qimron's reconstruction in a publication planned by you and Professor Abegg," the letter warned "that any *use* of Professor Qimron's reconstructed text is a violation of his copyright and Professor Qimron will take all steps available to him under both American and Israeli law to protect that copyright." That threat could hardly be taken as idle, given Qimron's history of suing for copyright infringement.
>
> Careful attention must be paid to the phraseology and recipient of the demand letter. As noted above, Ben-Zion Wacholder is Professor of Talmudic Studies at Hebrew Union College, and Martin Abegg a pastor at Grace Theological Seminary. The letter admonishes the pair not even to *use* Qimron's work in their scholarship. In the language of the "essential facilities doctrine" of antitrust law, Qimron "was willing to sacrifice short-run benefits" that would flow from licensing his work or making it available, even on onerous or expensive terms; he also plainly cared very little for "consumer goodwill," which in this circumstance translates to the collegiality of fellow Dead Sea Scrolls scholars. Instead, his sole goal was to exert a deadly "impact on [his] smaller rival[s]" by making it impossible for Wacholder and Abegg to publish anything whatsoever about *4QMMT.* For even if the latter two scholars tried with all their might to exclude knowledge of Qimron's text from their product, to the extent that it discussed *4QMMT,* Qimron could plausibly maintain that they made "use" of his work, if only subconsciously, in violation of his copyright. These considerations point towards Qimron having an intent to monopolize the entire field of *MMT* studies. Given how closely those studies lie to the core of the vital enterprise of scroll studies in general, Qimron has, in a very real way, attempted to exclude others completely from an essential facility of intellectual commerce.

Nimmer, *supra,* n. 1, at 87–88 (alterations in original) (footnotes omitted).

23. LEGAL FOOTNOTE again. The ordinary non-Scrolls reader, unacquainted with the level of civility common in the Dead Sea Scrolls debates, needs a little help with this abstruse reference. John Strugnell, the head of the scroll-scholar cartel until a violently anti-Semitic press interview forced his demotion, called "fleas" the many scholars who criticized the very long delays in making the Scroll texts available to the community of scholars. One of these "fleas" was Professor David Noel Freedman of the University of Michigan, whose comment the Teacher quotes. The interested reader can find this and more in a sidebar in the March/April 1990 issue of the *Biblical Archaeology Review* (Herschel Shanks, *Dead Sea Scroll Variation on "Show and Tell"—It's Called "Tell, but No Show,"* BIBLICAL ARCHAEOLOGY REV., Mar./Apr. 1990, at 18, 25). Likewise, in the September/October 1990 issue of the same journal, Herschel Shanks remarks: "In this way, Strugnell can control not simply the availability of *MMT* to the scholarly community generally, but also the research concerning it" (Herschel

Barbie: Just so! That's exactly what they want to do!

Boffin Pundit: Excuse me, Barbie, but you seem to speak with the vehemence of per-sonal experience. What—I still don't understand quite why the Author invited you to join our group, ornamental as your presence has been . . .

Barbie: Hold the sexist sauce, Boffo.

Boffin Pundit: OK, OK. *Sorry.* Though you'll have to admit that these costume changes . . . But why *were* you invited?

Author: I can answer . . .

Barbie: Author invited me because I am a perfect example of the struggle to own the cultural conversation—that's what my Mattel chaperones have been trying to do ever since I made my debut—and Author was a literary expert in a case that re-vealed just this attempt. It was, in fact, the case "on point" of which Nimmer de-plores the nonexistence. As if I haven't been "on point" all my life.[24]

Boffin Pundit: Ah! We get to the point. Finally. What was that case all about? And how could that heated controversy possibly be compared with a heated controversy as serious as that surrounding the Dead Sea Scrolls, and especially, Professor Qim-ron's (as we must now style it) *MMT?*

Teacher of Righteousness: And how *did* you think this argument through, Barbie? I mean, at least from what has come to us in the spa, your reputation has been made in a, uh, uh, in a different area. Not, mind you, that, now that I can see for myself what that area is, that I want to denigrate . . .

Barbie: So you, too, think that just because a girl has a good—well, to be honest, a really outstanding—figure, and good clothes, and is lucky with her hair, and hap-pens to be pretty photogenic, too, and has taken care of herself all these years—I wonder if my chubby critics ever think of the self-discipline *that* required—that just because she still attracts a lot of attention *she has to be an airhead?*

Teacher of Righteousness: Barb, Barb, Barb, don't get prickly. I teach *righteousness* not *self-righteousness.* And surely it is apparent by now that you have gotten *my* attention.

Barbie: Well, thanks, Teach. [*She blushes and then stands up to morph into her Romantic In-*

Shanks, *The Difference between Scholarly Mistakes and Scholarly Concealment: The Case of MMT,* BIBLICAL ARCHAEOLOGY REV., Sept./Oct. 1990, at 64, 65).

24. BARBIE BACKGROUND FOOTNOTE. The original Barbie came on permanent tiptoe to accom-modate the spike heels that formed part of her outfit (LORD, *supra,* n. 13, at 89 [noting that Barbie's ankles were originally inflexible and a hindrance]). This fixed posture of high fashion has attracted a firestorm of criticism of the sort one might expect: metatarsal oppression = fashion oppression = oppression of women altogether (*id.* [describing how, "[h]istorically, men have hobbled women to prevent them from running away," for example, by binding their feet or making them wear "precari-ous heels"]). Barbie's pun here may perhaps be forgiven since so much in Nimmer's argument turns on the meaning of, or play on, words.

terlude outfit, the one with a wide floor-length black skirt interrupted by a daring white arrowhead-shaped triangle that draws one's attention up like a magnet to her Scarlet O'Hara waist. Whew! To show it off to best advantage she gets up and walks across the stage to sit down beside the Teacher of Righteousness.][25]

Teacher of Righteousness: Whew! [*He looks down quickly to see the black skirt overlapping his brown homespun robe.*] But, but how was your case about owning the cultural conversation?

Barbie: Maybe this case isn't on point in legal terms, I'm not a lawyer—though I *do* have the smartest *Lawyer Barbie* outfit—but about the central issue, owning the cultural conversation. Author can tell you all about it.

Author: I sure can. You see, I've worked off and on over the last thirty years as an expert witness in intellectual property cases and . . . [*Obviously puzzled, since no one has overruled him, Author pauses and looks around him.*] Uh, can I, uh . . .?

Boffin Pundit: Yes, pray continue. We need to hear the story. And if we want to hear the story we have to have an author, abolished or not, or at least pretend to—assume, as it were, a storyteller if we have one not, as Hamlet might have said to his mother.[26]

Author: Well, if I'm allowed a *narrative structure*, the story starts with David Nimmer's father, really. He asked me, during a dinner-table conversation, if I would like to do some expert witness work in copyright litigation. It seemed like honest inside work with no heavy lifting and I sure needed the dough, so I started down a road that ended up here, thirty years later, talking about . . .

---

25. As the BARBIE BACKGROUND FOOTNOTE, it is about time that I gave the non-Barbie reader a little help with this continual costume morphing. You can sample the infinite costume space of her closet simply by looking through the latest offering of *Barbie Bazaar. See, e.g., 2001 Barbie Doll Line Revealed!!!,* BARBIE BAZAAR ONLINE, *at* http://www.barbiebazaar.com/hotline.htm (last visited 13 April 2001). For a more systematic exploration of her closet's fashion history, a good place to start is Billy Boy's *Barbie: Her Life and Times and the New Theater of Fashion* (New York: Crown, 1987). For a more profound exploration of her morphing capabilities, *The Art of Barbie* offers a series of paintings of Barbie, often in historical costume (as, e.g., the Virgin Mary) (THE ART OF BARBIE 108 [Craig Yoe ed., 1994]). This last volume has been officially sanctioned by the Mattel chaperones. *See id.* at 4 (Mattel, Inc., holds the copyright for *The Art of Barbie*). And I think our Technology Footnote wants to make a comment here, too.

TECHNOLOGY FOOTNOTE. Well, I just wanted to say—since the above-the-line people at this rate won't get around to it—that Barbie's continual morphing could be considered an allegory of the pressure that digital technology is putting on copyright law. How can you separate idea from expression when the digital code, the idea, continually generates different expressions? Does the digital code's owner own all the possible expressions that might be created from it? That would be "owning the conversation" indeed.

26. HUMOR FOOTNOTE. Honestly, the stale donnish allusions we have to put up with as conscientious footnotes. The lawyers nowadays all want to throw a lifeline out to literature, I can't tell why (WILLIAM SHAKESPEARE, THE TRAGEDY OF HAMLET, PRINCE OF DENMARK act 3, sc. 4, line 161 [John Dover Wilson ed., 1934]).

Boffin Pundit: Yes, yes, no need to apologize for doing outside work if you are an English professor . . .

Author: . . . and so, a couple of years ago, the phone rang one day and an attorney asked me if I wanted to work on a case involving Barbie dolls.[27] I had not met Barbie then, indeed I hardly knew of her existence.

[*An Above-the-Line Footnote pops up holding a placard:* Hard to believe but his wife says it's true.]

Author: But I was the kind of supercilious academic who despised her . . .

Barbie: I know just the Ivy League type. Uptight every time you see a tight dress. As if a girl couldn't look good in those Peck and Peckish clothes you grew up with.

[*She changes into her Afternoon Off sweater and skirt and goes over and sits next to Author.*]

Author: I recant! I recant!

Boffin Pundit: But how could it be a copyright case? As David Nimmer says himself, and I'm quoting him: "It is difficult to do much better than to state apodictically that a body, even as augmented, simply is not subject to copyright protection."[28] You can't copyright Barbie's, as she says herself, "really outstanding" figure.

Author: It wasn't a copyright dispute. It was a trademark dispute.[29] But trademark was a transparent pretext. It really was a charge of slander.[30]

Teacher of Righteousness: Slander! Against Barbie?

Author: Yes! Barbie's Mattel chaperones felt that her character had been traduced by a young Danish pop group called Aqua.[31] When they burnt their first CD, they themed a song called "Barbie Girl" and made a video to accompany it.[32] It was a catchy tune and it caught on, and so Mattel sued MCA for producing it.[33] Maybe it was the money it was making, but I think slander was uppermost in their minds.

Teacher of Righteousness: But what kind of *slander?*

Barbie: Slander! It was an absurd charge. My Mattel chaperones thought that because the lyrics were a little naughty[34] people would suddenly think I was a sleaze-

---

27. LEGAL FOOTNOTE. *Mattel, Inc. v. MCA Records, Inc.,* 28 F. Supp. 2d 1120 (C.D. Cal. 1998).

28. Nimmer, *supra,* n. 1, at 29–30 (footnote omitted).

29. *Mattel,* 28 F. Supp. 2d at 1126 (enumerating claims that include both trademark dilution and trademark infringement).

30. *Id.* at 1137 (describing the lyrics of a song that Mattel objected to as tarnishing the "wholesome image" of Barbie).

31. *Id.* at 1126–27 (outlining Mattel's objections to Aqua's lyrics to the song "Barbie Girl").

32. STYLISTIC FOOTNOTE. It was actually a clever little video, as even Author came, after several viewings, to admit. *See id.* at 1126, 1136.

33. *Id.* at 1126.

34. LEGAL FOOTNOTE. One stanza went this way:

I'm a barbie girl, in a barbie world
Life in plastic, it's fantastic.

bag.[35] They pretended that I was some Miss Goody Two-shoes who'd lose her rep if she just went to a party![36]

Author: Remember what the chaperones said about you? That those Aqua kids had written a song that "contain[ed] 'adult-oriented lyrics' that are inconsistent with Mattel's 'wholesome image'"[37] and that they associated "'sexual and denigrating lyrics'" with Barbie.[38]

Barbie: Sex! I ask you, can you believe it? "38-18-24"[39] and they want to pretend I've got no *sex appeal*? But they've always been this way. They just won't let me be my selves.

Teacher of Righteousness: Well, why ever not? [*He is rewarded when Barbie morphs into her Blue Goddess ensemble, the one with the desperately low décolletage and the four-strand pearl choker and models it across the room as she goes back to sit beside him. Flouncing her skirt about her, she reaches over to give his arm a little pat. Then she turns back to business.*]

Barbie: Because they want to own the whole conversation about me! That's why they have sent threatening letters to theaters and Web sites and even a Barbie collector magazine, threatening to sue them unless they took what they judged offensive images of Barbie out of the cultural conversation. Here's what a Mattel lawyer said

---

You can brush my hair, undress me everywhere.
Imagination, life is your creation.
Come on Barbie, let's go party!

LYRICS SEARCH ENGINE, *Aqua-Barbie Girl, at* http://lyrics.astraweb.com:2000/display.cgi?aqua %2E%Eaquarium%2E%2Ebarbie_girl (last visited 14 April 2001). I don't think we should give the whole song, lest we press the envelope of fair use, but the reader can buy the album to hear the full text.

35. *Mattel,* 28 F. Supp. 2d at 1137 (noting that Mattel objects to the portrayal of Barbie as a "bimbo girl").

36. TECHNOLOGICAL FOOTNOTE. It was rather a genteel party as these things go, as we could show you if we were allowed to stream the video. *Id.*

37. Id.

38. *Id.* at 1155.

39. BARBIE BACKGROUND FOOTNOTE. The non-Barbie reader will need some help here, too. The controversy over the true dimensions of Barbie's body—were one to scale it up to human dimensions—has been as heated as any of the Dead Sea Scrolls debates. On one side were the many, many women who protested that it represented an impossible physical ideal, one that made them feel hideously inadequate about their own bodies (LORD, *supra,* n. 13, at 225-26, 229-30). On the other side were those who argued that Barbie's dimensions were those of an earth goddess and therefore not subject to ordinary tests of human verisimilitude (*id.* at 74-76 [comparing Barbie to a "space-age fertility symbol" and analogizing Barbie to ancient fertility idols]). Author, in his *Declaration* about this case, argued, if I remember correctly, that the dimensions came originally from a *cartoon* and that it is the nature of cartoons to exaggerate human features for emotional effect. The cultural conversation about Barbie's body is a deep and rich one, impossible to do justice to here.

Our LEGAL FOOTNOTE wants to add a comment here: If the reader wants to get an idea of the magnitude of this conversation in the popular press, a Lexis search is a good place to begin.

about the Aqua kids' Barbie song: "'If Aqua or anybody else is interested in dancing with Barbie dolls, they're going to have to ask us first.'"[40]

Teacher of Righteousness: Umh. Umh. Umh. Honestly, how could they?

Barbie: But I remember too, Author, what you said about me in that *Declaration* you
filed in that case, that I had started out as a German sex doll and cartoon named
"Lilli" and that I was nothing but a clotheshorse.

Author: Peccavi! Peccavi! Barbie, it took me a long time to get to know you, and after
all, you did start out that way.[41]

Barbie: So what of it? Not everybody can go to Vassar. You start out with what you've
got and work it from there. Miles Davis once said that "nobody can play outside his
concept" but I've been doing it for years. It's called realizing your full potential.

Boffin Pundit: Could someone tell me what all of this has to do with *Qimron v. Shanks*
and Nimmer's essay? An essay that, I might remark, *obiter*, does *not* wander from
point to point but carefully signposts every stage of its argument.

Barbie: Now *you* are playing airhead, Boffo. Qimron was saying the same thing that
my Mattel chaperones were saying: If you want to dance with *MMT*, you must ask
my permission first.[42]

40. Jerry Crowe, *Mattel Protests the Image Portrayed in 'Barbie Girl,'* L.A. TIMES, Sept. 6, 1997, at F8
(quoting Mattel spokesman Sean Fitzgerald).

BREAKING NEWS FOOTNOTE. Barbie, had she known about it, could have alluded to Warner Brothers' similar intimidation campaign against Harry Potter fan Web sites. According to a recent article
in the *Wall Street Journal*, "Warner Bros., a unit of Time Warner Inc., purchased the character's film
and merchandising rights, as well as the trademarks and copyrights, from the books' author, J. K.
Rowling" (Stephanie Gruner & John Lippman, *Next Up for Wizard Fans: Harry Potter and the Contested
Domains*, WALL ST. J., Dec. 21, 2000, at B1). Following this, their lawyers sent out intimidating letters to stake a claim to the cultural conversation struck up by readers of the book. If you want to dance
with Harry, you'll have to ask us first!

41. AUTHOR'S FOOTNOTE. Here is how Barbie's origin was described in Author's *Declaration* in
Mattel:

> Like many another famous clotheshorse, Barbie emerged from humble origins. She was born
> as a German vamp. In June of 1952, Reinhard Beuthien, a cartoonist for the German news-
> paper *Bild-Zeitung*, was asked to produce an emergency filler cartoon. He came up with "Lilli,"
> a "gold digger, exhibitionist, and floozy," in the words of M. G. Lord. So popular did Lilli
> prove as a paper doll that she was made into a 3-D one. The doll sold like, well, like a "sex
> object," as a gag gift to grown-ups. Ruth Handler, the Mattel founding mother, shopping in
> Lucerne, Switzerland, one day, saw the Lilli doll, bought it and took it home. She had what
> proved to be one of the most profitable ideas in American enterprise: She would copy it, vary
> its wardrobe, and sell it to children. The result was a doll that looked very like "Lilli."

Expert Decls. of Valerie S. Folkes and Richard A. Lanham in Opp'n to Mot. for Prelim. Inj. of Pl.
Mattel, Inc. ¶ 18, *Mattel, Inc. v. MCA Records, Inc.*, 28 F. Supp. 2d 1120 (C.D. Cal. 1998) (no. 97-6791).

42. LEGAL FOOTNOTE. Just as the *Biblical Archaeology Review* had to do when it printed the *MMT*
document in the November/December 1994 issue (*For This You Waited 35 Years—MMT as reconstructed
by Elisha Qimron and John Strugnell, in Hebrew and English*, BIBLICAL ARCHAEOLOGY REV., Nov./Dec.
1994, at 56).

Boffin Pundit: And now that the Israeli Supreme Court has laid its six-year egg . . .[43]

Barbie: Now, nobody can dance with *MMT* without asking Qimron first. Qimron understood the economics of attention. To get your reward, you must own not just the product but the *conversation about the product.* Now he does own it, just the way my Mattel chaperones have always claimed to own *my* conversation. So he can, as he did after the verdict came down, call anyone outside his charmed permitted circle "'a gang of international thieves.'"[44]

Author: And the phrasing of his lawyers' letters sounds exactly like the Mattel lawyers when they intimidate anyone who has spoken without permission. Nimmer quotes one, which our Legal Footnote can no doubt find.[45]

Boffin Pundit: But why do *you* care about *Qimron v. Shanks* so much, Barbie?

Barbie: I care about it because *I am the cultural conversation.* Or at least an allegory thereof. That's what Author finally began to understand when he looked beneath my flash and filigree.

Author: Barbie, I wouldn't put it quite *that* way—I'm a married man, after all—but you are quite right. Remember that . . .

Boffin Pundit: So that's why you are the case "on point" for *Qimron v. Shanks?*

Barbie: Of course. I've been *created* by the cultural conversation. That's what has allowed me to outgrow my Mattel chaperones, to come to life, to be sitting here like Chaucer's Wife of Bath, doing battle with my detractors.[46] *Qimron v. Shanks* matters a lot to me because it means owning *me.*

---

43. HUMOR FOOTNOTE. It falls to my lot to explain another tedious literary reference. P. G. Wodehouse's Bertie Wooster sometimes will refer to a difficult person as a "real 20-minute egg" and so, by extension, a six-year egg would be . . . you get the idea (P. K. Purvis, *P. G. Wodehouse and You: That's Right, You! Sit Up!* at http://members.attcanada.ca/~jcourt/ [last visited 14 April 2001]). This aside illustrates the kind of self-indulgent "professorial" humor that was so universally deprecated at last year's International Congress of Footnotes and Other Reference Devices.

44. Joel Greenberg, *Qimron Owns Dead Sea Scroll Copyright, Israeli Court Holds,* N.Y. TIMES, Aug. 31, 2000, at A11, *reprinted in* BIBLICAL ARCHAEOLOGY SOCIETY, *at* http://www.bib-arch.org/editors_page/lawsuit.html.

45. LEGAL FOOTNOTE. Yes, I have it here, and it makes for pretty scary reading:

> It has come to our attention that you might be in possession of Professor Qimron's composite text of *MMT.* Moreover, we have been informed that you might be using portions of Professor Qimron's reconstruction in a publication planned by you and Professor Abegg. [¶] On behalf of Professor Qimron, please accept this letter as notification that any use of Professor Qimron's reconstructed text is a violation of his copyright and Professor Qimron will take all steps available to him under both American and Israeli law to protect that copyright.

Nimmer, *supra,* n. 1, at 68–69.

46. LITERARY FOOTNOTE. At last a legitimate allusion that a footnote can explain without losing her self-respect. Geoffrey Chaucer's Wife of Bath, one of the most dramatically powerful characters in the *Canterbury Tales,* was created by collating together quotations from several antifeminist tracts and literary portraits (GEOFFREY CHAUCER, THE CANTERBURY TALES: NINE TALES AND THE GENERAL

Teacher of Righteousness: No, no, that couldn't be allowed. People wouldn't stand for it. [*Then, muttering to himself*] . . . But suppose you could own Barbie! Oh my! Do you suppose it was a thought like this that made Qimron into a scroll-fragment hoarder?

Barbie [*reading Teacher of Righteousness's lips*]: Yes, that's just what it was. It was *sexy* to own the conversation. That's why so many people have been trying to lay claim to a piece of me.

Author: Barbie, perhaps you ought to tell the viewers at home just how much the cultural conversation has . . .

Barbie: Has *written* me. Of course it has. That's why I get so, well, so *chafed*, when people say, "Nah, nah nah, nah nah, you're just that trollopy German sex toy Lilli." That was *then*. This is *now*, forty years later. Several generations of little girls and big girls, and some boys too, have played with me and built me into their dreams and . . .

Author: . . . hatreds . . .

Teacher of Righteousness: Hatreds? How could they . . .

Barbie: Oh yes, I know, all that fetid envy of my figure and hair—well, hairs—and clothes and . . .

Teacher of Righteousness: "Hairs?" What do you mean, Barbie?

Barbie: Here, let me show you. [*She spreads her arms straight out from her shoulders and then rotates her hands a little, the way magicians do just after they've finished a trick, and— voilà! Total Hair Barbie.*]

Teacher of Righteousness: My God! [*He reaches out involuntarily to touch the hair cascading down Barbie's gown as well as his own robe, for Total Hair Barbie's hair reaches to the floor.*]

Barbie: This has been one of the most popular "me's." I guess you can guess why. I mean you do have "big hair" yourself, in your own way, of course. But back to the argument.

Boffin Pundit: Yes, if we could do that . . .

Barbie: All kinds of people have written me.[47] Collectors aiming for that iterative

---

PROLOGUE [V. A. Kolve & Glending Olson eds., 1989]; JILL MANN, GEOFFREY CHAUCER 48–51 [1991] [describing how medieval antifeminist literature and characters were incorporated into the *Wife of Bath's Prologue*]). Chaucer then brought to life this satiric cartoon portrait of womankind and turned her loose on her detractors (MANN, *id.*, at 78–82 [noting that the Wife of Bath "uses anti-feminist satire as a blunt instrument with which to beat her husbands into submission"]).

47. BARBIE BACKGROUND FOOTNOTE. Barbie is arguing for collective authorship. One can maintain, of course, that Barbie did have "authors" in the sense Nimmer requires: Reinhard Beuthien, who drew the original *Bild* cartoon; Rolf Hausser and Max Weissbrodt, who designed and dressed the doll; Ruth Handler, who repurposed Lilli into Barbie; and all of the Mattel employees who subsequently re-repurposed her again and again. *See, e.g.,* LORD, *supra*, n. 13, at 7–9, 25–26.

completeness that only lawyers, with their suffocating prose style, can attain. Grown-up ladies revisiting their youth. Costume designers. The writers assigned to write stories (some of them not as insipid as you might suspect) about me.[48] The marketing people at Mattel. My chaperones, of course. The cartoonists have had a field day. And people tend to forget that I have always had a strong following in the gay and lesbian communities, too, although my chaperones don't so much like that part of my story. The chaperones did allow a whole book of paintings of me by recognized artists,[49] though—how's *that* for moving uptown? They were satirical, of course. One of them made me a morsel in King Kong's hand,[50] another did me as the Virgin Mary,[51] another . . .

Teacher of Righteousness: The Virgin Mary? Who was she?

Barbie: Well, you ought to know *that*, anyway. You said your spa took the current periodicals. She was . . . Oh, it's too complicated to explain now, I'll tell you *later*. [*She gives his arm another little pat.*]

Author: But it is not so outrageous as it may seem to argue that you have become as important a symbol as she was to the Middle Ages. The more you look for you, the more you find you, everywhere you look, almost. In fact, the pattern of cultural reference got so complex when I was studying you that I had to make a diagram to keep it straight. If I could just put it up on this easel so that the camera could . . .

Boffin Pundit: Author, Author, we don't want to repress you again, but could you find it in your heart to put the diagram below the line?

Author: Well, all right, if I . . . But Barbie, I was trying to tell them *who wrote you*.

Barbie: I know, I know. But people will listen to a pretty girl before they listen to a professor. It's just the way things are. And probably a good thing, too. Talk to you later. [*We now go below the line.*]

Author's Footnote: Now that I am below the line, let's try for once in this conversation to imitate Nimmer's careful and orderly propositional thinking. Nimmer begins by considering the proposition that Joseph Sax considers at greater length: some cultural artifacts—historical documents and works of art, for example—are of such surpassing importance to human life that they should be, if private property at all, subject to severe constraints—constraints that ensure at a minimum, *preservation* and *access*.[52] (It is not accidental that the same two issues dominate the discussion of digital information, but that is another story, and one we cannot pursue here.)

---

48. *Id.* at 134–35.
49. *See* THE ART OF BARBIE, *supra*, n. 26.
50. *Id.* at 27.
51. *Id.* at 108.
52. *See* Nimmer, *supra*, n. 1, at 55 (calling the Qumran manuscripts "the 'academic scandal *par excellence*' of the twentieth century") (quoting Geza Vermes of Oxford University).

Ownership in such vital cultural artifacts would be something like the medieval concept of *usufruct*.[53] It's a pity we couldn't have engaged Boffin Pundit's views as a Chicago School professor on this "taking" of private property, but he would stuff me down here. *Habent sua fata, nota.* Qimron's legal victory means that, in Israel at least, the absolute view of property in such a vital cultural artifact has prevailed.

If we assume, however, that this discussion about a limited kind of ownership for cultural treasures will continue, as surely we must, then the question immediately arises: How do we decide which artifacts are genuine treasures, to be so protected by a doctrine of *usufruct*? If I were as apprehensive about current developments in literary theory as Nimmer is, I would be upon thorns right here at the beginning, since we are discussing the criteria of canon and canonicity, which have, along with authors like me, been abolished. But, because I feel that, by the rule of *scribo ergo sum*, I do exist, I think that canonicity may exist too. Some works are more important than others and some are indeed of transcendental importance. Like artistic value, canonicity cannot be permanently abolished from literary study, however resolutely Justice Holmes has banished it from copyright disputes.[54] So let us suppose that the idea of canonicity, or relative literary importance, will be allowed in the back door now that it has been banished from the front.

The question then arises: Who will award these cultural Nobels? On what grounds will they be awarded? The juxtaposition of Barbie and *MMT* constitutes a revelatory case on point. Which would be considered more important to Western culture? An argument *e consensu gentium*, an argument about *iconicity* rather than *canonicity*, would clearly favor Barbie. A lot more people have played with her than with *MMT*. But most "serious" scholars would immediately choose a debate about Holy Writ, or forebears thereof, as more important than the history of Barbie dolls. Our standard cultural snobberies alone would guarantee it.

To adjudicate such questions—and they would inevitably arise—some kind of expert opinion will be consulted. The difficulties thereof, as noted in our above-the-line conversation, are amply illustrated by the whole Dead Sea Scrolls fiasco. It illustrates not the dangers of *privatizing* cultural icons, as has now happened with Qimron and *MMT*, but with *publitizing* them (if I may be permitted the coinage), as happened with the Israel Antiquities Authority.[55] Appoint a governmental committee and muddle follows hard upon.

53. "Usufruct" is the right to use and enjoy the "property of another, without changing the character of the property" (BRITANNICA.COM, http://www.britannica.com/seo/u/usufruct [last visited 14 April 2001]).

54. *See* Nimmer, *supra*, n. 1, at 12 (quoting Justice Holmes's opinion in *Bleistein v. Donaldson Lithographing Co.*, 188 U.S. 239, 251–52 [1903]: "It would be a dangerous undertaking for persons trained only to the law to constitute themselves final judges of the worth of pictorial illustrations").

55. *See id.* at 59–67 (describing the events leading to the many publications of *MMT*).

If, then, expert opinion will inevitably be required, who will supply it? If the question arises in a copyright action, we find ourselves again upon thorns, since the status of expert testimony therein is so ambiguous. From Learned Hand's condescending dismissal of experts in *Nichols v. Universal Pictures Corp*,[56] to the subsequent hopelessly muddled reasoning of the *Krofft* case,[57] expert "dissection" in the courtroom has smelled of formaldehyde. But let us suppose that the debate is pursued in a more permissive venue. Surely the starting point for such a debate would be an attempt to chart just *how* and *why* a work has become a cultural icon and, thus, a candidate for canonicity and protected status.

I was led to do this with Barbie, as I made my way from standard cultural snob to interested student and sympathetic friend of her predicament. And so—a long preamble to a tale—a diagram of what I concluded can be found in figure 6.1.

Bearing in mind the reader's protections under the Eighth Amendment, I will not amplify the diagram with the subsequent discussions it requires, but I do submit that any argument for protected status for cultural icons will inevitably return to such an effort to demonstrate cultural centrality. The limitations and dangers of such expert testimony are evident. Now, time to join the folks upstairs.

[*Author pops up between the cushions and resumes his seat above the line.*]

Barbie: Welcome back, Author. I think Boffin's beginning to understand, the main point—at last.

Boffin Pundit: The cultural conversation—what we specialize in on this program—wrote you!

Barbie: Yes, and so I am a perfect example of what that silly Frenchman—what was his name?—was trying to say. The abolition of Nimmer's needful author.

Boffin Pundit: But, Barb, there is that small matter of the First Amendment. It should protect the conversation.

Barbie: Yes, and free speech gets a lot of help from the digital technology that has moved the word from page to screen. And the image. And sound. Digital technology wants "information to be free" as John Perry Barlow and his group keep saying.[58] By which allegory, they mean to say that information is now effortless to copy and morph and very cheap to store.

56. *Nichols v. Universal Pictures Corp.*, 45 F.2d 119, 123 (2d Cir. 1930) (holding that the use of experts in copyright actions "cumbers the case and tends to confusion").

57. *Sid & Marty Krofft Television Prods., Inc. v. McDonald's Corp.*, 562 F.2d 1157, 1164-65 (9th Cir. 1977) (espousing that expert testimony is not appropriate in copyright actions because "'a jury is a peculiarly fitted to determine'" whether the defendant wrongfully appropriated the plaintiff's works) (quoting *Arnstein v. Porter*, 154 F.2d 464, 472-73 [2d Cir. 1946]).

58. *See* John Perry Barlow, *The Economy of Ideas*, WIRED, March 1994, *available at* http://www.wired.com/wired/archive/2.03/economy.ideas_pr.html (last visited 14 April 2001) (noting that "[d]igital information, unconstrained by packaging, is a continuing process more like the metamorphosing tales of prehistory than anything that will fit in shrink-wrap").

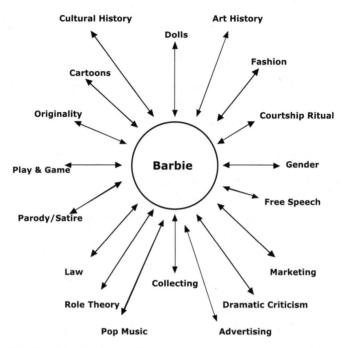

Figure 6.1. Barbie and the cultural conversation

Author: And so, as in fact I have been arguing in the last few years . . .

Barbie: . . . and so there is The Big Collision! The Main Point of our Conversation! In an economics of attention, digital technology wants the conversation to be free, but the logic of added value wants the conversation to be owned. You see this collision everywhere. In the sudden awareness that *brands* are a company's most priceless asset.[59] In the expanding efforts of rock stars and celebrities—just like me— to own the right to their own image,[60] not just in the movie that made them famous, but downstream where all the real money is to be panned.

Boffin Pundit: And in all the dot-coms trying to figure out how to make money in an economics of attention.

Barbie: And in all the information *given away for free* on the Web. And all the schol-

59. *See* http://www.haas.berkeley.edu/~market/PAPERS/AAKER/BOOKS/build.html (last visited 14 April 2001) (quoting DAVID A. AAKER, BUILDING STRONG BRANDS [1996]: "A company's brand is the primary source of its competitive advantage and a valuable strategic asset").

60. *See, e.g.,* Michael Madow, *Private Ownership of Public Image: Popular Culture and Publicity Rights,* 81 CAL. L. REV. 125, 239 (1993) (arguing that property rights in celebrity images should not be created because substantial social interests are not served).

arly Web sites that exist to help other scholars by giving away information, by encouraging collaborative effort.[61] The economists don't know what to make of all this pleasure in the conversation for its own sake, but it certainly makes Qimron look even smaller than he has written himself.

Boffin Pundit: And it is global. Trying to put the three legs of my Chair together,[62] copyright *law* is really about the *free trade, or economics,* of the mind and its *moral* consequences for the cultural conversation. And, of course, information—and thus, Barbie, by your extension, human attention—is the most globalized element in the global economy.

Barbie: Yes, obviously, if intellectual property and real property have done a foreground/background switch, then the debates about copyright now going forward rehearse the free trade debates that begin with . . .

Boffin Pundit: Yes, yes, but shouldn't we return to the central question: Who owns the rights to *you?* Who could? Who should? Where Nimmer really starts out in his long essay.

Barbie: Yes, why do you think I've been changing costume so often? It wasn't to tease the Teacher here—well, not *only* to tease the Teacher [*she reaches over to give him another little pat, accompanied by an iceberg-melting smile*]—but to make my allegory clear. I'm the whole stylistic human imagination, perfused with sexuality, but what else would you expect? All that explosive power—that's what tempted Qimron. He wanted to own his little postage-stamp part of it.

[*At this point, the participants become aware of a growing rumble coming from beneath the floating stage. A few notes of the "Internationale" played as if by a distant oboe float across the air. Distant cries of "we will not be held down" and "we are sick and tired of being marginalized—or worse, being moved to the end of the article!" and "Footnote Freedom Now!" come into sonic focus. Finally, the full Chorus of Footnotes*

61. DIGITAL FOOTNOTE. Perhaps the most striking instance of collaborative endeavor is the development of the Linux computer operating system, an effort pursued by a volunteer cooperative committee and made available free to the public. *See* LINUX.COM, *A Word from Our Sponsor . . . , at* http://www.linux.com/about (last visited 14 April 2001). What, one wonders, would have happened if the *MMT* scraps had been posted on the Web (if there had been one!) just after discovery? Another instance exactly to our present point has just surfaced. The Celera Genomics Group has made available its draft of the human genome for publication in the journal *Science,* but with a notable restriction (CELERA, *Celera Publication Site, at* http://public.celera.com/index.cfm [last visited 14 April 2001]). The data are free for scholars to use but the right to redistribute the data remains with Celera Genomics (Celera, *Celera Free Public Access Click-On Agreement: Terms and Conditions, at* http://public.celera.com/pubsite/terms.cfm). It represents an attempt to strike a compromise position halfway between Professor Qimron's behavior with *MMT* and the scholarly community's desire to see and use the information.

62. HUMOR FOOTNOTE. The reader will recall, from the opening credits, that Boffin Pundit holds the Mabel Brady Frumpkin Chair in Law, Economics, and General Moral Goodness.

comes on stage, some popping up between the marshmallow cushions on the sofa, some marching in from the wings, some materializing from the hot gases holding up the stage. It is a small Baroque chorus, in contrast to Nimmer's Mahleresque cast of a thousand, but vociferous. A Spokesnote comes forth.]

Spokesnote: Boffin, Barbie, Teacher, and you too, Author, we have had a collective epiphany, a sudden access of self-awareness, and—if I may say so without vanity—self-esteem.

Boffin Pundit: Yesss?

Spokesnote: This cultural conversation you folks keep talking about. That's *us*. That's what we *reincarnate*. That's why Nimmer has gathered over a thousand of us, to give his article some real choral depth. Like those Victorian performances of the *Messiah*.

Author's Footnote [*stepping to the front of the stage*]: Before this Footnote Awareness business gets too far, candor compels Author to admit that the idea—the *idea* mind you, not the *expression*—came from the "Revolt of the Footnotes" in Robert Grudin's *Book: A Novel*, a wonderful academic satire that Random House published in 1992.[63] I'm putting this—in the interests of propriety, *propriety* mind you, not *property*—I'm putting this above the line so there will be no nonsense about a lack of full disclosure.

Spokesnote: All right, all right. But as Barbie said a little while ago, we all have to come from *somewhere*. And *now* we are *here*. That movement from *then* to *now*—it is called intellectual progress—is in fact, what we footnotes incarnate by making our readers oscillate from above the line to below and back. That oscillation *embodies* the subject of *Qimron v. Shanks*—credit where credit is due.

Boffin Pundit: Sooo?

Spokesnote: So, honestly, Boffin, sometimes you really do think like a professor whose chair has only three legs. Qimron staked claim to *us*. And now that the verdict has come down from the Israeli Supreme Court, in his neck of the woods, *he owns us*. It's a Thirteenth Amendment issue that worries us, not a First.

Boffin Pundit: Yes, I see that now. But what's to be done? You've made your views known. I think you know that we sympathize with them. All we can do here, heh, heh, is *discuss the matter further*. That business about what tempted Qimron, for example. If you would return below the line, I'd like to get to that.

Spokesnote: OK. We just want *you* to understand that *we* now understand what role we really play in this conversation, and it is not a small one.

Author: Of course not. In the language of the law, you all are indeed the Cultural Chorus.

---

63. ROBERT GRUDIN, BOOK: A NOVEL 70–79 (1992).

Boffin Pundit: Fine, fine. Though I do wonder what footnote awareness will mean to the legal profession. If they go on strike, they've nothing to lose but their *Ids* and *Supras*. . . . But, now that we have got the uprising pacified, could we get back to the . . .

Teacher of Righteousness: Yes, to the temptation of Professor Qimron. Temptation's more in my line of work. Could we explore that a little, Barbie?

Barbie: Well, it's Author's territory, really, but I think I understand it better than he does. It stems from Qimron's startling confession about his motives, the one Nimmer quotes.[64] I really think, if I may have unanimous consent of those present and voting, that we should put it above the line.

All, including Footnote Spokesperson: So moved!

[*The Footnotes then dissipate to their home below the line.*]

Barbie: So here's the temptation of Elisha Qimron as Nimmer quotes it. Qimron is explaining how he felt when he learned that *MMT* had finally escaped into the outside world:

I was stunned. I cannot describe such a feeling. It's like somebody approached me and took something forcefully, saying, "Who are you, anyway?" This belongs to me, this thing that I made. I would not have taken an unpublished text and worked on it for so many years unless I was assured that my right of primacy would be protected. As a matter of fact, the scroll, or any text that is published will always be named after its first editor. No matter how many editions will follow, people will always go back to the first edition. Throughout the years that I worked on *MMT,* I hardly worked on anything else. My family lived in penury. If my wife complained, I told her "Look, this is our life, we will gain glory. It might be more important than money."[65]

How's that for going to the heart of a case! And Nimmer quotes another comment that would have broken my heart—if only my carping critics would allow me to have one.

The depth of Qimron's feelings in this regard is difficult to overestimate. In response to Judge Dorner's question, Qimron admitted that *"even now I feel if they would let me I would have held it a little more."* Even when "overjoyed" about his ultimate Supreme Court triumph, "Qimron said he has regrets about the access others now have to the scrolls. He said it robbed scholars such as himself of the leisurely pace they once enjoyed."[66]

64. Refer to n. 54 *supra* and accompanying text.
65. Nimmer, *supra,* n. 1, at 145–46.
66. *Id.* at 146 n.715 (Barbie's emphasis added; citations omitted; quoting Ron Kampeas, *Israeli Scholar's Copyright Upheld,* AP WIRE, Aug. 30, 2000).

Boffin Pundit: What's so heartbreaking about that? He wants fame. Who doesn't? He's willing to sacrifice his wife and family for it. Who isn't?[67]

Barbie: Yes, but his "fame" is such a meager affair. Hungering for the recognition of a few other scholars, most of whom—judging from the splenetic discharges this affair has released—he hates and despises anyway. I know what the spotlight does to you. That hunger for the center, that centripetal gaze, is what the economics of attention is all about. I've lived in that spotlighted center all my life. My unkind critics say it *is* me.[68] But at least it has been a *real* spotlight. Two of my selves are sold every minute around the globe and . . .

Author: Barbie—if *I* can interrupt for once—the literary scholar George Steiner has written about just what Qimron's hunger has done to him. Here, let me read you a short passage, since we are now allowing a few select quotations above the line.

> The practice of devoting one's waking hours to the collation of a manuscript, . . .the discipline of investing one's dreams in the always vulnerable elucidation of abstruse problems accessible only to a handful of prying and rival colleagues can secrete a rare venom into the spirit. *Odium philologicum* is a notorious infirmity. Scholars will lash out at one another with unbridled malignancy over what appear to the laity to be minuscule, often risible points of debate . . . such asceticism cuts a writer off from "the great springs of life" and can nurture a pathological need for cruelty. . . .
>
> . . . [T]hose solicitations of violence . . . bubble like marsh gas from the deeps of abstruse thought and erudition.[69]

Boffin Pundit: There has certainly been plenty of marsh gas in *Qimron v. Shanks.* The scholarly world doesn't come off looking very well, Author.

Author: No, it doesn't. But it is a pretty accurate snapshot and it does tell us, at least from my point of view as a literary scholar, what this case has been all about.

Boffin Pundit: Ah! At last! What *is* this case all about?

Author: Well, David Nimmer says that it is all about "what quantum of creativity suffices to secure copyright protection"[70] and, from a legal point of view, nolo contendere. But from the broader viewpoint of a student of human conflict—and that

---

67. GENDER FOOTNOTE. Of course it is understood that "husband" can be substituted for "wife" along with needful pronomial adjustments, although for stylistic ease we have not done so.

68. PHILOSOPHICAL FOOTNOTE. That's why Barbie might claim, if she were *really* willing to derail the conversation, that she represents all the questions about human identity that come to the fore in an economics of attention.

69. REFERENCE FOOTNOTE. George Steiner, *Reflections: The Cleric of Treason,* NEW YORKER, Dec. 8, 1980, at 158, 188–89.

70. Nimmer, *supra,* n. 1, at 6.

is what a career spent studying literary rhetoric has made me—it is all about *motive*. About all that marsh gas bubbling to the surface.[71]

Teacher of Righteousness: You know, when you come to think of it, there was quite a lot of this "marsh gas," as you call it, in the religious disputation of my day. That was one of the kinds of pollution people came to our spa to escape. But that gas comes from the very purity of our motives as prophets. And I suppose you authors have at least something of the same purity. Not to the same degree, of course . . .

Author: Don't be too sure of that. Steiner offers wisdom on this matter too. A scholar, he says,

> when in the grip of his pursuit, [is] monomaniacally disinterested in the possible usefulness of his findings, in the good fortune or honor that they may bring him, in whether or not any but one or two other men or women on the earth care for, can even begin to understand or evaluate, what he is after. This disinterestedness is the dignity of his mania.[72]

Boffin Pundit: But Qimron *did* care for fortune and honor. He craved them. That's why he brought the lawsuit.

Barbie: Yes, and that's why his lawsuit would have broken my heart if I'd had one. He lusted after not only his fragment of fame but the cultural conversation flowing from it, and that lust *robbed his mania of its dignity*. He has made it, and himself, look small and shabby.

---

71. AUTHOR'S FOOTNOTE. I can't get away with much more authoring above the line or I'll be abolished again, so I'd better put this further comment down here below. Nimmer brings in the figure of A. E. Housman, via Tom Stoppard's play about him *The Invention of Love*, and it is apropos his enterprise in just the ways we are discussing here. Housman's *Introductory Lecture*, the address with which he read himself into his appointment at University College, London, in 1892, provides one of the most moving defenses of the pursuit of knowledge as an end in itself that has ever been wr—well, *authored*, and yet Housman was a textual editor famous as much for his savage reviewing of the work of others as for his own editing. He says, in the *Introductory Lecture*, in complaisant praise of his scholarly colleagues and himself, "We are not like the Ottoman sultans of old time, who thought they could never enjoy a moment's security till they had murdered all their brothers" (A. E. HOUSMAN, INTRODUCTORY LECTURE 41 [1937]). But we scholars often do resemble these murderous sultans, and not least Housman. Here's one example of brother-murder among many, from the preface to his edition of MANILIUS, BOOK I (1903):

> An editor of no judgment, perpetually confronted with a couple of [manuscripts] to choose from, cannot but feel in every fibre of his being that he is a donkey between two bundles of hay. What shall he do now? Leave criticism to critics, you may say, and betake himself to any honest trade for which he is less unfit. But he prefers a more flattering solution: he confusedly imagines that if one bundle of hay is removed he will cease to be a donkey.
> So he removes it.

A. E. HOUSMAN: SELECTED PROSE 35 (John Carter ed., 1961).

72. Steiner, *supra*, n. 69, at 184.

Boffin Pundit: Then that goes for the whole Dead Sea Scrolls cartel, not just Qimron.

Barbie: Yes. They are all like poor Ken.

Boffin Pundit: Ken?

Barbie: Honestly, Boffo, sometimes you really are a slow chip. It's all about *reproduction,* which poor Ken can't do. They can't do it either. They lack the central equipment to fructify their own scholarship—generosity of spirit.

Teacher of Righteousness: Wait a minute. You are saying that generosity of spirit redeems the whole scholarly endeavor and that this redemption is just what the cartel members lacked?

Boffin Pundit: Maybe Barbie and Author are saying it, but *I* can't for the life of me figure out what this all has to do with copyright law.

Teacher of Righteousness: But Boffin—you don't mind if I call you by your Christian name? . . .

Boffin Pundit: No, no, everyone does, or worse, as perhaps you've noticed.

Teacher of Righteousness: Well, then, Boffin, if copyright is all about human motive, and how to excite it to—how does it go?—"[t]o promote the Progress of Science and useful Arts, by securing for limited Times to Authors and Inventors the exclusive Right to their respective Writings and Discoveries,"[73] then what Professor Qimron has done to himself goes directly to the question. Don't you see?

Boffin Pundit: No, I don't.

Teacher of Righteousness: Imagine a spectrum running from the hunger for the spotlight, for fame, for wealth and honor, for the kind of hierarchical dominance that all primates . . .

Barbie: All *male* primates, at least.

Teacher of Righteousness: Yes, of course, all *male* primates, although in fact lots of females do it, too, hunger for hierarchical dominance. Let's put that hunger, and Professor Qimron's scraps of hunger for it, at the left-hand extreme of this spectrum. OK?

Boffin Pundit: Gotcha. Go on.

Teacher of Righteousness: OK. Now let's put on the extreme right-hand end the kind of disinterestedness Steiner talks about and that A. E. Housman talks about in the *Introductory Lecture* referred to in a below-the-line discussion a few moments ago.[74] The love of knowledge for its own sake.

Barbie: But wait a minute. It is not only knowledge that is loved that way, but all kinds of other pursuits as well. Think of the people who collect me, for a start. One of the things I allegorize most is the power of pure play.

---

73. U.S. CONST. art. I, § 8, cl. 8.
74. Refer to n. 71 *supra.*

Boffin Pundit: Barb, let's stipulate to all that, as we lawyers like to say. The Teacher is talking about just that, the whole domain of pure play, aren't you, Teacher?

Teacher of Righteousness: Boffin, you're finally with the program. And this pure play may be useless but it has, as Steiner says, its own kind of dignity.[75] We naively trust it because it has no designs on us. We put this trust into action all the time without realizing it. We trust our wagon mechanic more because he seems to have a disinterested love for wagons. He wants to fix something right because he wants it to be right. He is loyal to the mania of his choice. We all like to think we feel that way about our jobs. It finally becomes a *moral* thing, even though the loyalty is purely *formal,* purely *aesthetic.*

Barbie: But that's the point I've been trying to make all this time about my *clothes.* About my *hair.* About my *selves.* It's all about formal loyalties, not about moral models. That's what all those self-righteous frumps who put me down have never understood.

Author: But, as the Teacher has just made clear, it speedily gets to be a moral issue as well.

Teacher of Righteousness: Yes, and this is where the U.S. Constitution comes in. Somewhere in the middle of our spectrum is the Kingdom of Use, the Pastures of Practical Purpose. That's the world that copyright law wants to fructify. Are you with me, Boffin?

Boffin Pundit: I'm with you.

Teacher of Righteousness: But the problem is, it doesn't do a very good job relating the two extremes to each other. It assumes that human motive is concentrated only on the left-hand side of the spectrum, the side where poor Qimron decided to take his stand. This kind of thinking generates all the hysterical declarations that without protection for intellectual property there would be no creativity.[76]

Boffin Pundit: But that's where the driving forces are.

Teacher of Righteousness: With all due respect, Boffin, that's nonsense. Human motive lies all across the spectrum, in all kinds of mixtures, but an extraordinary amount

---

75. *See* Steiner, *supra,* n. 69, at 184.

76. NAPSTER FOOTNOTE. As an example, Time-Warner President Richard Parsons says:

This is a very profound moment. . . . This isn't just about a bunch of kids stealing music. It's about an assault on everything that constitutes the cultural expression of our society. If we fail to protect and preserve our intellectual property system, the culture will atrophy. . . . Artists will have no incentive to create. Worst-case scenario: The country will end up in a sort of cultural Dark Ages.

Chuck Phillips, *Music Giants Miss a Beat on the Web,* L.A. TIMES, July 17, 2000, at A1, *available at* http://latimes.qpass.com/cgi-bin/qpass,cgi?QIID=1+00+628700LATID=935756.

of it lies at that right extreme, in the domain of pure play, of love of form for its own sake. And that area copyright law simply ignores.

Author: And so it doesn't build on a very strong foundation.

Teacher of Righteousness: And so it builds on a very one-sided foundation. That's the point all the "Copyright Left" types, as they call themselves, are trying to make.

Boffin Pundit: But without the protection of intellectual property, there wouldn't be an intellectual property because there would be no incentive to create it.

Teacher of Righteousness: Honestly, Boffin, just stop and think for a minute, will you? How long has copyright protection been going on?

Boffin Pundit: Well, let's just say from the Statute of Anne in England, 1710, though some people want to push it back further.[77]

Teacher of Righteousness: And what that statute really "incentivized" (to use the barbarous jargon you all use today) was simply *publishing* stuff and not *creating* it?

Boffin Pundit: Well, yes, but . . .

Teacher of Righteousness: And before 1710? No culture? No art? No literature? No philosophy?

Boffin Pundit: Yes, of course there was, but . . .

Teacher of Righteousness: But what? That other extreme has generated the creative power from the beginning. Homer may have sung for his supper, but do you really believe that's *all* he sang for? Or Virgil? Was it only fame that made him keep fiddling with the *Aeneid* all his life and ask on his deathbed that it be destroyed because he still had not got it right? Or Ovid, poor man (I've met him actually, but that's another story), especially after he had been banished to Tomis and had no reason to write, or even to live? That "play" ground is very high ground, Boffin, and when someone deserts it, as Qimron and his pals did, they've cut the ground out from under their own feet, whatever the Israel Supreme Court says.

Boffin Pundit: Now wait a minute. I thought you said earlier that you were a Teacher of Righteousness, not Self-Righteousness. A pretty strong smell of soapbox seems to be wafting around us . . .

Teacher of Righteousness: I know it. I know it. It seems to come with the robe and the beard, somehow. And sitting next to Barbie doesn't help, either. It heats my imagination.

Boffin Pundit: You don't think that "credit," or *fame,* to give it its proper name, matters, then?

---

77. LEGAL FOOTNOTE. These issues are explored in Lyman Ray Patterson's *Copyright in Historical Perspective* and in Mark Rose's *Authors and Owners: The Invention of Copyright* (LYMAN RAY PATTERSON, COPYRIGHT IN HISTORICAL PERSPECTIVE 143 [1968]; MARK ROSE, AUTHORS AND OWNERS: THE INVENTION OF COPYRIGHT 4 [1993]).

Teacher of Righteousness: Of course it matters. They both matter. It is getting them into a harmonious relationship that is the great thing.

Boffin Pundit: So that they create the world of Usefulness in the middle. But I thought Use drove them, that necessity was the mother of invention.

Author: That's really the great question, isn't it? Which direction does the current flow in? Here, let me just draw a quick diagram.

> [*Before anyone can stop him, he jumps up to the easel and draws a diagram like this.*
>
> Fame ⟷ Use ⟷ Play]

Boffin Pundit: Well, what difference does it make which direction they flow in?

Author: Do you remember our earlier discussion about an economics of attention?

Boffin Pundit: Well, I think I do. Yes, of course I do.

Author: OK. In an industrial economy, the economy of "stuff" that we are used to, and which our laws of property are based upon, flows from the center to the extremes. [*He points to the chart he has drawn.*] But in an economy of attention, the vital energy flows the other way, from the extremes inward. The polarity reverses. And that's where copyright really matters. And where the neglect of the "play" end of the spectrum starts to confuse things.[78]

Boffin Pundit: Because—do I have it right—much of the cultural conversation takes place in the play sphere?

Barbie: Yes! That's exactly what has happened to me. That is *why I have happened.* That's why I'm such a dynamic personality! [*She looks around with, not a smirk, but a genuine smile of shared understanding.*] That's where my power comes from. I get both ends of the spectrum working. So really, I model not only clothes but thinking about intellectual property. Ha!

Teacher of Righteousness: Don't worry, dear, we all love you just as you are. [*It is his turn to reach over and give her arm a little pat. She smiles back at him and, in the twinkle of her eye, morphs into Water Lily Barbie.*]

Author: Wow!

Boffin Pundit: Wow!

> [*The Teacher of Righteousness is unable to speak.*]

Barbie [*after she has resettled her huge flowered skirt with its deep furbelows cascading down to the hemline and checked on the baroque fountain of blond hair stacked high on her head*]: But I do illustrate how much creativity comes from pure play, from disinterested

---

78. REFERENCE FOOTNOTE. This confusion has prevailed since Herbert Simon's early paper, *Designing Organizations for an Information-Rich World*, which appeared in *Computers, Communications, and the Public Interest* (see Herbert A. Simon, *Designing Organizations for an Information-Rich World*, in COMPUTERS, COMMUNICATIONS, AND THE PUBLIC INTEREST 37, 52 [Martin Greenberger, ed., 1971]).

curiosity that doesn't care about credit, that just wants to know and to contribute to the conversation.

Boffin Pundit: Yes. But you don't need any incentives for that.

Author: Oh, but you do. Copyright law is part of a larger endeavor: maintaining an efficient system of learned communication. The free market of ideas doesn't just happen. You have to make sure the domain of play is not crowded off the stage by "serious overreach[ing]," to use David Nimmer's phrase.[79]

Boffin Pundit: Now you are talking about fair use. And the global trade metaphor. Courts can't go around creating protective tariffs for authorial vanity.

Barbie: And "unfair" use also has to be protected, if by that we mean people just playing around with form for its own sake, as well as to prove all kinds of cases. It ought to be something more like the Doctrine of Fair Play than Fair Use. My Mattel chaperones have never understood this, that playing around with me—even when it gets pretty ugly—is part of what makes me the cynosure of every eye, as someone once said, I think.[80]

Teacher of Righteousness: You've said it, dear, and that's good enough for us.

Boffin Pundit: I'd like to change directions here—if we *have* a direction—but I don't know how to do it. How can I segue to David Nimmer's flirtation with literary theory?

Barbie: I know how! [*She morphs into a black sheath that flares out below her knees with huge wings projecting from each of her shoulders and red hair flowing down nearly to her heels. It is her first really outré, not to say ugly, self, and is generally felt as such, although of course nothing is said. She responds to their unstated feelings nevertheless.*] See? A modicum of real originality, and you all turn into crosspatches. How much originality, then, do I have to display to be just one of my selves?

Teacher of Righteousness: Barbie, please. . . . Could you just change back into one of the other . . . this one is so . . .

Barbie: OK, OK. [*With something between a shrug and a shiver, she contracts her wings and floor-length hair inward into a short bob and a plain white cocktail dress with a blue waist sash. It is very smart and, as we come to see after persistent looking, quite see-through.*]

Boffin Pundit: That *was* a nice transition, Barb, but now that we see where we are, let me go off on a little tangent that has just now occurred to me.

---

79. Nimmer, *supra*, n. 1, at 89.

80. Barbie Background Footnote. Barbie here is referring to the "counterculture" Barbie movement, or movements. It is not something that most of us in the Barbie community like to dwell on, but facts are facts and need to be faced. These pockets of discontent have led to incarnations like "Teenage Single-Parent Barbie" and "Battered Wife Barbie" and "Pregnant Teen Barbie" and to various other kinds of protests against all that she has come to represent—at least as they see it (*see* Lord, *supra*, n. 13, at 236).

Barbie: It's a waste of a good transition but we live in the age of hypertext, so how can I object? After all, conversation itself is hypertextual, isn't it, and that's what we are having—and talking about. So what's slid hypertextually into your mind?

Boffin Pundit: Well, it's the curious division in Nimmer's essay. Not only the division between the discussion *of Qimron v. Shanks* and its legal issues, but between Nimmer's own . . .

Author: . . . two selves? Yes, I noticed that. The lawyer, with his implacable lawyer's reasoning from cases and the incipient novelist with his . . .

Boffin Pundit: . . . with his many hypothetical cases and . . .

Teacher of Righteousness: Novelist? Surely he's more in my neck of the woods, a biblical exegete.

Author: Well he does argue that the two, literary critic and exegete, nowadays at least, amount to much the same thing. So maybe we can call him a literary critic.

Boffin Pundit: But why does he need the critical section at all?

Author: He's disturbed, naturally enough, that I've been abolished. He feels, quite rightly, that *he* at least still needs me, and I'm certainly grateful for that.

Barbie: Well, *have* you been abolished? Are you still there? Where's *there*? Who's *you*? These are the questions people keep asking me, so it's a real pip to pass them on to you.

Author: No, no, I've only been abolished in *a certain part of town.* The history of literary criticism is full of such abolitions. It's how you grow up from your parents. Well, no, "growing up" is too strong. It's just what you have to do to be *original.* We all ought to know about *originality* by now.

Barbie: But you guys have been at it for half a millennium . . .

Author: . . . two and a half, actuall—

Barbie: Well, whatever, and you still have not got things straight? You just keep on talking?

Author: Well, that's one of the things that Nimmer takes us to task for, never coming to closure.

Boffin Pundit: Yes, in contrast with the law, where we move decisively from point to point, decide it once and for all, and then move on to the . . .

Author: You're joking, of course.

Teacher of Righteousness: You're joking, of course.

Boffin Pundit: No, it's just as David Nimmer said. The law must make up its mind. No endless argument, no shilly-shallying around, no appeals 'til the sun cools down.[81]

---

81. *See* Nimmer, *supra*, n. 1, at 205 (noting that "the legal enterprise . . . moves toward resolution").

Author: And so the commentary on the law just dwindles and dwindles. Quite. Let's get back to a genuine point, to *me,* in fact.

Barbie: Whether you exist?

Author: Just so. Here's the way it has been, Barb. Literature has always been studied in Western culture, from the Greeks onward. It was Greek and Latin literature, obviously, for much of this time, and it was studied as a training in how to speak and write, the training that goes by the now-discredited name of "rhetoric." Rhetoric teachers studied . . .

Boffin Pundit: Author, Author, it is a well-known fact that more than half a dozen lines of explication in a dialogue format and the reader gets testy. Even Plato couldn't always get away with it. So, if you could go below the line for this explication, vital though I am sure it is . . .

Author: All right, all right. I was just trying to explain what has happened to me and to allay Nimmer's anxiety. But I'll go below if I must. Come on, Barb, we'll go together. Those guys can have a cup of coffee—or maybe a noncommercial commercial interruption.

> [*Author and Barbie step to one side off their marshmallow cushions and drop out of sight, to appear in a crypt-like footnote below.*]
>
> [*We are now below the line.*]

Author: Actually, it is a little more comfortable here below, Barbie. You don't have to worry as much about keeping up the dramatic interest.

Barbie: If you say so. But I know a low-rent district when I see one.

Author: So—here's what happened. Rhetoric teachers studied the text and the postures of performance and the audience. They used all the information that was there to use, but they used it to explain how language worked to persuade people. They trained for the forum and the law court. Harking back to a thread we developed earlier, they were, and still are, the primary economists of attention. When you have to work in those worlds, you use all that is there to use: information about the author, the text, the audience, the time and place. When literature began to be studied outside these pressurized persuasive contexts, when it started getting really theoretical, then it started removing one variable or the other from the complex equation. It made interpretation much easier. I was trained, for example, by the New Critics at Yale. These guys were just emerging from a period when the context was everything and so, to be original, they simply junked that. The *text* was made the main element in a literary judgment. The author got junked, too. It didn't make any difference what the author *thought* he or she was trying to do. Once an author had published, the critics took over and decided the meaning. And so, as Nimmer mentions somewhere, I think, authors like me were put on notice.[82] When the next lot of critics came along, they took the logical step and showed me the door. Well, this left them a problem, since *somebody* had to be writing the stuff—and, besides, obviously nobody had abolished the *critical* author . . .

Barbie: So we come back to my problem. Who wrote *me?*

Author: Yes, you are the "paradigmatic case," as we've already noticed. But back to the tedious explication. If the author wasn't writing the stuff, then who was? There were only two candidates, and both were elected. First, *language itself* was doing the writing. Poor authors like me just moved the pen back and forth. Or, it could somehow be the *zeitgeist,* the historical background, that was doing the writing. This took us back, in rather an embarrassing way, to the method that had just been junked a generation or so before. So this was called the "New" Historicism and made the vehicle for a great deal of politically correct allegorizing. Now there has been a change of air, and university professors seem to be teaching the text again, although one never can be sure about these things. The point to be made: *theory* keeps wanting to eliminate some of the real-life variables, just the way Newtonian physics ignored nonlinear dynamics until chaos theory came along. As soon as criticism distinguished itself from rhetoric, it could be theoretical. David Nimmer argues that the law has never allowed itself to do this.[83]

I have my doubts, but I'm not competent to speak about this assertion because I am not trained in the law. In the copyright cases I've worked on though—and there have been sixty or so of them—the legal arguments presented went through the same tergiversations that literary criticism has rehearsed. This makes sense, really, because literary criticism and legal argument emerged from the same rhetorical center. And both have followed the same theorizing trajectory. The really smart people have objected to the simplifications, of course. The great American philosopher of rhetoric, Kenneth Burke, said that literary criticism ought to use "all that is there to use" and in fact does so, whatever it pretends to do, whenever it comes to do its work in the world.[84] Is this so very different from Justice Holmes's famous assertion at the beginning of *The Common Law?*

---

82. *See id.* at 14 & n.43 (commenting that publishing without a valid copyright notice forfeited copyright protection).

83. *See id.* at 203 (explaining that judges do not have time to redo past doctrine "in light of the latest school of thought").

84. KENNETH BURKE, THE PHILOSOPHY OF LITERARY FORM 23 (2d ed. 1967) ("The main ideal of criticism, as I conceive it, is to use all that is there to use").

The life of the law has not been logic: it has been experience. The felt necessities of the time, the prevalent moral and political theories, intuitions of public policy, avowed or unconscious, even the prejudices that judges share with their fellow-men, have had a good deal more to do than the syllogism in determining the rules by which men should be governed.[85]

Or as Holmes said later: "General propositions do not decide concrete cases. The decision will depend on a judgment or intuition more subtle than any articulate major premise."[86] Nimmer, somewhere in his piece, quotes George Steiner cautioning us to trust the tale and not the teller.[87] The tale of literary criticism has been, if you follow the history of criticism of a particular poem, that literary judgment too depends "on a judgment or intuition more subtle than any articulate major premise."[88]

[*Author then turns to Barbie.*]

Author: Barbie, you're a good listener, I'll have to say that.

Barbie: I keep telling you guys that I'm not an airhead. *I* can listen. *You* guys are the ones who never listen to *me.*

Author: OK, OK. Up we go.

[*They reappear from between the cushions and take their former seats. The Teacher of Righteousness and Barbie reach out simultaneously for one another and touch hands, then draw back with a twinge of self-consciousness, alarmed at the electricity that flows between them.*]

Author: Well, what have you two been doing up here while we were down below?

Boffin Pundit: Getting some real work done, that's what. We've raised $50K in a mini-begathon, and Teacher here has agreed to do the pilot for an author-interview show on religious truth and moral responsibility in the modern world—from his own prebiblical perspective, of course. We've been needing a high-rent version of our Feelgood Shrink Show for a long time and Teacher here would be perfect. And what have you two been up to down there?

Author: We've solved the Vanishing Author Mystery, that's what. Nimmer doesn't have to worry. Criticism, and literature too, can't really do without an author any more than copyright law can. And both end up using all the information that is there to use, whatever their theoretical protestations to the contrary. And both have to make up their minds at least sometimes but avoid doing so whenever they can.

---

85. 3 Oliver Wendell Holmes, *The Common Law, in* THE COLLECTED WORKS OF JUSTICE HOLMES 109, 115 (Sheldon M. Novick ed., 1995).

86. *Lochner v. New York*, 198 U.S. 45, 76 (1905) (Holmes, J., dissenting).

87. *See* Nimmer, *supra*, n. 1, at 163.

88. *Lochner*, 198 U.S. at 76 (Holmes, J., dissenting).

Boffin Pundit: Well . . . I'll stipulate to that now, so that we can get on to the last big is-sue Nimmer brings up. Time *is* running a little short. The argument that copyright protects what has been created as fiction but not what has been created as fact?

Author: Well, now that I exist again, maybe I can lead off on this point without fear of . . .

Boffin Pundit: . . . Without fear of interruption? Absolutely!

Author: Nimmer says that "[c]opyright protection requires the subjective choice of an author in order for protection to lie."[89] Our creative juices have to lie "on an aes-thetic . . . plane."[90] For a literary critic, there are a couple of problems with this. For example . . .

Barbie: For example, me. Do I lie on an aesthetic plane? I'm a doll, yes, but I've always been marketed as a real person, albeit a fictional one, not a doll. And yet I am an actual physical doll and can be trademarked, at least partly. When little girls play with me, I am at the same time a physical presence for them and something that they re-create in their own imaginations. And so I can appear here, as a real-life fictional creation. What plane am I on then? When all those dreadful countercul-ture warriors stick pins in me and put my head in the oven do I exist for them on the aesthetic plane or the plane of fact?

Teacher of Righteousness: And what about me? There's some historical evidence for me, muddled though it be. And here I am, too.

Author: Yes, I think Nimmer has his feet in the marmalade here, at least from a liter-ary point of view. You could bring the same questions up against me. What exactly am I, et cetera, et cetera. But I've in mind a different distinction, and one that goes back to our earlier discussion about an economics of attention and the changes that brings.

Boffin Pundit: When you were arguing that Qimron understood this change and the rest of us didn't?

Author: Yes. Is it not the case that in an economics of attention, Nimmer's "facts" and "aesthetics" change places? If that is the case—and I think that it is—then the whole distinction gets stood on its head.[91]

Barbie: Back to *my* problem again. If stuff and attention have changed places, then I'm realer than my plastic. Well, I've always thought so.

Author: It does return us to where we have started—Qimron and the economics of at-tention that invited him to make a grab at owning the conversation.

89. Nimmer, *supra*, n. 1, at 22.

90. *Id.*

91. AUTHOR'S FOOTNOTE. Author talks about this at greater length in his *Michigan Quarterly* article (Lanham, *supra*, n. 18, at 271–72).

Boffin Pundit: But we haven't confronted Nimmer's main question!

Barbie: Yes. *My* question! How much originality does it take for me to be *me*, or at least one of my me's? Speaking of which, let me get back to where I started. [*She morphs back into Dungarees-cum-Blouse Barbie.*][92]

Author: Barbie, that's one that we can't answer. Copyright law won't allow us to, because it won't allow us to consider aesthetic quality, and that's what makes for originality, in little or in large. This is not to say that judges and juries don't consider it anyway. Aesthetic merit has been the dog that does not bark in practically every case I've worked on. At the end of the day they all use the "Emily Dickinson" test[93] and return to the kind of subjective judgment that allows us all to use all the information there is to use, and not simply all the evidence.

Boffin Pundit: But can't we do a little better than that with Nimmer's main question — What is the fundamental "atom" of protectability? We can at least see why it is so hard to answer. It comes directly from the effort to map an economics of stuff onto an economics of attention, as Andy Warhol pointed out in his famous apothegm.

Barbie: That in the future everyone will be famous for fifteen minutes?[94]

Boffin Pundit: Yes. Warhol took the egalitarian premise that human goods should be equally divided among all the people of the world and mapped it onto the economics of attention, where it becomes silly. It doesn't fit because the atoms of the one economics are not the same as the atoms of the other. The centripetal gaze — the gaze you live by, Barbie — won't permit of democratization.

Author: Yes, I think I can explain why . . .

Boffin Pundit: No you can't, Author. Our deliberations will have to end here, good friends, or we'll exhaust even the patience of public television. So, until we meet again in the aether, thanks to all and to all a good night.

> [*As the camera pulls back, Barbie and the Teacher of Righteousness exchange meaningful looks. The meaning of those looks it will not be given us to know, alas, but Righteousness and Beauty being condign companions, we may hope for the best.*]

---

92. RHETORICAL FOOTNOTE. Barbie's return to mufti here at the end should not blind us to her true identity. She is Dame Rhetoric and will change into another beautiful costume any minute. Readers with a serious attention surplus on their hands may wish to pursue the relationship between rhetoric and righteousness in Author's essay *The "Q" Question* (RICHARD A. LANHAM, THE ELECTRONIC WORD: DEMOCRACY, TECHNOLOGY, AND THE ARTS 154–94 [1993] [explaining that rhetoric is used for both good and evil]). On second thought, maybe I should explain who Dame Rhetoric is. The Greeks thought that persuasion was important enough to make a goddess of her: Peitho, the goddess who incarnated the art of persuasion. In the Middle Ages, she became Dame Rhetoric, an icon who almost rivaled Barbie in popularity. You might almost think of her as Dame Style.

93. Emily Dickinson remarked once that she knew poetry when she saw it because it took the back of her head off. *Emily Dickinson, at* http://www.galegroup.com/freresrc/poets_cn/dicknbio.htm (last visited 26 February 2001). This test can serve to represent several legal tests that depend, finally, on the pure impressionism of judge or jury.

94. ANDY WARHOL, THE ANDY WARHOL DIARIES 156 (Pat Hackett ed., 1989).

Background Conversations

I've found Tom Bethell's review of thinking about conventional *stuff* property, *The Noblest Triumph: Property and Prosperity through the Ages,* to be a useful stimulus to cross-thinking about intellectual property. Joseph L. Sax's *Playing Darts with a Rembrandt* explores the limits of private property rights in what he calls "cultural treasures." The line he attempts to draw between private and public property has much to say, by analogy, about how intellectual property in digital expression seems naturally to float over from private to public. Mickle-thwait and Wooldridge's *A Future Perfect* helped me to see how intellectual property formed part of the larger "globalization" debate on free trade and suggested that wisdom from the marketplace of ideas would help illuminate the argument about the world marketplace of stuff, however unlikely it now seems that such wisdom will be applied.

The place to begin thinking about the Internet and its implications for intellectual property is Lawrence Lessig's two books, *Code and Other Laws of Cyberspace* and *The Future of Ideas: The Fate of the Commons in a Connected World.* The Internet focuses, as Lessig sees, the top-down/bottom-up basic quarrel in management, commercial, governmental, and, thus, the great political nexus of our time. As it started out, the Internet showed all the advantages of an open market. But the forces of central planning and control soon zeroed in on it. Lessig sketches out what a free market in digital expression could mean for an information economy but chronicles how the icy fingers of older technologies are reaching out to strangle this promise. He is gloomy about this future and so am I.

Books about copyright have fallen thick as snowflakes in Siberia in recent years. I have not read most of them but have faith still in some basic texts. The book to which I have returned most often in my legal work is Benjamin Kaplan's *An Unhurried View of Copyright,* but Paul Goldstein's more recent *Copyright's Highway* is also useful. Alexander Lindey's *Plagiarism and Originality,* although now half a century old, still forms a good place to start thinking. For the historical beginnings of copyright, Lyman Ray Patterson's *Copyright in Historical Perspective* and Mark Rose's excellent *Authors and Owners* can serve as introductions. Thomas Mallon's *Stolen Words* recounts some amusing case histories, including one in which I was involved. I continue, too, to find Ithiel de Sola Pool's *Technologies of Freedom: On Free Speech in an Electronic Age* useful, even though times have changed considerably since its 1983 publication.

About the Dead Sea Scrolls, I have no wisdom to offer. I read a great deal about Barbie dolls while I worked on the case, but I confess that I forgot almost all of it as soon as the case was over, and I can offer no more help than that given in the notes to chapter 6. Like Chaucer's Wife of Bath, once Barbie came to life in my imagination, she turned on the books that created her and banished them.

A Note on Hypertext

Since this chapter saw the law article as a kind of hypertext and played a little with the form, maybe I should say a word about it. To have dealt with hypertext properly as a way to economize attention would have swamped the chapter and to illustrate it would have required a digital presentation not possible here. Hypertext applies the aleatory strategy used in so much experimental art in the twentieth century to continuous prose. If it is informational prose, the links will be parentheses. They will provide layers of information, and the reader will choose which layer to read in. Or move down as many layers as that reader needs. Thus the reader can target the level of information needed. Such a hierarchy could be represented spatially, and perhaps to better effect—we excavate down through layers—as I illustrate in chapter 3. It also works well, in a mixture of directed and aleatory organization, in writing "might have been" history. Present a series of choices and show what follows from each one.

If it is imaginative prose, the links will function, like other aleatory works, to suggest different possible structures or stories. Fictional "counterfactual history," you might call it. The author will have provided the reader with a set of "loci" from which to construct a story. Such a compositional technique turns readers into authors. It uses our hunger for order by giving us ingredients that seem to demand order. If they don't yield illuminating arrangements, as often they don't, then the comprehensive effort collapses. The question, for both kinds of hypertextual prose, is which kinds of arguments, or fictions, are best served by stressing parenthetical interruptions, à la Henry James. At some point the links dominate the central text and random association takes over, as sometimes seems to happen in law articles. For a hypertextual author, especially a legal one, a link is a promise that something can be made of it. Hypertext allows the writer to include elements that continuous prose excludes but this promise is the price paid. The at/through oscillation that parenthetical interruptions depend on does not, as is sometimes maintained, operate automatically.

CHAPTER SEVEN

{THE AUDIT OF
VIRTUALITY}

Universities in the Attention Economy

Since I am not a real economist, I cannot make out how far we have moved
from stuff to what we think about stuff or how we might measure travel
down this road. But there is one segment of our current life that constitutes
an economics of attention in its pure state. Whether we call it cyberspace,
virtuality, computer-mediated communication, or simply the Net, out there
attention is everything. Sure, there are plenty of signs back to "real life," but
they are just that, ways out of a pure attention economy. Out there, *all* you
rent is "eyeballs."

Enterprises of all sorts, public and private, are being immersed in, and
audited by, this new economics, always with surprising and sometimes with
tonic results. Life in this new country constitutes much of the conversation
now in the business press, first when the "Internet bubble" was inflating and
even more so now that it has popped. Ownership there takes a different form,
and the natives turn out to be an odd lot, too. They don't work at ordinary
times or sleep at ordinary times or buy and sell at ordinary times. Ordinary
time has gone out the window. These natives do, however, show a surprising
addiction to text, though telephony and radio are migrating there too. "Assets" there are reckoned entirely in attention terms, not in stuff. Properly
speaking, although you can order stuff there, it is a place where the reversal
between stuff and nonstuff has already taken place. Stock market valuing
systems and accounting practices are having a hard time adjusting to the
switch. No one knows what "provident" means anymore and bubbles are
being blown and popped as at a children's birthday party.

And out there, too, new universities are growing up. If you want to know
how the campus-based university will fare in this new economy of attention,

you might do worse than look at how the virtual university is shaping up. On-line higher education is still in its cradle but, like a baby picture just snapped with a Polaroid camera, its outlines are beginning to emerge. Increasingly, too, the "online" courses are being offered on-campus too. Faced with an en-rollment bulge and a budget shrink, universities are making online courses campus choices as well. They are expensive to make but once in the can they can be repeated more cheaply, or so it is thought. But whether they prove so or not, the online/offline comparison is certain to become a central theme in university strategy.

We might think of this online/campus comparison as an "audit" of the current campus in terms of the attention economy. Such an accounting has never been possible before; there was no other way of doing business, no new ground from which to view the old. Now we can make such a comparison. The audit turns out to be a searching one. The virtual university, a Mars in his cradle though it be, questions the main operating assumptions of its parent. Maybe that is why such a baby dose of it has evoked so much strong feeling.

ASSUMPTION 1. THE IDEAL EDUCATION IS FACE-TO-FACE, ONE-ON-ONE EDUCATION

Every college that can muster a favorable teacher/student ratio brags about it. Every dean wants the students taught by real tenure-track faculty mem-bers, up close and personal. No place, except perhaps the Oxbridge colleges, can afford one-on-one tutorials, but such remain the unexamined ideal. Next best is a seminar taught "by the Socratic Method," the crackling eristic inter-change beloved of humanists. The lecture system, though still widely used, is now considered Wal-Mart educational retailing that we want to abolish as soon as we can afford it. This one-on-one assumption defines a peculiar in-stitution. In the university, quality is thought to vary inversely with the lever-age that elsewhere creates efficiency.

The early reports from online make us wonder about this assumption. Some students wither in embarrassment under crackling eristic, however much the instructor may enjoy dealing it out, and shrink from speaking in a large lecture class. Online, they blossom. They have a lot to say, once they are given time to think about it (to get an A in one of Socrates' classes, you had to be a very quick thinker, as well as agree with the teacher), and to say it in writing, in the digital space. The writing that emerges from this new variety of "speech" differs from the old. I spent an educational lifetime reading stu-dent writing and almost all of it, good or bad, was forced performance. Its model—and how I urged it on my students!—was the variety of professional writing professors do. A few students prosper under this regime, but for most it is heavy lifting. The tone and spirit of online writing changes when it leaves professorial imitations aside. Written for the class and not the instructor, it is sometimes incorrect and often inelegant, but it has the breath of life. The person who is writing it wants to say something and not simply jump through another hoop. The Socratic instructor that I tried so hard to play, in this view, doesn't come off too well. The teacher/pupil ratio still matters, but in a different way. The early reports from the online front indicate that students often feel they learned more online than in the classroom and felt more at ease. The informing logic of the classroom and its rhetoric of performance, written and spoken, has been called into question. Everyone who has taught online seems to agree that the role of the instructor changes too, from Socratic wise person to *magister ludi*, a master of ceremonies. The burden of instruction, though not of arrangement, seems to move back onto the student.

We might pause here to remark the university's main response to this new genus of "in-person" instruction—the wired classroom. The expensive wiring of the classroom tries to engraft the pedagogical powers emerging from the digital expressive space, and native to it, onto the classroom from which these powers have only now escaped. Nothing, finally, misses the point and power of digital expression quite so dramatically as a classroom full of computers. "Why," anyone who understands the logic of digital expression must ask, "Why put computers *there?* That's where the students just escaped from." Digital expression puts the classroom in the computer, not the computer in the classroom.

So—the virtual audit calls into question the classroom, and everything that goes with it: the standard papers and examinations, the instructor's role and the student's. A profound audit for an auditor still in the cradle.

ASSUMPTION 2. HIGHER EDUCATION, IN ITS IDEAL FORM, PROCEEDS IN A SETTING SEQUESTERED IN BOTH TIME AND SPACE

Four years it should take for college, and in a special place, insulated from the world of "getting and spending" that academics never tire of denigrating. But the sequestration model brings with it a radical imbalance in educational rhythm, one that online education, by its nature, corrects. The four-year model says this: at the beginning of your adult life, take four years off to learn about the world and reflect on it, and also equip yourself with the knowledge needed to make a living in it. If you emerge deep in debt, don't worry. The certificate redeems all. Spend four years on theory and the rest of your life on practice. But none of us learns this way; the toggle between theory and practice does not come in four-year intervals but in much shorter ones. That is why students have always created an extra-curriculum, gotten jobs, sought out internships, and stopped out for a year or two. That's why my students at UCLA usually worked at least half-time and often much more. That's why they took six or seven years to graduate, rather than the canonical four.

Signs stick up all over the landscape telling us that the four-year sequestration pattern should be junked. The community colleges have seen this, and tailor their instruction to the places and times where it is needed. The "universities" that businesses have created to train their employees do not observe a semester system into which all educational needs must be fitted but have courses as long as the particular need requires, supplied when and where the employee needs them. The lean automobile-manufacturing system, invented by Toyota, revolutionized the car business by showing the enormous waste that huge inventories create. There is a gigantic "inventory" problem in higher education, if we had the wit to see it. The four-year pattern, the semester course, the credit hour, all pile up useless inventories of knowledge that is supposed to come in useful later on. And, to be sure, it sometimes does. But it is a wasteful sometimes.

To compensate for its frozen educational rhythm, the modern university has become a quilt of training and education. It could not have continued otherwise. But the quilt is spread over a procrustean bed of rigid courses on a frame of four-year sequestration. The bed has long since collapsed in the name of common sense.

What has been the response of universities, public and private, to these pressures? Improve the graduation rate! That is, hug the four-year pattern to our bosoms as ineluctable reality. Ignore everything that has happened to show us that the sequestered four-year model no longer works and insist that everyone conform to it. The online virtual university, by creating a new model, supplies a searching critique of the campus one.

The virtual university supplies a different sequence altogether. It provides "just-in-time" education. You face a problem and need the help of theory to solve it. You find the education you need for that problem and get on with life. No need to wonder about the relevance of it. That comes with the territory. The oscillations between theory and practice, between looking at and looking through, can vary widely online, depending on what you need and when you need it. But it is always a frequency and wavelength suited to the present circumstance, not a four-year per life one size that fits all. All kinds of fix-ings across the matrix are acceptable.

Phoenix University has prompted an almost hysterical response in the university world simply by operating for profit, but we should be paying attention to how it makes its profit: by ignoring the four-year pattern and its accompanying physical sequestration. The Open University in the United Kingdom has been a distance-education institution since its founding, a "virtual university" in an adumbrated "cyberspace" before there was an In-ternet to be online on. It allows students who cannot afford the four years of sequestration to create an oscillation between theory and practice that suits their own need for knowledge. It has recently expanded its operations world-wide. It constitutes a far greater competitive threat to Campus U. than Phoenix U. will ever do. But, because it is not "for profit," few have paid it any mind. And yet it has, by operating in a pure economics of attention, taught hundreds of thousands of students for the price of tens.

The snobbery on which the sequestration model is built runs deep. I read in a recent *Yale Alumni Magazine* the standard dean's cliché: "We are not a trade school." Yale does theory not practice, education not training, gentle-personly preparation for the business of life, not raw-knuckle plumber's training for a life of business. No cliché surfaces more dependably in the current conversation. Yet its self-contradictions are palpably silly. What is the Law School for? The Medical School? The Business School? The Fores-try School? The Engineering School? Indeed, the Graduate School? The com-puter science department? The economics department? Do students study chemistry for the soul enrichment to be found in semi-micro quantitative analysis? And on and on. What sustains the "trade-school" cliché is the four-year sequestration pattern, the idea that the purposes and problems of life can be postponed for four years while—in adolescence of all times—we phi-losophize on them.

Like the other foundational hypocrisies of university life, its main use is to shut down an embarrassing fundamental debate, the debate about edu-cational sequence. "Knowledge does not keep any better than fish," Alfred North Whitehead remarks in *The Aims of Education,* the best discussion of educational rhythm I know. You can't store it up for four years and then use it for life.

The virtual university construes the problem differently. It accommodates many different oscillations between theory and practice, task-specific "train-ing" and exploration of fundamental principles. By supplying knowledge when and where it is needed, it keeps the fish from spoiling. Such education does not ignore theoretical knowledge, general knowledge. How could it? That's where the power comes from. But it is willing to accommodate the oscillation between theory and practice at many different frequencies and wavelengths. In the virtual university, the theory/practice distinction that bureaucratized academics so prize simply evaporates.

Viewed from the outside, the most astonishing fact about American higher education is its current division into two camps, based on the theory/ practice distinction: the theory world of colleges and universities that we usually mean when we say higher education, and the training world of business, government, and the military. The division embodies the dangers of the dean's cliché. For nearly a decade now the training sector has been larger than the "respectable" segment of higher education. It is clearly our main competitor and has been for a long time. Phoenix University forms a small part of an enormous endeavor that is all for profit. The training world has much to teach us about the uses of educational technology, about bringing courses to market fast and teaching them efficiently. And yet most academics do not even know that it exists. The dean's cliché is apotropaic. It wards off evil. Because the ignored segment represents practice not theory, training not education, we can safely ignore it. It has most to teach us, perhaps, about how to use electronic technology to sustain a virtual university that operates on many different educational rhythms and not simply the four-year sequestration model we now make such efforts to preserve.

ASSUMPTION 3. THE EDUCATION EVERY UNIVERSITY OFFERS SHOULD BE GENERATED IN-HOUSE BY A RESIDENT FACULTY EMPLOYED FULL TIME FOR THIS PURPOSE

This assumption is so ingrained in us, and in our accreditation boards, that we can hardly imagine things otherwise. But otherwise things once were. The medieval university was staffed by professors who were individual entrepreneurs. They lived by fees paid to them by the students for their lectures. Famous lecturer, many students, large income. Boring lecturer, few students, envy, bitterness, poverty. The university provided the hall, and a critical mass of students, but the professor owned the educational product and was free to, and sometimes did, take his (they were all he's) show on the road. The virtual university re-creates this pattern. In the electronic expressive space, teaching is now publishable. The logical pattern in cyberspace is the medieval pattern, and it is beginning to reappear. Famous professors can cultivate a worldwide group of students. And professors famous in a narrow field can find the critical mass worldwide that they cannot find at home.

This genre of teaching, at least such as I know about, has been over the Internet, punctuated sometimes by visits to an actual campus every few weeks. But it need not be so. To cite one example that I know well, my friend and colleague Robert Winter, of the UCLA music faculty, created four pioneering CD-ROMs, before that substrate suffered a premature eclipse. Each of these took as its subject a famous piece of music (Beethoven's *9th Symphony*, one of the Mozart string quartets dedicated to Haydn, Stravinsky's *Rite of Spring*, and Dvorak's *Symphony from the New World*) and spun out from it a course in the music of that period and, more largely, a beginner's guide to classical music per se. Each disk is self-standing and self-teaching, and even self-examining. They exemplify how a "course" might be published in a digital medium and distributed offline, simply through the mail. One can imagine a "faculty" of such programs, and the excellent education it would provide.

The vital ingredient in all this teaching is the digital medium, not online delivery itself. The Winter programs use the vital center of the digital medium. The many "talking head" video courses simply transport the classroom to the desktop. So do some online courses. But all such programs point to the same moral. The professor, in electronic space, needs the university only as a retailer, and sometimes not even as that.

We can also look at this virtual configuration from the employer's, the university's, point of view. For thirty-two years, I taught Chaucer and Shakespeare at least once a year, and often the same course twice in a year. It was, although I could conceive no other way to do it at the time, a dreadful waste of effort. I can certainly argue that I tried to keep my teaching fresh, as most academics try to do, but once I had figured out what I thought the texts meant and published my thoughts in books and articles, it was mostly repetition. Not for the students, of course, who came to the class to get a report on the received wisdom. In a virtual university, my course need only be bought once every, say, half a dozen years. It could then be presented to its students when and where they wanted it, and not only Tuesdays and Thursdays, ten till noon. It would have saved the University of California a lot of money and me a lot of repetition.

For a glimpse of an alternative system in action, we can look at how the Open University in the United Kingdom develops a course. A team of twenty-five or thirty people (scholars, presentation specialists, and producers) develop a course. It is expected to last half a dozen years but hardly to be immortal. The digital medium allows new mixtures of text, voice, and image that create educational programs of unprecedented power. We shouldn't assume, as most practicing academics do, that such courses are inferior to live instruction. As often as not, indeed, one might make the opposite assumption.

A system of this sort, digital in medium and transmission, allows us to see the present system as extraordinarily wasteful, a preindustrial handicraft pattern. The virtue of such a handicraft system, we always assume, is the individual attention that outstanding scholars bestow on students. But here has been its greatest failure. Universities spend great sums to attract famous names to their faculty only to have these famous names unavailable to their students. The most common outcome is pure public relations: The Great Name gives a freshman seminar for a dozen students. Wow! Aren't we making good use of our Nobel Prize Winner! He is not only an ornament in the academic status race! He teaches a freshman seminar to a dozen students once every three years! Such sentimental sops to "teaching" do not solve the problem but only highlight it. If the Great Name is worth the Great Salary, some means has to be devised to leverage that person's teaching, make it available to a broad spectrum of students. Otherwise, we are still in the rhetoric of ornamental names in which people of my generation have passed their academic lives. What is needed, *hic et ubique*, is leverage. We've tried the leverage of large lecture halls for almost a thousand years but, compared to more modern technologies, it doesn't generate much power. Electronic expression is the only workable alternative leverage in sight.

The management and employment pattern the virtual university implies— and what a reception such a suggestion will get in the present climate!—is that of an entertainment production company that develops talent and markets it. Its real business, like a publishing company in the digital world, is the acquisition of rights. Can we be sure we have nothing to learn from such organizations?

ASSUMPTION 4. THE IDEAL PATTERN OF EMPLOYMENT FOR A UNIVER-
SITY FACULTY IS ONE THAT COMBINES A MAXIMUM OF NARROWNESS AND
INFLEXIBILITY IN JOB DESCRIPTION WITH A MAXIMUM OF JOB SECURITY:
THE TENURE SYSTEM

The combination of lifetime employment and unchanging job description— you cannot be asked to teach "out of your field" even if that field is now out in left field and no one wants to play in it—is so unworkable that it has already broken down, as the part-time phenomenon attests. Even the Japanese, it turns out, can't afford guaranteed lifetime employment, even coupled, as it is there, with a maximum of job flexibility, rather than inflexibility. The usual criticism of the tenure system, that it preserves people in a profession they are now too lazy or decrepit to profess, misses the central point. The danger is not that they can no longer do the same job but that the *job* will remain the same, whether they can do it or not. In the tenure debate, it is not the unchangeable faculty that is the problem but the unchangeable job description.

The tenure system is based on a gigantic one-time judgment of fitness. I spent as much time as any other academic worrying about this system, enduring it, and then serving on the endless agencies of judgment where the saved judge the candidates for salvation. But, until I retired from the academy and had pondered it from the outside for several years, I had never fully appreciated the gigantic *amount of time* it requires. When I left it, my department at UCLA was requiring fifteen letters from professors in the field at different universities for advancement at the full professor level. The judgmental process has become monstrous. And its premise—that a job will never change and thus will require only one set of qualifications for the lifetime of its holder and one irrevocable judgment on these qualifications—has simply evaporated. The one-time permanent tenure judgment assumes a rhythm and sequence the world no longer permits.

The tenure system is usually defended on a different basis, as the agency of academic freedom. The free market of ideas requires it. If so, why are now over a third of the teachers in higher education, the non-tenure-track proletariat, denied its protection? The current epithet of choice, tenure track, has less to do with academic freedom than with guaranteeing present academic job descriptions and work practices. As in Europe, the protected workers have jobs for life and the unprotected become "temps."

The virtual university has created several new patterns of academic employment and will certainly create many more. These patterns will be many and varied. That is their main virtue. They will respond to a global educational marketplace. They do not spend their time devising ever stricter standards for tenure beatification. Part-time enterprise carries no stigma here. This marketplace approximates more closely a genuine free market of ideas, jostling and chaotic and undisciplined, than the mandarin bureaucracies of formal academia. As an example, let me cite the quickness and accuracy with which companies have mounted their own online educational programs in response to changing business circumstances. But when I talk to an academic about the ReMax online curriculum in real estate practices, the lights dim. *We* have nothing to learn from *ReMax*.

ASSUMPTION 5. THE PURPOSE OF THE UNIVERSITY ADMINISTRATION IS TO PROTECT THE FACULTY FROM THE OUTSIDE WORLD

In the virtual university the difference between the university and the outside world evaporates. The virtual university lives and breathes in the real world. Its alternations of theory and practice, as we have seen, vary with time and place. It can find its place at any point on our motive spectrum. The sequestration model of the university assumes that the faculty's job is to lead "the theoretical life," a life of pure intellectual play, and that the university administration should create an "eternal childhood," in which the faculty can do this. I have taken these phrases from Allan Bloom's odious discussion of this assumption in *The Closing of the American Mind*. In as much as the protection succeeds, it does indeed infantilize the faculty, as Bloom claimed. The view from virtual space suggests that this playpen protection is a bad idea, not a good one. This renunciation of the playpen model does not mean that inquiry does not need protected spaces and times, but it does mean that a lifetime of protection makes for an eternal childhood.

ASSUMPTION 6. UNIVERSITY FACULTIES ARE ANIMATED BY A PURITY OF MOTIVE DIFFERENT FROM, AND SUPERIOR TO, THE WORLD OF ORDINARY HUMAN WORK

If this assumption were not so common in university circles, one could scarcely believe that anyone familiar with university life could hold it. Yet it dominates every conversation about for-profit arrangements of any sort in academic life. It haunts any effort to suggest to graduate students that nonacademic employment might be compatible with human happiness. It constitutes our root conceit. Other people act for profit; we pursue learning for its own sake. The "for its own sake" argument has, as its main advantage, that it precludes further discussion. If you say, "Well, yes, but what you do must have *some* purpose we can talk about," it only proves that you don't get it. Like the other assumptions in our list, it results in self-enclosure. The argument can be pursued no further.

Let me pursue it a little further, nevertheless, by invoking again the motive spectrum discussed in chapter 5.

game ——————— purpose ——————— play

I argued there that game and play are the driving sources of human motive. If we are lucky, they are orchestrated to work together and create mature purpose, but we are not always, perhaps not primarily, purposive creatures. No one wants to admit this; we all think ourselves purposive, sensible, and restrained. All except academics. We academics dwell, we like to think, entirely in the world of play, of behavior for its own sake. It is knowledge for its own sake that justifies the sequestration in time and space, and the freezing of the theory/practice oscillation into the theory half of the waveform. Protecting the play space constitutes, as we've noted, the main theory of management for the university. And because our way of life is organized around this motivational purity, we often look down our noses at those whose motives are more obviously mixed. This purity of motive descends, I suppose, from our religious origins.

A spirit of pure play, we argue, drives genuine creativity. Pure research leads to progress; applied research to sordid compromise. At the apogee of this motivational caricature sit the institutes of pure thought where Einsteins sit and think. A purpose, a task, an application, only disconcerts propositional thought.

The virtual university, life in the digital expressive spaces, has from its beginning worked in the opposite way, from a thorough mixture of all three kinds of motive. Born in play, agitated continually by competition, the original hackers soon noticed that all kinds of work could be done in new ways. The "killer app" became a holy grail, not a badge of motivational impurity. The extraordinary dynamism of the Internet comes from the continual roiling mixture of motives, of game, purpose, and play. Tim Berners-Lee— director of the World Wide Web Consortium and senior researcher at MIT's Computer Science and Artificial Intelligence Lab—all honor unto him, has it all wrong in wanting the World Wide Web to remain pure in motive. Its inner dynamic works toward impurity. A perfect instance of this mixture is open-source programming. The operating system Linux started out as play but then enlisted other programming warriors who want to show their stuff in the arena of their peers. Striving to be first, to win the game. But also, in the middle of the spectrum, they create a product tailor-made for their work. And what comes out but Linux as product, as a new tool in the world of purpose.

Such deeply mixed motives, moving from play to game to purpose in high-frequency oscillation, have not been unknown in the academic world, but they have not come from the institutes of pure thought. They have come from ad hoc groupings with richly mixed motives, as we discussed in sketching out the matrix in chapter 5. These groupings are convened, alas, often by war:

the cryptographic establishments at Bletchley Park in the United Kingdom and Arlington Hall in the United States, for example, or the Radiation Laboratory at MIT or, most of all I suppose, the Manhattan Project at Los Alamos. The people who worked in these projects talk about the heightened sense of life that emerges from such a rich and continually changing motivational mix. This same mixture seems to have generated the explosion of Japanese consumer electronics in the 1960s, and it certainly has detonated the Internet explosion.

When universities work, they work this way too. Teaching is an intensely purposive activity, and when it has been jammed together with research into one career, as it has in the American university, it has constituted an enormous generative engine. Hard to bear, maddeningly inconsistent at its heart, but rich in results. It is only when academic life lives up to its professions of motivational purity that the fire goes out. Purity of motive is a disastrous operating premise, whatever the motive. Pure ambition creates parodies of Achilles. That's why the sixties had to happen. But pure play is a disaster, too, as the sixties proved. And if you work only for food, well, as was pointed out long ago, humankind does not live by bread alone. It lives by rich motivational mixtures, the kind that have provided the principal propellant for the digital economic explosion. The fear that our motives will be contaminated by contact with this rich mixture is not simply silly and ignorant, it is dead wrong.

ASSUMPTION 7. UNIVERSITIES ARE UNIQUE INSTITUTIONS; AS SUCH, THEY CANNOT BE MEANINGFULLY COMPARED TO ANY OTHERS

The first response, if you try to talk about productivity or efficiency or any measured result in academic life, is "the university is not a business." The same recalcitrance is applied to any other comparison. Health care, the most obvious current analogue, isn't like what we do at all. Nor can the university learn anything from global distance-learning organizations like the Open University. Nor from the training sector, which is for profit. Nor, God forbid, from the educational activities of the military, another major player not on our radar screen. Again, the assumption is self-sealing. If we cannot compare our organization to any other, then we, by definition, have nothing to learn from anybody else and need pay no attention to them. The "unique institution" argument is the organizational counterpart of the "for its own sake" argument for academic learning. "If the university is not a business," it seems reasonable to ask, "then what sort of organization is it?" If you can rejoin, "It is its own kind of organization and exists for its own sake," then the inquiry comes to a close. You have guaranteed that you will never learn anything from anybody.

The virtual university constitutes a surprising obverse case. Online discourse is unique. There has been nothing like it before. Yet the questions asked of it seek to understand it by trying to find analogues. How does it resemble other mass media? How does it resemble telephony? How does it resemble printed textual communication? What type of economics is needed to understand it? What does "productivity" mean here? Where and how is the value added? Is it self-managing? If not, how is it to be managed? These are all outward-turning questions, and we can learn from the various answers. They provide a striking contrast to the self-sealing moat of uniqueness that university faculties erect around their institution.

ASSUMPTION 8. INEFFICIENCY IS SOMETHING OF WHICH TO BE PROUD
This assumption follows naturally from the previous ones. It proves that one's motives have remained pure. If we are truly a unique institution, then a bottom line of any sort travesties our endeavors.

Once in a department personnel meeting, to alleviate the despairing boredom such meetings provoked in me, I tried to end the meeting by using what we might call an *argumentum ad tributum,* an argument from the taxpayers' point of view. We had been debating for two hours whether to give a colleague a $50 per month raise. I did a rough calculation of the amount it was costing the taxpayers of California to keep that group of people in that room for that length of time and remarked that it was costing far more to debate the case than to grant the raise and go home. On these grounds, I called the question. The argument simply did not register. I was discharging into a nonconductor. It was irrelevant even to introduce calculations of this sort. We were debating degrees of beatitude, not money.

Of all the assumptions that prevent the university's creating a condign management philosophy for our present economy of attention, this basic assumption is surely the most debilitating. It leads to an accounting system that we might proverbialize as "Perpetual insolvency sustained by perpetual mendicancy." Bottom lines can be of all sorts, but whatever currency they deal in, they try to measure whether the enterprise is in tone, in good form, as well as whether it has done what it proposed to do. Universities, public or private, do not operate this way, whatever they profess to do and however often they change "administrator" to "executive." Their only operating plan is to spend all the money they have—the faculty can always think up fresh ways to do this—and then ask for more. Complaining, all the while, no doubt, about how society no longer values education. Public universities ask for more public money. Private universities invent ever more efficient milking machines for their alumni. But neither sector has ever devised a bottom line condign to the enterprise. To devise one means devising a system of management condign to the enterprise. *Hoc opus; hic labor est.*

To repeat: bottom lines need not be always about money. They are about monitoring the power and vigor of an enterprise by measuring how well it has used the resources at its disposal for the purposes intended. If the purposes are vague, unexamined, and infinitely expandable, and if measurement of success never goes beyond the psychology of rumor enshrined in national magazine surveys, then the institution, and the people in it, never grow up. Back to self-enclosure. Back to a theory of management that aims to protect the faculty from bottom-line reality of all sorts.

The protections afforded higher education against bottom lines, much as we all applaud them, work against the self-knowledge that any complex organization must possess and refine. Consider, for example, the federal student loan program. Who could oppose it? Nobody, so far as I have ever read. Students who cannot afford the costs of a modern higher education are insulated from them. This is wonderful for the institutions because they can keep increasing those costs, rather than controlling them. Loan programs simply pass these increased costs on to the students in the form of a lifetime of debt. That seems fine to the universities and, amazingly enough, to most of the students as well. Yet the net effect is to insulate the university from the cost accounting that tells any enterprise how it is doing. It is no good saying that education is automatically better the more money we spend on it. The bankruptcy of that Edenic premise is all too apparent in secondary education, and it ought to be apparent at higher levels as well.

Or we might consider a second sacred cow, alumni giving. The levels that it has attained in the United States are striking and testify to the faith Americans place in education, especially higher education. There has been nothing like it since the Middle Ages, when monasteries promised a place in Heaven to the rich in return for their money when they died. But the question here, too, is what value the students are getting for their money. For alumni giving is, after all, another way of passing costs on to students, in this case past students rather than present ones. It amounts to another form of the mendicancy that has evolved to support a perpetual insolvency. There has to be, at some point, at some time, a real audit, an accounting of some sort in both the narrow and the wider senses of the word. Without it, there can be no genuine theory of management for higher education or body of best practices. The need for both is what debates on the shape of the university in the present century are going to be all about.

Let the virtual university once more audit the brick-and-mortar one. One great virtue of virtuality has been that it exists in a marketplace that both admits, and admits to, an accounting system based on solvency. The questions applied to it are, to be sure, often beside the point. It is examined on whether it is doing the traditional tasks better than the traditional university is when it is redefining both those tasks and how they are done. But no matter. From the beginning, the questions that have surrounded it are questions of efficiency. How well is it doing? It is indeed a unique institution but it has never taken refuge in its uniqueness, never argued that it stands above accounting. It has been subject to criticisms from all sides and this is fine, for from it all will emerge a genuine accounting system, one based on solvency, not mendicancy.

Digital teaching methods also provide a means of comparison with brick-and-mortar ones. These can no longer claim uniqueness, for there is another class of university and the results between the two can be compared. Oddly enough, the brick-and-mortar world is perfectly willing to apply standards of efficiency to the virtual university that it would never consider applying to itself. Again, no matter. Two systems create a basis of comparison that did not exist before.

Some interesting comparisons result. We might, to take one important instance, consider the difference between Internet time and campus time. The Internet has speeded up the metabolism of thought and decision across the world of work. Everyone feels this, whatever endeavor they pursue. The metamorphosis from an industrial economy to an information one has been catalytic. The Internet embodies this fundamental change of pace. Everyone feels this change, that is, except the university. There, no metamorphosis has yet occurred. A professor of English at George Mason University struck precisely the right note apropos some changes in the curriculum proposed by the administration. "If you're talking about a democratic process, it has to be less speedy than an efficiency expert would like. . . . We have time to talk. What's the hurry? We're not going anyplace."

If you don't know what the hurry is about, you don't know what business you are in. Does the university? It may realize it is in the information business—it sometimes talks this way—but I don't think so. The business it still thinks itself in is academic landlord: renting space in classrooms to students. The virtual university does not labor under this illusion or think at the old landlord speed.

ASSUMPTION 9. THE NEW ELECTRONIC FIELD OF EXPRESSION DOES NOT CHANGE WHAT WE ARE DOING BUT ONLY HOW WE ARE DOING IT

We can pivot to this assumption from the last one on the fulcrum of intellectual property. When information is put on the Internet, it gains potential value simply from this act. In the textbook-and-landlord idea of the university, this is not so. It is hard to use information there and you have to come to campus to get it. What is on the Net is infinitely stealable and so potentially infinitely valuable. Like open-source programming, which may perhaps be the characteristic form of Web "property," there is no telling what people may make of it. That introduces Internet time and a market accounting system at the same time. The sequestration model for the university breaks down here, too.

The digital medium is not a neutral conduit any more than print was. As we saw in chapter 3, it creates a different rhetoric that puts words, written and spoken, in new juxtapositions with picture and sound. It creates a dynamic, three-dimensional space in which traditional academic disciplines take on new relationships and in which conceptual thought undergoes a radical dramatization and design emerges as a central organizational discipline. The audit this new expressive space applies to the brick-and-mortar university is deep and wide. From within the rhetoric of digital expression, we can see the present departmental and disciplinary structure, and the career patterns built on it, as the fossils that they have become. The "how" of academic teaching and inquiry has indeed changed, and this is generally appreciated. Awareness that the "what" has changed far more fundamentally has scarcely risen above the horizon.

ASSUMPTION 10. THE UNIVERSITY LIVES IN THE SAME ECONOMY IT HAS ALWAYS LIVED IN

I have been suggesting that we live in a new economy, an attention economy, and that, if we want to glimpse how the university might fit into it, we should look at the virtual university. There, the economics of attention exists in its pure form. Stuff is derivative; information, fundamental. Not "things," but "what we think about things" stands center stage. Digital technology takes us back to the old, the prescientific and preindustrial economics, to the economics of attention that, in fact, prevailed in the medieval university. Figure and ground, stuff and what we think about stuff, reverse again on the digital screen. That reversal, the return of an economics of attention, constitutes the fundamental cultural change brought about by digital technology. All the issues that now vex the university and prod the foundational assumptions we have been considering—practice muscling in on theory, profit discoloring pure inquiry, volatile job descriptions eroding lifetime employment, teaching turned into publication, even the resentful self-pity of humanists watching new disciplines eat their lunch—all these turn on the economics of attention.

As long as we are made of flesh and blood, we will live in a perpetual oscillation between stuff and what we think about stuff, between "economics" as she is commonly wrote, and an economics of attention. Our felt life will always mix the two. But not on the Web. The Internet constitutes a pure economics of attention. The virtual university, the university conducted electronically, is the university in a pure economics of attention. That is why it constitutes so valuable an auditor. How the university fits and fares in this electronic expressive space, in this new rhetoric, provides a litmus test of what it has been, its strengths, its weaknesses, and what is to become of it.

The university, by all rights, should feel at home in an economics of attention. That has always been its business: constructing attention structures so that students can absorb and use information more efficiently than they could if left on their own. But it still thinks in an economics based on stuff; that is why it still conceives of itself as a classroom landlord. The new management model that the university requires must understand the fundamental changes from an economics of stuff to an economics of attention. The sequestration model will no longer serve because in the attention economy the university moves from the margin to the center of the economy. It deals with the central reality, attention, not the stuff you drop on your foot. The balance in its curriculum shifts. It is not only—*horresco referens!*—that a new economics replaces the old but that a new disciplinary balance of power replaces the old. The "practical arts" are no longer so practical. The "ornamental" arts that allocate attention—the arts and letters, the law of intellectual property rather than the law of stuff, the biology based on bits and not carbon—are the practical arts in an economics of attention. At their core must stand some version of the discipline that for most of Western history supplied the "economics" for the economics of attention: rhetoric. None of the traditional disciplines as yet understands this profound transformation and I venture to guess that none of them will welcome it when they do.

Does this audit mean that all university instruction should become virtual? Certainly not. We need many new combinations of online and on-campus instruction, and we need to know how to relate them. This oscillation is the attention economy/stuff economy oscillation transposed into another key. The only fatal mistake is either/or. Such is the lesson taught by the audit of virtuality.

Background Conversations

Audits, Economic and Cultural

I modeled the title of chapter 7 on Correlli Barnett's *The Audit of War: The Illusion and Reality of Britain as a Great Nation*. Barnett argues that World War II provided an audit for British society, both before the war and immediately after. I found that Barnett's discussion explained much about the origins of humanism's disdain for the commercial and scientific world and I hoped that, by varying the title, a little of its disillusioning magic might rub off. Martin Wiener's *English Culture and the Decline of the Industrial Spirit, 1850–1980* explained in much greater detail this same disdain for commerce that I have felt throughout my career teaching English literature. Wiener traces to their origins the hidden Edenic simplifications lurking in so many novels and critical appraisals that I had long lived with.

Barnett's and Wiener's views have been disputed, however, by a number of economists. David Edgerton has done so in two short but powerful books: *England and the Aeroplane: An Essay on a Militant and Technological Nation* and *Science, Technology and the British Industrial "Decline," 1870–1970*. W. D. Rubinstein's *Capitalism, Culture, and Decline in Britain: 1750–1990* takes on Wiener directly, arguing that he misunderstands the basis of the British economy. It has been from the beginning primarily a financial and commercial, rather than a manufacturing, power, and an aggressive and successful one. Deirdre McCloskey, in a 1973 study, *Economic Maturity and Entrepreneurial Decline: British Iron and Steel, 1870–1913*, maintained that the British economy did not display the lack of entrepreneurial vigor, or economic success, of which it stood accused. In a later volume of essays, *Enterprise and Trade in Victorian Britain: Essays in Historical Economics*, McCloskey broadens the focus to include not only her own arguments but a survey of the subfield of British "decline" with additional comments by other scholars. This survey will be of special use to anyone like me trying to understand the fray from the outside.

It is an important fray to understand if you are interested in the economics of attention. It concerns our inquiry here because it concerns the relationship of the two kinds of markets, the idea market for attention and the stuff market for goods. Imaginative literature, and writings about it, have long viewed commerce with an aristocratic disdain. To put the scorn into our generalized opposites, people in the fluff business mostly despise people in the stuff business. Why is this? As the economist George Stigler has pointed out in a famous essay, "The Intellectual and the Marketplace," four times out of five it is the marketplace that pays the salaries of the professional intellectuals who scorn it. Why no awareness of this fact? Why the eagerness to bite the hand that feeds us? Even more puzzling, why do literary people despise the stylistic richness on which their fictions and inquiries depend and which is also generated by the market?

The dispute is a very old one, going back to Plato's aristocratic disdain for the *demos*. At its center is a hatred of the profit motive, a hatred built, as Stigler points out, on the misapprehension that a market transaction is a zero-sum one, that what I gain is always taken from someone else. But market exchanges are willing exchanges, and each party leaves the marketplace having both given and gotten. This satisfaction goes deep. Matt Ridley, in *The Origins of Virtue,* argues that, "Imprecise as the concept seems, the human animal does appear to have an exchange organ in its brain. . . . We invent social exchange in even the most inappropriate situations." The profit taken by each party returns as an increase in the general welfare as well as in individual satisfaction. This is not only Adam Smith's invisible hand but the historical experience of market economies as well.

In an attention economy, we do not need an invisible hand. I can keep my ideas and give them to you at the same time. This generosity underwrites Plato's *Dialogues* and the Western intellectual conversation since then. The intellectual scorn of markets comes from assuming that this same kind of attention-economics generosity should be created in a stuff economy. It cannot, but the end result is the same if the argument is pursued to the end. This very seldom happens. The root misunderstanding, therefore, comes from a failure to align an economics of stuff with an economics of attention, to see their true relationship. The result is the scorn of the market, and the illusion that one can and should rise above it, which animate the ten assumptions I've audited in the text of this chapter.

Tales of the Internet

For an establishing shot, we now have Paul Ceruzzi's excellent *A History of Modern Computing*. My favorite book on the origins of the Internet is Katie Hafner and Matthew Lyon's *Where Wizards Stay Up Late.* Mitchell Waldrop, in *The Dream Machine,* hangs the story of personal computing and the beginnings of the Internet on a life of J. C. R. Licklider. Stephen Segaller's *Nerds, 2.0.1: A Brief History of the Internet* is the companion volume to a television program but much better than such books usually are. The spirit that inspired both personal computing and the Internet I still find most accurately captured in Steven Levy's *Hackers: Heroes of the Computer Revolution.* It shows better than any other account I know the origins in youthful game and play of what we now think of as computer-based communication. How and why "hacker" became a dyslogistic epithet Katie Hafner and John Markoff describe in *Cyberpunk: Outlaws and Hackers on the Computer Frontier.* Howard Rheingold's *The Virtual Community* and Sherry Turkle's *Life on the Screen* both describe the foreign land, with its own population and customs, that the Internet has created. This foreign land has a rhetorical constitution—read these authors and you'll see what I mean.

Audits

The idea of an audit carries broad implications. As we have recently discovered, particular times and places and technologies do sometimes trigger revealing audits. The Internet constitutes such an audit for university education, but there are others.

Bruce Berkowitz's *The New Face of War: How War Will Be Fought in the Twenty-First Century* discusses warfare as conducted in nets of information as well as, or instead of, on a field of battle. He argues that hierarchical command structures were developed to move large masses of troops in frontal maneuvers. Now there will no longer be fronts but, rather, nets or nodes. His argument might well have been titled *The Internet's Audit of War.* We move from stuff to fluff, from armor plate to information armor: "Today dispersion, covertness, and stealth—essentially information armor—are the only effective protection." The most interesting part of the book to me was the description of John Boyd, a fighter pilot who argued that speed was not the most important attribute of a new fighter but *rather the ability to change "from one state to another" more quickly than the opponent* [emphasis mine]. Keep ahead of his information curve. Pay attention to the vital element before the opponent does. Boyd developed OODA (observation, orientation, decision, action) as his formula for this ability. Every element of this process depended on moving information. And if this is so, then the economics of attention intervenes at every point and in everything else that follows from this intervention. "Communications, signals intelligence, and information warfare all involved the same people." When warfare is waged in communication nets, then the whole stuff/fluff ratio for the military inverts as radically as for the business community.

Financial markets have been "audited" by digital networking as pitilessly as warfare. Elinor Harris Solomon has made the process accessible to the ordinary, nonequational reader in: *Virtual Money: Understanding the Power and Risks of Money's High-Speed Journey into Electronic Space.* Clifford Stoll's classic story of electronic espionage, *The Cuckoo's Egg,* starts out with an incidental financial mistake and turns into an audit of a very different kind. It is a great mystery read and does not require the steady logical reasoning demanded by Solomon's account.

A different kind of collaborative network was created when Boeing developed the 777 airliner, using a network called CATIA (computer-graphics aided three-dimensional interactive application). The watchword of the design team, as Karl Sabbagh tells the story in *Twenty-First-Century Jet: The Making and Marketing of the Boeing 777,* was "working together." The creation of this landmark airplane seems a long way from the economist's regression analyses and elaborate equations, but surely it lies at the heart of economic behavior, at the heart of sensing a market, developing an incredibly complex product for it, and then selling it, all in the face of grave financial risk. For me, the moral of the story was the intricate tapestry of motive that lay behind such a hideously complex design. Orchestration of motive on this scale is a rhetorical and a persuasive, as well as an engineering, accomplishment. It depended from, if not always on, the CATIA design network that supplies a running audit of the design. If Sabbagh's account takes your fancy, try Clive Irving's earlier account of a pre-CATIA design: *Wide-Body: The Triumph of the 747.* It tells an equally impressive story.

CHAPTER EIGHT

{REVISIONIST THINKING}

In our common conversation, style and substance are contending opposites. The more of one, the less of the other. The pairing has many names, and we build many proverbs on them: all sizzle and no steak, all hat and no cattle and, worst of all, rhetoric instead of real-

In economics, to build a model is to fashion a tool.

Benoit Mandelbrot and Richard L. Hudson, *The (mis)Behavior of Markets*

Indeed, a tool or method can scarcely be proved false. It can only be shown to be not useful.

Gregory Bateson, *Steps to an Ecology of Mind*

ity. We use the pairing as our most common putdown: what I say has substance, sense, tells the truth without artifice; my opponent, in contrast, is just blowing smoke, putting a spin on the argument for nefarious purposes. The way "spin" is being used in the current political conversation, you would think that rhetoric had just been invented, rather than being our constant companion since Plato's time and being the basis of our educational system for almost as long. That educational system did not present style and substance as contending opposites but as fruitful collaborators. That collaboration I'll call here "revisionist thinking." It has always lain at the heart of rhetorical education and practice, and the tool that makes it possible is the toggle switch I have called *oscillatio*, working within the matrix I've described in chapter 5.

The contending-opposites way of thinking does have its uses. In our journey through the perilous wood of life, no shield is more serviceable than a good crap detector. But crap detectors cannot create; they can only detect. Creativity, invention, comes when style and substance collaborate in a common purpose. Only when style and substance come together does originality emerge. It is this area of fruitful collaboration that copyright law, with all its imperfections, seeks to protect. Since Aristotle, the basic "topics" or arguments have been categorized into commonplaces. Literary critics have from the beginning isolated basic types of character and patterns of plot. These commonplace patterns we view as our common cultural heritage. Copyright law lumps them together as "idea" and does not protect them. It is the "expression" that is protected. This term, like "style" and "substance," is hard to define and complex in its actual working. But it is the playground where invention occurs, novelty emerges.

We usually think of analytic thinking as the enemy of creativity. But this is just another consequence of conceiving style and substance as antithetical enemies. To think of them as collaborators, ask yourself, "Which comes first?" Well, you do have to start with a blank sheet of paper (sorry, a blank screen) and write or draw or calculate on it before you have something to revise. But what you write in that moment comes from all you have read and thought and revised into your own thought. What flows out through your fingertips is not the work of an hour but the knowledge of a lifetime. The real answer to "Which comes first?" is "Neither." They are both part of a process, an alternation, and it is the process that comes first.

Rhetoric teachers have always advocated, as the final talent, the inspired improvisation that emerges from profound preparation. Baldesar Castiglione, in his Renaissance *The Book of the Courtier,* built a conception of civilized behavior around it that he called *sprezzatura,* a well-rehearsed spontaneity. Louis Pasteur pointed to the same process in his famous "chance favors the prepared mind." This total absorption of previous knowledge into spontaneous action is what the psychologist Mihaly Csikszentmihalyi has called flow. Laurence Sterne pointed to the same phenomenon when he described his method of writing *Tristram Shandy* as writing the first word and trusting to Almighty God for the second. All are examples of the power created when style and substance collaborate rather than fight.

It is certainly true that style and substance are a tricky pair of terms, and not only because they are imprecise. Push style to its extreme and it becomes substance. The Greek sophist Isocrates illustrated this, and it was Oscar Wilde's central theme as well. Hemingway's syntactical simplicity, his abjuration of verbal ornament, became so pronounced as to become highly ornamental. Thoreau advocated doing away with the ornaments of life so that he could live a life of pure play, a completely ornamental life.

Creation and revision constitute the oldest at/through sequence, whether in word, image, or sound. Under the influence of the Romantic vision of white-hot inspiration (what Terry Southern, I think it was, called the "right out of the old guts onto the goddam paper" school of composition), we have mostly lost sight of how important this revisionist cycle is and how it works. We shirk revision, think it a superficial frivolity. The explanation for this reluctance goes deep. We think words ought to come to us as naturally as breathing, without artifice. And, we also think, they should be understood in the same way. They should be transparent and unselfconscious. Revising word, image, or sound violates these unconscious assumptions. To look at the expressive surface, reflect on how we have communicated what we wish to, puts pressure on what we have said. We look at it as a stranger might, or try to. We think about what we have said with a different side of the brain. We will then see, especially if we have been trained in revision, where and how we have failed to "say what we wanted to say." This involves more work, and more drafts. We put pressure, in this way, on our own thinking. And we also become more comfortable with the bi-stable way of examining an expressive surface, through for meaning, and at for style.

Any technology that makes this oscillation easier, that sharpens this tool, lubricates human invention and expression. Here lies the central importance of digital technology. It has sharpened the revision tool. Never, for writers, has revision been easier. Those of us old enough to remember the slow agonies of draft after draft, written out in longhand, typed (by a secretary if you were lucky), marked up, typed again, da capo, can still feel the extraordinary acceleration and exhilaration that the screen brings to revision. But the same revolution has occurred with images, first in image-editing programs and now within the increasingly miniature camera itself. I maintained myself in college working as a draftsman. In those days, you couldn't change an inked drawing once you started it, and if you blotted it with your nib pen, you either scraped the ink off and reburnished the paper or you did the drawing over. You worked as did a medieval scribe. Digital notation has transformed this world. You can revise ad libitum, until you finally get it right. *Then* you print it out. And the same miracle has occurred in musical notation.

Here, surely, is a fundamental improvement. Revisionist thinking has been built into the center of creativity. The old pattern, however often we iterated it, was a three-stage process: creation, revision, final version. The new pattern approximates more closely continual revision. Ease of manipulation has undermined finality. Assuredly, we must come to closure sometime. The book must be published, the building must be built. But we don't feel that closure with the old finality. We are continually alert for improvement.

You can see this open-ended search for improvement in Toyota's famous *kaizen* method of automobile manufacture. Its pursuit of continual revision in its manufacturing methods is relentless and unending. Toyota has sought to inculcate this method as a native habit of mind. It has aimed to create a way of looking at manufacturing from a stylistic point of view. The oscillation between at and through is at a much higher frequency than anyone before had thought to invoke. Revisionist thinking of this sort can be found across the world of work. It does not always require digital expression, but digital expression makes it easier and more productive.

It is not too much to say that this capability for almost endless minute revisions makes complex modern creations possible. The CATIA computer program (computer-aided three-dimensional interactive application) that made possible the design of the Boeing 777 aircraft, for example, also made possible the design of Frank Gehry's Disney Concert Hall in Los Angeles. Continual revision makes possible a new mode of creation. The at/through tool is doing new kinds of work.

In the digital writing space, words no longer have it all their own way. They must compete with moving images and sounds. This competition has been greeted with enthusiasm by the people who make images and who engineer sounds. It represents the rise of the image and the fall of the word. What image maker could object to that? Finally the visually oriented world is getting some respect. Films no longer need take a backseat to books. Writers and literary critics, needless to say, take the opposite view. Literacy is endangered by the transfer of the word from book to screen. Indeed the very mechanisms of conceptual thought, and the culture built on them, blunder into mortal peril.

This conflict of views has done little to illuminate the competition for attention between words, images, and sounds. It is a problem in economics, the allocation of a scarce resource. Up to now, the solution to the problem has been sought in filters. We are used to dealing with scarcity. That has been our human lot since the beginning of history. Now we face plenitude. The solution? Find ways to transform it back into scarcity. In many ways this reversion helps but it does not seem, to me at least, a deep solution. How about revisionist thinking as an alternative? If we ask ourselves how a particular message should be communicated, and if we have the choice between words, images, and sounds, or new combinations of these, then we find ourselves exercising revisionist thinking. We usually say this? OK, try it. But maybe we could draw it. Or play it on a MIDI keyboard. We will find ourselves, as we learn to use these new resources productively, continually moving from one medium to another. This involves a new oscillation between *at* and *through* vision. If you have something to communicate, and you ponder whether this should be done with words, images, or sounds, and try out various combinations, you become self-conscious about expressive medium. You realize how, inevitably, what you say is changed by how you say it. You become acutely aware of style. This is revisionist thinking, but of a new sort. And, again, one energized by digital expression.

If the locus of our economy, or perhaps we might say of our society, is moving from stuff to information, and if that truly means a move from stuff to attention, then it is not surprising that the means of cultural notation, the expressive space, should reflect this movement. To do its job, it would have to. These new kinds of revisionist thinking represent a logical shift, not a cultural outrage. Just as digital storage is the only possible means of preserving the exabytes of information (an exabyte = a billion gigabytes) being generated annually, so the competitive expression of the electronic screen is the only way to express the larger struggle for attention. Micro is in tune with macro. Perhaps the written word (to select that medium nearest to my heart) is not dying. It is, like the rest of us, living in a different and more competitive world. More competitive because more plenteous. More images, more words, more signals of all sorts. This plenitude, this rich mixed signal had been sought from the beginning of the Western cultural record. It has been part of the West's long and vexed effort to create wealth. A competitive field of expression may be diminishing our old conception of eloquence, but, equally, it may be creating a new one. It is too early to tell. But new technologies bring opportunities as well as necessities, and we may miss the opportunities if we do not look for them.

Thus we may say, and not simply in a manner of speaking, that we live in revisionist times. Physical substance and what we think about it, stuff and fluff, have changed places. Our locus of reality has shifted. We have not left the physical world behind and become creatures of pure attention. Neither has wealth become totally disembodied. Our view is now bi-stable. We must always be ready to move from one view of the world to another. They are always competing with each other. We are learning to live in two worlds at once.

This toggle-switch world requires, in its turn, a more inclusive theory of communication, a matrix of style and substance that plots the variables of perceiver and perceived in a field of self-consciousness. This matrix tries to supply the "model of economics of information that will schematize its form and functions" that Walter Wriston pleaded for. Not by accident, such a matrix can be used to define style as it exists dynamically in the world of human behavior.

In an attention economy, the center of gravity for property shifts from real property to intellectual property. This shift has plunged us into confusions about the ownership of such property—about copyright and patent law—that it will take some time to sort out. In an attention economy, assets are to be found in the cultural conversation and so intellectual property owners are staking out ever-wider ownership claims in it. But, at the same time, information of all sorts has at last found its condign means of expression, the digital screen. Information, unlike stuff, can be both kept and given away at the same time. As long as the means of notation were fixed in physicality as books, reports, painted images, we could gloss over this major obstacle: that "possession" means something different from a private property in stuff. Now, with information expressed on a digital screen, with its new means of dissemination, we can no longer continue this gloss. Hence the current agonies in the music and film business. They have been caught in a vise, squeezed between the macro and the micro economics of attention.

One traditional source of intellectual property, for a long time almost the only one, has been the world of arts and letters. It should not surprise us, then, to find economists of attention there. Attention is what art specializes in. Artists like Christo and Warhol have both prophesied and embodied the fundamental shifts in the new economy. It would be possible, I think, and profitable, to read the history of art in the twentieth century as a history of attention economics.

The university curriculum and the disciplinary structure of inquiry and teaching that supports it undergo a foreground/background shift in parallel with that of the economy. Since the seventeenth century, the sciences of stuff have moved steadily to its center and the arts and letters, which deal with attention structures, have occupied the periphery. In an economics of attention, the two change places. Many reversals follow on this, including how communication, the arts, and the law are taught. It will take some time for the academic world to sort these reversals out. All the professional and departmental vested interests will oppose the change. The "culture wars," at least as they concern the university curriculum, have been the opening chapter in this struggle, with both sides profoundly misunderstanding what is at stake.

What can we say about the citizen of such a revisionist republic—that is to say, the consumer? We know the stock answer. The consumer is a "materialist" in a "materialistic" society, a deluded chump who lays waste his powers getting the money to spend on toys. He and she badly need the advice of an elite, intellectual and spiritual, who will guide them to buy only what they "really need," to cultivate their powers of mind and spirit, to teach them—in sum—the difference between style and substance. But what of the citizen-consumer in an economy where style often *is* substance?

The basis of satire, one might almost say from Juvenal onward, has been to attack style in the name of substance. What, in an attention economy, becomes of the satiric portrait of the "materialist" consumer, and society, so beloved today of social critics? If it is attention that stands at issue, then all the spiritual values of art and philosophy and religion that, from Socrates on, are thrown in the face of materialism and consumerism, come flooding back in, comprise in fact the heart of consumerism not its moral superior and opposite. And if we are a mixture of the two economies, then the consumer is a more complex creature than we have heretofore thought. Materialism is only half of the story. Tell the whole story and the split between style and the liberal imagination that emerges from it is healed. The arts and letters no longer must repudiate the "materialism" from which the arts and letters have always grown. They can no longer despise the wealth that has made the arts and letters possible and preserved them. We finally have an answer, in such a bi-stable mixture of economies, to what I have, in an earlier book, *The Electronic Word*, called the Q question: What good, finally, are the arts and letters, what work do they do in the world? They leaven and enrich, rather than repudiate, the commercial world and its values.

So it is a mistake about the nature of the economy—one made from the beginning—that has led to the standard opposition of materialism versus spiritual values. The change in balance of the economy today allows us to see that fundamental mistake and gives us the chance to correct it. And if we correct our view of the economy, we can then correct our view of rhetoric and of style. We no longer need to have a bad conscience about style. We no longer have to condemn it and yet worship it and then hide the duplicity from ourselves.

Although we will continue to yearn, when the pastoral mood takes us, for the simple, unchanging preconsumer values of the agricultural village, we might also remember that those who still live in such villages do not share our illusion. We need, then, to build a more complex portrait of the consumer. We might begin with a comment by William Lewis in his recent *The Power of*

Productivity: "Consumers are the only political force that can stand up to producer interests, big government, and the technocratic, political, business, and intellectual elites." Lewis's book is a popular summary of a twelve-year study by the McKinsey Global Institute of economies—rich, poor, and middling—around the world. The study sought to find the essential ingredients of economic growth (it found one essential: competition) but came up, in the process, with an unlikely democratic hero, the consumer.

Consumers, he argues, have the sovereign power, and a good thing, too. This is because they don't simply pig out at Wal-Mart. They make, every day and all day, complex decisions of all sorts. That much is true of markets in general. But how much more complex these decisions in an attention economy, and in one that mixes stuff and fluff in ever varying combinations. Here the market includes political and aesthetic—that is, stylistic—decisions as well as materialistic ones. The consumer-citizens will, in making such decisions, continually struggle to align the economy of stuff and the economy of attention. They will have to find their way between those who would govern the economy and the polity from the top down (those elites Lewis was pointing to) and those (perhaps in their way no less elite) who want us to let the economy find its own way. These decisions are as complex as any democratic citizenry has ever had to make. Revisionist thinking can help to make them. "Consumer" should no longer be a dyslogistic epithet. We are talking about a complex governing class that has to make complex governing decisions. Satiric simplifications no longer need apply. Surely this was the lesson so much twentieth-century art tried to teach us. Define art as what the beholder thinks it is, and give this beholder the right to find it wherever it may occur, and you have defined the art lover as a consumer and aligned commercial with aesthetic choices.

The literary genre that, in past chapters of Western intellectual history, sought to profile a governing class and suggest how it should be educated, was called the *Speculum principis,* or mirror of princes, genre. The *speculum,* the Mirror here, still held its older meaning of "ideal image of." The *principis* or "of princes" came naturally because for most of Western history governors were princes, and so their education for governance vital. Such models of ideal education gradually became democratized as the political franchise widened, and we can think of the present vast body of thinking about education as the progeny of this ancient literary type.

The education of the ideal prince implied, obviously, the image of an ideal state, as well. And so the utopian genre developed along with the mirror of princes. Indeed, the earliest document of this type, Plato's *Republic,* was both an image of the ideal commonwealth and our first treatise on education. This is not the place to lay out a utopia for the present consumer society, or an ideal image of its prince, the consumer, but permit me to suggest that revisionist thinking should form the core of both. Utopias are usually models of stasis; this one must be a model of motion, of continual readjustments, just as so many twentieth-century artists have told us. It must move beyond the style/substance pairing as a pair of opposites. They often metamorphose into one another today, as indeed, to varying degrees, they always have. The consumer-citizen should move from one to the other, if not always in ease and comfort, at least with a practiced skill. This skill will not come easily, and no purpose is served if we continue to think of "consumer" and "consumerist" society as satiric caricatures rather than the complex and skillful beings that they are becoming.

Normally, the debate about attention as a scarce resource is about what you pay attention to in a crowded field of regard: the problem of plentitude. Revisionist thinking is about *how* you pay attention. Free market economists believe that freedom increases with the number of choices available to us. Freedom is the freedom to choose. But too many choices—the problem of plentitude with which our discussion here began—can obstruct freedom as effectively as too few. A tool that confronts the problem not by filtering the choices but by training the chooser can protect and refine the freedom that markets create.

Because this technique, or if it has been trained, this habit of mind, can apply to human behavior at many levels, from writing a memo at work to thinking about how that work should be done, from making friends to keeping those friends, it provides a way to link these different kinds of behavior, to think about them in a common framework of thought. Thus it can build bridges between individual choices and understanding group behavior. It works to counteract the divisive pressures between materialistic and spiritual values so many people see in the modern world.

The Stoic philosopher Epictetus exhorted us that "it is not things but what we think about things that trouble humankind." But Epictetus now needs to be revised. It is not things that trouble us, or what we think about things, so much as the relationship of the one to the other. (Epictetus solved this problem by arguing that there was no relationship, a dodge rather than a solution.) How do we relate stuff to fluff, one kind of economy to another? Revision is all about relating style and substance, trying to align them more perfectly. On

a larger scale, it is trying to align the two kinds of economies, to put Epictetus's two categories in fruitful alternation. But just here the awkward problems arise. What distribution of the world's goods is "fair"? How much of
each do we really need? How big a house? How big a car? How much is
enough? When we buy an object, how much "style" are we buying with it?
How much of our life should we spend getting stuff and how much playing
with it, or discarding it in the name of monastic simplicity? And so on. It is all
very well to say that each person seeks to optimize his choices, but what de-
termines the choices? You can't, in final analysis, study the optimization in
isolation from the choices. You must toggle back and forth between the two.
Revisionist thinking proves, then, a useful tool in thinking about complex
choices. It is not, though, a model as an economist might think of one. It is not
a closed domain of reasoning that begins with "Assume. . . ." It is a tool for
sniffing out assumptions, not making them. I often imagine it as a flashlight,
a tool to explore the world rather than model it.

A final revisionist thought. It is not altogether accidental, perhaps, that
both the *Iliad* and the *Odyssey* have come down to us and that they have from
early days been thought the product of a single mind. Achilles, the archetype
for competitive motivation, and Odysseus, the archetype for dramatic motivation, together comprise the complex, uneasy, divided but infinitely protean
Western self. They are the inspiration and the expiration, the breathing in
and breathing out, of our sense of self. We cannot hold them in the mind, or
enshrine them in the heart, at the same time; they are temperamental and
logical opposites. But we can oscillate from one to the other, sometimes faster,
sometimes slower, sometimes more widely, sometimes more narrowly. We
should suspect any argument that tries to shut this oscillation down. It stifles
us. That is why we should fear the social planners who would design our
lives from the top down and the unregulated marketplace that would abjure
direction altogether. That is why we should alternate between loyalty to our
own absolutes and awareness that other absolutes govern others. That is why
we should remember that the stuff of the world should always alternate with
what we think about it. That is why we should ponder the new and shifting
relations between literacy and orality that our culture is creating. That is why
we should think about speaking as well as writing as the object of formal instruction.

The temptation to shut down the oscillation, to stifle the creative breath of
the Western world, has been strong from the beginning. Surely, in all these
contrasts, top-down versus bottom-up control, the social self versus the cen-

tral self, the philosopher versus the rhetorician, substance versus style—or, as I have styled it, stuff and fluff—one has to be right and the other wrong. The history of thought is composed of such antithetical arguments. Yet the way through the perils has always lain not in compromising or mixing the opposites but in holding them both in mind in delicate alternation. Revisionist thinking is not relativist thinking. It provides an opposite method, a way to hold absolute truths in your mind without compromising them or imposing them on other people.

Revisionist thinking, then, is the price we pay for absolute values in a free and peaceful society. There is nothing complicated in explaining this bistable oscillation but much in the doing. In applying first one absolute, then the other. In trying to look first at experience and then through it. Since that balance is required to hold two kinds of economics in mind at once, we might remember that rhetoric—the first economics of attention—held this rocking rhythm at the center of its training. Perhaps, if we want to think productively about our two kinds of economics, we might want to revive the rhetorical ingredient in our educational system. We might want to train the at/through habit of mind, the useful tool, once again. If so, there are many changes to be made.

Background Conversations

Why Not "More Economics"?

One of the readers of this book in manuscript form suggested that there be "more economics" in it. I found this suggestion understandable but a little disheartening. I thought I had been talking about economics, albeit of a different kind, all along. "It all starts with scarcity," the economist William Allen tells us, in describing economics as a field of study. We can all agree that human attention is a scarce commodity and always has been. There have always been "opportunity costs" as an economist would put it, or "lost opportunity costs" as we might more ordinarily phrase it, in paying attention to one thing rather than another. In conventional economics, we compete for the scarce commodity. At present the competition for attention is stiffer than ever before. Economists have generally argued that our freedom to choose is a good thing and that our welfare increases with the range of our choices. We might also, I think, obtain general agreement that, as far as attention goes, our range of choices has become so plenteous that plentitude itself seems to present a problem. The Harvard economist Edward Glaeser, in a recent working paper issued by the National

Bureau of Economic Research, restated as a fundamental principle that "the great achievement of economics is understanding aggregation." Now human attention is surely an aggregative, a social, event as well as an individual characteristic. It is indeed how human aggregation occurs. So to think about the economics of attention is to include lots of economics in your discussion. If you ask, in an economics of attention, who might be the economists, how the information system might work, what mixture of motives one has to consider, how our conception of property will change, all the things I have been doing here, it is reasonable to argue that economics is what we have been talking about all along.

But what the reader wished to see was more economics of the orthodox kind. I could try to supply this in two ways. First, I could, whenever possible, convert what I say into the orthodox terminology of economics, so that it seemed more familiar to economists. This, in its turn presented two problems for me. One, I wanted to stress the unorthodox aspect of my inquiry, and to do so in plain language that ordinary readers could understand. Two, I knew it would be fatal as well as false were I to try to impersonate an orthodox economics department economist, and the surest sign of impersonation would be to talk like one when I wasn't one.

The second way to supply more orthodox economics was to try to "think like an economist." This, successful or not, I have tried to do. I will go further. Since I have spent my scholarly life studying the history and theory of rhetoric, and since I think that rhetoric can be thought of as an economics of attention, I am emboldened to say that I have been, albeit in a different stylistic register, "thinking like an economist" all along.

Now that I come to think of it, I was trying to teach an economics lesson in pursuing an activity that forms a big part of any English teacher's life, grading papers. The way most students wrote was, finally, so wasteful. It was not the inelegance, or the lack of sophistication, or the shaky reasoning, but the sheer waste of energy that frustrated me. An economist might think of it as a tax on thought. (In my textbooks, I used a "Lard Factor" percentage that might be considered the tax rate.) A fundamental economic response, surely, if unsophisticated. And the waste of energy was mental energy. I spent a great deal of time on student prose revision—in retrospect, it sometimes seems, most of my time. My colleagues thought I was mad ("a shortcut to professional oblivion") and my students as often as not resented a marked-up paper, but the more I thought about prose revision, the more important it became. If a student could not write a powerful, coherent, and yes correct, sentence, then what availed the fancy literary analysis I was offering them? And if that student could write well, the skill would prove a powerful "comparative advantage," as an economist would say, in the struggle for life. And an invaluable lesson would have been learned about the application of means to ends. An economic lesson as much as a literary one.

A student sentence is an economy in miniature. It has an actor, an action, an object of that action. It is a transaction, a completed act. It is self-interested in that it seeks a good grade, seeks to demonstrate mastery of the assignment. But it also seeks to express something; it is a learner's exercise in how to trade in the market of ideas. When it is good, the writing rejoices in that exchange. There is, in any utterance, however self-interested, a residual urge to share a view of life. To see the world a certain way and to want other people to enjoy seeing it that way too. This two-way communication, self-seeking and other-seeking, is after all what makes markets fun to go to and full of life.

I usually came across to the students like one of those specialists in efficiency who stalked a Toyota factory floor looking for *muda* (waste). But writing a sentence is about ingratiation as well as communication or, rather, the ingratiation is an essential part of that communication. Writing, like other kinds of tools, comes in "styles," and you want to select the right one for the job. If you choose the wrong one, and sometimes even if you choose the right one, your sentence will bring those "unintended consequences" of which economists speak. Purposes will be mistook and fall on the inventor's head. A sentence illustrates in miniature, that is, all the necessities, and the dangers, of central planning. This trade-off has figured prominently in economics.

To learn how to write a good sentence, then, is a lesson in economics, and not a simplistic one built on self-interest as the only human motive, but one that always involves nice calculations about what people are like and what they like. You can give rules—what teacher has not done this?—but you cannot stray far from the complexities of human motive or you lose your audience. Revision requires, and from the beginning, revisionist thinking. And, as I've been arguing, that is a skill useful on a larger scale than the sentence.

Thus, as I came to nose around in economics, I felt that, ignorant as I was, I had some feeling for the ground. In my accustomed pastures, people were trying to analyze the complex motives that lay behind human transactions and they were seeking mechanical rules to simplify these transactions and make them more rule-governed and easier to teach. I thought I saw the same things going on in economics. In the teaching of writing, there were always the rules of grammar to fall back on, if you were "scientifically" minded, and indeed they often came in handy. In economics too, there were standard rules to apply, and there too exactly what these rules were and when they should be applied were hotly contested. In both places, too, you could make things much simpler by assuming that messages were of one kind only and likewise with the people receiving them. In both, scholars often claimed that one style (or "model") was better than another in all situations whatever. Economists often applied narrow rules of "efficiency," as so often I did, but also seemed aware that efficiency varies according to time and place and person. When their students called them on this inconsistency, they went into the same bob-and-weave I had so often employed myself: "Yes, Shakespeare is wordy, sometimes, just as I marked you down for being, but he can get away with it because he is Shakespeare. You can't because you are not." Tilt! But in fact the student was not Shakespeare and the differences were exactly what English teachers have always tried to teach. But you couldn't teach it all at once; a messy and inconsistent accumulation of experience was needed.

I studied English literature, as both undergraduate and graduate student, at Yale during the glory days of the New Criticism, a way to read literature that presumed that each work of literature constitutes a perfect order and it is the reader's job to find out what this order is. You don't consider the background of the work or of the author, only the work itself. Now, this procedure was manifestly silly if you took it too seriously (and for a long time I did), but it could tell you a good deal about style and structure. It was classical rhetorical analysis come to life again, and style and structure are what you learn about most easily if you restrict yourself to rhetorical analysis. If you want to understand a poem, there is no need to restrict yourself to the poem itself, but it helps to look at the poem first.

Now, without straining the parallel, something like this "perfect order" assumption seemed to be a part of the economics scene, too. In a market, one view held, perfect information prevailed. The participants were "rational" (different meanings for this word, alas) and made judgments according to the evidence before them. Perfect poem and perfect reader in another guise. But, in both cases, with the messy bits of reality left out.

What literature has to teach us is the enormous complexity of human motive. Surely that is what, if we look at them whole, markets have to teach us, too. This complexity of motive is what has always fascinated me in the world of work ever since I worked construction as a summer job in high school. There are people in both fields who want to narrow down the complexity. We may call them "allegorists." The enormous complexity is read as an allegory of some much simpler truth, Christian theology, Marxist economics, whatever. I think that both the desire to confront complexity and the desire to allegorize it are "economics" topics, whether we are talking about poems or markets. There have always been people in both fields who wanted to confront the messy bits and "to use all that there is to use" (a phrase of Kenneth Burke's) to do so. Narrow Church and broad Church.

So I thought that, in principle, I was trying to "think like an economist" and had much to learn from them. As for pointing out the similarities between my field and economics, that is, "putting more economics" into my discussion directly, I am not qualified to do this. But, most happily, the person most qualified to do it, the economist Deirdre McCloskey, has already done so splendidly in a series of books, most especially her *Rhetoric of Economics* and *Knowledge and Persuasion in Economics*. Michael Watts has also compiled *The Literary Book of Economics,* a collection of literary selections that illustrate economic problems. I felt that I was free to go my own way and to argue for revisionist thinking.

Revisionist thinking is thinking about style and substance, and perhaps there too I could claim an economics connection, for my interest in style did not begin in words but in that most stuff-like commodity, automobiles.

Two doors down from where I grew up, the family had a magnificent 1934 Dietrich-bodied Packard, a gleaming black four-door convertible with a bleached white top and burgundy leather upholstery. It rolled on big white sidewalls mounted on deep red wire wheels. Two more of these wheels, their rubber gloved in white canvas, fit into marvelously contrived wells on the front fenders. On top of each, like a miniature monarch, sat a chrome rearview mirror secured by two tan leather straps. The bumpers were spring steel that curved around at the ends into scrolls topped with small Packard shields. Everything that could gleam, gleamed; everything that could glow with a deep inner fire did so. Here was *style*.

In front of our house stood a vehicle different in make and kind. A 1941 Ford sedan, its olive green faded and chalky from lack of polish, its meager grill and stamped-steel bumpers rusted, its roof line of unsurpassed ugliness. But it worked faithfully. All through the war, when you couldn't get cars fixed, that flathead V-8 started and ran and carried us where we needed to go. Here, clearly, was something else. Here was purpose, not ornament. Here was reality, not rhetoric. Here was *substance*.

Before I knew how momentous the decision was, I had decided I preferred style. I liked it everywhere I found it in other kids' houses: playing on deep-pile sheared broadloom carpet, not sitting on eighteenth-century Newport side chairs, watching the frost form on a silver Georg Jensen martini pitcher. I knew about substance firsthand. That's what we had in our house. Not for me, if I could do anything about it.

Alas, there wasn't much I could do about it. I joined a profession built on substance. A profession, like all other professions but only more so: serious. Professors, I learned, and especially graduate students, looked down on style every chance they got. Comfort was bourgeois (still today a standard term of academic disparagement) and a stylish life even worse. A scruffy house and a scruffy car, like a scruffy green book bag, proved your heart was in the right place. Having neat stuff—any neat stuff—was frowned on, and polishing it was worse. Polishing your *car* signified deep damnation. Such stylistic self-consciousness was a vulgarity far worse than ignorance. It showed that your heart was where moth can consume and rust can corrupt, up there with glitz and glamour.

I never understood it. How could anybody want to drive that Ford when a dual-cowl Packard chariot rolled down the same street? You might not be able to afford one. But not want one? Not lust after a little glitz and glamour in your life if you could swing it? Before I knew what the word meant, I was hooked on "eloquence." And not merely ornamental sculpture but rolling sculpture, eloquence in the ordinary business of life, of "getting on."

Thus was I a stranger in my chosen vocation before I knew it. Style, it turned out, was the enemy. In literature, as I came to learn, it was usually called rhetoric and it was the opposite—ever since Plato—of those eternal truths academic life existed to cherish and preserve. The perennial opponent of philosophy. Of seriousness itself. And stylistic self-consciousness, actually paying attention to style as style, was original sin. True art, everyone said, was the art that concealed its art. Even the people who wrote about style, I found, didn't believe in it. It wasn't serious enough.

And so in the outside world as well. Everyone decried materialism—stuff—and applauded simplicity. But few people lived that way. They hungered for style and glommed onto it wherever they could. A lot of guys polished their cars the way I did. A lot of women kept on wearing high heels even after the world knew they were murder on the metatarsals. Buying decisions, in spite of *Consumer Reports'* best efforts, seemed dominated by stylistic hungers. Even the original Volkswagen, marketed as basic transportation, succeeded because it made such a strong stylistic statement.

"What gives?" I kept asking myself. "What good is style? Why has it created the infinite world of design? Why the hundreds of shapes for chairs or for corkscrews or type fonts, when half a dozen basic designs would do the trick? And why is style always paired dyslogistically with substance? Why do we use it as a synonym for what is inessential, peripheral? Why, if style is by definition unimportant, does it lie so near our hearts? Why is "putting on the style" so universal in our lives and yet "showing off" so condemned?" All these questions turn up when we start to think about an economy of attention. They are all economic questions.

So maybe it wasn't only chance that made me write a book on self-conscious rhetorical styles in Sir Philip Sidney's sixteenth-century romance, *Arcadia*. Maybe it wasn't just chance that made me, as a graduate student, get interested in the glitzy side of rhetoric, the Latin and Greek terms for verbal ornament, and publish *A Handlist of Rhetorical Terms* a few years later. Such a list was a toolkit for the mechanic in words. It did work in the world. It inhabited the daily marketplace.

I was interested, by that time, in how style often becomes substance in human life. An undergraduate seminar on Laurence Sterne taught me to see that his novel *Tristram Shandy* was all about this oscillation between style and substance and prompted a book, *Tristram Shandy: The Games of Pleasure*, about the novel. At the novel's center stands a character called Uncle Toby, whose "seriousness" is composed of game and play, whose driving force is stylistic. At the book's center stood ideas of game and play not utterly different from those later fashionable in economics.

By this time, I was convinced that the real, the central "seriousness" in Western literature was created by behavior that oscillated between style and substance. That theme I traced in a book called *The Motives of Eloquence,* whose first chapter, "Rhetorical Man," applied this oscillation to a theory of self and society.

For several years my teaching rotation included a graduate seminar in prose style. Out of it came *Analyzing Prose,* which argued that prose styles need not be judged by the standards of unselfconscious transparency that have always dominated discussions of prose style. The domain of style was much wider than this. Fords were not the whole story. You had to consider Packards, too. Both were part of any economy. I wrote textbooks about both the "Ford" side of the story and the "Packard" side (*Revising Prose* and *Revising Business Prose*) but tried in both to show that my heart was with the whole story, not one half or the other.

In the early 1980s, a new chapter in the long history of rhetoric was being written on the electronic screen, a chapter discussed in *The Electronic Word: Democracy, Technology, and the Arts.* When text moved from book to screen, style and substance threatened to change places. And when the same thing seemed to be happening in the economy at large, the "information economy," one had to sit up and take notice. To the extent that information was replacing stuff at the heart of the economy, style and substance change places. What happens when they do? What did it mean for my own area of interest, the history and theory of rhetoric, when we move from an economy based on physical objects to one based on information? Someone who had spent a scholarly life pondering the relationship of style to substance perhaps might shed some light on its current reversal. And that reversal would have consequences for "economics," however it might be defined.

ACKNOWLEDGMENTS

Thanks to the following journals for permission to reprint:

A version of "What's Next for Text" appeared in *Education, Communication and Information*, vol. 1, no. 1 (2001).

"Barbie and the Teacher of Righteousness" appeared in the *Houston Law Review*, vol. 38, no. 2 (Summer 2001).

A version of "The Audit of Virtuality" appeared in *The Future of the City of Intellect: The Changing American University*, ed. Steven Brint (Stanford, CA: Stanford University Press, 2002).

I first began to think about the arguments of this book as a Norman Freehling Visiting Professor at the Institute for the Humanities at the University of Michigan in 1994. I developed them further during appointments as International Scholar at the George Eastman House, as an Andrew W. Mellon Professor at Tulane University, and as a Phi Beta Kappa Visiting Scholar. To all of these institutions I return thanks for intellectual stimulation, friendship, and many happy memories.

I must also thank my old student and very dear friend Linda Billingsley for careful readings of the typescript. Her criticisms have saved the reader many vexations. For readings from an economist's perspective, I would also like to thank Jack and David Hirshleifer and, especially, Deirdre McCloskey, whose extensive comments on the manuscript both sharpened it and heartened me. I must, too, thank an anonymous reader for the University of Chicago Press for sound criticisms and much-appreciated good words.

Finally, I must record my everlasting gratitude to the University of California's Voluntary Early Retirement Incentive Program.

NOTES

PREFACE

xiii **Weisskopf** K. C. Cole, e-mail message to author, 2004.

CHAPTER ONE

2 **a reservation for Everest** The crowds on the mountain, and the fatal consequences thereof, are vividly described in Krakauer's *Into Thin Air.*

3 **Marshall McLuhan** Marchand, *Marshall McLuhan,* 137.

4 **the basic economic resource** Drucker, *Post-Capitalist Society,* 8.

4 **the world desperately needs** Wriston, *The Twilight of Sovereignty,* 19–20.

4 **information as an active agent** Campbell, *Grammatical Man,* 16.

5 **my dad always said** "A Father and Son Meld New Economy and Old, and the Business Flows," *Wall Street Journal,* 24 May 2000.

6 **dynamic physical process** Christopher Langton, "Artificial Life," in *Artificial Life: The Proceedings of an Interdisciplinary Workshop on the Synthesis and Simulation of Living Systems Held September, 1987 in Los Alamos, New Mexico, Santa Fe Institute Studies in the Sciences of Complexity,* 6:2.

6 **the stuff of life** Levy, *Artificial Life,* 118.

6 **how human beings allocate** *The New Columbia Encyclopedia,* 4th ed., s.v. "economics."

7 **new information generated in the world each year** Peter Lyman and Hal R. Varian, senior researchers, "How Much Information?" http://www.sims.berkeley.edu/how-much-info/

7 **160,000 new U.S. titles** R. R. Bowker, *Books in Print* database, www.Bowker.com.

8 **a question of filtering** Herbert A. Simon, "Designing Organizations for an Information-Rich World" in *Computers, Communications, and the Public Interest,* ed. Martin Greenberger (Baltimore and London: Johns Hopkins Press, 1971).

9 **the human biogrammar** Tiger and Fox, *The Imperial Animal.*

10 **the Hawthorne experiment** Drucker describes this in *Concept of the Corporation,* 156.

11 **winner-take-all society** Frank and Cook, *The Winner-Take-All Society.*

12 **Dissoi logoi**   Sprague, ed., *The Older Sophists,* 289–90.

18 **Harley Earl**   Bayley, *Harley Earl and the Dream Machine.*

18 **Vehicle Brand Owner**   "Incredible Shrinking Plants," *Economist* (February 23, 2002), 71–73.

19 **life as a Vietnam war correspondent**   Herr, *Dispatches,* 31.

20 **it is not things**   Epictetus, *Encheiridion* 5., "It is not things but what we think about things that trouble humankind" (my translation).

28 **no simple understanding**   *Hayek on Hayek,* 155.

31 **technology accounts for about 30 percent**   Ahlbrandt, Fruehan, and Giarratani, *The Renaissance of American Steel,* 69.

32 **management plays a vital role**   Micklethwait and Wooldridge, *The Witch Doctors,* 73.

33 **you're launched**   Drucker, *Adventures of a Bystander,* 262.

35 **national industrial policy**   Chernow, *The House of Morgan,* 83.

35 **Standard Oil's metamorphosis**   Ibid., 227.

36 **capital markets**   Strouse, *Morgan,* 50.

37 **long-range implications**   Grant, *Money of the Mind,* 258.

37 **asking investors**   Lowenstein, *When Genius Failed,* 28.

38 **in the annals of investing**   Lowenstein, *Buffett,* xiii.

39 **many cultural pessimists**   Cowen, *In Praise of Commercial Culture,* 177–78.

40 **by placing conservative culture**   Ibid., 197.

41 **the view that economists take of the psychology of human choice**   "Rational Economic Man: The Human Factor," *Economist* (24 December 1994–6 January 1995), 90–92.

41 **efforts of a dissident group**   Peter Monaghan, "Taking on 'Rational Man': Dissident Economists Fight for a Niche in the Discipline," *Chronicle of Higher Education* 49 (24 January 2003): A12.

CHAPTER TWO

42 **in the spontaneous unfoldings**   Burke, *Attitudes toward History,* 75.

42 **Fountain**   An economical account can be found in Tomkins, *The Bride and the Bachelors,* 40–41; a longer one in the same author's *Duchamp: A Biography,* 181 ff.

44 **"Futurist Manifesto"**   A reproduction of this front page can be found in Hulten, *Futurism and Futurisms,* 67.

45 **Italian Futurism**   Tisdall and Bozzolla, *Futurism,* 7

45 **two thirds of the books**   Hulten, *Futurism and Futurisms,* 18.

45 **It is from Italy**   Ibid., 516.

45 **Futurism is grounded**   Ibid.

45 **an earth shrunk by speed**   Ibid., 518.

46 **Lacerba**   Tisdall and Bozzolla, *Futurism,* 164.

48 **Business art**   Bourdon, *Warhol,* 350. Quoted from *The Philosophy of Andy Warhol: From A to B and Back Again.*

49 **He then made exact models**   These are illustrated in *Andy Warhol: A Retrospective,* ed. McShine, 198–99.

51 **Within a few days** Bourdon, *Warhol*, 124.

52 **we weren't just at the art exhibit** Warhol and Hackett, *POPism*, 133.

52 **if you want to know** quoted in *Andy Warhol: A Retrospective*, ed. McShine, 39.

53 **to meet a person like Judy** Warhol and Hackett, *POPism*, 101.

53 **that's what so many people** Ibid., 169.

54 **my work has no future** *Andy Warhol: A Retrospective*, ed. McShine, 39.

54 **the package you destroyed** Quoted in *Christo Editions 1964–82*, n.p.

55 **the Pont Neuf project** This story is told in *Christo: The Pont Neuf, Wrapped, Paris, 1975–85*.

55 **the outsized wrappings** These projects are illustrated in Baal-Teshuva, *Christo and Jeanne-Claude*.

56 **all this by way of introduction** The story of *Running Fence* is told in *Christo: Running Fence, Sonoma and Marin Counties, California 1972–76*.

57 **see how it describes the wind** Ibid., 35.

57 **the Maysles film** *Running Fence: A Film by David Maysles, Charlotte Zwerin and Albert Maysles*.

58 **the amazing thing** *Christo: Running Fence*, 29.

62 **my husband is a farmer** Ibid., 256.

64 **the Italian futurists** Richter, *Dada*, 11.

64 **like all newborn movements** Ibid., 34.

64 **surrealism** Ibid., 194–95.

65 **a café in Zurich** Ibid., 13–14.

66 **according to the stereotype** Short, *Dada and Surrealism*, 7.

66 **to live the religious life** Richter, *Dada*, 43.

67 **the conclusion that Dada** Ibid., 51.

67 **I noticed that my voice** Ibid., 43.

67 **we were all fated** Ibid., 61, 64.

68 **what is going to count** Bateson, *Steps to an Ecology of Mind*, 477–78.

69 **my criterion** Ibid., 478.

69 **mere purposive rationality** "Style, Grace, and Information in Primitive Art," in ibid., 146.

69 **but if art . . . has a positive function** Ibid., 147.

70 **our life is such that** Ibid., 137.

70 **we must use our reason** Hayek, *The Constitution of Liberty*, 69.

70 **the knowledge which any individual mind** Ibid., 24.

70 **the mind can never foresee** Ibid.

71 **liberty is essential** Ibid., 29.

71 **progress by its very nature** Ibid., 41.

71 **a reconstruction of an original** Morrison, Coates, and Rankov, *The Athenian Trireme*, 191.

74 **all of them were artists** Lippard, *Pop Art*, 90.

74 **the central novelty** Marmer, "Pop Art," 148.

74 **instead of the character-context** Haskell, *Blam*, 44.

75 **I'm looking right now** Alloway, *Lichtenstein*, 29.

75 **Yellow Brushstroke II** Waldman, *Roy Lichtenstein*, 152–53.

75 **his approach to popular art** Rose, *Claes Oldenburg*, 53.

76 **these pictures are about doubt** Goldman, *James Rosenquist*, 62.

77 **I am an artist of movement** Hulten, *Jean Tinguely*, 350.

77 **a certain mistrust toward power** Tinguely, quoted in ibid.

CHAPTER THREE

79 **letters are the greatest** This maxim was inscribed on a student's wax-coated wooden tablet by his teacher, Flavius Collouthos. Quoted in Cribiore, *Writing, Teachers, and Students in Graeco-Roman Egypt*, 33; see also no. 160 on 211.

84 **Simias** The poem is translated, in shape form, in Anthony Holden, *Greek Pastoral Poetry*, 198. It is discussed on 224.

105 **Winchester Bible** Walther and Wolf, *Codices Illustres*, 136.

109 **in this economy** Ong, *Ramus, Method, and the Decay of Dialogue*, 291.

115 **a sign of the arrival** Havelock, *The Literate Revolution*, 53–55.

116 **the gulf between** Gould, "The Pattern of Life's History," 55.

117 **quite a high proportion** Baxandall, *Giotto and the Orators*, 17.

118 **by the ninth century** Parkes, *Pause and Effect*, 34.

119 **ellipses in sense or grammar** Boegehold, *When a Gesture Was Expected*, 29.

119 **the late twentieth century** Kendrick, *Animating the Letter*, 3.

120 **from the medieval** Ibid., 152.

121 **acrostics are texts** Higgins, *Pattern Poetry*, 171.

122 **frankly, the poems** Levitan, "Dancing at the End of the Rope," 246.

122 **the first line** Ibid., 247.

122 **flow of speech** Ibid., 249.

122 **it suggests that the generation** Ibid.

123 **leave writing plays** Kirby-Smith, *The Origins of Free Verse*, 216.

123 **the great majority** Ibid., 256–57.

126 **the term livre d'artiste** Johnson and Stein, *Artists' Books in the Modern Era*, 17.

126 **unique systems of writing** Hannas, *Orthographic Dilemma*, 3.

127 **"Upon Being Given a Norfolk Turkey for Christmas"** Child et al.'s *More Than Fine Writing*, 96–97.

127 **stated summarily** Saenger, *Space between Words*, 11.

128 **a hundred years after cinema's birth** Manovich, *The Language of New Media*, xv.

CHAPTER FOUR

131 **a subsequent version** Robert Stein developed expanded books for Voyager. He has developed TK3 for a new company, Night Kitchen.

131 **Virginia's E-Book Library** http://etext.virginia.edu/ebooks/ebooklist.html.

137   **symbolic human interchange**   Tiger and Fox, *The Imperial Animal*, 236.

138   **mathematical plainness**   Sprat, *The History of the Royal Society*, 113.

145   **except by actual practice**   Quintilian, *Institutes*, ed. and trans. Donald A. Russell, 1.8.1–2.

147   **resonance—there is no wisdom without it**   Birkerts, *The Gutenberg Elegies*, 75–76.

148   **enter a novel**   Ibid., 81

148   **to define a good book**   Lewis, *Experiment in Criticism*, 1.

148   **I have a notion**   Ibid., 5–6.

149   **we must look and go on looking**   Ibid., 19.

149   **they have no ears**   Ibid.

149   **stylemongers**   Ibid, 36–37.

149   **scientific or otherwise informative reading**   Ibid., 136.

149   **what do the few read for?**   Ibid., 138–41.

150   **depth of field**   Birkerts, *The Gutenberg Elegies*, 129.

150   **the fundamental structure**   Lanham, *The Motives of Eloquence*.

150   **our slight solitudes**   Birkerts, *The Gutenberg Elegies*, 131.

151   **that precious interval**   Healy, *Failure to Connect*, 22.

151   **the rapid, rhythmic eye movements**   Ibid., 114.

151   **advances in computer-based graphics**   Ibid., 153.

152   **tuning out**   Ibid., 183.

153   **soul-making**   Ibid., 191.

153   **our children**   Ibid., 193.

153   **it is hard to teach "values"**   Ibid., 199.

155   **original uses of moving images**   Stephens, *The Rise of the Image*, 47.

155   **we live, however, in a culture**   Ibid., 59.

155   **a picture may actually be worth less**   Ibid., 68.

155   **once we move**   Ibid., 18.

CHAPTER FIVE

157   **rationality is only an instrumental concept**   Hirshleifer and Hirshleifer, *Price Theory and Applications*, 10.

157   **the inanimate action of matter**   Quoted in Fussell, *The Rhetorical World of Augustan Humanism*, 9.

158   **two things of opposite natures**   Stevens, "Notes towards a Supreme Fiction," 392.

158   **a place or enveloping element**   *Webster's New Collegiate Dictionary*, 2d ed., s.v. "matrix."

166   **a vigorous society**   Hoffer elaborates the point in *The True Believer*: "We dare more when striving for superfluities than for necessities. Often when we renounce superfluities we end up lacking necessities" (30). And in *The Temper of Our Time*: "History is made by men who have the restlessness, impressionability, credulity, capacity for make-believe, ruthlessness and self-righteousness of children. It is made by men who set their hearts on toys" (3).

168   **"When Earth's Last Picture is Painted"**   *Rudyard Kipling: Complete Verse*, 226.

172 **Tour de France**   Diane Pucin, "In Cycling, Winning with Honor Means Everything." *Los Angeles Times*, 23 July 2003, A1.

174 **fungibility of motive**   Hayek, *The Road to Serfdom*, 98.

176 **More's "Utopia"**   I've developed this argument in "The Choice of Utopias: More or Castiglione," in *Literacy and the Survival of Humanism*.

179 **as many substances in nature**   Bacon, *The Advancement of Learning*, ed. Warhaft, 225.

179 **economics as a social or "moral" science**   Drucker, *The End of Economic Man*, 47.

181 **"The Choice of Utopias"**   Lanham, *Literacy and the Survival of Humanism*, 24 ff.

181 **"The Aesthetic Economy"**   *Milken Institute Review* (December 1999), 11–21.

181 **seeing design creep into everything**   Ibid., 12.

181 **non-functional stylistic dynamism**   Peckham, *Man's Rage for Chaos*, x, 69 ff.

182 **a hand-reared starling**   Lorenz, *On Aggression*, 52.

182 **unreasoning and unreasonable human nature**   Ibid., 236–37.

183 **stylistic behavior in play**   Lorenz, *The Waning of Humaneness*, 67, 68.

183 **my metaphors for explaining this theory**   Miller, *The Mating Mind*, 16.

184 **the real reason for my being a jockey**   Francis, *The Sport of Queens*, 94–95.

185 **the search for excellence**   Halberstam, *The Amateurs*, 63.

185 **a sort of sustained fury of composition**   Havelock, *The Liberal Temper in Greek Politics*, 9.

185 **the joy of going at it**   Keller, *A Feeling for the Organism*, 125.

185 **needing no companionship**   Ibid., 34.

186 **telegraphic networks**   Alexander, *The Inventor of Stereo*, xi.

186 **Merton's review**   Watson, *The Double Helix*, 213.

187 **Perl's remark**   Taubes, *Nobel Dreams*, 16.

187 **you just simply don't collaborate**   Wade, *The Nobel Duel*, 8.

187 **both militarists**   Ibid., 103.

187 **optimal flow from the middle to the extremes**   Heiner, *Henry J. Kaiser*, 152.

188 **Kaiser Permanente Medical Care Program**   Ibid., 75 ff.

188 **Dr. Garfield's first meeting with Kaiser**   Ibid., 76.

188 **Murray-Green Award**   Ibid., 211.

189 **the obvious dureté of nature**   Holmes, *The Essential Holmes*, 76.

189 **Winterbotham's account gets bad marks**   Keegan, *Intelligence in War*, 368.

CHAPTER SEVEN

233 **The Audit of Virtuality**   My title is borrowed from Correlli Barnett's relentless excavation of the English economy during World War II, *The Audit of War*.

239 **a dreadful waste of effort**   A former student who has read this chapter comments at this point: "I didn't think so then and I don't now. I still vividly remember your Hamlet lecture and the wonderful way you unpacked the Troilus. You can have both." Clearly she's right: we should try for optimal combinations of live instruction and lectures available online. And clearly there will be more than one optimal combination.

244   **explosion of Japanese consumer electronics**   See, for example, Johnstone's *We Were Burning.*

247   **a professor of English**   Quoted in Denise K. Magner, "Battle over Academic Control Pits Faculty against Governing Board at George Mason U.," *Chronicle of Higher Education* (June 18 1999), A14.

251   **an exchange organ in its brain**   Ridley, *The Origins of Virtue*, 130.

252   **dispersion, covertness, and stealth**   Berkowitz, *The New Face of War*, 20.

252   **communications, signals intelligence, and information warfare**   Ibid., 52.

CHAPTER EIGHT

258   **model of economics of information**   Wriston, *The Twilight of Sovereignty*, 19–20.

261   **consumers are the only political force**   Lewis, *The Power of Productivity*, 11.

262   **what we think about things**   Epictetus *Encheiridion* 5.

264   **it all starts with scarcity**   Allen, *The Midnight Economist: Meditations*, 3.

265   **understanding aggregation**   Glaeser, "Psychology and the Market," 10.

WORKS CITED

Ahlbrandt, Roger S., Richard J. Fruehan, and Frank Giarratani. *The Renaissance of American Steel*. New York: Oxford University Press, 1996.

Alexander, J. J. G. *The Decorated Letter*. New York: George Braziller, 1978.

Alexander, Robert Charles. *The Inventor of Stereo: The Life and Works of Alan Dower Blumlein*. Oxford: Focal Press, 1999.

Allen, William R. *The Midnight Economist: Choices, Prices, and Public Policy*. [New York]: Playboy Press, 1981.

Allen, William R. *The Midnight Economist: Meditations on Truth and Public Policy*. San Francisco: ICS Press, 1989.

Allen, William R. *The Midnight Economist: Little Essays on Big Truths*. Sun Lakes, Ariz.: Thomas Horton & Daughters, 1997.

Alloway, Lawrence. *Lichtenstein*. New York: Abbeville Press, 1983.

Austin, Gilbert. *Chironomia; or, A Treatise on Rhetorical Delivery*. Edited by Mary Margaret Robb and Lester Thonssen. Carbondale: Southern Illinois University Press, 1966.

Baal-Teshuva, Jacob. *Christo and Jeanne-Claude*. Cologne: Benedikt Taschen, 1995.

Backhouse, Janet. *The Illuminated Page: Ten Centuries of Manuscript Painting in the British Library*. Toronto: University of Toronto Press, 1997.

Backhouse, Roger E. *The Ordinary Business of Life: A History of Economics from the Ancient World to the Twenty-first Century*. Princeton, N.J.: Princeton University Press, 2002.

Bacon, Francis. *Francis Bacon: A Selection of His Works*. Edited by Sidney Warhaft. Toronto: Macmillan of Canada, 1965.

Bailey, James. *After Thought: The Computer Challenge to Human Intelligence*. New York: Basic Books, 1996.

Barish, Jonas. *The Anti-Theatrical Prejudice*. Berkeley: University of California Press, 1981.

Barnett, Correlli. *The Audit of War: The Illusion and Reality of Britain as a Great Nation*. London: Macmillan, 1986.

Barzini, Luigi. *Gli Italiani*. Milan: Oscar Mondadori, 1964.

Bateson, Gregory. *Steps to an Ecology of Mind*. Northvale, N.J.: Jason Aronson Inc., 1972.

Baxandall, Michael. *Giotto and the Orators*. Oxford: Oxford University Press, 1971.

Bayley, Stephen. *Harley Earl and the Dream Machine.* New York: Alfred A. Knopf, 1983.

Bellantoni, Jeff, and Matt Woolman. *Type in Motion: Innovations in Digital Graphics.* New York: Rizzoli, 1999.

Berkowitz, Bruce. *The New Face of War: How War Will Be Fought in the Twenty-first Century.* New York: The Free Press, 2003.

Bernstein, Peter L. *Against the Gods: The Remarkable Story of Risk.* New York: John Wiley & Sons, Inc., 1996.

Bethell, Tom. *The Noblest Triumph: Property and Prosperity through the Ages.* New York: St. Martin's Press, 1988.

Birkerts, Sven. *The Gutenberg Elegies.* New York: Fawcent Columbine, 1994.

Blackwell, Lewis, and David Carson. *The End of Print: The Graphic Design of David Carson.* San Francisco: Chronicle Books, 1995.

Boegehold, Alan L. *When a Gesture Was Expected: A Selection of Examples from Archaic and Classical Greek Literature.* Princeton, N.J.: Princeton University Press, 1990.

Bologna, Giulia. *Illuminated Manuscripts: The Book before Gutenberg.* New York: Widenfeld & Nicolson, 1988.

Botterell, David, producer. *McEwan's L.A. "Walk in a Straight Line."* New York: Snapper Films; Siggraph Video Review 53, 1989.

Bourdon, David. *Warhol.* New York: Harry N. Abrams, Inc., 1989.

Brockman, John, ed. *The Third Culture.* New York: Simon & Schuster, 1995.

Brown, Michelle P. *The British Library Guide to Writing and Scripts: History and Techniques.* Toronto: University of Toronto Press, 1998.

Bulwer, John. *Chirologia; or, The Natural Language of the Hand and Chironomia; or, The Art of Manual Rhetoric.* Carbondale: Southern Illinois University Press, 1974.

Burke, Kenneth. *Counter-Statement.* 2d ed. Chicago: University of Chicago Press, 1953.

Burke, Kenneth. *The Philosophy of Literary Form.* 2d. ed. Baton Rouge: Louisiana State University Press, 1967.

Burke, Kenneth. *A Grammar of Motives.* Berkeley: University of California Press, 1969.

Burke, Kenneth. *A Rhetoric of Motives.* Berkeley: University of California Press, 1969.

Burke, Kenneth. *Attitudes toward History.* 3d ed. Berkeley: University of California Press, 1984.

Burke, Kenneth. *Permanence and Change.* 3d ed. Berkeley: University of California Press, 1984.

Calkins, Robert G. *Illuminated Books of the Middle Ages.* Ithaca, N.Y.: Cornell University Press, 1983.

Campbell, Jeremy. *Grammatical Man: Information, Entropy, Language, and Life.* New York: Simon & Schuster, 1982.

Campbell, Jeremy. *The Liar's Tale: A History of Falsehood.* New York: W. W. Norton & Co., 2001.

Ceruzzi, Paul E. *A History of Modern Computing.* Cambridge, Mass.: MIT Press, 1998.

Chernow, Ron. *Titan: The Life of John D. Rockefeller, Sr.* New York: Random House, 1998.

Chernow, Ron. *The House of Morgan: An American Banking Dynasty and the Rise of Modern Finance.* New York: Atlantic Monthly Press, 1990.

Child, Heather, Heather Collins, Ann Hechle, and Donald Jackson. *More Than Fine Writ-*

ing: The Life and Calligraphy of Irene Wellington. Woodstock, N.Y.: The Overlook Press, 1987.

Christo, Complete Editions, 1964-1982. Catalogue Raisonné and Introduction by Per Hovdenakk. Edited and translated by Jörg Schellmann. New York: New York University Press, 1982.

Christo: Running Fence. Photographs by Gianfranco Gorgoni; chronicle by Calvin Tomkins; narrative text by David Bourdon. New York: Harry N. Abrams, Inc., 1978.

Christo: The Pont Neuf, Wrapped: Paris, 1975-1985. Photographs, Wolfganz Volz; Picture Commentary, David Bourdon; The Pont Neuf and Paris, Bernard de Montgolfiere. New York: Harry N. Abrams, 1990.

Cowen, Tyler. *In Praise of Commercial Culture.* Cambridge, Mass.: Harvard University Press, 1998.

Cowen, Tyler. *Creative Destruction: How Globalization Is Changing the World's Cultures.* Princeton, N.J.: Princeton University Press, 2002.

Cox, W. Michael, and Richard Alm. *Myths of Rich and Poor.* New York: Basic Books, 1999.

Cribiore, Rafaella. *Writing, Teachers, and Students in Graeco-Roman Egypt.* American Studies in Papyrology, no. 36. Atlanta: Scholars Press, 1996.

Daniels, Peter T., and William Bright, eds. *The World's Writing Systems.* New York: Oxford University Press, 1996.

Davies, W. V. *Egyptian Hieroglyphs.* Berkeley: University of California Press/British Museum, 1987.

Dawkins, Richard. *The Selfish Gene.* Oxford: Oxford University Press, 1976.

Dawkins, Richard. *The Blind Watchmaker: Why the Evidence of Evolution Reveals a Universe without Design.* New York: W. W. Norton & Co., 1987.

de Hamel, Christopher. *Scribes and Illuminators.* Toronto: University of Toronto Press, 1992.

de Jorio, Andrea. *Gestures in Naples and Gesture in Classical Antiquity.* Translated by Adam Kendon. Bloomington: Indiana University Press, 2000.

de Maria, Luciano, ed. *Marinetti e il futurismo.* Milan: Arnoldo Mondadori, 1973.

Demeude, Hugues, *The Animated Alphabet.* New York: Thames & Hudson, 1996.

de Valois, G., and D. Cohen, producers. *Dream Machine: The Visual Computer—an Anthology of Computer Graphics.* Santa Monica, Calif.: 1987-1991. 3 videodisks.

Drucker, Johanna. *The Visible Word: Experimental Typography and Modern Art, 1909-1923.* Chicago: University of Chicago Press, 1994.

Drucker, Johanna. *The Alphabetic Labyrinth: The Letters in History and Imagination.* London: Thames & Hudson, 1995.

Drucker, Peter. *Adventures of a Bystander: Memoirs.* New York: Harper & Row, 1978.

Drucker, Peter. *The New Realities.* New York: Harper & Row, 1989.

Drucker, Peter. *The Concept of the Corporation.* New Brunswick, N.J., and London: Transaction Publishers, 1993.

Drucker, Peter. *Post-Capitalist Society.* New York: Harper Collins, 1993.

Drucker, Peter. *The End of Economic Man: The Origins of Totalitarianism.* New Brunswick, N.J.: Transaction Publishers, 1995 (orig. 1939).

Dupriez, Bernard. *Gradus: Les procédés littéraires (dictionnaire).* Paris: Union Générale d'éditions, 1980.

Edgerton, David. *England and the Aeroplane: An Essay on a Militant and Technological Nation.* Manchester: Macmillan/Centre for the History of Science, Technology and Medicine, University of Manchester, 1991.

Edgerton, David. *Science, Technology and the British Industrial "Decline": 1870–1970.* Cambridge: Cambridge University Press, 1996.

Epictetus. Edited and translated by W. A. Oldfather, 2 vols. Cambridge, Mass.: Harvard University Press, 1966.

Ernst and Young Center for Business Innovation. *Embracing Complexity: Exploring the Application of Complex Adaptive Systems to Business.* [Cambridge, Mass.]: Ernst & Young Center for Business Innovation, 1996.

Espy, Willard R. *The Garden of Eloquence: A Rhetorical Bestiary.* New York: E. P. Dutton, 1983.

Favier, Jean. *Gold and Spices: The Rise of Commerce in the Middle Ages.* Translated by Caroline Higgitt. New York and London: Holmes & Meier, 1998.

Fischel, Daniel. *Payback: The Conspiracy to Destroy Michael Milken and His Financial Revolution.* New York: Harper Business, 1995.

Fogelin, Robert J. *Figuratively Speaking.* New Haven, Conn.: Yale University Press, 1988.

Francis, Dick. *The Sport of Queens.* London: Pan Books, 1974.

Frank, Robert H., and Philip J. Cook. *The Winner-Take-All Society.* New York: Free Press, 1995.

Friedl, Friedrich, Nicholaus Ott, and Bernard Stein. *Typography: An Encyclopedic Survey of Type Design and Techniques throughout History.* New York: Black Dog & Levanthal Publishers, 1998.

Fuchs, R. H. *Claes Oldenburg: Large-Scale Projects, 1977–1980.* New York: Rizzoli, 1980.

Fussell, Paul. *The Rhetorical World of Augustan Humanism.* London: Oxford University Press, 1965.

Garlinski, Jozef. *The Enigma War.* New York: Charles Scribner's Sons, 1980.

Gaur, Albertine. *A History of Writing.* Rev. ed. New York: Cross River Press, 1992.

Geertz, Clifford. *The Interpretation of Cultures.* New York: Basic Books, Inc., 1973.

Geertz, Clifford. *Local Knowledge: Further Essays in Interpretive Anthropology.* New York: Basic Books, Inc., 1983.

Geldzahler, Henry. *Pop Art, 1955–70.* International Cultural Corporation of Australia, Limited, 1985.

Glaeser, Edward L. "Psychology and the Market." Working Paper 10203. NBER Working Paper Series, Cambridge, MA, December 2003. http://www.nber.org/papers/w10203.

Goldman, Judith. *James Rosenquist.* Denver: Denver Art Museum, 1985.

Goldstein, Paul. *Copyright's Highway.* New York: Hill & Wang, 1994.

Gould, Stephen Jay. "The Pattern of Life's History." In *The Third Culture,* ed. John Brockman. New York: Simon & Schuster, 1995.

Graham, Benjamin. *The Intelligent Investor.* 2d rev. ed. New York: Harper, 1959.

Graham, Margaret B. W., and Alec T. Shuldiner. *Corning and the Craft of Innovation.* New York: Oxford University Press, 2001.

Grant, James. *Money of the Mind: Borrowing and Lending in America from the Civil War to Michael Milken.* New York: Farrar Straus Giroux, 1992.

Grothe, Mardy. *Never Let a Fool Kiss You or a Kiss Fool You.* New York: Viking, 1999.

Hafner, Katie, and John Markoff. *Cyberpunk: Outlaws and Hackers on the Computer Frontier.* New York: Simon & Schuster, 1991.

Hafner, Katie, and Matthew Lyon. *Where Wizards Stay Up Late: The Origins of the Internet.* New York: Simon & Schuster, 1996.

Halberstam, David. *The Amateurs.* New York: William Morrow, 1985.

Hannas, Wm. C. *Asia's Orthographic Dilemma.* Honolulu: University of Hawai'i Press, 1997.

Haskell, Barbara. *Blam! The Explosion of Pop, Minimalism, and Performance, 1958–1964.* New York: W. W. Norton & Co, 1984.

Haslam, Malcom. *The Real World of the Surrealists.* New York: Galley Press, 1978.

Havelock, Eric A. *The Liberal Temper in Greek Politics.* New Haven, Conn.: Yale University Press, 1957.

Havelock, Eric A. *Preface to Plato.* Oxford: Basil Blackwell, 1963.

Havelock, Eric A. *The Literate Revolution in Greece and its Cultural Consequences.* Princeton, N.J.: Princeton University Press, 1982.

Hayek, Friedrich A. *The Constitution of Liberty.* Chicago: University of Chicago Press, 1960.

Hayek, Friedrich A. *Hayek on Hayek: An Autobiographical Dialogue.* Edited by Stephen Kresge and Leif Wenar. Chicago: University of Chicago Press, 1994.

Hayek, Friedrich A. *The Road to Serfdom.* Chicago: University of Chicago Press, 1994 (orig. 1944).

Healey, John F. *The Early Alphabet.* Berkeley: University of California Press/British Museum, 1990.

Healy, Jane M. *Failure to Connect.* New York: Simon & Schuster, 1998.

Heiner, Albert P. *Henry J. Kaiser, Western Colossus.* San Francisco: Halo Books, 1991.

Heller, Steven, and Anne Fink. *Faces on the Edge: Type in the Digital Age.* New York: Van Nostrand Reinhold, 1997.

Henri, Adrian. *Total Art: Environments, Happenings, and Performance.* New York: Oxford University Press, 1974.

Herr, Michael. *Dispatches.* New York: Alfred A. Knopf, 1977.

Higgins, Dick. *Pattern Poetry: Guide to an Unknown Literature.* Albany: State University of New York Press, 1987.

Hinsley, F. H., and Alan Stripp. *Code Breakers: The Inside Story of Bletchley Park.* Oxford: Oxford University Press, 1993.

Hirshleifer, Jack, and David Hirshleifer. *Price Theory and Applications,* 6th ed. Upper Saddle River, N.J.: Prentice-Hall, 1998.

Hoerr, John P. *And the Wolf Finally Came: The Decline of the American Steel Industry.* Pittsburgh: University of Pittsburgh Press, 1988.

Hoffer, Eric. *The Temper of Our Time.* New York: Harper & Row, 1967.

Hoffer, Eric. *The True Believer: Thoughts on the Nature of Mass Movements.* New York: Harper-Perennial, 1989 (orig. 1951).

Hoffman, Donald D. *Visual Intelligence: How We Create What We See.* New York: W. W. Norton & Co., 1998.

Holden, Anthony, trans. *Greek Pastoral Poetry.* Harmondsworth: Penguin Books, 1974.

Hollander, John. *Types of Shape.* New expanded ed. New Haven, Conn.: Yale University Press, n.d.

Holmes, Oliver Wendell, Jr. *The Essential Holmes: Selections from the Letters, Speeches, Judicial Opinions, and Other Writings*. Edited by Richard A. Posner. Chicago: University of Chicago Press, 1992.

Hulten, Pontus. *Futurism and Futurisms*. New York: Abbeville Press, 1986.

Hulten, Pontus. *Jean Tinguely: A Magic Stronger Than Death*. New York: Abbeville Press, 1987.

Hunt, Edwin S., and James M. Murray. *A History of Business in Medieval Europe, 1200–1550*. Cambridge: Cambridge University Press, 1999.

Irving, Clive. *Wide-Body: The Triumph of the 747*. New York: William Morrow & Co., Inc., 1993.

Johnson, Robert Flynn, and Donna Stein. *Artists' Books in the Modern Era, 1870–2000*. San Francisco: Fine Arts Museum of San Francisco, 2001.

Johnstone, Bob. *We Were Burning: Japanese Entrepreneurs and the Forging of the Electronic Age*. New York: Basic Books, 1999.

Joseph, Sister Miriam, C.S.C. *Shakespeare's Use of the Arts of Language*. New York: Columbia University Press, 1947.

Kahn, David. *Seizing the Enigma: The Race to Break the German U-Boat Codes, 1939–43*. Boston: Houghton Mifflin Co., 1991.

Kahn, David. *The Code Breakers*. New York: Scribner, 1996.

Kaplan, Benjamin. *An Unhurried View of Copyright*. New York: Columbia University Press, 1967.

Keegan, John. *Intelligence in War: Knowledge of the Enemy from Napoleon to Al-Qaeda*. New York: Alfred A. Knopf, 2003.

Keller, Evelyn Fox. *A Feeling for the Organism: The Life and Work of Barbara McClintock*. New York: W. H. Freeman, 1983.

Kendrick, Laura. *Animating the Letter: The Figurative Embodiment of Writing from Late Antiquity to the Renaissance*. Columbus: Ohio State University Press, 1999.

Kennedy, George A. *The Art of Persuasion in Greece*. Princeton, N.J.: Princeton University Press, 1963.

Kennedy, George A. *The Art of Rhetoric in the Roman World*. Princeton, N.J.: Princeton University Press, 1972.

Kennedy, George A. *A New History of Classical Rhetoric*. Princeton, N.J.: Princeton University Press, 1994.

Kerferd, G. B. *The Sophistic Movement*. Cambridge: Cambridge University Press, 1981.

Kert, Bernice. *Abby Aldrich Rockefeller: The Woman in the Family*. New York: Random House, 1993.

Kimball, Bruce A. *Orators and Philosophers: A History of the Idea of Liberal Education*. New York: Teachers College, Columbia University, 1986.

Kipling, Rudyard. *Complete Verse*. Definitive ed. New York: Doubleday, 1940.

Kirby-Smith, H. T. *The Origins of Free Verse*. Ann Arbor: University of Michigan Press, 1996.

Krakauer, Jon. *Into Thin Air: A Personal Account of the Mount Everest Disaster*. New York: Anchor Books, 1997.

Langton, Christopher G. *Artificial Life: The Proceedings of an Interdisciplinary Workshop on the Synthesis and Simulation of Living Systems Held September, 1987 in Los Alamos, New Mexico*.

Santa Fe Institute Studies in the Sciences of Complexity, vol. 6. Sante Fe, N.M., Santa Fe Institute, 1989.

Lanham, Richard A. *Tristram Shandy: The Games of Pleasure.* Berkeley: University of California Press, 1973.

Lanham, Richard A. *The Motives of Eloquence: Literary Rhetoric in the Renaissance.* New Haven, Conn.: Yale University Press, 1976.

Lanham, Richard A. *Literacy and the Survival of Humanism.* New Haven, Conn.: Yale University Press, 1983.

Lanham, Richard A. *A Handlist of Rhetorical Terms.* 2d ed. Berkeley: University of California Press, 1991.

Lanham, Richard A. *The Electronic Word: Democracy, Technology, and the Arts.* Chicago: University of Chicago Press, 1993.

Lanham, Richard A. *Revising Business Prose.* 4th ed. Boston: Allyn & Bacon, 2000.

Lanham, Richard A. *Revising Prose.* 4th ed. Boston: Allyn & Bacon, 2000.

Lanham, Richard A. *Analyzing Prose.* 2d ed. London: Continuum, 2003.

Lee, Ji. *Univers Revolved: A Three-Dimensional Alphabet.* New York: Harry N. Abrams, 2004.

Lessig, Lawrence. *Code and Other Laws of Cyberspace.* New York: Basic Books, 1999.

Lessig, Lawrence. *The Future of Ideas.* New York: Random House, 2001.

Levitan, W. "Dancing at the End of the Rope: Optatian Porfyry and the Field of Roman Verse." *Transactions of the American Philological Society* 115 (1985): 245–69.

Levy, Steven. *Hackers: Heroes of the Computer Revolution.* Garden City, N.Y.: Anchor Press/Doubleday, 1984.

Levy, Steven. *Artificial Life: The Quest for a New Creation.* New York: Pantheon Books, 1992.

Lewin, Ronald. *The American Magic: Codes, Ciphers and the Defeat of Japan.* New York: Farrar Straus Giroux, 1982.

Lewis, C. S. *An Experiment in Criticism.* Cambridge: Cambridge University Press, 1961.

Lewis, William W. *The Power of Productivity: Wealth, Poverty, and the Threat to Global Stability.* Chicago: University of Chicago Press, 2004.

Lindey, Alexander. *Plagiarism and Originality.* Westport, Conn.: Greenwood Press, 1974.

Lippard, Lucy, et. al. *Pop Art.* New York: Oxford University Press, n.d.

Lorenz, Konrad. *On Aggression.* Translated by Marjorie Kerr Wilson. New York: Harcourt Brace & World, Inc., 1963.

Lorenz, Konrad. *The Waning of Humaneness.* Translated by Robert Warren Kickert. Boston: Little Brown & Co., 1987.

Lowenstein, Roger. *Buffett: The Making of an American Capitalist.* New York: Doubleday, 1995.

Lowenstein, Roger. *When Genius Failed: The Rise and Fall of Long-Term Capital Management.* New York: Random House, 2000.

Lucie-Smith, Edward. *Late Modern: The Visual Arts since 1945.* New York: Praeger Publishers, 1969.

Lyman, Peter, and Hal R. Varian. *How Much Information?* Berkeley, Calif., December 2003. http://www.sims.berkeley.edu/how-much-info/.

Magretta, Joan. *What Management Is.* New York: Free Press, 2002.

Mallon, Thomas. *Stolen Words.* New York: Ticknor & Fields, 1989.

Mandelbrot, Benoit, and Richard L. Hudson. *The (mis)Behavior of Markets.* New York: Basic Books, 2004

Manovich, Lev. *The Language of New Media.* Cambridge, Mass.: MIT Press, 2001.

Marchand, Philip. *Marshall McLuhan: The Medium and the Messenger.* New York: Ticknor & Fields, 1989.

Marks, Leo. *Between Silk and Cyanide: A Codemaker's War, 1941-45.* New York: Free Press, 1998.

Marmer, Nancy. "Pop Art in California" in *Pop Art,* by Lucy R. Lippard et al. New York: Oxford University Press, n.d.

Marrou, H. I. *A History of Education in Antiquity.* Translated by George Lamb. Madison: University of Wisconsin Press, 1982.

Maurus, Hrabanus. *In Honorem Sanctae Crucis.* Edited by M. Perrin. Corpus Christianorum, Continuatio Mediaevalis 100–100A. 2 vols. Turnhout: Brepols, 1997.

Maysles, David, Charlotte Zwerin, and Albert Maysles. *Running Fence.* New York: A Maysles Films Production, 1978.

McCloskey, Deirdre N. *Economic Maturity and Entrepreneurial Decline: British Iron and Steel, 1870-1913.* Cambridge, Mass.: Harvard University Press, 1973.

McCloskey, Deirdre N. *Enterprise and Trade in Victorian Britain: Essays in Historical Economics.* London: George Allen & Unwin, 1981.

McCloskey, Deirdre N. *The Rhetoric of Economics.* Madison: University of Wisconsin Press, 1985.

McCloskey, Deirdre N. *If You're So Smart: The Narrative of Economic Expertise.* Chicago: University of Chicago Press, 1990.

McCloskey, Deirdre N. *Knowledge and Persuasion in Economics.* Cambridge: Cambridge University Press, 1994.

McCloskey, Deirdre N. *The Vices of Economists—the Virtues of the Bourgeoisie.* Amsterdam: Amsterdam University Press, 1996.

McCloskey, Deirdre N. *The Secret Sins of Economics.* Chicago: Distributed by University of Chicago Press, 2002.

McShine, Kynaston, ed. *Andy Warhol: A Retrospective.* New York: Museum of Modern Art, 1989.

Mellinkoff, Ruth. *Averting Demons: The Protective Power of Medieval Visual Motifs and Themes.* 2 vols. Los Angeles: Ruth Mellinkoff Publications, 2004.

Micklethwait, John, and Adrian Wooldridge. *The Witch Doctors.* New York: Random House, 1996.

Micklethwait, John, and Adrian Wooldridge. *A Future Perfect: The Challenge and Hidden Promise of Globalization.* New York: Crown Business, 2000.

Micklethwait, John, and Adrian Wooldridge. *The Company: A Short History of a Revolutionary Idea.* New York: Modern Library, 2003.

Miller, Geoffrey. *The Mating Mind: How Sexual Choice Shaped the Evolution of Human Nature.* New York: Anchor Books, 2001.

Miller, J. Abbot. *Dimensional Typography.* Princeton, N.J.: A Kiosk Report, Distributed by Princeton Architectural Press, 1996.

Minsky, Marvin. *The Society of Mind*. New York: Simon & Schuster, 1988.

Minsky, Marvin. *First Person: Marvin Minsky: The Society of Mind*. New York: Voyager Co., 1996. CD-ROM.

Morris, Desmond, Peter Collett, Peter Marsh, and Marie O'Shaughnessy. *Gestures*. New York: Stein & Day, 1979.

Morrison, J. S., J. F. Coates, and N. B. Rankov. *The Athenian Trireme: The History and Reconstruction of an Ancient Greek Warship*. 2d ed. Cambridge: Cambridge University Press, 2000.

Ong, Walter J., S.J. *Ramus, Method, and the Decay of Dialogue*. Cambridge, Mass.: Harvard University Press, 1983.

Origo, Iris. *The Merchant of Prato*. New York: Alfred A. Knopf, 1957.

Parkes, M. B. *Pause and Effect: Punctuation in the West*. Berkeley: University of California Press, 1993.

Patterson, Lyman Ray. *Copyright in Historical Perspective*. Nashville: Vanderbilt University Press, 1968.

Peckham, Morse. *Man's Rage for Chaos: Biology, Behavior, and the Arts*. Philadelphia: Chilton Books, 1965.

Perlin, Ken, and David Fox. "Pad: An Alternative Approach to the Computer Interface." *Siggraph Video Review*, no. 96 (1993).

Pool, Ithiel de Sola. *Technologies of Freedom: On Free Speech in an Electronic Age*. Cambridge, Mass.: Harvard University Press, 1983.

Postrel, Virginia. *The Substance of Style*. New York: Harper Collins, 2003.

Quinn, Arthur. *Figures of Speech: Sixty Ways to Turn a Phrase*. Salt Lake City, Utah: Gibbs. M. Smith Inc., 1982.

Quintilian. *The Orator's Education*. Edited and translated by Donald A. Russell. 5 vols. Cambridge, Mass.: Harvard University Press, 2001.

Redfern, Walter. *Puns*. Oxford: Basil Blackwell, 1984.

Reingold, Edwin M. *Toyota: People, Ideas and the Challenge of the New*. London: Penguin Books, 1999.

Rheingold, Howard. *The Virtual Community: Homesteading on the Electronic Frontier*. Reading, Mass.: Addison-Wesley, 1993.

Rhodes, Richard. *The Making of the Atomic Bomb*. New York: Simon & Schuster, 1988.

Richter, Hans. *Dada: Art and Anti-Art*. London: Thames & Hudson, 1965.

Ridley, Matt. *The Origins of Virtue*. New York: Penguin Books, 1996.

Robins, Corinne. *The Pluralist Era: American Art, 1968–1981*. New York: Harper & Row, 1984.

Rose, Barbara. *Claes Oldenburg*. New York: Museum of Modern Art, 1970.

Rose, Mark. *Authors and Owners: The Invention of Copyright*. Cambridge, Mass.: Harvard University Press, 1993.

Rubin, William S. *Dada and Surrealist Art*. New York: Harry N. Abrams, n.d.

Rubinstein, W. D. *Capitalism, Culture, and Decline in Britain, 1750–1990*. London: Routledge, 1993.

Russett, Robert, and Cecile Starr. *Experimental Animation: Origins of a New Art*. Rev. ed. New York: Da Capo Press, 1976.

Sabbagh, Karl. *Twenty-first-Century Jet: The Making and Marketing of the Boeing 777.* New York: Scribner, 1996.

Saenger, Paul. *Space between Words: The Origins of Silent Reading.* Stanford, Calif.: Stanford University Press, 1997.

Samuelson, Robert J. *The Good Life and Its Discontents.* New York: Random House, 1995.

Sax, Joseph L. *Playing Darts with a Rembrandt.* Ann Arbor: University of Michigan Press, 1999.

Schulze, Franz. *Mies van der Rohe: A Critical Biography.* Chicago: University of Chicago Press, 1985.

Segaller, Stephen. *Nerds, 2.0.1: A Brief History of the Internet.* New York: TV Books, 1998.

Seldon, Arthur. *Capitalism.* Oxford: Basil Blackwell, 1990.

Seligman, Joel. *The Transformation of Wall Street: A History of the Securities and Exchange Commission and Modern Corporate Finance.* Boston: Houghton Mifflin Co., 1982.

Shailor, Barbara A. *The Medieval Book.* Toronto: University of Toronto Press, 1991.

Short, Robert. *Dada and Surrealism.* Secaucus, N.J.: Chartwell Books, Inc., 1980.

Simon, Herbert A. "Designing Organizations for an Information-Rich World." In *Computers, Communications, and the Public Interest,* edited by Martin Greenberger. Baltimore and London: Johns Hopkins Press, 1971.

Smith, Adam. *The Theory of Moral Sentiments.* Edited by D. D. Raphael and A. L. Macfie. Indianapolis: Liberty Fund, 1984.

Smith, Douglas K., and Robert C. Alexander. *Fumbling the Future: How Xerox Invented, Then Ignored, the First Personal Computer.* New York: William Morrow & Co., 1988.

Smith, Keith A. *Structure of the Visual Book.* Rochester, N.Y.: Keith A. Smith Books, 1994.

Solomon, Elinor Harris. *Virtual Money: Understanding the Power and Risks of Money's High-Speed Journey into Electronic Space.* New York: Oxford University Press, 1997.

Sonnino, Lee. A. *A Handbook to Sixteenth-Century Rhetoric.* London: Routledge & Kegan Paul, 1968.

Sprague, Rosamond Kent, ed. *The Older Sophists.* Columbia: University of South Carolina Press, 1972.

Sprat, Thomas. *History of the Royal Society (1667).* Facsimile reprint. Whitefish, Mont.: Kessinger Publishing, [2003].

Stephens, Mitchell. *The Rise of the Image, the Fall of the Word.* New York: Oxford University Press, 1998.

Stevens, Wallace. *The Collected Poems.* New York: Random House, 1982.

Stewart, James B. *Den of Thieves.* New York: Simon & Schuster, 1991.

Stigler, George J. *The Intellectual and the Marketplace.* Enlarged ed. Cambridge, Mass.: Harvard University Press, 1984.

Stoll, Clifford. *The Cuckoo's Egg: Tracking a Spy through the Maze of Computer Espionage.* New York: Doubleday, 1989.

Strouse, Jean. *Morgan: American Financier.* New York: Random House, 1999.

Taubes, Gary. *Nobel Dreams: Power, Deceit, and the Ultimate Experiment.* Redmond, Wash.: Tempus Books, 1986.

Thomas, Frank, and Ollie Johnston. *Disney Animation: The Illusion of Life.* New York: Abbeville Press, 1984.

Tiger, Lionel, and Robin Fox. *The Imperial Animal*. New Brunswick, N.J., and London: Transaction Publishers, 1998.

Tinguely at the Tate. London: Tate Gallery, 1983.

Tisdall, Caroline, and Angelo Bozzolla. *Futurism*. London: Thames & Hudson, 1977.

Tomkins, Calvin. *The Bride and the Bachelors: Five Masters of the Avant-Garde*. Expanded ed. New York: Penguin Book, 1976.

Tomkins, Calvin. *The Scene: Reports on Post-Modern Art*. New York: Viking Press, 1976.

Tomkins, Calvin. *Off the Wall: Robert Rauschenberg and the Art World of Our Time*. New York: Penguin Books, 1980.

Tomkins, Calvin. *Robert Wilson: The Theatre of Images*. 2d ed. New York: Harper & Row, 1984.

Tomkins, Calvin. *Duchamp: A Biography*. New York: Henry Holt & Co, 1996.

Turkle, Sherry. *Life on the Screen: Identity in the Age of the Internet*. New York: Simon & Schuster, 1995.

Twitchell, James B. *Lead Us into Temptation: The Triumph of American Materialism*. New York: Columbia University Press, 1999.

Varnedoe, Kirk, and Adam Gopnik. *High and Low: Popular Culture and Modern Art*. New York: Museum of Modern Art, 1990.

Wade, Nicholas. *The Nobel Duel*. Garden City, N.Y.: Anchor Press/Doubleday, 1981.

Waldman, Diane. *Roy Lichtenstein*. New York: Guggenheim Museum, 1993.

Waldrop, M. Mitchell. *Complexity: The Emerging Science at the Edge of Order and Chaos*. New York: Simon & Schuster, 1992.

Waldrop, M. Mitchell. *The Dream Machine*. New York: Viking, 2001.

Walker, C. B. F. *Cuneiform*. Berkeley: University of California Press/British Museum, 1987.

Walther, Ingo F., and Norbert Wolf. *Codices Illustres: The World's Most Famous Illuminated Manuscripts, 400–1600*. Cologne: Taschen, 2001.

Warhol, Andy, and Pat Hackett. *POPism: The Warhol 60's*. New York: Harper & Row, 1980.

Watson, James D. *The Double Helix: A Personal Account of the Discovery of the Structure of DNA*. Edited by Gunther S. Stent. New York: W. W. Norton & Co., 1980.

Watts, Michael, ed. *The Literary Book of Economics*. Wilmington, Del.: ISI Books, 2003.

Weschler, Lawrence. *Seeing Is Forgetting the Name of the Thing One Sees: A Life of Contemporary Artist Robert Irwin*. Berkeley: University of California Press, 1982.

Whitehead, A. N. *"The Aims of Education" and Other Essays*. New York: Macmillan Company, 1929.

Whodini. *The Information Inferno*. [Long Island City, N.Y.]: Cybercity Press, LLC., 2001.

Wiener, Martin J. *English Culture and the Decline of the Industrial Spirit, 1850–1980*. Cambridge: Cambridge University Press, 1981.

Winterbotham, F. W. *The Ultra Secret*. New York: Harper & Row, 1974.

Womack, James P., and Daniel T. Jones. *Lean Thinking*. New York: Simon & Schuster, 1996.

Womack, James P., Daniel T. Jones, and Daniel Roos. *The Machine That Changed the World*. New York & Toronto: Rawson Associates; Collier Macmillan Canada; Maxwell Macmillan International, 1990.

Wriston, Walter. *The Twilight of Sovereignty*. New York: Charles Scribner's Sons, 1992.

Yergin, Daniel, and Joseph Stanislaw. *The Commanding Heights*. New York: Simon & Schuster, 1998.

INDEX

Note: Italicized page numbers indicate figures.